ANXIETY – The Inside Story
How Biological Psychiatry Got it Wrong

By Niall McLaren, M.D.

Future Psychiatry Press

Ann Arbor, MI

ISBN 978-1-61599-410-6 paperback
ISBN 978-1-61599-411-3 hardcover
ISBN 978-1-61599-412-0 eBook

Library of Congress Cataloging-in-Publication Data

Names: McLaren, Niall, 1947- author.
Title: Anxiety--the inside story : how biological psychiatry got it wrong /
    by Niall McLaren.
Description: Ann Arbor, MI : Future Psychiatry Press, [2018] | Includes
    bibliographical references and index.
Identifiers: LCCN 2018035209| ISBN 9781615994106 (pbk. : alk. paper) |
ISBN
    9781615994113 (hardcover : alk. paper) | ISBN 9781615994120 (eBook)
Subjects: | MESH: Anxiety Disorders--therapy | Anxiety Disorders--
psychology
    | Physician-Patient Relations | Models, Psychological
Classification: LCC RC531 | NLM WM 172 | DDC 616.85/22--dc23
LC record available at https://lccn.loc.gov/2018035209

Future Psychiatry Press is an imprint of
Loving Healing Press
5145 Pontiac Trail
Ann Arbor, MI 48105
USA

http://www.LHPress.com
info@LHPress.com

Tollfree 888-761-6268
Fax +1 734 663 6861

Disributed by Ingram (USA/CAN/AU) and Bertram's Books (UK/EU)

Contents

Table of Figures

Preface

This is a book on a common, destructive and widely misunderstood topic, written for anybody with a good high school education. It is not a "self-help" book; in fact, there are warnings that readers should *not* attempt to diagnose and treat themselves. It is not a text-book, although medical students and others should be able to learn a lot from it. There are practically no statistics, no diagrams of brains and only a few explanatory graphs. There are no randomised controlled trials, no A-B-A-B trials, no surveys, no genome-wide associations studies, no talk of imbalances of brain enzymes or neurotransmitters, none of that. Instead, it looks at the lived experience of being an anxious person, how it develops, how it wrecks lives and how to understand it. From this understanding comes a rational treatment model although this book doesn't focus on treatment.

It does, however, focus on the signal failure of mainstream psychiatry to take anxiety seriously. In particular, it looks at how psychiatry rediagnoses anxiety as a range of other conditions, then commits sufferers to a life of drugs which can never be effective. This explains why the consumption of psychiatric drugs is rising rapidly throughout most of the world, yet the rates of suicide and disability pensions for psychiatric reasons are also rising, even faster.

This book is built around actual cases taken from my files. After patients give consent, the histories are rewritten so that all facts are obscured. The files are then put away with no record of who they represent. Many months or even years later, long after I have forgotten who they are, the cases are inserted into the relevant chapters of the book. This is a bit of a problem because, apart from about three cases, I have no way of checking on their further progress but that's the way it is. I am grateful to the people who consented to appear in this book and hope it helps them and others.

Thanks are due to Allan Patience of Melbourne University, who diligently read the manuscript and suggested hundreds of improvements, only one of which wasn't incorporated. I think without his encouragement, I would probably have given up. Chris Sprudzans resolutely pushed me to adopt this particular style and to "lighten up" in general. Also thanks to my daughter, Cynthia, who did the artwork and graphics for the covers, and to my wife for patiently putting up with yet another book.

Mainstream psychiatry abhors criticism and will do anything it can to avoid it, or if it can't, to evade acting on it. One of the oldest ways of avoiding criticism is to pretend that it doesn't exist. This takes the form of psychiatric journals steadfastly refusing to publish critical material. The next step is to launch attacks on the critic. One of the most common I hear is that I am "anti-psychiatry," which allows psychiatrists to reject everything I have written before they read it. There are two responses to this ploy, the first being that this sort of *ad hominum* attack is proof of the intellectual desolation of those who use it. The second is that whoever complains I am "anti-psychiatry" clearly doesn't have the first clue what the expression means. Anybody who did know wouldn't be so silly as to make such a basic mistake. For myself, I am fighting for the right of young psychiatrists to think.

I hope this book contributes to the start a long overdue critical re-evaluation of psychiatry, its models and treatments, and above all, its inhumane and often brutal treatment of the mentally disturbed.

PART I –
Anxiety: How Did We Get Here?

1 — Why Would any Sensible Psychiatrist Bother with Anxiety?

Modern mainstream psychiatry really can't be bothered with anxiety. For orthodox psychiatrists, anxiety is not an SMI (Serious Mental Illness) so it is generally treated as second rate and handed to psychologists. Very often, it is called 'comorbid,' meaning it occurs with something else, mostly depression but also alcoholism and other addictions, chronic pain and so on. The way psychiatrists use the word 'comorbid,' they mean 'trivial, irrelevant, a sideshow which need not be taken seriously.' In this book, I will argue that anxiety is not a sideshow, it is the biggest show in town and it has to be taken very, very seriously. Anxiety is much bigger, much more dangerous and much more difficult to understand and manage than, say, depression. But before I set out my case, it would help if you had some background so you can understand how I arrived at this almost sacrilegious position.

I studied medicine in Perth, Western Australia, which takes pride in its reputation as the most isolated capital in the world. But I was the only student in my year who came from a country high school, all the rest had been to school in the city. I was the first of my entire family to complete high school, the first to go to university, and I knew just one person in the city when I arrived there. As a scholarship boy, I was able to attend the most prestigious residential college but right from the beginning, it was clear to me, and to everybody else, that I didn't fit in. What spoiled it was that not only did I not fit in, but I had no intention of fitting in. And this continued throughout my studies. I spent my summer holidays working on isolated farms far from the city, I took history, politics and religion and other Big Ideas very seriously and slowly, it dawned on me that I didn't like anybody with power or money. I liked ordinary people, I was at one with them and that hasn't changed.

Throughout the six years of my medical course, my plan had been to train to become a country general practitioner. I never intended nor expected to stay in the city longer than I had to but in my first posting of my first year, that all changed. I was sent to the neurosurgery unit and loved it, to the extent that two years later, I managed to get another three months on the unit. It was a busy life. In the good old days, we were rostered on duty in the hospital for as much as 103hrs a week. If you slept for a few hours here and there, you were lucky. On several posts, I was routinely rostered on continuous duty from 8.00am Friday to 6.00pm Monday. It was not unusual to work until sunrise on Saturday, or even longer. Yes, it was dangerous but there was no point complaining as many of our consultants had served in the Second World War and they scorned anybody who complained about being tired. Convinced that I had found my purpose, I applied to begin the training. A neurosurgeon must do the same training as a general surgeon, then a further two years in his specialty. I threw myself into the reading program, essentially basic medical school again, anatomy, biochemistry, physiology, pathology, with a big emphasis on neuroanatomy and neurophysiology.

At the end of my three years as a junior medical officer, just before I was due to start formal surgical training, I was given the choice of yet another term in the emergency department or going to the psychiatry ward. *Psychiatry?* It seemed that would be helpful for a neurosurgeon so that's what I chose. My first day wasn't much fun, it was difficult to reconcile all this talking with the idea of cutting heads open but within a few days, I realised that this was what I had always been interested in: Big Ideas. And psychiatry, of course, deals in the biggest ideas of all: mind, reality, the lot.

After three months, I left to go to another hospital to start as a surgical registrar, or trainee (resident, in the US). I'd already had nearly three years of surgical jobs so it was back to the routine of dealing with lumps and bumps, blood and pains, smashed bodies, burns and the like. During the afternoon of my second day, halfway through the second gall bladder and before I started on my list of haemorrhoids, I realised I couldn't spend the rest of my life doing this. Two hours later, I left the operating theatre and rang the head of the psychiatry department in my old hospital to see if he could give me a job. Yes, he said, we're very short, when can you start? I had to wait three months but this time, I knew exactly what I wanted. There were two things that psychiatry could give: Big Ideas, and real contact with people. Remember this was the 1970s, there were lots of Very Big Ideas being tossed around at the time. One of them was Always Be Nice to Each Other. It would be very nice, I thought as I drove home, to be among people who care about humans and are hooked on Big Ideas.

Most psychiatrists had decided during medical school, or even earlier, what they wanted to do. As soon as possible, they began their specialist training, which took them out of the mainstream of medicine. My route into psychiatry was rather circuitous, and it took just two and a half days for this to show. Our training program was held in the university department of psychiatry every Wednesday afternoon. On my first afternoon, I met my new colleagues who had started three months before me, and settled down to await with great interest the first lecture in my new career, on depression.

It was not at all what I had expected. The professor, a taciturn man who clearly had little time for human beings, came in, stood at the lectern and immediately started to talk about brain chemistry.

With my colleagues industriously copying his every word, he announced that depression was caused by an imbalance of what he called biogenic amines in the hypothalamus. Antidepressant drugs were therefore used to correct that imbalance. The symptoms of depression were just the effects of a molecular brain disorder, just as a hyperglycaemic state was the effect of not enough insulin, or inflammation was the effect of a foreign organism in the body. The psychiatrist's role was to ask the patient for his symptoms, here you see them in this list, in fact you can hand the patient the list and get him to tick the relevant boxes himself, then you add up his score. If it's over 25, that says he's got depression and you give him the drugs or ECT (electroconvulsive therapy, or shock treatment) or both. Any questions?

Well, yes sir, I have some questions. For a start, I've just spent an extra three years studying the brain and I can state flatly that what you said about the neurochemistry of the hypothalamus is simply not true. Also, the neural pathways you showed in your slides are out of date, and nobody knows enough about the hypothalamus to be sure of its role in emotion. And is depression the sort of thing you can "get" like you get syphilis, or is it a frame of mind? Sir.

With a strange look, which I later learned was caused by grinding his teeth, he picked up his files and stalked out, muttering over his shoulder something about next week's lecture as he went.

"What do you think you're doing?" the other registrars hissed as the door slammed shut behind him. "If you want to get kicked off this program, that's a great start. Don't ever, ever disagree with him. You'd better learn to knuckle under or start looking for another job."

But knuckling under had never been my strong suit and, aged nearly twenty-seven, it was a bit late to start learning.

By the end of my first week, my thoughts of a fascinating career in an atmosphere of genteel intellectual camaraderie had turned to dust. I realised that the only way to survive in what was little better than an academic cat fight was to know the stuff better than everybody else. That meant hitting the books and fortunately, I'm good at that. I've never watched TV or played cards or most of the other distractions that medical students indulge so I started at one end of the section of psychiatry in the library and set to work.

In those days, certainly in Australia, psychiatry was seen as a very mild-mannered endeavour, a flea on the tail of the medical dog, you could say. Psychiatrists were seen as other-worldly, often lazy, if not half-crazy themselves, and generally irrelevant to medicine's real job of fixing sick people. The psychiatry department was tolerated only because nuisance patients or the genuinely insane could be sent there before they wrecked the place: out of sight, out of mind. The subject matter of psychiatry was airy-fairy, an amorphous mishmash of some Freudian stuff, which was good fun because it allowed junior doctors to talk about their favourite subject, a bit of "rats and stats" and some hard stuff like shocking brains or cutting them. That bit I knew about. In my anaesthetics term, I had put many people to sleep so they could be given electrically-induced fits and, in neurosurgery, I had actually assisted at almost the last leucotomy (lobotomy) operation performed in Western Australia, on a 34yo man. But the rest was new and fascinating.

In those halcyon days, there were three themes in psychiatry. The first I'd met in my first lecture, the notion that all mental disorder is just a special sort of brain disease. People who believed this called themselves biological psychiatrists and spent their time talking to patients and junior doctors about brain enzymes and drugs and ECT and psychosurgery. They saw themselves as the hard, rational and sensible wing of psychiatry, the psychiatrists of the future, and made no attempt to conceal their distaste for all this wishy-washy talk about feelings and caring and all that.

"Does a surgeon," they scoffed, "need to worry about his patient's feelings as he cuts open his belly?"

Not at all, he does his job calmly and dispassionately, the patient gets better and everybody is happy. This is the way of medicine, you have to be cruel to be kind, and they saw themselves as very much in the mainstream of medicine rather than wandering about in some tender-hearted haze.

Some distance away were the behaviourists, who followed the theories of the Russian psychologist, Ivan Pavlov and his modern disciple, Hans Eysenck, and the American psychologist Burrhus F Skinner. The Pavlovian tradition is well known to everybody from his experiments with dogs salivating to the lunch bell. We learn by conditioning, the process of pairing events and responses that controls behaviour. Skinner's approach was slightly different. The organism emits behaviours which provoke responses from the world which in turn reinforce the behaviour. Reinforcement can be positive or negative (also known as punishment) and by this process, behavioural patterns are shaped and maintained. Both schools of behaviourism were sure that, if there was a mind, we certainly couldn't talk about it or study it rationally. Skinner was (mostly) of the view that there is no such thing as the mind. Even such quintessentially humanist concepts as freedom and dignity were artefacts of more or less random reinforcement of our naive behaviour. In the late 1970s, the behaviourists were Big. Skinner was one of the most highly-awarded researchers in the US but his ideas were seen as so threatening that they were parodied in Anthony Burgess' book and film, *A Clockwork Orange*.

Behaviourist psychologists staked out the rational ground for themselves, their goal being to give a full scientific explanation of all normal and abnormal life. However, they weren't the first to make this claim. Fifty years before their heyday, Sigmund Freud, a Viennese neurologist, began publishing a revolutionary theory of mind and mental disorder, the psychoanalytic theory. Freud said that the mind is a real if somewhat unusual sort of thing. It is divided in three parts, id, ego and superego. All observable behaviour, including what we think and do and feel, is the outcome of herculean battles, mostly deep in the subconscious and unconscious. We are not, he said, as rational as we would like to think and most of our behaviour can be traced back to infantile sexual conflicts. If left unresolved, these can result in adult neurotic problems, or worse.

You can see the issues at stake here. On one hand, we have the Freudian notion that there is a mind, that it causes behaviour and, because it can go wrong, it has to be taken very seriously. Even though it is very complex, the mind can be analysed and sorted out by the process of talking, although it was very time-consuming, generally taking years.

Not so, scoffed the behaviourists, all talk of mind is pre-scientific mumbo-jumbo. As scientists, we cannot talk about something we can't see or verify independently, and nobody can see minds. Thus, we have one group of psychiatrists saying that there is a mind and we can work with it, while another group said either that there isn't a mind, it's all an illusion, or there may be but we can't even talk about it because it isn't a proper subject for science. Finally, we have the biological psychiatrists who said there is a mind but, as a matter of scientific fact, it is nothing more than the brain. Everything we need to know about mental disorder can be learned by studying the brain in the laboratory, exactly as we study every other organ in the body.

For me, biological psychiatry didn't last long just because it seemed counter-intuitive. How could such intensely mentalist concepts as religion, the rule of law and the national debt be rewritten in biological terms? It didn't do me much good raising these questions in our lectures as everybody else simply accepted it as given: one fine day, ordinary physical science will give a complete description of mental disorder with no questions left unanswered. At the time, I knew this sounded phony but it was years before I learned that it is called promissory materialism, and it is indeed phony. Unfortunately, the great majority of psychiatrists in the world today still firmly believe this and bristle at anybody questioning them.

Behaviourism went the same way. The concept of conditioning didn't make sense to me. How could this account for creativity, or novelty, or even the depths of human depravity? Hitler and Stalin were both pretty horrible characters but nobody would say that they were trained to do what they did. That took real creativity and determination. So as soon as I had time, I went back to Pavlov's original publications. And there it was. Just before he died in 1936, Pavlov published two papers which academic psychology somehow seemed to have overlooked. In these, he said flatly that he wasn't a psychologist, he despised psychologists as his techniques could never be expanded to the point where they could explain all behaviour. Skinner's theories went the same way. In 1959, the linguist Noam Chomsky showed that Skinner's theory of language was little better than a word game and had no scientific value at all. That started the rot and by the early 1980s, behaviorism had tumbled into the history books.

At the same time, psychoanalysis wasn't doing well. My own experience was that, having dispensed early with biological psychiatry, and having an intense interest in what I later learned was humanism, I wanted a genuine theory of mind to use as the basis for my work in psychiatry. So I jumped the 'B for Biological Psychiatry' section in the library and went straight to 'P for Psychoanalysis.' Unlike the US, Freud's theories were never very big in Australia, so that while we had to have some idea what it was all about, we were only expected to be well-read in the topic, not experts.

Most of my colleagues settled for a series of books written by a chap called Calvin Hall, who wrote little primers on the main figures in psycho-analysis. I looked at one and thought it was complete rubbish, so I borrowed what was always known as the Bible of Freudian theory, Otto Fenichel's *Psychoanalytic Theory of Neurosis*. Anybody who was serious about psychoanalysis had to have read this door-stopper. I read 29 pages and gave up, convinced that nobody could make the sorts of claims they were making. How could anybody say what a newborn baby felt about being born? Who could say what a ten day old baby felt about being breast-fed, about being separated from the mother, about having a poo each day? To me, it was nothing more than fairy stories even though, at the time, I didn't have the technical knowledge to be able to say why.

Thus, I soon reached the point where I was adrift in my chosen field. If anything reliable had ever been said about the nature, causes and manage-ment of mental disorder, I hadn't heard it or seen it, and nor had any of my teachers. But, worryingly, the professors and my fellow-trainees didn't seem to be bothered by this. They were busy sorting themselves into one or other camp and had no time for "compulsive nay-sayers," as I was being called.

After four years and more final warnings than anybody I have ever known, I graduated in psychiatry. Four days later, I went to the library and decided on my next project. I wanted to find, for once and for all, the correct, scientific theory of mental disorder and its treatment. I had no doubt there would only be one theory, that it would be a psychological theory, and the treatment would be a form of psychotherapy, or talking. In no time, this led me to questions of the nature of mind, the nature of science and, indeed, the nature of knowledge itself. These, as you will recognise, are absolutely central questions in what is called philosophy.

Soon after, I left the hospitals and began to work in prisons, which was good because I was more or less on my own and nobody bothered me with their silly ideas about mental disorder. It was actually a relief to talk to prisoners rather than academics: the inmates knew all about mental disorder, they had lived it and breathed it all their lives. Before long, I began formally studying philosophy which meant that I parted company with my psychiatric colleagues. I gave a few lectures at research seminars but these started a pattern which has continued to this day: generally, I couldn't finish my talks. As I presented my material, people began shifting in their chairs, then muttering to each other and finally, I was shouted down or people actually came to the front and snatched the microphone out of my hand.

In 1983, I enrolled in a PhD program jointly in philosophy and psychiatry but I couldn't get any supervision in psychiatry. My first supervisor, a very kindly chap, looked at the first chapter and laughed. It sounded fascinating, he said, but he didn't understand a word of it. In 1987, completely discouraged by the total lack of interest in what I thought was a critically important matter, I decided on a total change of career. I left Perth for the remote Kimberley region of Western Australia, nearly 3000km away, as the first psychiatrist to work in the region. The purpose was to reduce the numbers of Aboriginal people who were being sent to the mental hospitals in Perth, where nobody spoke their languages or knew anything about them, and they felt they would die of the cold. As it turned out, I was the first truly isolated psychiatrist in the world, and the most isolated. I had no staff, no beds, and for the first three years, not even an office. My job was to travel around this huge and spectacular region, finding mentally disordered people in their villages and dealing with them on the spot.

From the point of view of the Health Department, it was very successful. From my point of view, it was partly successful and partly a dismal failure. The success was that I learned to practice psychiatry without relying on security wards, detention orders, hospitals, ECT and all the trappings of modern psychiatry. The failure was that dealing with another and totally different culture forced me back to the most basic concepts of what we mean by mental disorder, and back to philosophy. I learned there's no escaping philosophy, you think you can practice science without it but all you're doing is making the same old mistakes again.

For the next ten years, I was studying, writing and publishing on the application of the philosophy of science to psychiatry. Over the years, this project broadened to a general theory of mind, which is another book. But what counts here is the broad conclusion forced on us by the philosophy of science: mainstream modern psychiatry has no scientific basis whatsoever. Modern psychiatry has no theory of mind, no theory of mental disorder, no theory of personality and no theory of personality disorder. Its treatment, especially physical treatments such as drugs, ECT, other forms of brain stimulation or surgery, is little more than blind poking. At the very best, psychiatry is a protoscience, a vague indicator of where we ought to be looking for the correct theory of mental disorder. At worst, it is pseudoscience, misleading, dehumanising and destructive. As a profession, psychiatry is in much the same position of general medicine before, say, the work of Louis Pasteur. Unfortunately, telling that to other psychiatrists is a sure way to be shown to the door.

2 | Treatment in Psychiatry

At half past three on an ordinary Thursday afternoon, the operating suite on the sixth floor of Royal Perth Hospital is busy-busy. Patients are wheeled in and out, staff move around, quietly tending to the drips and beeping machines, muted phones ring... Everything moves ahead smoothly with none of the drama you'd expect from watching hospital shows on TV. Even if—heaven forbid—there's a cardiac arrest, there's no shouting, no alarm bells, everybody knows what to do and does it with a minimum of fuss.

We're working in Theatre 4 which gives us an expansive view over Perth's beautiful Swan River. A lovely day for an operation, everything is ready, the patient is wheeled in and shifted to the operating table under the huge circular light. The anaesthetist checks whether we're ready then speaks quietly to the patient. I watch closely, everything is interesting, everything is valuable, it's essential to know every step of the procedure. In a minute or two, the patient is asleep and connected to the respirator and ECG monitors. The anaesthetic technician and I lift the patient's head and position him for a frontal approach. We shave him and drape him just as the surgeon enters, pulling on his gloves, then it's my turn to scrub. I'm as quick as I can be, I don't want to miss any of the operation because it's unusual, there's only one surgeon in town doing them. Better still, we're short of a registrar so even though I'm only an intern, I'll be allowed to do a lot more than most juniors. The surgeon marks the skin for the incisions then takes the knife.

"You've done these before?" he mutters.

"Yes sir."

"Right," he says, handing me the scalpel, "then four burr holes at those points."

I make the incisions, cauterise the bleeders, insert retractors to hold the scalp back and take the drill. It looks like an ordinary carpenter's augur except it's highest quality stainless steel, so it can be put in the autoclave and sterilised. The drill bit is just like the bits I have in my tool box at home, a flat 10mm bit that will go only through the skull itself and no further. In less than a minute, the first hole is in place, then the others follow quickly. Four neat holes over the frontal poles of the young man's brain. We can see the cerebral tissue pulsing pinkly under its coverings.

My part over for a few minutes, I stand aside and the surgeon takes over. The nurse hands him an instrument called a leucotome, Greek for a tool that cuts white things, but it looks just like a thin stainless steel biro (ballpoint pen). He inserts the instrument through the hole, pushing it down, deep into the brain substance. For me, this is pretty shocking: neurosurgeons normally guard the brain as though it were their own but here he is, shoving a steel dart deep into the brain and wiggling it around. But it's all in the interests of scientific medicine. This patient has a crippling neurotic illness.

Over nearly fifteen years, our patient had had every treatment in the book but nothing had made any difference. He'd had dozens of drugs, a hundred or more ECT, a variety of different psychological programs, even a course of the justly-feared deep sleep therapy, but nothing worked. I spoke to him before the operation to get him to sign his consent. He was 34yrs old, intelligent and I got on well with him as he was from a small country town in the wheatbelt. He had been to school in the city and started to train as a teacher but he could not continue. He was severely anxious, disabled by obsessions and compulsions and suffered recurrent depressive states. He had made several attempts on his life but this only increased his guilt. He had been advised to consent to psychosurgery, as it was called, as a last-ditch attempt to gain some quality of life.

He asked me what I thought but I had to admit I knew nothing about the operation and next to nothing about neurotic problems. During my few weeks of psychiatry as a medical student, we had hardly touched on them. We spent most of our time in the mental hospital talking to middle-aged people with chronic schizophrenia, when they could be convinced to stay at the table and stop talking to their voices. This man was nothing like them. My job was only to witness him signing that he had been given full advice about the operation, and to certify that he was alert and aware of his actions. With a resigned shrug, he signed consent to a modified rostral leucotomy, the Scoville operation, and a few minutes later, I left him.

That was in 1971, shortly after I had graduated in medicine. I don't know what happened to him, but later I saw other people who had had the same operation. While it was true that they were in no particular distress, they were also little more than shells of humans. They were unable to work but attended day centres where they took part in elementary activities. They needed a lot of attention otherwise they would simply sit in the corner and smile vaguely into space. Some of them wet themselves but didn't seem to be aware of it. The few I saw were all older people so they would have had families to look after, which was lucky because they couldn't look after themselves. Maybe I just saw the bad ones but who would know? Nobody kept any figures and the operation simply faded out. The one I assisted at was one of the last in Western Australia but I don't know how many were done there. We do know that, from 1937 to about 1972, over 100,000 people around the world had parts of their brains damaged or removed in the attempt to relieve mental distress. It did, but at the cost of what most of us would recognise as being human.

What's this thing called 'psychosurgery'? What sort of thing is the psyche that you can perform surgery on it? But let's go further back: what is this thing called mental disorder? Is it the sort of thing you can "treat" anyway? These are very important questions because they underpin the entire psychiatric industry.

Historically, the battle over the cause of mental disorder was between those who saw it as a religious matter, mostly meaning possession by evil spirits; those who saw it as a matter of weak morals, usually involving masturbation; and those who saw it as a type of brain disease. Benjamin Rush (1745-1813), one of the signatories of the US Declaration of Independence, was a Philadelphia physician with an interest in mental disorder. He was firmly of the view that mental disorder was essentially physical, and that physical treatments were essential. He insisted that patients should be treated just as humanely as other sick people, and kept busy rather than left to languish, chained and locked in wards little better than dungeons. His physical cures were harsh (bleeding, purging, spinning to "improve" blood flow, etc) but there was nothing else available.

Over in the UK, the disagreeable and opinionated Henry Maudsley (1835-1918) exerted a huge influence over the development of the new "science of mental disorder." At only 23yrs of age, soon after he had graduated in medicine, he became superintendent of a small mental hospital, then another until he retired to private practice at the age of thirty. However, he wrote prolifically and, in the same year, became editor of the *Journal of Mental Science*, later renamed the *British Journal of Psychiatry*. In 1870, he declared that all mental disease is brain disease, setting orthodox British psychiatry on a course it has held to the present:

> Mental disorders are neither more nor less than nervous diseases in which mental symptoms predominate, and their entire separation from other nervous diseases has been a sad hindrance to progress....

Have no doubt: in making this profound statement, Maudsley knew little or nothing about mental disorder, about the brain, neurophysiology, pharmacology, genetics, or anything. All he had was a supreme confidence in his own judgement, which remains part of the English-speaking professorial tradition. The concept of psychosurgery, of removing or disabling parts of the brain to alter the course of mental disorder, comes straight from this. When the operation of leucotomy or lobotomy was devised in 1937, there really wasn't much more known about how the brain works. But let's go back a bit to talk about treatment in general.

For hundreds of years, mad people were either kept in their homes, hidden from view, or hounded from their villages. On the streets or wandering abroad, they were in grave danger and most didn't last long. Gradually, in Western Europe, each parish was required to provide a workhouse for the destitute such as widows and orphans, and also for the insane, but conditions in the workhouses ranged from poor to bestial. Local taxpayers resented having to provide for strangers and did everything they could to make life difficult for the unfortunates who ended in them. We are not talking about the distant past: George Orwell wrote of his experiences as a tramp in England in the 1930s. One of the worst features was that a homeless man could not spend two consecutive nights in a poorhouse: regardless of the weather, he had to walk to the next parish then queue for a place. Quite often, there were none.

In the nineteenth century, national governments took over responsibility for providing for the insane. This led to a massive building program in Europe, North America and in the European colonies. People were incarcerated, often for life, in appalling conditions, while death rates from a dozen communicable diseases were extremely high. Added to this was the cruel or depraved behaviour of the wardens and wardresses, combined with terrifying and/or dangerous forms of treatment such as cold water baths, restraints, various chemicals and purgatives, diets and so on. For example, at its peak in the early 1950s, the Knowle Asylum in Hampshire, southern England, held up to 2,000 patients. From the time it opened in 1852 to the time of the last burial in its associated cemetery in 1971, at least 5,500 patients were known to have died in the hospital, although the number was almost certainly larger as there were often as many as four corpses interred in each grave. Some years, there was up to 10% death rate among its inmates.

In the latter half of the nineteenth century, medicine began its long, slow climb out of these pits of atrocity. A major impetus came from the work of one of my heroes, the brilliant Spanish neuroanatomist, Santiago Ramón y Cajal. As a child, Santiago was a holy terror. He was transferred from school to school because he argued ferociously with the teachers, even the Jesuits. At age eleven, he made a cannon and tested it by firing at their neighbour's gate. It worked first time, blowing the gate to bits, so young Santiago was hauled off to prison by the police for the night. At fourteen, his father, an anatomy demonstrator, despaired of his son's education and apprenticed him to a cobbler and then a barber but he didn't last long as he argued with everybody. At his wit's end, his father took him to a cemetery to find bones to draw. Immediately, Santiago found his vocation, so he was sent to medical school and later became one of the truly great scientists of the century. He devised accurate but selective stains that isolated individual neurons. For the first time, people could actually see these amazing cells in their entirety.

Driven by changes such as Pasteur's germ theory and antisepsis, by anaesthesia, by pathologists such as Rudolph Virchow and microbiologists such as Robert Koch, it seemed that the rapid advance of medical science would soon confirm Maudsley's dictum, that all mental disorder is a physical disorder of the brain. Psychiatrists tried all sorts of experimental treatments, most of which would make modern people recoil in horror. For example, the neurologist and pathologist, Julius Wagner-Jauregg, developed the concept of pyrotherapy or heating people to cure mental disorder. I have no idea where this idea came from, maybe it's part of European folk medicine but almost from the time he graduated in medicine, Wagner-Jauregg was experimenting on heating mental patients. He used a variety of chemical and infective agents, trying to induce fevers high enough to cure them. When it didn't cure them he reasoned that they needed more of his treatment, not that there was anything wrong with his idea (this is a very persistent trope in psychiatry). Eventually, he settled on malaria, which was transferred to mentally-disturbed people by direct blood transfusions from infected people. It had no benefit on people with what we would now call schizophrenia but, by chance, it did work on another scourge, tertiary or cerebral syphilis.

At the time, large numbers of people admitted to mental hospitals were suffering the ravages of syphilis. This was invariably slowly fatal. It was young Julius's good luck that the organism, *Treponema pallidum*, is highly sensitive to temperature. Giving the patient a fever of up to 42C, which malaria does, killed the treponemes and stopped the progress of this dread condition. For this, Wagner-Juaregg was awarded the Nobel Prize in 1927. He didn't stop there as he was convinced that schizophrenia was caused by masturbation, so he sterilised and castrated large numbers of patients to stop their evil habit. This fitted neatly with the concept of eugenics, then terribly popular in Europe and the US, which led to many hundreds of thousands of psychiatric patients being sterilised to improve the national breeding stock.

Eventually, an energetic but neurotic young Austrian painter named Hitler took this to its extreme, helped, as it transpired by some of Germany's most influential psychiatrists. Between 1933 - 39, some 360,000 mentally-afflicted people were sterilised in Greater Germany. This led to a further program called *Aktion T4*, after Tiergartenstrasse Vier, the address of the building in Berlin where it was planned. This program, approved at the very highest levels of the Nazi government, set out to cleanse the Reich of all mentally deficient or defective individuals—by euthanasia. At first, they were killed by injection but this was too slow so they settled on gassing them with carbon monoxide, then cremating the bodies. By the end of the War, something like 95,000 people had been murdered in this way, and the program became the model for the Final Solution. Psychiatrists figured highly in all of these programs, although trainee psychiatrists are never told that.

But we're racing ahead. The 1920s were heroic times for physical treatments in psychiatry, and one of the most persistent themes related to artificial convulsions. It had long been known that people with epilepsy didn't seem to suffer schizophrenia at the same rate as the general population. Conversely, people with schizophrenia who also suffered fits seemed to improve somewhat after a series of seizures. In the late 1920s, a Hungarian neuropathologist, Ladislav Joseph Meduna, found that the brains of people who died of epilepsy showed widespread gliosis or scarring, which is evidence of neuronal death. At the same time, he found that people dying with schizophrenia showed much lower counts of gliosis. Meduna reasoned that inducing seizures to cause neuronal death should be effective in treating schizophrenia. He experimented with a variety of drugs, soon settling on injections of camphor. However, this took about 45 minutes to cause seizures, during which time the patients were gripped by a rising sense of terror. They pleaded to be spared this torture so, after further work, Meduna found a derivative of camphor, cardiazol (Metrazol, 1934), which could be given by IV injection. This reliably induced seizures after only 30-60 seconds of overwhelming terror. He published his results, claiming almost miraculous cures, and the treatment was very quickly adopted in Europe and North America.

At about the same time, an Austrian psychiatrist in Berlin, Manfred Sakel, began experimenting on drug addicts and psychopaths using low doses of insulin. His goal was to reduce the blood sugar level, thereby starving the brain to slow it down, or perhaps to overfeed it by driving sugar from the blood into the neurons (or something, I've never seen his rationale). This went nowhere but it seems he read Meduna's work on chemically-induced seizures and realised that giving larger doses of insulin would cause seizures due to the very low blood sugar levels. Once again, this quickly became popular to that by the early 1950s, practically every reputable psychiatric centre in the world was using insulin treatment.

Unfortunately, it was hugely expensive in terms of staff time: a small group of patients got the latest treatment while the rest mouldered in the lunatic asylums, but the psychiatrists loved it. In 1935, an influential British psychiatrist, Ian Skottowe, announced that insulin treatment was effective in schizophrenia because it pushed glucose out of the blood into the neurons of the frontal region of the brain, thereby energising them. It sounded very scientific but there wasn't a word of truth in it. In 1953, a very junior medical officer in London, Harold Bourne, published a paper in the prestigious medical journal, *The Lancet*, arguing that insulin treatment was totally ineffective. Any positive results came from the enormous investment of time and energy in the carefully-selected group of patients who received it, and the placebo effect which, of course, works on staff just as well as it works on patient (placebo effect is the old "water injection" effect. If you give a patient some inert treatment and tell him it will be effective, he will start to feel better).

Needless to say, the British psychiatric establishment didn't take this lying down. A few weeks later, the journal published irate letters from such luminaries as William Sargant and Eliot Slater (who had studied under Ernst Ruedin in Munich, the architect of the T4 program). They took the very strongest exception to Bourne's diligent analysis of the outcomes of insulin treatment, arguing that their vast clinical experience and judgement demolished his "mere figures." In their view, the psychiatrist really was God. Professor (later Sir) Martin Roth, some-time president of the Royal College of Psychiatrists, was totally impervious to Bourne's case and persisted in using insulin treatment on his unit until at least the early 1960s. Bourne was absolutely right, of course, but the Establishment got its own back by preventing him working in the UK. He eventually went to New Zealand and thence to Italy, where he remains to this day.

By the mid-1930s, insulin and cardiazol shock treatments were widely practised. Their drawback was the uncertainty of the seizures and the huge expense of caring for the patients until they recovered from each day's treatment. In 1938, an Italian neuropathologist, Ugo Cerletti, chanced by a pig slaughterhouse on his way home from work. As he watched, the pigs were stunned with an electric shock to the head, causing a seizure, after which their throats were easy to cut. Intrigued, Cerletti experimented on inducing seizures in humans using electricity. Finally, in 1938, he and his psychiatrist associate, Lucio Bini, developed a machine that delivered controlled shocks to the brain, reliably inducing seizures. This quickly took over from chemicals as quicker, safer and less unpleasant.

At first, ECT was used mainly in schizophrenia but by 1941, it was being used more and more in depression. There was, however, never any doubt that it worked by causing diffuse physical damage to the brain. At a time when actual destruction of the brain by "lobotomy" was seen as modern and merciful, nobody worried about it. It was only in the 1970s, when the idea of deliberately causing brain damage on unwilling patients fell into disrepute, that psychiatrists moved to the idea that ECT doesn't cause brain damage.

And so we arrive back at one of the most appalling episodes in psychiatry's grim history, psychosurgery, the idea that inflicting damage on the brain will cure mental disorders. The person who is generally credited (or blamed) for introducing it was a Portuguese neurologist, Antonio Egas Moniz. Egas Moniz was already famous for introducing the technique of cerebral angiography, in which dyes are injected into the carotid arteries just as X-rays are taken, allowing the blood vessels to be outlined. There are various stories of how he came to the idea of cutting brains but what seems to have convinced him was a neurology conference he attended in London in 1935. Some American researchers described how they had removed the frontal lobes of two chimps, which caused profound changes in their behaviour. Instead of normal chimp behaviour (when locked in small cages in laboratories) of irritability and tantrums, they became placid and tractable. Intrigued, Egas Moniz went home and convinced a psychiatrist friend of his to lend him twenty patients for an experiment of removing the frontal poles of their brains. Egas Moniz pronounced the operations a success and before long, it was being performed in many different countries, including the US. The psychiatrist apparently was horrified but nobody listened to him.

An American psychiatrist, Walter Freeman, became a fanatical supporter of psychosurgery and spent the next twenty years performing and publicising the operation. However, he was too impatient to be bothered with the standard method of drilling holes in the head and poking in a knife to cut the brain, he wanted to do it in his office. He developed the technique of lifting the upper eyelid and shoving large needles up through the thin bone at the top of the orbit or eye socket, into the brain, and wriggling them around to destroy the connections of the frontal region. After the operation, patients became placid, apathetic and disinterested. Left to their own devices, they would sit in a corner, grinning amiably, and do nothing. They showed no distress but also no initiative, curiosity or creativity. They were simply not the same people, their personalities had been destroyed, or worse. Pres. John F Kennedy's sister, Rosemary, who suffered brain damage during birth, had one of the first lobotomies performed in the US but she was left severely disabled and lived in an institution in Wisconsin until she died in 2005.

We should mention one more travesty, the so-called "deep sleep therapy." Influenced by the irrepressible William Sargant in Britain, a couple of Australian psychiatrists developed the technique of putting patients to sleep for up to six weeks using a cocktail of large doses of a variety of drugs. They used a private hospital in Sydney called Chelmsford, and were making a lot of money for themselves and the hospital because they could guarantee to keep all the beds completely full. Unfortunately, they were also bumping off a lot of patients who developed pneumonia or had strokes while comatose and didn't wake up. At least nineteen people committed suicide after their "treatment." The scandal grew and grew because the institutions that were supposed to be ensuring proper standards of treatment were either asleep on the job or too busy protecting their own interests. After as many as 85 deaths, DST was banned and the psychiatrist responsible for a large part of it, one Harry Bailey, committed suicide.

The whole saga of psychosurgery was and still is a ghastly scandal. There was absolutely no scientific justification for it, just because it was not based in any scientific model of mind or of mental disorder. Society wanted cures, the patients wanted cures so, predictably, a few psychiatric adventurers moved in. The rest is history, but it's forgotten history, carefully and very discreetly airbrushed from the record, a little quirk in the long-distant past that we needn't bother ourselves with. In this, psychiatry differs from general medicine and surgery, which are proud of their history. The difference is that mainstream medicine uses its history to show how far it has come, how its ideas have changed and developed as scientific knowledge advances.

Psychiatry is different. If its history were widely known, psychiatrists would have to say: "Well, yes, we used to do some pretty dreadful things to people but guess what? Nothing much has changed because we're still using the same old theory that mental disorder is caused by brain disorder."

The orthodox position in modern mainstream psychiatry is very simple: All mental disorder is caused by disturbances of brain function, so that a full understanding of the function of the brain will tell us everything we need to know about mental disorder, leaving no questions unanswered.

However, before we go any further, we need to ask the following question:

> Is it true that all mental disorder is caused by disturbances of brain function?

No, it is not true that all mental disorder is caused by disturbances of brain function, because we know that some aren't, for example, the acquired or post-traumatic anxiety state, now know as PTSD.

No, it is not true because no person, psychiatrist, psychologist, neuroscientist, philosopher or poet, has ever written a biological theory of mental disorder, nor even a suggestion of what such a theory would look like. In technical terms, the claim that biology will explain mental disorder is an example of promissory materialism, i.e. the hope that one fine day, somebody will come running from a laboratory shouting "Eureka." It won't happen.

To go a step further, it is not true because the most scrupulous analysis of the possibility says "No go." Physicalism, the philosophy that ultimately, everything has a physical explanation, fails just when things start to get interesting. It cannot account for mental life, which was the reason physicalism got a run in the first place, namely that we don't have an account of mentality. We'd like to be able to explain mental life but physicalism won't do it.

So we can forget biological psychiatry. Trouble is, an awful lot of people have an awful lot of money invested in giving biological treatments for mental disorder, and they won't give it up without a fight. Worse still, there's an awful lot of high-flying academic psychiatrists around the world who have invested their entire careers, and their egos (which is much worse), in claiming that mental disorder is biological in nature. They will fight tenaciously to save their jobs and their reputations. So we're stuck with biological psychiatry for a while. Just because it's been proven wrong doesn't mean it will fade away overnight.

The value of biological psychiatry is that it isn't necessary to talk to a patient beyond asking a few standard questions to work out which disease he has, and that can easily be done by a nurse armed with a questionnaire. This will give a diagnosis which then dictates the drugs he should have. There are lots of psychiatric drugs these days, antipsychotic drugs, antidepressants, tranquillisers, the group known as "mood stabilisers," stimulants such as amphetamines, hypnotics and others. Antipsychotics and antidepressants are the really big money-spinners, but if you give people the list of side-effects, they don't want them. Side effects include drowsiness, confusion, emotional blunting, manic bouts, suicidal and homicidal ideas and impulses, massive weight gain, loss of sexual interest and function and above all, addiction. And they don't actually work as they are supposed to. Antidepressants are effective in about 65% of cases but placebos are effective in about 55-62% of cases. And placebos don't wreck your sex life.

However, let's assume our patient has answered his dozen questions and a diagnosis has rolled out. He is prescribed a couple of drugs and off he goes. A few weeks later, he's back complaining he doesn't feel any better or, quite as often, he actually feels worse. Aha, says the psychiatrist, you've got a very severe case of depression, you need more drugs in bigger doses. When that doesn't work, he will get a new diagnosis, called "treatment-resistant depression." Thus labelled, he can choose from the following list (actually, he won't get to choose, he'll be told what he's getting. If he's in Queensland, he'll get it whether he wants it or not because "unreasonably refusing treatment" is a trigger to being detained and getting it as an involuntary patient).

First, there is ECT, that "valuable, essential and effective" treatment which is widely used in some countries (mostly English-speaking) and hardly or not at all in others (most of the rest).

Second is a newcomer, transcranial magnetic stimulation (TMS), which uses powerful alternating magnetic fields to do something to the brain, nobody's quite sure. The most recent case of TMS I've met was a young lady who had had 63 sessions over nearly 50 days in hospital, at a total cost of about $82,000. Even though the psychiatrist was happy it had improved her, she wasn't convinced it had worked and took herself off for a second opinion. Another young man had 43 sessions with no discernible improvement (total cost of three admissions $165,000) so his family doctor sent him to see another psychiatrist who sorted him out for $1500.

Third is another novel treatment, transcranial direct current stimulation of the brain (tDCS). Patients are wired up and get a trickle of DC electricity through the brain. There is a lot of work being done at present to see what works safely. Wikipedia sums it up: "tDCS appears to be somewhat effective for depression." However, it's useless for everything else so it isn't clear why all this money is being spent on it. Nobody has any idea how long its effect lasts, and everything I've seen says that patients lose interest long before the psychiatrist does (but then the patients aren't making money out of it).

It must not be forgotten that simply taking an interest in a patient and giving him something to think about is also "somewhat effective for depression." Just for background, tDCS was first used in 1801, by one Giovanni Aldini, nephew of the well-known Luigi Galvani. Nothing came of it although Aldini showed an uncommon degree of initiative by trying it on himself. Afterwards, he recorded that he couldn't sleep for days.

Next, we have a crop of transcranial somethings, tACS (transcranial alternating current, of course), tPCS (pulsed current), and tRNS (random noise), where the frequency of the alternating current varies (there's no noise involved, it just means a random frequency generator).

These days, with permanently implanted nerve stimulators for pain, we have moved on to try the same thing for brains that ache. Permanently implanted electrodes can be used to tickle the pleasure centres but this is still classified as experimental and, fortunately, is severely restricted. If you have a problem with foolish people texting while driving, imagine what would happen if they could give themselves a touch of electronic bliss on the freeways?

Alert readers will be aware there hasn't been much fanfare in the new psychiatric drugs department lately. This is because there aren't actually any new drugs. To make it worse, most of the big companies seem to have given up on psychiatric drugs. Partly this is because it's too difficult as they don't have a theory to guide them and partly because of some very well-founded fears of what the long-suffering patients might do when they realise that people who take psychiatric drugs in the long term will die, on average, 19yrs (in Australia) to 25yrs (in the US) younger than their undrugged peers. This is correct.

As the consumption of psychiatric drugs rises, so too does the death rate from complications of taking the drugs. People who take these drugs get very fat and get all the complications of being overweight, including diabetes, hypertension and high cholesterol. But in a nifty piece of public relations, the drug companies managed to convince some academic psychiatrists to name this the "metabolic syndrome." This spectacularly meaningless expression shifts attention away from the drugs to the patient's metabolism and thus his genetic make-up, a variant on the old ploy of blaming the victim.

In the absence of any new drugs, psychiatrists have had to fall back on some old ones. These days, all the money is on the dissociative anaesthetic agent, ketamine, which, not entirely coincidentally, is also very popular among trendy young party-goers. The idea that ketamine is an antidepressant seems to have come from desperate attempts to relieve chronic pain, which it didn't do very well but it made some people with chronic pain somewhat less unhappy. There is now a thriving industry giving keta-mine infusions to the morose. Its effect, at a cost per infusion ranging from a few hundred to about $10,000, lasts anywhere from a minute to a week. There's even a new version of ketamine which you squirt up your nose for instant euphoria.

An enterprising Australian company, Aura Medical, even started selling kits consisting of eight syringes of ketamine for IV injection as a do-it-yourself cure for self-diagnosed depression. At $150 per injection, or $1200 for each kit, they felt they had a winner. Since eight injections of ketamine can produce addiction, they could hardly fail, especially as the wholesale price of ketamine in India, where it is manufactured, is 17rupees per 50mg injection. That's about... wait for it... 35c per injection. That's some profit (for the mathematically-challenged, it's about 45,000%). Needless to say, lots of teenagers were queuing to get their "Special K" kits to make sure they weren't too depressed to go to the rave party. Aura Medical is no longer in business.

These days, antibiotics are old drugs but there's always a rush to find new uses for old drugs, because that means their patents can be extended by another twenty years. In the pharmaceutical industry, patents are a licence to print money. Different psychiatrists are using different antibiotics to treat different unsuspected infections, the only common factor being their cer-tainty that their program will amount to a silver bullet for "treatment-resis-tant depression." Others have decided that mental disorder is caused by inflammation of the brain and are using a range of anti-inflammatory drugs to block cerebral inflammation. They're very keen to pursue this line, so keen that they haven't actually waited for the evidence that there is any inflammation in the depressed person's brain. One of the substances being investigated is curcumin, the active ingredient in turmeric, a form of ginger. Oddly enough, the incidence of depression has apparently risen sharply since the most potent anti-inflammatory drugs of all, steroids, were intro-duced, just as the widespread use of antibiotics hasn't led to a general levity in the national mood.

Finally, we get back to... pyrotherapy. That's right, the very latest idea—hot off the press, you could say—comes from a Canadian psychiatrist, that heating people lifts their mood:

> A 2016 study led by Dr Charles Raison found that raising the body temperature of depressed volunteers through whole-body hyper-thermia treatment improved their symptoms of major depression for up to 6 weeks.

Warming frigid Canadians may make them a little less glum but I'm not sure it would work very well here in sunny Australia. Dr Raison also teaches "compassion meditation," whatever that is, but I suspect my cynical countrymen would prove resistant to that, too. How did he get the money to do that research? Easy, the people who dish out the grants are all dyed-in-the-wool biological psychiatrists. If it's biological, they're most likely to approve it.

This brief survey suggests treatment in psychiatry isn't all it's cut out to be. My case is simple: the treatment fails because it isn't mandated by a formal, articulated and tested model of mental disorder. Instead, it is driven by an ideology of mental disorder, the totally unsubstantiated conviction that mental disorder can somehow be explained by a full understanding of the physical structure of the brain. That conviction is totally and tragically wrong.

In the remaining chapters, we will look at anxiety as a pure psychological disorder, a severe disturbance of mental life that arises in a perfectly normal brain.

3 Anxiety – The Very Idea

My case in this book is that anxiety is a deadly serious condition which must be taken very seriously. Its significance lies partly in its devastating effect on people's lives but also its crucial, central role in driving practically all other mental disorders. This, of course, is the polar opposite of the standard position in psychiatry, which is that each and every one of the ever-growing number of psychiatric diagnoses is a separate and distinct category of illness, with no crossover or blurring of the borders. The rationale behind this belief is that each category of mental disorder will eventually be mapped down on to the genome, where it is caused by a unique genetic defect. Thus, it will be amenable to a specific treatment, just as insulin is specific to diabetes. Of course, each patient may have lots of separate diagnoses, each of which will require its specific treatment, but that's just his bad luck in the great lottery of genetics.

I believe that's rubbish, so let me state my position clearly. I believe that...

- ...Mental disorder is real;
- ...Mental disorder has no physical basis in disease or disturbance of the brain. It is wholly a psychological phenomenon (Philosophically, this position is known as dualism);
- ...Although drugs can be helpful at times, the correct treatment for mental disorder is psychotherapy, or the talking cure. If this is implemented early, there is no need and no theoretical justification for so-called physical treatments of the brain—ECT, TMS, psychosurgery etc.;
- ...Anxiety is the most fundamental and most powerful of all emotions. It is the only recursive emotion, i.e. it can act back on itself, which is the basis of the anxiety state;
- ...Once people become anxious, what really counts is how they try to manage it; and...

- ...The essential basis of any form of psychotherapy is a relationship
  of trust between patient and psychotherapist (note that trust does
  not imply affection or even friendship).

In assessing a new case, I take what is called a semi-structured psychiatric history. The questions are essentially the same for every patient,
worded the same, in the same order and, where possible, with the same
intonation. It is very important to follow this process to avoid bias. If you
don't feel comfortable with or don't like a patient, as happens from time to
time, you'll cut the interview short and not let him speak. But if you do let
him speak, you'll see the real person underneath, and he'll feel he's had a
fair hearing. The exact questions I use are found in the Appendix. I let the
patient speak for a minute or so, then start the questions but I control the
interview throughout. If a patient starts to talk about something irrelevant, I
bring him back to the question I'd asked. By the end, we have covered his
whole mental state in the present, with quite a detailed survey of his life.

The questions fall naturally into clusters so we'll follow those.

Case 3.1 – Melissa, 19yo female

Melissa F, aged 19yrs, lives with her parents and younger brother in a
fairly expensive outer suburb and is studying occupational therapy. She
drove to the appointment in the car her parents had given her when she
finished high school. She was referred by her general practitioner (GP) after
she had been seeing a psychologist for about a year, with no improvement.
She was not sure what approach was being followed but the psychologist
had told her she needed antidepressants. As she came into the interview,
Melissa was decidedly wary. She had heard that everybody who saw a
psychiatrist would be prescribed drugs but she made it clear she didn't want
them.

Presenting Complaints:

She said she had come because she had suffered "years of anxiety
and stress." In general, she was feeling "not OK." With regard to
vegetative functions and appetites, her sleep was "really bad." She
went to bed very late, about 3.00am or even later, and was able to
get to sleep fairly quickly but she didn't wake until midday or even
later. Her sleep was broken but she wasn't sure why although it
wasn't due to pain, noise or bad dreams. She couldn't sleep earlier
because of "a lot of anxiety and thinking." Her appetite was poor but
she didn't think she had been losing weight. Her levels of energy were
"really low" and she had very little interest, or motivation to get anything done. This included her studies and her private life. Socially, she
didn't mix well: "I try to avoid people, I've never been good at
mixing." Asked about her sexual interest, she shrugged dismissively.

Cognitively, her memory was good but she had a lot of trouble
concentrating, especially if she became upset. She found her mind

wandered from study and she couldn't explain what she did with the time. She had always had trouble making decisions and delayed them whenever possible. She often had trouble thinking clearly as under any sort of pressure, she became confused and flustered. The only time she could think clear enough to study was after the rest of her family had gone to bed at about 10.00pm. Her thought content was dominated by "worrying over everything." There were no disturbances of perception.

Asked to describe her mood, she said: "I'm not good enough." She was feeling low and miserable about 80% of the time. This was often "overwhelming," by which she meant she was sick of things as they were and felt she couldn't go on without a major change of some sort. She was often sick of life itself and had the feeling that if she dropped dead or didn't wake up, it would be a great relief. However, she said she had no actual suicidal ideas and wouldn't act on them anyway. She felt the unhappiness was caused by "relationship troubles but also it's just me."

Q: *Do you ever have bouts where you feel fantastic, full of energy and on top of the world for no good reason?*

A: No way, I wish I did.

Q: *Do you have bouts where you feel tense and jittery or you get agitated?*

A: Yes, just about all the time.

Q: *What do you experience during them?*

A: I get worked up and I can't do anything, I can't settle, got to keep moving.

Q: *That's restless. Do you ever get worked up to the point where you start to shake?*

Yes, a lot, in my hands.

Q: *Do you get sweaty?*

A: Yes, my hands and my face, it's embarrassing.

In response to direct questions, she agreed that when she is agitated, her stomach churns and she is unable to eat. Her heart races and she feels short of breath. She gets a dry mouth, she has a tightness in her throat so she can't talk or swallow properly and she stammers and loses her words. With these symptoms, she feels lightheaded and unsteady on her feet and has the feeling that she doesn't fit in, that the world is normal but she isn't.

During the bouts of agitation, she feels frightened and very irritable. She has to get away from whatever is bothering her and hide until it settles. She has "heaps" of bouts of agitation each day, often lasting up to an hour or two although sometimes a bad one can go on all day and only starts to settle when she is alone after midnight.

They are caused by "overthinking and worrying about everything, the boyfriend..."

Q: *In your ordinary daily life, is there anything you're frankly scared of, like heights, confined spaces, wide open spaces?*

A: I'm scared of being abandoned.

Q: *What about thunder and lightning, sudden noises, being touched unexpectedly?*

A: Sudden noises, and being touched. My brother does it to me, he sneaks up behind me when I'm not expecting it.

Q: *You startle easily?*

A: Yes, very badly, that's why he does it.

She is not comfortable in the dark and always has a night light in her bedroom. She is frightened of snakes although they are the only animals that bother her. Socially, she is fearful of crowds, standing in queues and of public speaking, which causes her great difficulty at school. She becomes agitated by appointments and interviews, and before tests or exams. She is frightened of public transport and never uses it, and of meeting strangers. She doesn't like to speak on the phone, especially if she has to ring an office to ask for something. She is quickly agitated by any sort of threat or criticism and by arguments or disputes, even if they don't involve her. She avoids any sort of confrontation and can't say No to people. She is very fearful of letting people down, of causing trouble or giving offence. She always tries to keep the peace, even when it causes her a lot of trouble. She is frightened of loneliness, humiliation and disapproval, and of making mistakes or failing at anything. The thought of making a mistake is enough to stop her trying something new, especially if people will be watching her. She fears the idea of mental illness and also feels faint when she has to have an injection. She is frightened of any sort of untrustworthy or shifty-looking people, and of aggressive people.

When she is out of her home, she has a very strong feeling that people are looking at her, talking behind her back and judging her. If somebody laughs nearby, she feels they're laughing at her. Around strangers, she always has the feeling that people are watching her or spying on her, or that she is under some sort of surveillance, but there was no sense of conspiracy or danger directed at her (i.e. these are signs of excessive self-consciousness but not frank paranoid symptoms). These feelings can be so strong that she has to leave whatever she is doing and go somewhere else, usually home to her room, before she can settle.

She checks doors, locks, keys, etc. very closely as she is always worried about security. She has to go back and recheck as she is frightened she may have made a mistake or she can't recall for certain whether she did it. She is not fussy about cleanliness, tidiness, order, punctuality or efficiency, but she is quite ritualistic in the order she does things like cleaning or putting things away, such as clothes or books. She has constant intrusive thoughts of impending trouble or of something serious going wrong but, at the time, these fantasies seem very real. She constantly imagines everything that could go wrong but she sees this as sensible, a matter of being prepared, and not as something to be resisted.

Physically, she has some low back pain but it has never been investigated and she doesn't take any medication for it.

Recent History:

She said she has been this way all her life, certainly throughout her schooling. There has been no recent change in her life apart from her relationship with her boyfriend, an engineering student. She met him two years ago and the relationship has never gone well. He drinks too much and smokes a lot of dope and they often argue. She is aware her parents don't approve of him even though they don't say anything.

Personal Background:

She was born and raised in New Zealand and migrated to Australia with her family at the age of eight. They have relatives here, including her paternal grandparents, and she wasn't worried by the move as she had been to Australia several times. Her father, who is now aged 49yrs, is a senior accountant with a large mining company. He is "a bit judgemental" and they get on fairly well except they tend to squabble, especially if she has been arguing with her mother. Her mother, a dental hygienist, is also aged 49yrs. She is "much like me, anxious and depressed." They argue quite a lot "due to her (the mother's) anxiety," which annoys her father. She has a 16yo brother who is in Year 11 at school and is "sporty and a bit nerdy" but otherwise he is "pretty normal." Again, they tend to argue, especially if he makes fun of her anxiety. She didn't know much about her family history. She thinks her paternal grandfather may have had bipolar disorder but she was fairly sure there was no history of substance abuse or of criminality.

She attended local state schools to the age of 17yrs, passing Year 12 with quite good marks. Asked how she got on with the teachers, she said she was very quiet and did her best to avoid any attention. She was "always" shy and nervous with the other children but had a few friends and said she could get on with most people. However, it was clear that this meant she did her best to avoid any sort of dispute or confrontation. In primary school, she liked sport but, by high school, had lost interest as she was "too anxious over being judged." She couldn't think of any particular interests she had at school. Her home life was unsettled as there was "a fair bit of arguing," although a lot of it was her arguing with her parents.

On leaving school, she went straight to university. She has passed all her units but felt she could do better if she were not so anxious. She has a few good friends but doesn't mix much socially. For four months last year, she didn't go out because of some argument with the boyfriend. She doesn't drink, uses no drugs, doesn't gamble and has no police record. Her general health is good with no infective conditions and no asthma.

Self-Assessment (Personality assessment):

Normally, she sees herself as "below everyone else." She said she is very nervous and is intensely bothered by guilt, shame and self-consciousness. She is unassertive and allows people to push her around. She is very wary of people and "never fully" trusts anyone, including the boyfriend. She is fairly tidy and organised, mostly patient, and follows rules as she doesn't want to attract attention. She wants to be able to mix with people but finds it very difficult and has to push herself. She is a bit jealous of people and tends to hold grudges: "I don't forget." She tries to keep a low profile to avoid any conflict with authority. She sees her temper as "quick, but only at home." Away from home, she simply gives in and avoids conflict. She sees her intellect as "average" and her self-esteem as "low, really low," due to "anxiety and overthinking."

Mental State Examination:

The mental state showed a slim, lightly-built young woman who would pass for about sixteen. She was dressed in clean sports clothes and joggers, with no visible tattoos, studs, scars or jewellery. She moved freely with no signs of pain but tended to sit still in her chair. At first, she was wary, edgy and unhappy and took some time to settle but by the end of the interview, she was able to laugh a little. She was somewhat guarded at first but was neither hostile nor suspicious. She spoke quietly with no speech defect, giving fairly brief answers to questions but did not appear to be withholding information. There were no psychotic features and nothing to indicate an organic impairment of brain function. She appeared to be of superior intellectual ability.

This case is fairly typical of patients referred to me. First point to note is that without a structured interview, the extent and severity of her anxiety symptoms would not have been found. Probably 99% of psychiatrists would have zeroed on her depressive symptoms and, of course, she has a full book: sleep disturbance, loss of appetite, low energy, inactivity, loss of interest and motivation, no social life, no sexual interest, poor memory and concentration, trouble thinking clearly, feeling low and miserable 80% of the time, feeling sick of things and of life itself and feeling death would be a relief. All that was lacking was suicidal ideas and impulses *but* she didn't want antidepressants or other psychiatric drugs.

By this stage, most psychiatrists would be reaching for the detention orders on the basis that she is clearly lacking insight and not capable of deciding what's good for her. I didn't. I didn't prescribe psychiatric drugs and she was managed as an outpatient with no compulsion. The reason is that depression is to be seen *not* as a thing in itself, but as a reaction to life events. In biological psychiatry, the line of causation goes directly from genes to neurons to mental symptoms. My case is that that concept is wrong, that for mental events, the line of causation starts with a prior mental event. And in Melissa's case, we don't have to look far for the prior mental events. It's the anxiety, as she said herself when she walked in.

So: By far the most common cause of a chronic or recurrent depressive state is an unsuspected anxiety state;

But: If you don't ask specifically about the anxiety state, you'll never know it exists. People don't volunteer it.

Next point is that her anxiety preceded the depression. In fact, it started so long ago that she couldn't recall ever being free of it. She had endured it for at least eight to ten years before she became depressed. Severe anxiety destroys people's lives and their self-esteem, and they react to these major life events with depression. If you want, you could say that her depression was a grief reaction to losing any hope for her life, to the endless losses with no prospect of life ever improving. If you look at it from this point of view, her depression is not an illness but it is the *normal reaction to massive losses*. A grief reaction is not a disease and, by the same token, since depression is the brain doing what it is designed to do, it is not a disease.

Third: if you don't ask, you won't be told. Anxious people have lived with their problem so long that they think it's normal. Quite often, people say: "But I thought everybody felt this way, but other people coped with it better than I do." No, most people have never experienced a panic attack, and many people (especially men) have little or no idea what anxiety is. It lies entirely outside their experience and they just don't get it. Remember that emotions are what philosophers and psychologists call "brute facts," or "raw givens," meaning something that can only be understood by direct experience as it cannot be further explained.

One panic attack can ruin your whole day. One a day for ten years forces you to give up hope for your life, and you will sink into black despair. If psychiatrists can't find an obvious loss to blame, they call it depression. It's pretty sad when you have to give up on life at nineteen but that's what anxiety does. But if nobody takes a proper history, nobody will find the anxiety or recognise its significance.

Take-home message: If you work out that a patient is depressed, congratulations. You're one third of the way there. Now all you have to do is find the cause, and deal with it.

The next case describes what it's like to live a life tortured by anxiety. Melissa's case tells us what anxiety *is*, now let's look at what anxiety does, or the *what* of anxiety.

Case 3.2 – Gerry T, 30yo male

Gerry T, an apprentice mechanic aged 30, was referred because of recurrent depression. Over the years, he had been seen several times by public mental health services and had been given a number of diagnoses: major depression, panic disorder, bipolar disorder and borderline personality. He was first prescribed antidepressants at age thirteen and had taken them on and off over the years but he didn't like them, partly because of side effects (weight gain, sexual effects, severe withdrawal) but mostly because they never seemed to work. His concern was that he had changed careers and had had several "turns" at work so he was worried about losing his job. He lived with his wife and two small children and was taking no drugs at the time.

Presenting complaints:

Questioning showed poor sleep and erratic appetite, with loss of energy, interest and motivation. His sexual interest was "OK, better than it has been." Socially, he was actively avoiding people, which had become normal for him. Under any sort of pressure, he was having trouble thinking clearly and he was delaying decisions where possible, for fear of making mistakes. The thought content was dominated by worries—money, family, work, everything. He was feeling low and miserable as much as half the time. It was "bad enough," meaning he was sick of things and had sometimes had the idea that it would be easier if he didn't wake up but there were no suicidal ideas. Sometimes on weekends or holidays, he would wake feeling good and would laugh and sing but it didn't last: "They told me it's part of my borderline personality."

However, he was regularly troubled by bouts of intense agitation, with shaking, sweating, churning stomach and racing heart. During them, he felt tight in the throat and tended to stammer and lose his words. He felt faint and had the feeling of the walls closing in. He was frightened and irritable during these attacks and tried to get away by himself. If he couldn't, he was likely to shout and throw things. When in these moods as a teenager, he recalled, he used to hurt himself but he hadn't done that for years. Most of his agitation happened at work. He was having 1-2 bouts a day, lasting half an hour or so, caused by worrying over his performance and, in particular, friction with two more senior people at work who were not actually in charge of him.

He had an extensive list of fears, all related to the human world. He feared crowds, queues and public speaking, interviews and appointments, tests and exams although this also depended on how he was feeling on the day. He didn't like meeting strangers or disputes of any sort, and was quickly agitated by criticism which he took as "very personal." He didn't like letting people down or causing trouble, and feared loneliness, humiliation and disapproval. In particular, he feared making mistakes or failing at anything. He was always frightened of the thought that he would develop a more serious mental illness. Socially, he quickly became agitated by having to deal with aggressive people, especially if he had his children with him. He was highly self-conscious but not paranoid, and there were no obsessive-compulsive features. He had been this way for most of his life.

Personal background:

His family life was very unsettled as his parents separated when he was nine but he maintained close contact with his father. His mother, who raised him, was "seriously anxious and depressed" and they used to argue but he got on reasonably well with his stepfather. He had a younger sister who was "like me, anxious and insecure." He didn't do well at school as he was very shy and nervous and was often teased. His marks were erratic, depending on what was going on at home or in the playground. In the main, he didn't get on well with the teachers as he often didn't try. His only friends were the "misfits that nobody liked." He feels his home life was poor and he spent as much time out of the house as possible.

By age thirteen, he was "very shy and suicidal" and saw a psychiatrist who prescribed antidepressants but there was no other treatment. By fourteen, he was smoking marijuana and drinking because it made him feel better. He left school at sixteen, after Year 11, but his work record was very unsettled. Mostly, he had worked as a driver and changed jobs whenever he became too anxious. His marriage was unstable and there had been several separations over the years, mostly due to his agitation. He stopped drugs and alcohol at twenty-four and had no police record.

Self-assessment and mental state:

He saw himself as someone who was "fairly nervous but tries to be a good person." In the past, he had been very unassertive and people took advantage of him but since his children were born, he had become assertive to the point of arguing. He was intensely bothered by guilt, shame and self-consciousness and was quite mistrustful of people so that he found it easier to keep to himself. He liked to follow rules and got on well with authority. His temper was "mostly placid," he saw his intellect as "average" and his self-esteem as "low, no confidence at all." The mental state showed a chubby chap of stated age, dressed in clean casual clothes with no tattoos etc. He was pleasant and keen to talk. There were no overt signs of mental disorder, and he was at least of bright normal intellectual ability.

This is a very typical case for office psychiatry. For seventeen years, he had been treated for depression but, even though he couldn't explain it, he knew all along that the real problem was anxiety. The cluster of fears he described is so common that we have to wonder why it happens so often. He had no fears of the natural world but his capacity to relate to people was seriously affected. What's going on? Why are humans so scared of other humans? It wasn't a fear of physical aggression: since his teenage years, he had known he could handle himself, and he hadn't been in a fight since he stopped drinking. Still, the thought of mixing with people caused him so much anxiety that he found it easier to stay home.

All his fears related to how he was performing, and how people were judging him, or what is known as performance anxiety. For Gerry, humiliation, disapproval, making mistakes or looking stupid were worse than somebody physically attacking him. This is extremely widespread but it is not cultural, nor is it related to age, sex, intelligence, size, or appearance, health or wealth. Fear of humiliation and scorn is absolutely basic and stems from the need to be accepted, to be approved. Humans are social animals, we feel better in groups. For us, the worst thing is to be excluded from the group. If you want to break somebody, you put him in solitary confinement while the ultimate sentence is exile.

But that's not true of all people. Most of us can handle a degree of disapproval. It isn't the end of the world if somebody doesn't like our clothes, or our face, or laughs at our cooking or work. The people who can't take it are those, like Gerry, who have no self-esteem. If a person has no self-approval, he is dependent on other people for approval, and is therefore automatically scared he isn't going to get it. So high levels of performance anxiety are almost always driven by low self-esteem. Trouble is, high anxiety causes mistakes, which reinforce the low self-esteem. A person with high self-esteem isn't much fussed by his mistakes because he looks to his achievements and feels better because of them. People with low self-esteem forget their achievements and focus all their attention on their failings, because they hurt so much. Quite often, they can't even think of one good thing about themselves but they can recite a long list of failings. If they look in a mirror, they don't see anything good, only blemishes.

So this is part of the unfairness of life: people who are blessed with good families arrive at school with good self-esteem, and everything acts to build on it, to strengthen and reinforce it. People feel good around the confident person, so he gets lots of invitations to birthday parties, he is asked to join the football team and life gets better and better. Pity the poor little mite who has been yelled at all his short life; he shrinks from contact, hides from the others and soon, nobody wants to be seen sitting near him. If he's really unlucky, some bully decides to get his kicks by teasing the lonely kid that nobody else will defend, and so it gets worse.

Anxiety is the most communicable of emotions. Sitting near an anxious person is unpleasant so naturally enough, everybody wants to be near the cheerful, expansive person who can make them laugh. Once again, we see a mechanism by which anxiety reinforces itself, but this time through its effects on other people in the social environment.

The message of this chapter is that anxiety is severe, destructive and persistent; it starts early and reinforces itself by a variety of social and psychological means. There is a close relationship between low self-esteem and high social or performance anxiety, and between severe, long-term anxiety and depression. The most common cause of an unexplained or recurrent depressive state is an unsuspected anxiety state. But it is only unsuspected because nobody bothered to take a proper history.

Modern psychiatry relegates anxiety to the level of a nuisance, it is an also-ran but not an SMI (Serious Mental Illness). Psychiatry is obsessed by depression, which it can't explain, and ignores anxiety, which it also can't explain because anxiety only makes sense in a cognitive model. The fact that Gerry had been diagnosed with major depression, panic disorder, bipolar disorder and borderline personality says only that nobody knew what was going on in his life. The reason they didn't know was mainly because they hadn't taken a history, but also because even if they had, they didn't have a model that could make sense of his symptoms. It's so much easier to smile indulgently and recite "Chemical imbalance of the brain" while reaching for the prescription pad. But that dismisses the patients' misery as of no account, it dehumanises them and leaves them feeling lost and alone. Which was more or less the story of these two patients' lives

.

PART II –
The Nature of Anxiety

4 The Role of Anxiety

It is said that a true panic is the most dreadful feeling we can experience and still survive. I believe that, but if it's so bad, why is it there? What role does it serve? The answer is very simple. Make a noise near the family cat and see what she does, or watch some birds in the garden when the cat goes out for a stroll. Touch a snail with a blade of grass, drop a small stone into a school of fish, clap your hands near a horse (no, don't do that) or unexpectedly brush your fingers lightly over the back of somebody's neck (preferably somebody you know well). In each case, the animal (including the human animal) shows a stereotyped response known as the alerting reaction or, if it's more intense, as the fight or flight reaction. That is, the animal's physiology is abruptly shifted from drowsily chewing on grass or gazing out the window to a state of high alertness or arousal. This gets them ready to deal with the world, whether it's good or bad, and that's more or less what we call anxiety. Remember that a person who has just won a match or passed a major exam is also highly aroused but she has no anxiety at all. Physiological arousal is not the same as anxiety but it's a close enough approximation.

A drowsy or unalert person is in a sort of torpor. His breathing is slow and moderately deep, his heart rate is slow, blood flow is directed away from the muscles to the abdominal viscera, his skin is warm and dry and so on. Mentally, his mind is unfocussed and he tends to drift from one thought to the other with no plan.

If, however, you jab him with a pin, or he realises he has to rush to catch the train, or he sees a snake or hears a sudden noise, his entire physiology changes. Instantly, he will become highly alert and focused. His heart rate accelerates rapidly, his breathing becomes much faster while the skin on his hands and feet becomes slightly sweaty. Internally, his blood flow is directed away from the abdomen to the heart, the brain and to to the physical muscles. His muscles tighten and he will start to tremble slightly. Mentally, he is highly aware of his surroundings, he is thinking very fast, jumping from topic to topic, and thinking of a wide range of possibilities. That is, he is ready to fight or run away.

From now on, I will talk of this as the anxiety response but remember that it doesn't have to be unpleasant. A hunter who suddenly sees his quarry will react in the same way (as will the quarry, of course). The arousal response gets you ready to deal with a challenge. The essence of the anxiety response is that it gets you ready to deal with a threat but arousal and anxiety are very similar. Essentially, we can define anxiety as follows:

> Anxiety is the reaction we experience in response to the perception of an impending threat.

This means that you can't experience anxiety without believing you are under some sort of threat. Conversely, if you feel anxious, you have perceived a threat somewhere.

A threat is always in the future, coming at you. You cannot be anxious about the past. You can be amused, or angered, or bored, or saddened by the past but since there is no way it can hurt you, you can no longer see it as a threat. If you feel anxious thinking of a past event, it will be because of your concern for its future consequences.

Just for completeness, we can define excitement in the same terms even though we won't be talking about it just yet:

> Excitement is the reaction we experience in response to the perception of an impending victory.

The physiological states of anxiety and excitement are very alike.

All animals can perceive threats. Some, like snails, react only to a physical touch. Snakes and fish respond to vibration. Most animals respond to a range of sensory inputs (sound, smell, vision, touch etc) but usually rely on one sensory modality more than the others. A threat means only that the animal must take evasive action to survive, it must change whatever it is doing before it ends up as somebody's breakfast. The alerting responses gets it ready to make those changes, either to fight or run like crazy. Remember that we don't have to invoke a theory of mind in order to use the concept of a threat. Dogs and cats perceive threats, birds perceive threats, fish, even worms don't like being poked. Monkeys, of course, are extremely alert to their surroundings and react to a wide range of potential threats.

We can use a simple, mechanistic model to account for the standard response to external threats in all animals, including humans. However, if you want to explain a threat response that won't go away, or keeps flaring up half a dozen times a day without any obvious threat, as Melissa's did, you will need a formal theory of mind. Biological psychiatry doesn't have a theory of mind, so it can't explain anxiety. For orthodox psychiatry, the only possible explanation for a mental malfunction is a brain malfunction. We will see that this is so simplistic as to miss the point entirely but first, we need a more substantial framework. The framework is known as psychophysiology, meaning the borderland between psychology and physiology.

Don't worry about the big words, the general principles are very straight-forward and you can always check them against your own experience. This raises a very important point: that any theory of anxiety must make intuitive sense. If your first response is "That sounds dumb," then you're probably right.

A person in a state of high arousal shows a broad range of characteristic biological responses. These affect every part of the body from the scalp (hair standing upright) to the soles of the feet (cold and sweaty). His heart rate is fast, his blood is circulating rapidly through the essential organs of heart, brain and muscles, at the expense of blood flow in the abdominal viscera and skin. His respiratory rate is higher and he is moving a greater volume of air with each inspiration, most likely by mouth-breathing. His mouth will probably be dry and he will experience a sense of a lump or tightness in his throat so that he has trouble swallowing and his voice may quaver. His muscles are tense and he trembles in the limbs. Even if a tremor can't be seen, he will have a sense of his muscles having turned to jelly or being weak in the knees. His skin is cool to cold, pale and sweaty, his pupils are dilated and his heart is racing. If he tries to speak, his voice may quaver and he is likely to stutter or stammer or lose his words. He may feel faint, light-headed or dizzy or be unsteady on his feet and clumsy in movements.

Anxious people will typically describe cognitive symptoms, such as feel-ing trapped or a sense of the walls closing in on them, or that the world somehow looks different (derealisation), or they feel different themselves. This may be that they feel different from other people (alienation), or differ-ent from their normal selves (depersonalisation). Asked how he feels, an anxious person will probably say he feels frightened or apprehensive, or that something terrible is about to happen. Equally, he may say he feels very irritable and annoyed. Behaviourally, he may try to get away from whatever is troubling him or, very likely, find some sort of chemical to reduce his fear. If he is irritable, he may start to shout and bang things or punch walls, pick arguments or get into a fight.

Mainstream psychiatry sees all anxiety states as different entities. A person who responds to anxiety with an urgent need to scrub things and put them away is seen as suffering the disorder called Obsessive-Compulsive Disorder while somebody else, who experiences exactly the same inner state, may start drinking and will be deemed to suffer a completely separate dis-order called Alcohol Abuse Disorder. This makes no sense at all. The inner state of anxiety is exactly the same, the only difference is how they handle it, or what they do to reduce it. Some people try to withdraw from life (Avoidant Personality Disorder); some people worry about their health (Somatisation Disorder, previously known as hypochondriasis); some people spend money or hoard things; some fight or cut themselves while others are promiscuous; some join cults or meditate; plenty of people gamble while others eat to calm their agitation. Many people, of course, use drugs of various sorts, experimenting until they find a chemical that reduces their anxiety. It is only a matter of personal choice, local culture and availability that decides whether a person uses tranquillisers such as opiates or benzo-diazepines, or stimulants such as amphetamines and cocaine.

It doesn't matter what they do, all these allegedly different categories of mental disorder are only superficial variations on a single theme, *anxiety*. All that counts is that they are gripped by fear and they have to do something, anything, to reduce it.

> I once said to a patient: "You don't have a primary depressive state, your main problem is that you're very anxious."
> "Oh no," she exclaimed, clearly frightened, "not anxiety! That's terrifying!"

Remember this: Anxiety is intolerable. There is only one sort of anxiety, the scary sort, but there's an infinite number of ways to try to reduce it. Practically all of them are unsuccessful.

There is an important relationship between your level of arousal (~anxiety) and your ability to perform in your daily life. This was discovered in about 1908 by some American psychologists who were doing nasty things to defenceless little rats. What they found, now known as the Yerkes-Dodson principle, is both simple and universal: There is an optimal level of arousal for each of us to perform our tasks. Below this level, we are too drowsy or bored to pay much attention and we make mistakes. Above it, we become too agitated to perform and we make mistakes. This point is absolutely critical to the concept of anxiety as a psychological, as distinct from biological, construct. We can see it clearly on the Yerkes-Dodson curve, in figure 4.1:

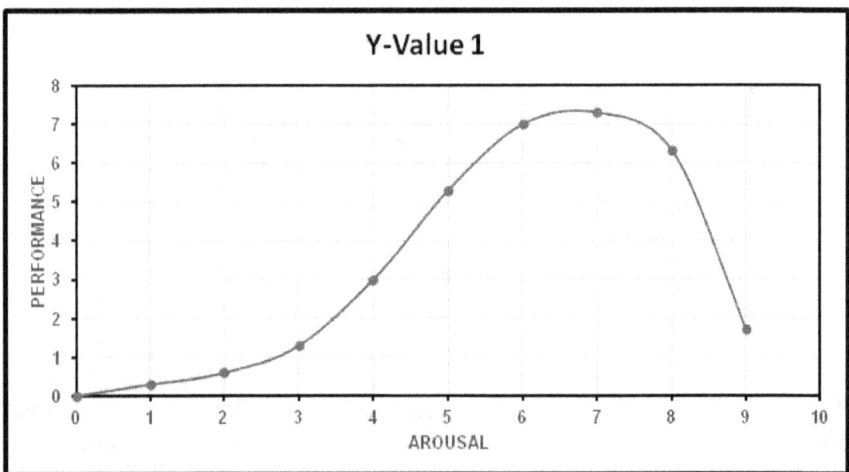

Figure 4.1: The Yerkes-Dodson Curve.

This curve graphs performance against arousal. Arousal we have defined above, essentially the difference between being drowsy and being alert and ready for action. Performance means exactly what you would expect, your performance on some task that can be measured. It might be tying your shoelaces or doing a crossword; filling your tax form or driving a big truck through crowded streets; giving a speech, attending a job interview or removing somebody's appendix. If your arousal is zero, as when you are asleep, your performance is necessarily zero. As you wake up and your arousal goes up one unit, your performance also goes up, but only by about a quarter of a unit. As arousal goes up another unit, the improvement in performance accelerates and goes up half a unit; next level of arousal, performance has gone up 1.5 units; one more unit of arousal, and performance is streaking ahead. However, it doesn't keep going up forever; at a certain level of arousal, your performance starts to plateau. If your arousal keeps getting higher and higher, then your performance starts to decline, slowly at first, then faster and faster until it is in free-fall. This is the stage of true panic where a person can't do anything, even to save himself. In panic, arousal is so high that the sufferer is likely to run in front of a bus without realising what he is doing.

This principle is universal: it applies to all humans at all times, and to all animals that have been tested. What is known as sports psychology, or exam psychology, or the sort of psychology taught to special military forces, aims to get the person to her optimal level and stay there, without going too high or too low. The fact that a person is making mistakes doesn't tell you anything about her level of arousal, it may be too low to perform properly or it may be too high. If her level of arousal is below her optimal level, the correct treatment is to make her more alert (remind her of the time, yell, shake her, etc) but if her arousal level is too high, these moves will make her worse. If she is over-aroused, the correct treatment is to calm her. This may be by talking quietly, or walking her away from the problem, or using a tranquilliser to reduce her arousal. That is, tranquillisers have an anomalous effect, in that they make some people go to sleep while they make others more functional. It depends on where they are on the curve.

For students, this is important. A student who is easily bored (as I was) needs a lot of stimulation to stay awake, whereas others who are taking their work far too seriously need something to calm them down. It's true of all workers but bored workers may decide to stir things up by doing something silly or risky (as I often did). When you understand this simple principle, you are halfway to understanding anxiety states. For the rest, look again at your family dog or cat. Rover and Puss-in-Boots are quietly snoozing in their favourite places in the house. Suddenly, there is a loud knock at the door. In an instant, Rover jumps up barking and runs to the door while the cat leaps in one mighty bound to the top of the bookcase. That is, they have become highly aroused and are acting defensively.

First point to note: the anxiety response is very fast. We are talking of just hundreds of milliseconds between the stimulus and the response. You can see this in figure 4.2, which graphs arousal vs time following a scary event. In the following graphs, the units are arbitrary. An arousal level of one is taken as the basal level while seven is taken as the level of dysfunction, as per the Yerkes-Dodson Curve (Fig. 4.1). Levels of arousal above this cause rapidly increasing disability which, crucially, compounds or feeds upon itself, i.e. poor performance causes further arousal, and thence further disability.

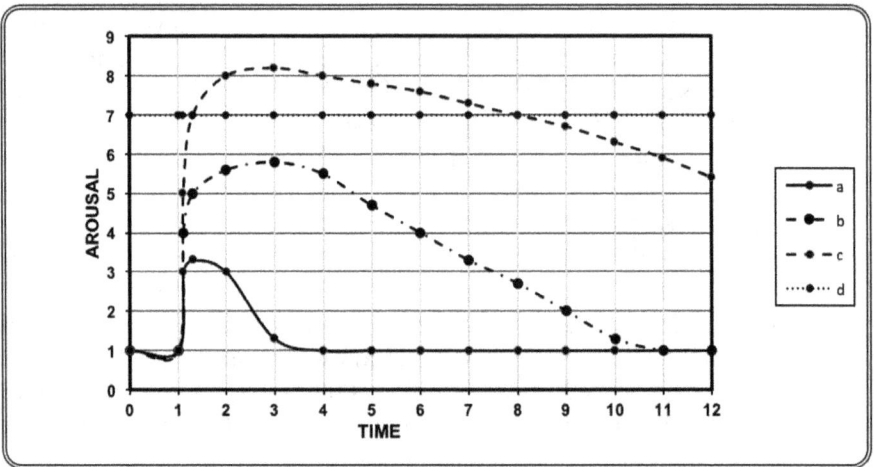

Figure 4.2: Acute arousal response.

In Figure 4.2, the curves have been compressed to show them together. In practice, the levels of arousal of a severe anxiety response to a major stimulus are more like ten or twenty times higher and last very much longer than those of a mild response. After a mild fright, a person may be back to normal in ten minutes while after a severe fright, it may be days or longer before he starts to get back to normal.

Second point: once aroused, we stay aroused for some time, as you see in Graph 4.2. The arousal or anxiety response doesn't stop just because nothing happens. Even if you yell out, "Shut up you stupid dog, it was the wind banging," he doesn't calm down immediately. Arousal rises quickly and drops slowly, for obvious reasons. It wouldn't do if you became aroused on seeing a crocodile, but when it disappeared into the water, you immediately stopped worrying about it. That's not how crocodiles hunt, they rely on stealth in the murky water (the rule for crocs is you only have to worry about the one you can't see). The role of arousal is to save your bacon, it keeps you alert and ready for action, forcing you to behave defensively even when the threat seems to have faded.

Point three. If something happens to cause further alarm while you are still aroused, your level of arousal will go much higher and will take a lot longer to settle. This causes a lot of confusion, which it shouldn't. Consider a typical case:

> While waiting for her bus, a young woman witnessed a traffic accident. A car banged into another then slewed across in front of a cyclist, knocking him to the ground. Her bus arrived and she had to get on but while recounting the story at work, a door slammed behind her. She screamed and began to cry, then fled the room and shortly after, left the building. People were annoyed, saying she was over-reacting to the door slamming, that she was histrionic or attention-seeking. Their view was that doors slam all the time, she should have been able to distinguish between a door and something more serious.

This sort of thing is common. People often think that the response to a startling stimulus or fright of any sort should never be more than "reasonable," meaning what they would expect from a person in a calm state. However, for a person who is already anxious, regardless of the reason, a further fright doesn't take them to the level they would normally experience for that event, it *adds to their existing level of arousal* and therefore goes well beyond "reasonable." This is also the case for each threat that you perceive: if you haven't settled from the last one, your arousal level goes up higher and higher with each threat. And higher. There is essentially no upper limit to arousal; it goes up and up until you do what is necessary to save yourself. We can call this a "cumulative stress reaction," as in Figure 4.3.

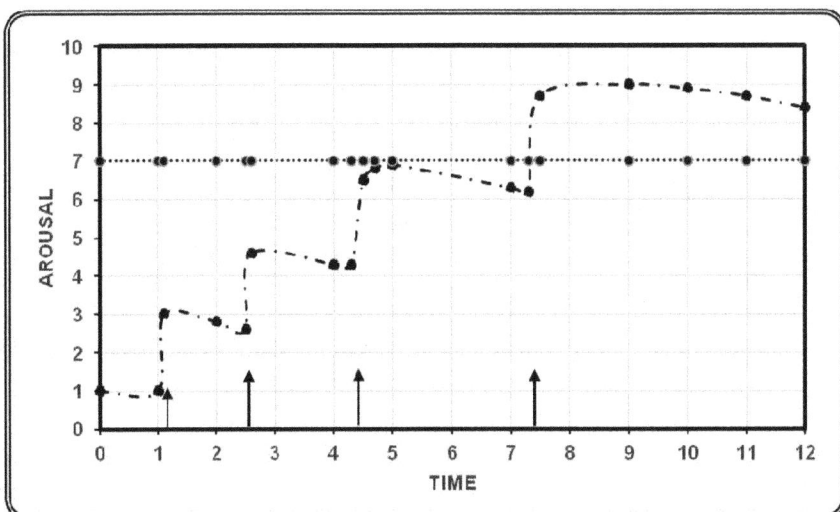

Figure 4.3. Cumulative Anxiety Response.

Here, there are four frights, roughly at Times 1, 2.5, 4 and 7. Because the arousal is already high at the fourth one, it is pushed above the level of clinical significance, shown as level 7. In ordinary life, each consecutive stress reaction is larger than the first, they amplify and exaggerate with time. Three relatively small stressors in rapid succession may even have a much stronger effect that one major stressor. This is more likely to happen if the person is suffering sleep deprivation after the first one, or is already sick or weakened, such as with illnesses like malaria, hepatitis etc, or is in pain.

The cumulative stress or anxiety reaction is far more common than you might think. It is often seen in soldiers who have been exposed to lengthy combat operations, to emergency workers and so on. Habitually anxious people normally function close to the level of disability, which means it takes only a minor stimulus to push them over the edge. That doesn't mean they are "weak characters," it means they are already highly aroused due to seeing lots of threats, which are just events in the environment that other people don't see as threats.

Point four. True panic or terror states are fortunately uncommon but they need to be seen as emergencies. People become so disordered that they don't know what they are doing. That is, their cognitive functions become disturbed to the extent of being non-functional. The terrified person is at serious risk of falling down the stairs or doing something desperate to relieve his agitation. As the state of arousal goes up and up, the mind begins to spin faster and faster, looking for solutions to the threat. People may come up with a good response but then, because their capacity to focus on a single point is so disturbed, they forget it and run off to try something else. Also, the memory of a person in a state of terror begins to fail. They can't recall things they should, and they can't take in anything new. You may say to a panic-stricken person: "Take the second passage and then open the green door." A few moments later, you hear back: "Did you say the green passage and then open the second door? I can't find a green passage, oh what am I going to do?"

Five. The terrified person is unable to sleep so before long, his state of panic will become complicated by sleep deprivation. One of the features of sleep deprivation is that people start to hallucinate, which means they slip straight into a dreaming state. This produces what is called a high-arousal psychotic state. It is very important to recognize this as it is *not* a permanent psychosis. The hallucinations will settle as his arousal returns to normal but there is reason to believe that prolonged administration of antipsychotic drugs can convert a brief psychotic reaction into a long-term disorder.

Point six. Nobody can endure terror for long. People have to do something for relief but because their thinking is scrambled, what they do may in fact make things get worse, such as get drunk, run into the night or attack somebody who is trying to help them. When I was at school, there was a case of a couple who were flying a light plane when they ran into a thunderstorm. The wife was terrified of lightning and insisted the husband put the aircraft down in a paddock. As soon as they stopped, she jumped out of the plane and ran into the whirling propeller, which killed her instantly. They were still in the thunderstorm, so where would she have run anyway? In her terror, she didn't think of that, but that's what panic does. At the highest levels of arousal, intellectual function is fragmented and the person may be more or less unaware of his surroundings and unable to act to help himself or to respond to the world.

Finally, it is the nature of the threat response that, when agitated, we look *out there* for the cause, not *in here*. When we are frightened, we do not sit down in an introspective state, scanning our inner workings to find out what is going on, we are fixated on the outside world. A frightened person's eyes dart around, he is highly alert to every sound, smell and touch. That's how evolution designed it. It does not represent stupidity, as in "Calm down, mate, your wallet is here, under your jacket, nobody's pinched it."

(A postscript: There are no degrees of panic. You're either totally consumed by it or it isn't panic. Don't ever use vapid expressions such as "moderate panic" or "extreme panic." That's like saying moderately dead or extremely dead. The word *extreme* means "at the limits of human experience, the point beyond which there is no return." You should only use it once a year. While we're splitting hairs, could I also point out that the word "marked," beloved by the editors of the *Diagnostic and Statistical Manual of Mental Disorders, 5th Ed.* (DSM-5), is an adjective, not an adverb. It means "noted," "specified," or "picked out," as in "a marked man." It does not mean "very," "rather," "intensely" or anything like that).

In practice, if a person is trying to conceal his level of arousal, it may be very difficult to be sure of it. There are plenty of people who don't want to reveal how anxious they are. At mild levels, they may simply be skittish and inclined to laugh too much. Quite often, anxious people come across as impulsive and disorganised. For example, they agree to go to a party but when it's time to leave, they suddenly decide they have to finish an assignment, or wash the dog or something that could have been done before, or could wait until tomorrow. Silly, irritating or childish behaviour is very likely driven by concealed anxiety. In high school students, the "class clown" is often a bright child, usually a boy, who has fallen behind and is too embarrassed to admit it and ask for help. Compulsive joking, especially practical jokes, or an inability to take things seriously, are often signs of an underlying anxious personality. One of the things they can't take seriously is their own anxiety, just because admitting it is too scary.

When these people become depressed, as anxious people mostly do, it seems to come from nowhere. When you ask, they will not be able to give any obvious reasons: nothing has changed, work is still there, family are still there, no particular money worries and so on, but this terrible depression has just swept in from nowhere. They present as rather edgy but physically agitated, unable to settle to anything, disorganised and impulsive. Their moods are very brittle, they try to laugh then burst into floods of tears which will dry as soon as they appeared:

> "I don't know what's wrong with me, I just can't stop this silly crying. It's not as if there's anything wrong in my life, I've got a lovely family, a lovely house, a good job or good husband..."

If you ask, "Are you an anxious person?" they will usually deny it with a bright laugh. However, a proper history will reveal that this well-known syndrome, previously called agitated depression but now mostly lumped under "bipolar disorder," is the predictable outcome of a carefully-concealed anxious personality. The reason it is concealed is because they see it as a moral failing, a sign of personal weakness.

In the past, people with agitated depression were treated with large doses of sedating antidepressants, often with ECT, and they appeared to respond very well, only for the same problems to return in a year or two. The reason they respond is because they want to be sedated or even given oblivion by the ECT, so they don't have to think about being anxious. Eventually, they present in another state of intense agitation, somebody labels them "bipolar" and they go on drugs for life. However, they never do well because the underlying anxiety problem is still there. It may be buried under a pile of drugs but it never goes away.

These people like the idea that depression is a biological disease of the brain, they prefer tablets to talking because talking about their anxiety is the last thing they want. Being told "It's not you, it's all those nasty chemicals playing up in your brain" is manna from heaven. They love psychiatrists who excuse them from responsibility for their moral failings ardently support the idea of biological psychiatry.

Often, these people join what seem to be community support groups for people with mental disorder. Invariably, the message is "You don't have to feel ashamed for having a chemical imbalance of the brain, take your tablets and all will be well." The websites for these groups look remarkably professional but if you check their financial statements, you will find they get large donations from... drug companies. They are sometimes called "grassroots organisations" and governments like their input for enquiries, but they are better seen as "astroturf" groups. This means totally synthetic and dropped from above, not developing naturally from below. But enough cynicism.

Let's look at another case which shows these features.

Case 4.1: Cameron S, 48yo male

This man is a district manager for IT services for a large government department whose IT division is notoriously disorganised. He was referred after he saw his GP to ask whether he should resume antidepressants. For five years after his first marriage ended, ten years before, he had taken escitalopram (Lexapro) but he wasn't keen on it as it caused huge weight gain and loss of libido. Also, he didn't believe he was really depressed. At some stage, he had been told he was suffering PTSD due to his first wife's "malignant narcissism" but he didn't know if he had been given specific treatment. He lived with his partner and their two small children, and also had joint custody of his two teenage children.

Presenting complaints:

"I've had ten years of issues because of PTSD from my first marriage to a malignant narcissist." His sleep was erratic and he often took up to 3hrs to get to sleep. He had been drinking as much as a bottle of wine to help him sleep. He had also been given a CPAP machine for sleep apnoea but he said it didn't work and he had stopped using it. During the week, he woke at 6.00am with an alarm but he felt groggy and exhausted. On weekends, he slept in a bit but the children were up early and woke him. After lunch at work, he often struggled to stay awake. His appetite was excessive and he had steadily gained weight over the years, from 70 to 100kg. He had little energy and didn't get much exercise although he helped with the children's sport. He didn't have much interest in things, either in his private life or at work, and his motivation to do things had waned. Socially, he had become quite withdrawn. At work, he got on well with most people although his two immediate supervisors infuriated him. He said his sexual interest was "not too bad for an old man."

He felt his memory and concentration were quite patchy but nobody else seemed to notice. He was having trouble thinking clearly as he tended to become confused and flustered under pressure, and there was a lot of pressure at work. His two bosses didn't like each other and each tried to use him against the other. Faced with decisions, he was tending to delay them where possible, which was not like him. He was preoccupied with the pressures at work and concerns over the possibility of losing his job, especially as so many services were being privatised. There were no disturbances of perception.

He described his mood as "pretty bad" as he had been feeling low and miserable about 20% of the time, mostly at work or when thinking about it. He was sick of things and felt trapped but was not sick of life itself and there were no suicidal ideas. The unhappiness was due to problems at work and the never-ending difficulties of dealing with his ex-wife. He had never experienced bouts of elevated mood but he had frequent episodes of feeling agitated and irritable. During these, he was shaky, sweaty and tremulous inside. His heart raced, his stomach churned and sometimes he felt he might vomit. He was short of breath and tended to gasp for air, his mouth was dry and he drank a lot of water. He tended to stammer and lose his words and sometimes felt light-headed and unsteady on his feet. During these bouts, he felt trapped and confused but there were no other cognitive symptoms. He was frightened and angry and tended to snap unless he could get away by himself until he settled.

On a good day, such as on holiday with the children, he might not feel agitated at all but on a bad day, he would wake feeling agitated and it would last until long after he went to bed. Mostly, the agitation was caused by trouble at work, including anticipating difficulties with his squabbling bosses, and also having to deal with his ex-wife: "She can wreck my day just be refusing to answer the phone, and she knows it." At home, his partner worked part-time and studied part-time so they were always under pressure and he had to do a lot of the housework at night or on weekends. His partner was very fussy about cleanliness, tidiness and order but he wasn't, which led to friction: "I'm a bit of a pig, actually, I'd rather take the kids to the beach than scrub the floors but then I wouldn't be able to enjoy myself because I'd know there'd be trouble when we got home."

On questioning, he was frightened of heights but most of his fears were social in nature. He feared crowds and didn't like standing in queues. In the past, he had always been very nervous before tests and exams, and he didn't like threats or criticism. He was fearful of any sort of dispute and couldn't say No to people. He hated letting people down, causing trouble or giving offence. He always went out of his way to keep the peace but this often made things worse. In particular, he feared making mistakes or failing at anything. He was frightened of death and mental illness, and of dealing with aggressive people.

At work, he had a strong feeling that people were watching him and judging him, and he often felt exposed to some sort of danger or risk. From time to time, he had the feeling that people were conspiring against him but this stopped when he was away from his office. He had always been fussy about punctuality but there were no obsessive-compulsive features. His physical health wasn't good as he was overweight and had been hypertensive at times.

He couldn't recall when these symptoms began, probably during his first marriage. After the separation, which he found "incredibly traumatic," he was referred to a psychiatrist who diagnosed "mild PTSD" and prescribed the antidepressant.

Personal background:

He had always lived in the same city. His parents were in their seventies. His father had been a salesman, described as "pretty strict" while his mother had worked part-time while indulging her hobby of china painting. She was "nice enough" and he kept in regular touch with his parents. One brother had left the city after his marriage failed and lived on an isolated small farm where he "brooded in his twisted way." The other was a school teacher in a distant town and was "pretty good" but they weren't especially close. There was no other family history of mental disorder, substance abuse or criminality.

He attended local Catholic schools to Year 12, passing with "quite good" marks. He said he got on well with the teachers but not very well with the other children. He was very small for his age and was often teased and bullied. He didn't play sport because of his size but liked making models. When he turned fifteen, he was able to join the military cadets and he did well at this. Compared with other children at his school, he felt his home life was "pretty good."

On leaving school, he went to a technical university to study engineering but he spent most of his time in student politics and didn't work very hard. He enjoyed the social life at university and was drinking fairly heavily. He was also in the military reserves and found time to train for his private pilot's licence: "I made up for all the bad times I'd had at school. Maybe I should have worked harder but what the hell, you're only young once." On graduating, he joined a government department and began work in IT but he found work was very different from university life and he started to become anxious again. He was in a relationship for four years but this ended when he was given a grant to travel overseas for extra study. He was away several years and married during this time.

When he came back to his former department, he was given a position below his previous level so, after months of dissatisfaction and irritability, he left. At about the same time, his marriage started to deteriorate. His wife became addicted to a variety of drugs and became "insanely jealous." She was mixing alcohol, narcotics and tranquillisers so he had to come home from work and care for the children as she was often incapable. She was ringing him at work, accusing him of having affairs, checking his phone and emails and was often physically aggressive. They were sleeping separately but he had to lock his bedroom door as she drank at night and would come in to berate him. Every time he tried to get some sort of help, she made out that there was nothing wrong with her, that he was the one with the problem. Eventually, she began to threaten to kill him if he didn't stop seeing all the other women so he left. The divorce was protracted and bitter and he was finally referred to a psychiatrist. Two years later, he began his present relationship and felt it was going well.

Normally, he drank moderately but he had been drinking a lot more lately. He used no illegal drugs, didn't gamble and had no police record.

Self-assessment:

"Mostly I'm fairly happy but a bit nervous." He agreed he was nervous and not very assertive. He was trusting, patient and "tidy enough." Normally, he was quite social and liked to mix but admitted he had to have a few drinks first. He was not inclined to be jealous and didn't hold grudges. He followed rules but was "not keen" on authority and tended to keep his distance. He felt his temper was "fairly even," his intellect "bright" and his self-esteem was "medium to low, always lacking confidence."

Mental state examination:

The mental state showed an overweight man of stated age, dressed in rumpled office clothes, with no visible tattoos, studs, scars or jewellery. He tended to move and fidget a lot and gave brief, dismissive laughs as though self-conscious. He was edgy but not depressed, hostile or suspicious. There were no psychotic features and he was probably of superior intellect.

Let's go back to his presenting complaint:

"I've had ten years of issues because of mild PTSD from my first marriage to a malignant narcissist."

First, there's no such thing as "mild PTSD." It isn't a mild condition. Next, the expression 'malignant narcissist' is pop psychology. It doesn't exist in psychiatry and most of the people who wear it (or boast it) are what we used to call psychopaths. Cameron's description of his ex-wife's behaviour was typical of what is known as pathological jealousy, or the Othello syndrome, and it is commonly seen in drug and alcohol abuse. It's one of the paranoid states and is quite likely the most dangerous of all psychiatric conditions. When she threatened to kill him, he had every reason to be scared. However, it can be very deceptive as it merges imperceptibly across the spectrum, from mild mistrust, to suspicion, to brooding preoccupation with infidelity, to constant accusations, whence it is but a small step to a full-blown paranoid psychosis with delusional jealousy. By the time she began threatening murder, she was clearly in the grip of a paranoid psychosis. It is also typical that these people can convince everybody that the other person has the problem.

Part of the trouble dealing with pathological jealousy is that you never know quite where the person sits on the spectrum. There is normally relatively good preservation of personality; jealous people can hold down jobs, run a family or business and often maintain a normal social life. But it's all front: underneath, the seething maelstrom of suspicion swirls into every aspect of life until eventually, it destroys everything. In Cameron's case, his wife's endless accusations that he was having affairs finally forced him to leave.

It's clear that he was suffering when the marriage was finally dissolved but the diagnosis of PTSD was incorrect. The first psychiatrist hadn't taken a complete history and didn't know of Cameron's long-standing anxiety symptoms. It wasn't the case that all his current symptoms were new and therefore attributable to the marriage. His marriage didn't cause his fear of heights, or exams, or his fear of failure; in fact, it was his fear of admitting failure that kept him in the marriage long after he knew it had no future.

As an adult, he lived with a constant, low to moderate level of anxiety, depending on what was going on around him. Specifically, his problem was his fear of upsetting people, of causing trouble and attracting criticism and, above all, of failing. This went straight back to childhood. He'd always been anxious; the only time he wasn't much troubled by anxiety was during his university years when he started drinking and stopped competing. Socially, he had finally grown to average height and was able to impress people with his high verbal facility and his sense of humour, well-lubricated by alcohol. At last, he was able to get by on his natural talent

Specific treatment of Cameron's anxiety led to a rapid improvement in his mental state. Without antidepressants, as he insisted. Perhaps if he had been seen as a teenager, his life would have been different. The next case had been seen as a teenager but it hadn't done him any good.

Case 5.2. Mark C, aged 27yrs.

This man was referred for assessment by the local probation office as he had been convicted of possession of small amounts of marijuana and amphetamines. His probation officer wanted to know if he was suitable for a drug diversion program as he had been diagnosed as schizophrenic at the age of 13yrs and his mental state was very unsettled. He had moved back to stay with his parents and had stopped all drugs, legal and illegal, although he later revealed he hadn't taken the psychiatric drugs for years as he didn't like them. Mostly he worked as a labourer on building sites but he had never been able to hold jobs and had been unemployed for over a year. Mark was of average height and weight, with long dark hair, unshaven and with extensive Yakuza-type tattoos over his arms and legs. He always wore heavy metal T-shirts and had several large skull rings on his hands. The striking thing about him was that he was never still. He moved and fidgeted a lot, his talk was jerky and impulsive while his eyes darted around the room constantly but rarely landed on the interviewer.

Presenting complaints:

"They say I'm Asperger's and schizophrenia, I used to hear voices when I was 13 or so, like an imaginary friend. Now I'm just angry and violent but mostly I'm depressed and fed up."

His sleep was very poor. He went to bed late, 1.00am or later, as he was unable to sleep earlier. His sleep was restless and broken and he woke about 9.00am feeling tired and sluggish but he didn't take naps by day as he was unable to settle with people around. His appetite had been poor while he was using amphetamines but had improved since he stopped them. He didn't have much energy or take regular exercise but he rode his pushbike around as he had lost his driver's licence. He had little interest or motivation and, since he was determined not to mix with the drug scene, he had no social life: "But I don't play well with others anyway, I'm always in fights." He had no sexual interest at all.

He felt his memory was "bad" and his concentration was "...worse, I've never been able to concentrate, at school they said I'm ADHD." He had difficulty making decisions as he didn't like to make mistakes. He had trouble thinking clearly around people as he was constantly edgy and worried over what could go wrong. However, alone late at night, he could think more clearly and played computer games. The thought content was dominated by endless worries of "battles with everybody, of not being able to make a go of my life." He was questioned closely about disturbances of perception, particularly what are known as the first rank symptoms of schizophrenia. There are eleven of these symptoms, first described by Kurt Schneider in the 1950s, which relate to the perception of loss of control of self: hearing your thoughts spoken out loud, feeling people can read your mind or put thoughts into or take them out of your mind, and so on. He did not show any of them although he said often talks to himself.

He described his mood as a bit better since he had stopped all drugs. He had been feeling very low and miserable most of the time but this had settled somewhat. He was still feeling sick of things and sometimes sick of life itself. The thought of death didn't concern him and if anything went wrong and he got angry, he started having vague suicidal ideas again: "I'm trying to get myself better but if anybody upsets me, I start thinking what's the point, I might as well be dead." Sometimes he felt good, "just good, not over the top," but it didn't last. Something would go wrong and he would "hit the skids again."

He said he experienced frequent bouts of intense agitation, "all nervous and jittery, since I was a kid, I can never sit still." When agitated, he shakes badly and sweats profusely, especially sweaty hands and armpits. His stomach churns and he can't eat in case he vomits. He is short of breath and his mouth is dry, he feels tight in the throat and his voice quavers. He tends to stammer and lose his words unless he screams but once he starts, he can't stop. He feels lightheaded and clumsy and has a sense of the walls closing in. At its worst, he feels the world has changed or is different in some vital sense, which scares him even more as he wonders if it means he's schizophrenic.

During these bouts, he feels frightened and angry. He yells, throws things, punches walls, argues with anybody near him and gets into fights: "I think of violence all the time." He has half a dozen bouts of agitation like this each day, most of them lasting 30-90 minutes but a bad one can last until he finally manages to get to bed. The only way he can calm himself from the agitation is to fight (giving him a sense of control) or to take drugs. The agitation is caused by having to deal with people, especially officials or people in any sort of authority, minor upsets such as delays or losing things, or disputes of any sort. In particular, he is inflamed by a sense of injustice, whether it involves him or not.

On questioning, he has a very extensive list of fears but only one fear of the natural world, rats. Practically all of his fears are of the human world, including standing in a crowd or a queue, or public speaking, interviews and appointments, tests and exams. He rarely uses public transport as he becomes too agitated by passengers sitting behind him and has to get off. He fears meeting strangers or dealing with anybody in an office or shop. He is instantly agitated by threats or criticism, by arguments, disputes or confrontation, especially saying No to people. Despite his record, he hates letting people down, causing trouble or giving offence unless he is already agitated, in which case he doesn't care what people think. He feels comfortable when alone but fears humiliation and disapproval, and is fairly sure that everybody disapproves of him even before they know him. He hates making mistakes or failing at anything and will avoid something new for fear of making a mistake, especially in public. He doesn't like hospitals and is very frightened of needles, so he has never used IV drugs. He is fearful of police and all people in authority, or anybody who looks aggressive.

When out and about, he has a strong feeling that people look at him and talk behind his back. He has a strong sense of being judged and if anybody laughs near him, he feels they are laughing at him. He often feels he is in danger, especially in crowds or from any aggressive people but he doesn't have any sense of being under surveillance ("Do you have the feeling that people are watching you or spying on you, you're under surveillance or bugged?"). Sometimes, he feels that people are deliberately trying to get him into trouble, for example, his brother.

He always checks doors, locks, keys etc. for security but is not fussy about cleanliness, tidiness, order, punctuality or efficiency. He is quite ritualistic in the way he likes to arrange things or put them away, and is annoyed if anybody moves his possessions. He has constant, intrusive thoughts of impending trouble but these are never the same and are tailored to his immediate surroundings. If he thinks something may go wrong, his first thought is to attack: "I'm always in combat mode, ready to fight. I've got to be a warrior instead of a normal guy, I'm obsessed with the Vikings."

Recent history:

He has been this way all his life. At school, he was told he had ADHD and should take tablets but he couldn't recall if he did. At 13yrs, he was seen at a professorial unit in a major hospital in Sydney and was diagnosed as having Asperger's syndrome and "mild schizophrenia." He was prescribed risperidone which he took for four years but he stopped it because it was no help, it affected his sex life and he was gaining a lot of weight. Over the years, he had seen various psychologists and some psychiatrists through the forensic mental health services or probation department but he didn't trust any of them and never told them what was happening to him. Since about fifteen, he had "self-medicated" with a range of drugs, mostly stimulants.

Personal background:

Mark was born and raised in an outlying suburb of Sydney. His father, who is now aged 65yrs, was a manager of a number of businesses. He was "pretty good" and doesn't drink. His mother, who is now aged 61yrs, worked part-time as a cleaner and is also "a good person." He said he gets on well with his parents. He is the sixth of seven children, four sons and three daughters. The eldest, a sister, is a teacher in her 40s but he feels she is "arrogant" and he has never had much to do with her (she is 15yrs older). His eldest brother is aged 42 and works as a cable TV installer. He is "charming and charismatic, the opposite to me" and has had lots of girlfriends but he has drug problems. They get on reasonably well. A sister in her late 30s is a cleaner in a country town but she is also very nervous and he rarely sees her. A 36yo brother who has always been single has not worked for years and is "mentally unstable, never goes out, the worst temper of all." A sister of 30yrs works in disabilities while the youngest brother, aged 25yrs, is also long-term unemployed and very nervous. This brother has not been in trouble with the police but never stays in one place very long. One brother has been in prison and he thinks they all use drugs at different times.

He attended local state schools to the age of fifteen when he was finally expelled. He hated school but his marks varied a lot, depending on whether he was interested. He didn't get on well with the teachers as he felt they often picked on him. If he had trouble with a teacher, he would refuse to go in the classroom or would even run away: "I couldn't go in, I wanted to hurt people." He didn't get on well with the other children as he was very shy and nervous and was often teased but this drove him to a frenzy and he would attack the children who were annoying him: "The other kids were scared of me, I'd go completely mad." He didn't play any sport as he couldn't get on with anybody and was too ashamed if he couldn't do something, like kick the football. Throughout his schooling, he was troubled by very poor sight in one eye which meant he had poor stereoscopic vision and couldn't tell where balls were. However, he trained in martial arts from fifteen and did well at it. He feels his home life was generally quite good but he recalls arguing a lot. He didn't know whether his parents had ever been to the school to check on his progress or his behaviour.

On leaving school, he started work in a business his father was managing but this didn't go well. Invariably, he got into arguments with the other men and stormed off the job or was dismissed. By this stage, he was drinking and sometimes drank at work to calm himself, which caused more trouble. He had had about seven jobs in all, the longest for four years as a removalist, but there were also long periods of unemployment. He had no trade qualifications. Socially, he had always been single. He had had two or three girlfriends but they never lasted more than a few weeks: "I get annoyed, they try to tell me what to do. I can see through women, they try to manipulate me." He drinks erratically, mainly drinking alone at night to help him sleep. He has used a lot of marihuana but also amphetamines, methamphetamine, ecstasy and some LSD. Sometimes he uses opiates to help him sleep but he doesn't like them as they make him dull and he feels he would be in more danger. He doesn't gamble. He has a record for possession but has never been imprisoned. Physically, he is healthy with no IVDU and no blood-borne infections.

Self-assessment:

He immediately said: "I'm not a bad person." He sees himself as very nervous and very much bothered by guilt, shame and self-consciousness. He is uncontrollably assertive, which constantly gets him into arguments. He trusts nobody and never has done. He is un-tidy and disorganised, impatient, impulsive and actively avoids mixing or dealing with people (he always stands outside our building rather than sit in the waiting room). With his few girlfriends, he was very jealous and he holds grudges "forever." He deliberately breaks rules and doesn't get on with authority. He sees his temper as "really, really bad," his intellect as "pretty smart" and his self-esteem as "low, terrible."

Mental state examination:

The mental state showed a fit young man of average height and weight, with long, dark hair and a week's growth. He was dressed in clean, plain, faded casual clothes and joggers, and had extensive, high quality tattooing over all limbs and on his chest. He was clean, with no dental decay. He moved and fidgeted constantly, jiggling his legs and picking at his fingers. He made only fleeting eye contact and was clearly uncomfortable doing so. His talk was quick and jerky, and he tended to smile or laugh quickly but it never lasted more than a few seconds. He was sweaty and tremulous and his pulse could be seen, at a rate of about 90. He was clearly forcing himself to stay in the interview and several times looked at the door as though deciding whether to stay or go. Despite his laughs, he was not happy. He was wary but not overtly hostile or suspicious. There were no psychotic features and nothing to suggest an organic impairment of brain function. He was at least of bright normal intellect, if not superior, but was educated well below his potential.

When asked what he thought was actually wrong, he said he didn't know. He didn't believe he was suffering schizophrenia but he wondered about autism as he couldn't get on with anybody. He had no idea what could have caused his problems: "Maybe that's the way the gods made me?" He didn't know what he needed as a remedy but he didn't want psychiatric drugs as they didn't work and he'd seen what they do to people.

It is essential to remember that there are two ways of looking at a person, the external or objective approach or the opposite, the inner or subjective approach. Both of them claim to be free of value judgements but they rarely are. By any objective measure, this man is an aggressive psychopath, a full-blown, tick-all-the-boxes antisocial personality disorder. Subjectively, he suffers terribly. Yes, he inflicts pain on others but his major goal in life is to find some sort of relief from the anxiety that rages within him. Practically every contact he has with people ends by causing him enormous distress but it doesn't stop. Once he becomes agitated, it doesn't relent, his rage feeds on itself until he either uses drugs for relief, gets into a fight or he gets away by himself and can slowly settle. Or all three.

Subjectively, he has a severely anxious personality with high levels of self-consciousness and paranoid thinking. From time to time, he becomes seriously depressed and the idea of suicide is never far away. He has since revealed that when he has a bad argument with somebody, he is filled with hatred for the world and his ideas flicker back and forth between taking brutal revenge or simply ending it all on the basis that life will never get better. These men are common; I see a lot of them, and a few women.

The standard, mental health service or forensic approach is to give him a label, put him on drugs and then do very little. This is exactly what was done for five of his teenage years and was the reason he had not sought treatment since. The problem with giving him a label is that it does nothing for him. It satisfies the institution but fails the individual. But institutions are incapable of dealing with these men. For a start, if he decided he would seek treatment, he might have to wait six weeks for an appointment. For somebody whose moods change by the minute, that is simply setting him up for failure. It would be almost impossible for him to find his way into a large institution, then sit in a noisy, crowded waiting room where deteriorated, long-term patients would bother him by asking for a smoke. If he made it that far, public services never run on time, and delays inflame him. Finally, he would see a nurse who would ask him a series of very basic questions while pecking away at a computer. He would then have to wait longer to see a junior medical officer who might ask a few more questions before prescribing a couple of drugs and telling him to come back in a month.

It doesn't work. There's less than 1% chance he would get through the various hurdles and traps without losing his temper and storming out or being dragged out by the police. It doesn't work because the rigid and inflexible imperatives of the institution always override the patient's needs, no matter how desperate. It doesn't work because junior staff simply don't have the skills or experience to negotiate the minefield of his arousal. And it doesn't work because ultimately, he's just another PD (personality disorder) and he has to learn to wait in line because institutions and we're busy people. If he says, as I have heard, "If I could wait in line, girlie, I wouldn't need to be here," that's further proof of his manipulative nature and he should be reminded there are seriously ill people here and if he chooses not to wait, he'll probably be detained. It's an amazing thing, you know, we have all these terribly clever people with large government grants to run programs to reduce suicides, but the people who are most likely to kill themselves are incapable of waiting in line to get into the program. Just because he's a psychopath doesn't justify treating him psychopathically.

However, the surface label of psychopath totally misses the point of the endless torment of his anxiety. It helps that Mark is reasonably articulate. Often, these men aren't. They sit and brood and mutter and mumble until finally, they storm out. Remember that these people are already highly aroused by the mere process of keeping an appointment; it is the job of the interviewer to recognise this and conduct the interview in such a way as to reduce his arousal, not add to it. Keeping them waiting adds to it; treating them like cattle adds to it; and treating them as moral defects rather than as damaged humans adds to it. That is, by failing to recognise and deal with the volcanic anxiety that drives his aggressive and unpredictable behaviour, we set him up for yet another failure.

Putting that aside, there is something very strange about this case. Throughout his adult life, he has been seriously disturbed so the question immediately arises: Why? He said his parents were good people, there was no suggestion of any mistreatment by them or anybody else yet five of the seven children in his family are either anxious or abuse drugs (presumably because they are also anxious). Doesn't this look like good evidence for a genetic theory of mental disorder? Superficially, yes, but bear in mind that they all speak English and nobody claims that speaking English is genetically determined. The capacity to communicate via language is genetic; what we say in any language isn't. The same goes for emotions: the capacity to experience emotions is the result of the brain's precise microstructure, which is coded into the DNA. Which emotions we experience and to what extent, is a product of life experiences. Anyway, neither of his parents is anxious.

Nonetheless, it would appear that he didn't have any major adverse experiences in childhood. That's perfectly consistent with the idea of psychogenicity of mental disorder: the whole point is that small disorders in childhood can amplify or self-reinforce through life to become major adult disorders. That is, it doesn't take much, an apparently minor upset at a critical stage of life, to produce significant mental disorder in adulthood. Most emphatically, there is not a one-to-one relationship between adult disturbance and childhood trauma. Psychologically, we are quite fragile. That's the bad news. The good news is that the reverse is also true: mental disorders can be corrected. This may be by judicious application of a specific remedy at a crucial moment, or it may be because life goes well and the person has a run of good luck which self-corrects the earlier pathological beliefs. We are an odd mixture of fragility and resilience, and the outcome is, to a very large extent, pure luck.

Of course, people who show stable mental balance always believe that luck has nothing to do with it. Like the rich, they are convinced that their happy lives are the result of their superior moral equipment: hard work, diligence, integrity, honesty, self-denial and so on. That's rubbish. 97% of wealth is inherited and while the wealthy like to affect a veneer of graciousness and benevolence, underneath, their attitudes are fairly putrid, mostly concerned with grabbing as much as they can and making sure nobody else gets the chances they had. Of the other 3%, the fortunes that people build in their lifetimes, have a look at the life of John D Rockefeller, that says it all.

But back to Mark: in fact, his parents were too busy to pay any attention to their rapidly expanding brood. His father always worked and was rarely home. Apart from discipline, he had little to do with his sons growing up. He wasn't a bad person, he just wasn't there. At different times of his life, Mark has gone as long as two years without speaking to his father. His mother had seven children over eighteen years, her first when she was barely eighteen. She was there, but she wasn't available. If parents are emotionally important (and I believe they are), these children were quite as deprived as any children in an institution. I don't think there is anything magic about this, that having parents in the room imparts some sort of calming aura, it is actually a very practical matter. It is a fact that all infants go through anxious phases. The first starts at about six months and lasts until about 24 months or even a bit older. It is not a natural process for children to emerge from these phases, they have to be trained out of it. If the parents are emotionally unavailable, then the child will never move to a non-anxious stage, i.e. he will never learn that the world isn't such a scary place after all and, above all, that he can cope with it by his own talents.

Look at a simple example: many children have a phase of being scared of what might be in the dark ("tigers under the bed"). The parent's job is to show him that there's nothing there, the darkness is safe, he can go to sleep and in the morning, he'll see that there was nothing to be scared of. The alternative is a roar from an angry parent: "Go to bed, you stupid child, and don't you dare get up again." So the child creeps back to bed, quaking in fear at what monsters might be lurking in the dark, but more from the fear of what will surely happen if he lets out another squeak. Our broad perceptions of the world and our place in it are often based on quite small events. If, by bad luck, these are reinforced, things can get worse very rapidly. Remember that we learn more from adverse events than from pleasant, that is, that we learn to be anxious more easily than we learn to be calm. There is a clear survival value in this stratagem.

Three final points. First, if you don't have a structured interview, you won't get past Square One with these men. The interview starts with neutral material ("What's your sleep like, your appetite, your energy...?") and slowly winds its way toward the sensitive stuff, rather than rushing headlong at his sore bits. This process reassures him that he will be heard.

Second, if you don't ask, you won't find out. I don't know how many times difficult patients have said to me: "I've been seeing psychiatrists and psychologists half my life but nobody's ever asked me these questions." And don't think it's just provincial hospitals or psychiatrists that cut corners. Some of my patients have been seen at the most prestigious centres, in Australia and overseas, and nobody has ever taken a proper history.

Third, maintain impartiality. It is not the psychiatrist's role to judge a person's actions, but to find out why they happened. Leave the judging to juries. Don't be punitive, and don't ooze sympathy, patients don't like it because they know it isn't genuine. A very disturbed policeman once said to me:

> I saw Dr X (a well-known lady psychologist) and started to tell her my story. After a few minutes, she burst into tears and said 'That's terrible, how dreadfully sad for you.' I laughed and walked out. If she couldn't handle that bit, she would fall apart with the bad stuff.

Nice, middle-class people may think they can fool patients with ersatz sympathy but it doesn't fool the streetwise.

Finally, you can see why most psychology or psychiatric programs fail when they try to deal with these men. Psychiatrists don't have a model of personality disorder, mainly because they don't have a model of personality (a true model of personality will dictate the nature of disordered personalities). They take a skimpy, superficial history, decide on "PD" and prescribe some drugs. Before long, the patient is taking six drugs and has acquired half a dozen diagnoses. Why prescribe drugs? Because that's all psychiatrists know. When, predictably, the drugs don't work, they change them and add a few more, which goes nowhere. Psychology programs, such as so-called 'anger management programs' completely miss the point of his explosive arousal.

> "Just try counting to ten."
> "Lady, he was on the ground bleeding before I'd taken a breath to count."

As with so many of these programs, they work tolerably well on moderately-impaired, well-educated, psychologically-minded people who are likely to get better anyway, but not on the severely impaired, the group who need it most.

At the core of most personality disorders is a volcanic anxiety. Mark had almost no fears of the natural world. His fears were of the human world, specifically how he was performing and how people were judging him. He feared disapproval because he needed approval so strongly, but he had never had it. But it always happens that whatever we fear most of all is what we bring about.

Generally speaking, people don't walk in and announce, "Hi, I'm anxious." Most people see anxiety as a sign of moral weakness so they try to conceal it. People would sooner say "I'm a drunk" than "I'm so nervous I can't go to work without drinking." They will often use jargon, or talk in odd or abstruse terms, deflecting attention from their symptoms to something else. They may complain about work, or marriage, or money or health, all sorts of things but the psychiatrist's job is to bring the attention back to where it belongs. Quite often, as with Mark, other people have decided what their problem is, especially for young people:

> "They say I'm Asperger's and schizophrenia."

He was neither. He is anxious, intelligent, artistically-inclined and easily humiliated. Understanding that, rather than labelling him, gives the clues to his management.

5 Anxiety as a Recursive Emotion

When we're talking about emotions, there are certain points to remember. First, emotions are like colours: you can know them only by direct experience. You can't explain a colour to a colour-blind person. Emotions are what we call brute facts or raw givens, meaning they can't be further analysed or explained in terms other than themselves. Mostly, we define emotions in terms of the experience that would most likely provoke or stimulate them in an ordinary person, what is called an ostensive definition. Grief is what you experience when you lose something precious. But if you've never lost anything precious, you will have no idea what that means. Anxiety is a sense of fear, or foreboding, as if you had to give a big talk or you looked over a cliff or if you thought somebody was lurking in the bushes. However, if you've never had a fright, you're at sea. So we have to assume everybody knows what it means to be scared. We can accept that apprehension/ trepidation/ foreboding/ anxiety/ fear/ dread/ terror/ panic are all degrees along the same scary axis.

Second, there are other emotions, of course—happiness and joy, anger and rage, and so on—but anxiety is far and away the most powerful of all human emotions and inner states. It has to be: its role is to save your bacon so it has to over-ride everything. It is more powerful than humour, sadness, hunger, tiredness, sexual arousal, anger, curiosity, pain, cold, you name it. When it comes to the toss, anxiety is always the winner, and to prove its point, it's the only emotion that doesn't fade away with time. You can only laugh for about 15 minutes, then it starts to hurt. Pain dulls, excitement fades, sexual arousal has its in-built dampener (fortunately), anger cools, passion gels and so on, but only anxiety builds up and up without limit. It intensifies until you give in and do what it wants, which is to get away from the threat. This is true of all animals.

Third, *Homo sapiens* differ from other animals in two vitally important respects. In the first place, animals need a direct external stimulus to become aroused. They have to smell or feel something, hear an odd sound or see a movement and so on. Until that happens, they just keep browsing or drowsing. We humans, however, have the capacity to activate our own anxiety systems from within. We can be quietly watching the clouds drift past then jump as we recall that we have an urgent appointment in the exam room tomorrow. We can feel a twinge or a lump somewhere and become anxious over what it could be. We suddenly recall we have overspent a little on the weekend and the electricity bill is due tomorrow. We look at the sky and start to worry over whether it will rain for little Johnny's birthday party. Our capacity to model the future means we can predict trouble without a direct stimulus, then we respond to it as though it were a reality.

The final point is closely related, in that we can become anxious about being anxious itself. This is the central point of the anxiety state, this is where anxiety is at.

A person may say, "I know this sounds silly, I know they're harmless and can't hurt me but I'm terrified of frogs."

The correct answer is: "No, you're not scared of frogs at all. You're scared of how you'll feel if you go *near* a frog, which is a totally different thing. You are, in fact, scared of your own fear state."

Fear of flying is surprisingly common: "I'm terrified of flying."

Answer: "You're not scared of flying, you're scared of being locked in a small space with lots of people watching, in case you start to feel panicky and can't get out and the people think you're a fruitcake."

Another young man loved fishing but was too scared to go in a boat. Why was he scared of going in a boat? Because he couldn't get off. Why would he want to get off? Because he might panic. And why would he panic? Because he couldn't get off. Thus the trap closed on him.

A fourth person says: "I'm absolutely terrified of heights, I can't even look at a picture of the view from a hilltop."

Answer: "No, you're scared of how you'll *feel* if you look over an edge."

The next person may say: "I have to present my project tomorrow but I'm already on the verge of panic. Speaking in public terrifies me."

Answer: "No, you're not scared of speaking in public. You're scared of making a mistake in public, which is a different thing. So why would you make a mistake? Because you're scared. You're scared you'll make a mistake but you only make mistakes when you're scared. You see the vicious circle you're trapped in?"

This is true of all performance anxieties:

> "I'm scared I'll blush" (but I only blush when I'm scared).
> "I'm scared I'll shake" (but I only shake when I'm scared).
> "I'm scared I'll sweat" (but I only sweat when I'm scared).
> "I'm scared I'll stammer and lose my voice" (but I only stammer and lose my voice when I'm scared).
> "I'm scared I'll look like an idiot" (but I only look like an idiot when I'm scared).

It is also the basis of sexual anxiety. The male version is:

"I'm scared I won't be able to perform."

The female version is:

"I'm scared this is going to hurt."

Guess what? That's exactly what happens, because anxiety is totally inhibitory of sexual function. It has to be, otherwise people wouldn't stop in time to run from the lion.

Lurking behind all performance anxiety lies a fear of disapproval:

"I'm scared I'll blush *because* people will see me *and* they'll think I'm a fool (*and* I'm scared of being thought a fool)."

There are always two or three steps to the cognitive process of activating one's fear response, but they are so fast that most people don't even realise there are any intervening steps.

The mechanism of anxiety states is expectation, and it is immensely powerful. If we predict trouble, we automatically become aroused just because trouble is a threat. But if the trouble we predict for ourselves is either fear itself, or the consequences of fear, then we are caught in a vicious circle. For the unhappy people who are stuck in vicious circles, this can be very difficult to see just because anxiety forces us to look out rather than in. Of course.

The concept of a self-fulfilling prediction doesn't stop at performing in front of people (performance anxiety), it also reaches inside:

"I'm so scared there's something wrong with my heart, I keep having palpitations."

But anxiety causes the heart to race, so the circle closes. It becomes worse if you try to take your own pulse while breathing rapidly because it will seem to miss beats.

Choking comes close to the top of the list of fears:

"I'm claustrophobic, if I can't get fresh air, I'm terrified I'll choke."

But anxiety causes rapid breathing and dizziness due to lowering the level of CO_2 in the blood, which gives the sense of choking.

"I can't hold anything down, I'm scared it means I've got cancer of the stomach."

But anxiety causes churning or butterfly sensations of the stomach, which the person interprets as evidence of cancer. It is no use saying to an anxious person: "There's nothing wrong with your stomach so stop worrying," because worrying just is the "disease." It's a neat trap because the "disease" of worrying causes its own symptoms. People worry about the symptoms of anxiety, thinking it's a disease, but anxiety produces the symptoms.

This is the whole basis of what is called hypochondria, or hysteria, or Briquet's syndrome, or somatisation, or any of those other expressions that means "unexplained physical symptoms in an anxious and miserable person."

Agoraphobia, or fear of leaving the house, is one of the more common specific fears and is terribly disabling. Some years ago, I saw a student who had been studying interstate for four years. When it came time to graduate, he had to tell his parents that he hadn't actually attended university in all that time as he was too anxious to leave his flat. His prediction was: If I leave my flat, I'll get dizzy and stumble, and people will think I'm some sort of nut case so I'll have to stay here. The thought of people thinking he was mentally disturbed was terrifying so, each morning, as it came time to leave, his anxiety level rose until he had to give in and stay home. It's the basis of school refusal, or of difficulty returning to work after accidents.

A 38yo master welder had been working inside a fuel tanker on a very hot day. Because of the intense heat, he felt dizzy and got too close to the wall of the tank. The earthed current shorted to the sweat on his cheekbone, hurling him to the floor and leaving a burn that required grafting. When it came time to return to work, he was unable to enter tankers as he felt faint and thought he would again stumble and be shocked. The anxiety about being shocked again caused him to feel unsteady on his feet, which convinced him it was likely to happen (for the record, his treatment took two sessions).

A 42yo female police inspector had been extensively investigated for urinary incontinence by urologists and gynaecologists but no cause had been found. She was booked for surgery but the urologist requested a psychiatric opinion as he was concerned she might react badly if the operation were not successful. This was very wise, as she wasn't incontinent at all. She had become anxious about the thought she would have to leave meetings *because of* the need to pass urine. The anxiety created the sense of urgently needing to pass urine. This could happen as often as every ten minutes. It was much worse when she had to chair a meeting or give evidence in court as all eyes were on her. It was pure performance anxiety, but focused on the need to pass urine (not stammering, sweating, shaking or blushing etc), which is much more common than people think. She recovered fully after three sessions and was most grateful as she had been able to avoid the operation. The urologist was also very grateful as he'd had a bad feeling that something would go wrong.

Another sound bite for those who like them:

The symptom we fear most is the symptom we create.

If fear of needing to pass urine is a bother, spare a thought for the many people who are rendered housebound for fear of needing to defecate. A 33yo mother of three young children could hardly leave the house, which meant her husband had to take the children to school, do all the shopping and so on. She had seen a number of psychologists and psychiatrists over the years but to no avail. At first, she insisted she had no idea how this had arisen, or what it was she actually feared about leaving her home. After several sessions and amidst huge embarrassment, she finally revealed her secret, that she would be "caught short" and would soil herself in public.

This fear developed at sixteen when she went on a school bus trip. During the trip, she felt the need to go to the toilet but, to her horror, the bus developed a flat tyre and stopped in the middle of a completely bare plain. She was too embarrassed to tell anybody and spent a tortured half-hour, dreading that she would lose control in front of everybody.

From that day forth, she developed a fear of going on buses, which soon spread, to trains, to school, to cinemas, shops, then to leaving the house. As soon as she knew she had to go out, she would experience an intense urge to empty her bowels. It didn't matter if she had just done so, it would start again within ten minutes of leaving the house. It would be nice to say that simply by talking about it, she was cured but that only happens on TV. It took months of slowly extending her trips away from the house until she felt she was free of her fear. Of course, for years, while she had kept her shameful secret, she had made no progress, but the mainstream psychiatrists had never bothered to check how it started. To them, it was fully explained by the idea that she had a genetically-determined chemical imbalance of the brain, so no further enquiry was needed.

Performance anxiety is always a self-reinforcing cycle. Very often, people can't recall when it started but they all confirm that it gradually gets worse, that it spreads to "infect" more and more of their lives until they are leading a desolate existence, hidden from the world.

I have never seen a patient with a single, isolated phobia. They may exist but I don't see them. Invariably, I find anxious people have a number of specific fears, most of them related to the human world. Not only do social fears far outnumber fears of the natural world, but they are much more damaging. People can usually live with fears of snakes or deep water, but a fear of criticism inevitably affects daily life. However, most people don't want to talk about their fears so, if you ask them directly, they may say they have none. Men in particular see anxiety as a moral failing and will do everything they can to conceal it. It is necessary to approach the question obliquely. It might seem that the order of questions asked in my history is random but it's not. I start with fears of the natural world because people have less trouble admitting them. Nobody worries too much about admitting a fear of heights and most men are fairly comfortable with it. Similarly, most people don't mind admitting fears of animals, which makes it easier for them to admit social fears.

During my training, we were hardly taught about anxiety disorders such as phobias. I remember the lecture extremely well. Our professor, a gloomy and humourless fellow, clearly didn't think much of phobias and dismissed them with a joke. A German officer, he said, was visiting a famous British regiment, whose CO boasted of his men's steely discipline.

"Why," said the Sandhurst graduate, "my men are so well-trained that I could issue them any order and they would follow it."

"Is that so?" sneered the German. "When I was training, my CO said that in their recruit training, they were ordered to eat faeces to prove they could follow orders. Could your men do that?"

"Nothing to it," boasted the Britisher. "Private Jones," he bellowed, "you heard, show our visitor what we're made of."

In no time, a plate of steaming faeces was placed in front of the ramrod stiff private. Without blinking, he began spooning it into his mouth. Suddenly, he stared at his plate, turned green and vomited.

"Ach so," gloated the German as he strolled off.

"Jones," shrieked the CO, "what do you mean by that? You let the entire regiment down."

"Dreadfully sorry, sir," stammered the miserable private, "but there was a hair on the plate."

That, I swear, was the only attempt at explanation in our lectures on phobias. The rest was statistics and some limp attempt at relating it to brain damage. Presumably, it was also the extent of the good professor's understanding of this crippling disorder. As he made absolutely clear from Day One, he saw mental disorder in terms of brain chemicals, not as a disturbance of mind. Without doubt, the concept of mental disorder as a function of recursive cognitive processes, as a self-fulfilling prophecy, was alien to him. You could say that it hadn't crossed his mind.

Psychiatry was and still is obsessed with depression. During my training, questions about specific fears were little more than an afterthought. We were taught to ask people directly: "Are you scared of anything?" Needless to say, this never seemed to go very far. Everybody said they were not so, satisfied that they weren't anxious, we went prowling along for something else.

Case 5.1: farmer, 54 yo

One day, I saw a 54yo farmer with a long history of recurrent depression. He had been in hospital half a dozen times over the years and had had ECT on at least three admissions. He was sitting in the waiting room, a tall, thin, weather-beaten and utterly mournful man in an ill-fitting suit, seated next to his small, thin and weary wife. When called, he clambered to his feet and shambled across the room as though ascending the scaffold. Without a word or glance of recognition, he walked to the door.

"Would you like your wife to come in with you?" I asked brightly.

"Nope," he muttered, pushing past.

I hesitated, then turned to ask her. Hardly had I said her name than she jumped to her feet. "Oh thank you so much," she called as she fairly flew across the room, "all the other doctors wouldn't let me come in."

In the interview room, the patient sat slumped in his chair, his head supported on his hand, eyes fixed on the floor, and gave brief, glum answers to the questions. Yes, he was seriously depressed; no, nothing had gone wrong; no, he had no idea why it happened, it's endogenous depression, didn't I know what endogenous meant? The interview limped along until I asked him about his sexual interest. At that, he seemed to freeze and shrink inside himself. "It's OK," he mumbled.

"What rot," his wife snorted. "He's never been interested. If it hadn't been for me, we wouldn't have had any children."

"Margaret, do you mind..." he groaned, covering his eyes.

"Well it's true," she snapped. "If you don't tell the doctor the truth, how do you expect him to help you?"

Joylessly, he admitted that his memory was hopeless, he couldn't concentrate or think, no, he couldn't make any decisions....

"I make all of them, Dr," his wife announced triumphantly, "I always have. It's got to the stage where I have to tell him when to start the ploughing."

And did he feel he was a nervous person?

"No," he croaked from somewhere deep and dark.

"You are so," his wife snapped, "you're a frightened rabbit. He's terrified, Dr, he always has been. Ever since he got back from the Army, they discharged him after a year. I don't know what they did to him but he was never the same."

"M-Margaret," he stammered miserably, "there's no need to bring that up, the doctor isn't interested in that..."

Slowly, and giving the impression of prising armour plate off a tank with a nail file, he revealed a huge list of specific fears, panics, phobias and terrors. He was a tortured individual who had tried to conceal his fears and carry on with life but, every few years, it became too much and he sank into a depressive state. His hospital records, which went back 20yrs, showed none of this. He had never once mentioned fears of any sort but that was most likely because nobody had ever asked him. As soon as he mentioned loss of appetite, early morning waking, loss of energy and interest, he was deemed to have what is now called major depressive disorder which, as everybody knows, is biological. Since they had the answer they needed, nobody bothered to ask further. They also had the answer he knew would stop the interview and keep them away from his shame.

At first, it seemed that he had been perfectly well when he enlisted in the Army at age nineteen but he was discharged as unsuitable after less than twelve months. Very reluctantly and only after a great deal of prodding, he described a shy and nervous childhood leading into his teenage years as the kid who stammered and blushed and always found an excuse not to go to parties or dances. Unfortunately, a relative convinced him that he should join the Army to overcome his fears so that's what he did. It was easy, he recounted, to conceal his mental trouble during recruitment, the interviewers were "really dumb."

For the first few months, he was excited and fairly sure that the Army had some special technique to cure anxiety but gradually, he realized they didn't. One day, when ordered to crawl into a small tunnel, he panicked. That was the beginning of the end. He tried his best but it didn't work. Totally ashamed and humiliated, he crept home again, married the girl next door and that was about it. After the strain of an hour of unburdening himself of his dire secret, he asked to go to the toilet.

No sooner had the door closed behind him than his wife leaned over. "What he said about his manly drive," she hissed, "that wasn't true. He didn't know what to do. I had to do it all. I had to masturbate him and pull him on, otherwise I would've died a virgin. We've got four children and they're all fine, thank God. But you mustn't dare tell him I said that, I'm sure he'd cut his throat from the shame."

Forewarned is forearmed; without ever mentioning the word, he was treated for severe anxiety and did reasonably well.

I often say that if you don't ask, you won't know but sometimes you can ask and still be misled. One of Sigmund Freud's earliest associates, Wilhelm Stekel, said that the psychiatrist must be like a detective, carefully following every suspicion because all too often, the patient will be trying to lead him away from the important stuff. Stekel didn't believe in the Unconscious, which was how he fell out with the irascible and self-righteous Freud. Instead, he said, patients generally do know what the problem is, they are simply unable to bring themselves to acknowledge it. There's a lot of truth in that because the one thing anxious people generally don't want to do is reveal how anxious they are.

Very often, people will go to great lengths to conceal their anxieties, especially men who tend to see anxiety as a sign of personal weakness and hate to admit it.

In any severe bout of anxiety, regardless of the cause, there are several stages. The first is the mental event of an expectation or anticipation that something is about to happen. That is, there is the perception of a threat. A threat doesn't have to be a big hairy man with a club, or a bear, or a precipitous cliff face, it can be any sort of situation, physical or social. All that counts is that this person sees that situation as a threat, even though the next person may think it's a breeze. The perception of a threat causes the first stirrings of anxiety, both physical and psychological but remember that all this takes place very fast. It may be so fast that the person may not be able to recall what started it, all he knows is that suddenly, his heart is starting to pound.

Now we move to the second stage, where the symptoms of anxiety themselves take over and become the new threat. That is, he is more scared of his heart racing and stomach churning, or of shaking and sweating, than he was of the original threat, whatever it was. This is true of all anxious people: they are more scared of their own fear state than they are of anything else (It can reach the point where people are more scared of being scared than they are of dying. Chronic anxiety is a major cause of suicide bids).

Immediately, he is caught in a vicious circle. Anxiety causes symptoms, and the symptoms feed back to produce more anxiety. This gives the clue to successful treatment but we'll cover that later. For the moment, our unhappy subject is caught in a rapidly intensifying state of fear. In a minute or even a few seconds, he is sweaty, shaky, nauseated, short of breath and feels he is about to faint. His heart is pounding violently in his chest, he stammers or loses his speech and has the feeling the walls are closing in on him. He may feel the world has changed in some sense and he is out of it, or that he has changed and he doesn't feel real. Mentally, his head is a mess. Most people complain of their thoughts racing, of too many thoughts tumbling through their heads and of being unable to complete a thought before it disappears and another pops in. Others say their heads go completely blank and they lose any sense of what they were about. As the anxiety intensifies, strange things start to happen.

There's a range of possible responses to an anxiety attack. The first is to try to get away from the threat, to run, or hide, or just sit quietly quivering in the corner and hope nobody notices. This is why cigarettes are so popular. If you start to get anxious in the office, you can always grab your smokes and head outside for a well-earned drag. That way, nobody knows you're going because you're terrified. It's better to be seen as an addict than as a nervous person.

Better still, you may be able to have a drink. Ah, I needed that. Anybody who says "Ah, I needed that" has a problem with alcohol, and an even bigger problem with anxiety. Alcohol is a highly specific and highly effective anti-anxiety drug, if not the most specific and effective of all. People who are drinking regularly by age fifteen are almost invariably seriously anxious, even if they conceal it, and will most likely become alcoholics. The same applies to illegal drugs which are almost all powerfully anxiolytic. Morphine, of course, has always been known as a tranquilliser and was used in medicine for hundreds of years for just this reason. Amphetamines and other stimulants are also highly effective in reducing anxiety: "I feel ten foot tall and bulletproof, I can do anything I like." That's exactly what an anxious person wants, it beats feeling like the rabbit in the spotlight, and that's why amphetamines are so popular.

The third option is to flip the anxiety into rage, the "fight" part of "fight or flight." A person who bursts into flaming rages over nothing is almost certainly severely anxious but he may not thank you for telling him: indeed, he may fly into a rage. And this raises a very important point, which requires a small digression into psychiatric theory because we normally think of anxiety as a "psychiatric illness" while rage is a "personality disorder." However, I'm saying they are intimately related. What, then, is the relationship between a formal mental illness (if there be such thing) and personality? Before we can answer that, we need to be able to say what personality is.

The broadest possible definition of personality is this:

> (5.1) Personality is the sum total of interactions between the individual and the environment.

Immediately, we see some practical problems with this. For a start, it's encyclopaedic, you would need a very large computer to record all the details. Second, it wouldn't be finished until the person is dead, which isn't much help. Third, it doesn't actually do what we want from a definition of personality. It's nice to know what a person has done in the past but what we really want is some idea of what she's likely to do in the future. That is, we're interested in her habitual modes of behaviour, because whatever she's done in the past, she's likely to keep doing in the future. A person who has habitually turned up to work on time is likely to continue doing that. On the other hand, a person who rarely gets to work on time is more likely than not to be late tomorrow. Thus, we restrict our definition to read:

> (5.2) Personality is the total of the *habitual* patterns of interaction between the individual and her environment.

This still doesn't tell us much, because people change as they get older. More importantly, under unusual or very difficult circumstances, they may behave in unexpected ways. So we add another restriction to arrive at this definition:

> (3) Personality is the total of the habitual patterns of interaction between the individual and the environment in the *stable, adult mode of behaviour.*

We're getting there but it's still very broad. We know that people who are sick, or who have had a knock on the head, or are intoxicated with any of a million substances will act strangely: out of character, we'd say. Our definition needs a further restriction:

(4) Personality is the total of the habitual patterns of interaction between the *healthy, sober* individual and her environment in the stable adult mode of behaviour.

Because personality is really about what distinguishes us one from the other, we want to exclude the common elements of behaviour, such as language, culture and so on.

(5) Personality is the *uniquely distinguishing*, habitual patterns of interaction between the healthy, sober individual and her environment in the stable adult mode of behaviour.

Now because these are habitual patterns, it is fair to assume that something is generating them. The model we are using is mentalist (cognitive in modern talk), which is very helpful because physicalist (biological) models can't say anything interesting about personality. By continuing this process, we will arrive at the final definition:

(6) Personality is the *total set of explicit and implicit mental rules* (including attitudes, beliefs, ambitions etc) *that generates* the uniquely distinguishing habitual patterns of interaction between the healthy, sober individual and her environment in the stable adult mode of behaviour.

Personality *just is* a set of rules. That's why you can't see it or experience it in yourself. Where are these rules? In memory. Can we think of them all? No, partly because there are too many, and partly because a lot of them were learned pre-verbally, or sub-verbally, as in a moment of agitation. And lots more are simply soaked up in much the same way as we learn a language. The great linguist, Noam Chomsky, says that human children can extract the general rules of their language from exposure to just a small sample of the possible sentences in the language. Children don't even know they have these rules but they're there, and that's true of most adults, too.

But this is also true of learning the myriad rules of behaviour, of our attitudes to ourselves and the world and our place in it. You could say that from very early in life, we are mining the environment (natural and social) for rule-like generalisations, using them to populate our mental lives. That is, the unique collection of rules, explicit and implicit, that generates the uniquely distinguishing habitual patterns in my stable, healthy, sober adult mode of behaviour *just is* my personality. It's the framework on which my sense of self is built. Fleshed out with memory, emotion, goals, ambitions and current experience, I assemble a coherent sense of self. This is important, because under certain circumstances, such as very high arousal, it can start to break down, which is terrifying in itself.

Personality is no more than a set of rules that govern how I interact with the world, how I behave, how I feel, how I initiate moves and how I respond to everything around me. As a first approximation, you could get away with calling it a program, and I wouldn't argue too strenuously but remember, it's unique. No two people on earth have exactly the same set of rules, that would be impossible. Similarly, nobody knows all the rules that govern his life, any more than he knows all the rules of language. Look at this pair of phrases:

A green great dragon.
A great green dragon.

Which one is correct, and why? Everybody older than about ten who speaks English knows that the first one is incorrect. Why? Because the order of adjectives in English says that size comes before colour (in fact, the order is opinion-size-age-shape-color-origin-material-purpose. Hardly anybody knows this explicitly, but everybody can tell when the rule is broken. The example comes from JRR Tolkien's first attempt to write a story, aged six).

This puts us in a good position to define personality order:

(7) An ordered personality is said to exist when the individual's set of rules is *both* internally coherent, thus generating a euthymic (pleasant) state, *and* consistent with the larger society's set of rules, thus leading to harmonious interactions.

That makes sense: a pleasantly normal personality is more or less what other pleasantly normal people in that community at that time say it is. This leads us smoothly to a formal, *explanatory* definition of personality disorder:

(8) Personality disorder exists when *either* the individual's set of rules is internally incoherent, thereby causing inner distress, *or* when it repeatedly brings him into conflict with the larger society, *or both*.

So much for personality, but that leads to another question; what does the American Psychiatric Association say about personality? Actually, they don't say anything at all about normal personality but they do talk about personality disorder. To my mind, that's a bit like trying to be a mechanic without knowing how normal engines work. It's a bit sad, really, the DSM-5 chapter on personality disorder is only forty pages out of about a thousand, stuck toward the end between Neurocognitive Disorders (granted, an important section but it's not actually psychiatry) and Paraphilic Disorders (getting the hots over rubber boots which, to my boring way of thinking, is fairly low down the list of psychiatric priorities).

If you get the impression that the authors of DSM-5 really didn't think much of personality disorder, you're actually right. They didn't, and still don't. One of the reasons they don't like it is because you can't prescribe drugs for personality disorder so, as we will discuss later, there is a very big push to rediagnose all personality disorders as mental disorders and put their owners on drugs. Not surprisingly, most of them don't get better or even get worse, and are often very ungrateful to boot, so they are rediagnosed as "borderline personality disorder" and get more drugs. But that's another story.

The other reason conventional psychiatrists don't like personality disorder is because they don't know what to do with it. For decades, they've been stuck with a categorical model of personality disorder, because that's how they set out to do it. Thus, you're *either* an avoidant personality *or* you're a schizoid personality, but you can't be both. That's their story, but anybody can see that there are no categories of personality disorder, you can have elements of this or that jumbled together. I saw one paper where they studied the personalities of 140 medical students. Most of the students met criteria for one personality disorder or another, lots met criteria for three, four or five, and one enterprising soul met criteria for no less than eleven separate personality disorders (perhaps he intended to make an academic career).

Clearly, that makes a mockery of the categorical concept so, early in the planning for DSM-5, they decided they would swap to what is called a dimensional model. We'll talk about that later but it all went pear-shaped. They found that if they abandoned categories of personality disorder, they had to abandon the whole concept of categories, which would have been difficult because it's baked into modern biological psychiatry. Take away the categories and the notion that there are separate genetic mental illnesses collapses in a heap. Thus, the dimensional model was discreetly dropped and we're stuck with the ludicrous notion of categories of personality disorder.

My case is that this schemozzle comes about because orthodox psychiatry doesn't have a model of personality, so a model of personality disorder doesn't actually follow. Their definition of personality disorder appears on page 645:

> ...an enduring pattern of inner experience and behaviour that deviates markedly (that word again) from the expectations of the individual's culture, is pervasive and inflexible, has an onset in adolescence or early adulthood, is stable over time, and leads to distress or impairment.

As far as definitions go, this is not what it seems to be. Firstly, it is highly repetitious: "enduring" means "inflexible... (early onset).... stable over time..." That's four separate ways of saying exactly the same thing. The purpose of all this verbal stuffing is to make you think you're reading something momentous, when in fact it's trite. Second, it is purely descriptive and not explanatory. Our definition (No. 6, above) is *explanatory*, i.e. it tells you precisely *how* the features of personality disorder arise.

Third, and most devastating of all, it actually misses most of the people we would like to label as personality-disordered. DSM-5 is good at labelling misfits, troublemakers, misery-bags, losers, drop-outs, eccentrics and such like, but it misses all the ghastly people who are making such a hash of modern politics and economics. Successful scoundrels, be they crooks, politicians, militarists, financiers or industrialists, are most certainly *not* distressed or impaired. In fact, they laugh all the way to their offshore banks.

Look at the former chairman of NASDAQ in New York, a Mr Bernard Madoff. Mr Madoff was a very successful financier and investor. He was hugely popular on the cocktail circuit, knew absolutely everybody who counted, donated to all the right charities and so on. Trouble was, he was also a thief and scoundrel of truly breathtaking proportions, like $65 billion worth of thief. Until he was arrested, no psychiatrist could have (or would have dared) label him as having a personality disorder, yet he surely had one. His personality was exactly the same the day before he was arrested as it was the day after but he was never distressed, he was never impaired, he was just a crook.

There are lots and lots of them. The behaviour of the former chairman of Lehman Bros, one Richard Fuld, was generally reckoned to be appalling. It was so bad that he was known as the Gorilla of Wall St, which apparently amused him greatly as there was a lot of competition for the title. A well-known magazine listed him on their *Worst American CEOs of All Time* list, describing him as "belligerent and unrepentant." His performance before the House enquiry into the Wall St crash certainly ran true to form. If he was ever distressed, it was only because he was caught, but everything says his distress didn't last. It was in fact his *lack* of distress (and regret, and remorse, and guilt, and empathy for all the people he ruined and his manifest delight in terrorising his underlings) that characterised him. That is, a total absence of distress is evidence of the most severe personality malfunction.

But the psychiatrists who wrote DSM-5 didn't want to put that in their book because they'd have a lot of very influential people in politics, business and the military on their case. This is why they got rid of the old and perfectly serviceable term 'psychopath.' In the old days, there were three variants of psychopaths. There was the well-known aggressive psychopath who fights, steals, shoots up, gets drunk, breaks laws, bashes his girlfriend, sires children and abandons them. There was a second sort, called the 'inadequate psychopath,' meaning he was always involved in some sort of shady or underhand deceit, commonly an alcoholic or addict who liked to push his missus around but burst into tears and apologised when caught. The third was known as a creative psychopath. Bernard Madoff met this definition perfectly: charming, seductive, given to highly creative dishonest schemes and utterly remorseless in the way he used people as objects to further his ambitions.

In fact, lots of very influential people in politics, business and the military meet it perfectly, which is why it had to go. They got rid of the creative psychopath, replacing it with 'antisocial personality disorder' which is conveniently defined it as a violent person with a criminal record, i.e. it is only for poor people. How embarrassing would it be if your new bible of psychiatry labelled half the governing class of the country as psychopaths? Good heavens, what would happen if it fingered some very well-known professors of psychiatry, including one from Harvard who told a Congressional enquiry he was only one rung below God in the pecking order? On second thoughts, perhaps we'd better leave this touchy topic and return to the main theme of this chapter.

Since anxiety is the emotion we experience in response to the perception of a threat, we can now define an anxious personality as *A person who habitually responds to neutral events in the environment as though they were a threat.* That is, he becomes anxious either too intensely or too often, more likely both (note that if he reacts aggressively, he's still an anxious personality, even though his behaviour is aggressive; ideally, treating his anxiety will reduce his aggression).

The *cognitive mechanism* of his anxious personality is that he has a rule which states that a particular event (say seeing a frog) will constitute a risk or threat. However, it's not just the frog which is the threat because he knows perfectly well that frogs aren't dangerous. There has to be more to it, and the extra bit is the risk that frogs are very likely to cause anxiety. That is, he is reacting to the risk of an anxiety attack and the thought of having an anxiety attack is very scary. The frog becomes scary to him just because it carries a significant risk that he will experience a threat response. Effectively, he is saying something like:

> If I do X, or if Y happens, inevitably I will feel anxious, and the mere *thought* of feeling anxious is itself very scary; insofar as X or Y makes me feel anxious, X or Y constitutes a threat to me.

That is, he unconsciously converts a non-threatening event in the environment into a threat but the *real* threat is his own fear state. This is the trap, the vicious circle of the anxiety state:

> If I try to speak in public speak, I may make a mistake;
> If I make a mistake, people will laugh at me;
> The thought of being laughed at is very scary;
> Therefore, public speaking is a threat.

The trap closes when he tries to speak in public and, according to the Yerkes-Dodson curve, becomes so anxious that he starts to make mistakes. Then his worst nightmare comes true.

You need to understand that all this is computed in a split second. Very few people will be aware of the intervening steps, just because they are standing inside the vicious circle. The notion of the vicious circle of anxiety is very slippery and takes people some time to comprehend. You could also call it a self-fulfilling prediction (that is, a prediction that comes true just by virtue of being made):

> I fear public speaking because I may make a mistake;
> If I make a mistake, I will look ridiculous;
> The thought of looking ridiculous fills me with dread.

As soon as you say "I will look ridiculous," you start to feel anxious because nobody wants to look ridiculous. Simply making the prediction starts to make it come true, which is the hallmark of a self-fulfilling prediction.

People solve this problem by different means. Some people use avoidance (cancel the talk), others have a drink, while others get aggressive. Some, of course, do all three: get drunk, fail to turn up and then blame the organisers.

It is important to know that the modern systems of diagnosis used in psychiatry do not recognise an anxious personality. In the American DSM-5, and in the World Health classification (ICD-10), anxiety is seen as a distinct illness in its own right, like depression and schizophrenia. I believe this is wrong, that being anxious constitutes an abnormal personality just because it satisfies the DSM-5 definition of a personality disorder given above:

> ...an enduring pattern of inner experience and behaviour that deviates markedly from the expectations of the individual's culture, is pervasive and inflexible, has an onset in adolescence or early adulthood, is stable over time, and leads to distress or impairment.

Yes, being anxious certainly meets every element of that definition, including the crucial ones of "distress and impairment." Being stuck in your bedroom 23hrs a day at 23yrs of age is certainly distressing and impaired, it lasts a long time and there isn't much you can do about it.

To summarise:

Anxiety is an emotion with two expressions, the mental, and the physical or somatic. The physical features of anxiety are the well-known and disabling symptoms of over-arousal: shaking, sweating, churning stomach, racing heart and so on. The mental features fall into two distinct categories, cognitive and emotional. Anxiety is a severe and seriously-underestimated condition that can have devastating effects on the individual's life.

Anxiety is not a disease state, i.e. there is nothing wrong with the brain. It is the body's normal alarm system functioning exactly as it is meant to, but it is accidently being switched on too often, and too intensely. The *cognitive mechanism* is that the individual has come to fear his own fear state, i.e. he is caught in a vicious mental circle in which feedback intensifies and maintains the anxiety state. Psychiatric drugs may suppress the anxiety response but they do nothing to change the underlying cognitive mechanism, and may lead to dangerous states of dependency or addiction. Correct treatment of anxiety states necessarily consists of cognitive and other forms of psychotherapy, with some assistance from drugs in the more severe cases.

Case 5.2: Adam B., 25yo

The next case shows how anxiety starts early and continues unabated until it is recognised and given specific treatment. Adam was aged 25 when he was referred but he had reports dating back to ten years of age. He also brought some questionnaires that his GP had administered. There is not the slightest doubt that he met all the criteria for personality disorder:

> "...an enduring pattern of inner experience and behaviour that deviates markedly from the expectations of the individual's culture, is pervasive and inflexible, has an onset in adolescence or early adult-hood, is stable over time, and leads to distress or impairment."

Actually, his disturbance went back to early childhood but he still qualified.

Adam was sitting in the waiting room with two people aged about sixty, whom I assumed were his parents. He was muttering as he came through the door. He was tall and thin, dressed in scruffy and ill-fitting clothes and he smelled. He dragged his chair around and sprawled on his arms across the desk, complaining that he was exhausted and nobody understood him. He said he was living with some friends and his father, who didn't get on, and he had lost his job. He was taking no medication. Practically every second word was a swear word, which is fairly normal in his area, so I have deleted most of it because it gets boring.

Presenting complaints:

"I've got unbearable multiple stresses, I'm not sleeping or eating." In general, he said, he was feeling "Shit." His sleep was very poor as he went to bed after midnight but still took an hour or two to get to sleep. He woke after a few hours and couldn't get back to sleep. When it was time to get up, he felt groggy and tired but he didn't take naps by day. His appetite was poor and he had lost a little weight. At 188cm and 63kg, his BMI was 17.8, meaning he was verging on "seriously underweight." He had very little energy and never exercised. He had practically no interest in things and had even stopped playing computer games. He was not motivated to do anything and didn't want to mix with people. Of his sexual interest, he first said he couldn't be bothered but then laughed and corrected himself, saying he had to satisfy his partner whether he felt like it or not.

With another laugh, he said his memory and concentration were poor but this was normal for him and he had been treated for ADHD at school. He had trouble thinking clearly as his mind jumped "...from fought to fought, all over the fuckin place," and he was usually unable to make decisions. The thought content was full of worries, mostly over how he could comply with requirements to look for work in order to get his unemployment benefits. There were no disturbances of perception.

He said he felt "weird, what comes from years of ignoring ADHD." He was low and miserable about half the time. He felt there was no point to life, that he was sick of life itself and that death would be a relief although he was not having any overt suicidal ideas. In the past, he had often been suicidal and he didn't want to get to that point again. The unhappiness was due to the "stress of life, getting nowhere." There were no other pressures such as court cases or physical illness. He never experienced good feelings as he was agitated "all the time." By agitated, he meant shaky, sweaty, racing heart, churning stomach and shortness of breath. His mouth was dry, his voice quavered, he stammered and stumbled over his words and was clumsy and unsteady on his feet. He was never able to settle and chewed his nails. At his worst, he had the feeling of the walls closing in on him and that he had changed in some sense and was different. He could not explain this further.

When agitated, which was a large part of the time, he was frightened and irritable and had to get away from whatever was troubling him. Often he started yelling and sometimes threw things around but he didn't get into fights. If he was doing anything, he had to stop because he shook so violently that he couldn't hold tools. He was having 3-4 bad bouts of agitation a day, lasting up to an hour each, but he never fully settled in between. They were caused by any sort of upset or friction with people, especially by having to deal with officials.

On questioning, he had a long list of specific fears. He was frightened of weapons but the rest of his fears were of the human world. He feared crowds, standing in queues and public speaking. He was frightened before interviews and appointments, tests and exams of any sort, and couldn't write while anybody was watching. He feared public transport, meeting strangers and talking to people by phone. He was instantly agitated by threats or criticism and by arguments or disputes, even if they didn't involve him. He feared confrontation and couldn't say No to people. He hated letting people down, causing trouble of any sort or giving offence. Even though he couldn't mix with people, he feared loneliness, as well as humiliation and disapproval. He always tried to keep the peace but this often ended up causing more trouble. In particular, he feared making mistakes or failing at anything to the extent that he often wouldn't try anything new for fear of making a mistake. He was very frightened of becoming mentally ill and feared dentists, hospitals, blood and needles. He was very frightened of police, drunks, junkies and any aggressive people, as well as people in authority.

Whenever he went out, he had a very strong feeling of people looking at him and talking about him, to the point that he often had to go home again. He had a very strong sense of people judging him but did not feel that people were a danger to him. Sometimes he had the idea that the police or Social Security were watching him but there was no sense of conspiracy.

He checked doors, locks, switches and gas taps etc. repeatedly: "I gotta, sumpfink could go wrong." He was fussy about punctuality but not about anything else and was untidy and disorganised, but he was ritualistic about cleaning things and always wanted them done in a certain routine. He tended to group things by colour or counted them into groups, and hated anybody moving them. He had recurrent thoughts and tended to blurt these out, which made people think he was odd: "Could be anyfink. I get some fought in me 'ead an' I gotta say it. Like, just crazy." In fact, the thoughts he mentioned were mostly lame or tasteless jokes.

Physically, he was well but was very unfit. He had been having the same mental problems as long as he could remember but felt it was steadily getting worse. At about age eight, he was diagnosed "ADHD and Asperger's" and was prescribed methylphenidate (*Ritalin*) which he took for about eight years. He felt it hadn't done anything.

Personal background:

He was born in a rural town but, from infancy, was raised in a working class suburb of the city. His parents separated when he was aged six and he stayed with his father. His father was then aged 60yrs and had worked as a labourer. He was described as "bad-tempered, arrogant, stubborn... domineering and homophobic." They lived in the same house but Adam lived upstairs with the landlady and the other man, a friend of hers, while his father lived downstairs. They didn't talk much. The father had been single since the separation. Adam had had no contact with his mother, a "pothead," since she left. He was the only child of his parents' relationship. He had an older paternal half-brother interstate but they had never met. There were no grandparents and he didn't know if he had any other relatives.

He had attended local state schools but there were many moves until he finished school at age fifteen. He wasn't sure how many schools he went to, at least a dozen. His marks were poor but he was recorded as passing Year 10. He didn't get on well with the teachers as he talked a lot. When he was given the diagnosis of "autism spectrum disorder" (ASD or Asperger's Syndrome), he was put in a special class, which he hated. He didn't get on well with the other children as he was shy and nervous and was often teased and bullied: "I was a loner, nobody wanted to know me, especially after they told everybody I'm Aspy's." He didn't play any sport and had no interest in his class work but he liked computers. He had one at home and played games endlessly. However, his home life was very unhappy as his father hardly ever spoke to him: "I 'ated bein' 'ome but it was OK wiff me computer 'cause 'e weren't interested in it." On leaving school, he had had one or two attempts to work but couldn't manage the interviews. He was given one job through Social Security but he was too nervous and had to give it up.

Socially, he had had one or two girlfriends in the past but they didn't last. He said the woman in the waiting room was his partner (she was aged 63yrs). He had rented a room in her house and, after some months, she invited him to stay in her room with her. He declined as he didn't want his father to find out. They had an intermittent sexual relationship but mostly, he didn't last or couldn't perform at all. He didn't drink, smoked a bit of dope "to keep calm," didn't gamble and had no police record.

Self-assessment:

He saw himself as "different, never able to fit in." He was intensely nervous, unassertive and very much bothered by guilt, shame and self-consciousness. In the main, he didn't trust people, especially women, but sometimes he would trust somebody blindly and get into trouble, such as lending them money. He agreed this was partly because he couldn't say No to people. He was very untidy but also had his habits of organising things. He was not social but also was unable to be completely alone: "I can't 'andle more than two or free people, any more an' I gotta sit in a corner and can't look at nobody." He was not inclined to be jealous but sometimes held grudges. He tried to follow rules as he feared getting into trouble. He was frightened of authority and was submissive and avoidant. He saw his temper as "moderate," his intellect as "a bit below average" and his self-esteem as "crap."

Mental state examination:

The mental state showed a tall, thin, youthful chap with long blond hair and a wispy beard, dressed in scruffy, mismatched and smelly clothes. He was pale, bony and gangly; he was wearing some chunky rings, had one tattoo and his fingernails were heavily chewed. He had gapped teeth and halitosis ("Have you cleaned your teeth lately?" "Not this year. Why?"). He was sweaty, tremulous and his pulse was visibly thudding in his throat. He moved constantly and fiddled with his face or picked at his nails. Strikingly, he finished my questions and blurted out answers but if they were wrong, he laughed. He was not depressed, hostile or suspicious. There were no psychotic features and he appeared to be of at least bright normal intellect, if not superior.

He had brought a number of documents, including two reports by paediatricians from when he was seen at age eight and nine. They were very brief, just a few lines, pronouncing him "ADHD and Asperger's Syndrome" and prescribing methylphenidate, a stimulant, which he took for some years. He also had two questionnaires which his GP had given him. One was the "Adult ADHD Self-Report Scale," or ASRS, and the other the DASS21, the 21 question version of the "Depression, Anxiety and Stress Scale." He scored highly on both tests which worried him as he thought he may have to take stimulant drugs, which he didn't like. However, there are a couple of things to remember about these scales.

First, the diagnosis of "adult ADHD" didn't exist until a few years ago. In the past, children who were diagnosed with ADHD miraculously got better when they turned eighteen. Unfortunately, that left ever-larger numbers of teenagers suffering withdrawals from stimulants so it wasn't long before there was a little bit of "diagnostic creep." Quite reasonably, it was argued that if, the day before his eighteenth birthday, a person needed certain drugs for a particular set of symptoms, then he would still have the same symptoms two days later. Therefore, and entirely coincidentally for the drug companies who sponsored all the research, he should rightly continue the drugs. So a condition that was once strictly limited to children is now spreading through the adult population, meaning lots more people have to take the expensive and highly addictive drugs.

Second, the criteria on the ASRS are, without exception, so vague and so general that you could diagnose a ham sandwich with ADHD. The same symptoms are also seen in severe anxiety, meaning people who would once have been diagnosed as neurotic and given no drugs, now get a diagnosis of a brain disease for which they need lots of expensive drugs. For life. Needless to say, if people are told by an expert that they have something wrong in their heads and they need to take drugs with a lot of unpleasant side effects, they tend to take them, until they're addicted, when it's too late. Adam was a bit unusual in that he stopped taking stimulants when he was about twelve, as he found he could get a very good price from all the seedy men who hung around the schools trying to buy "dexies." It's said that 40% of stimulants prescribed for children and adolescents end up on the black market. I'm sure that's true.

The next thing about both of these scales is that they look at the surface only. They ask certain questions about behaviour, such as whether you fidget or interrupt, or you're miserable or agitated, but they don't look deeper. That is, they make a surface assessment without any attempt to work out *why* the person fidgets, or interrupts, or is miserable or agitated. Until he was seen at age 25yrs, nobody had ever asked Adam what was happening inside to make him act in this way. But that's modern psychiatry: as far as they're concerned, there is nothing to explain. If the symptoms exist, they tell us everything we need to know about the patient. That is, they tell us there is a specific "chemical imbalance of the brain" which needs just this drug, so take it and be happy.

Finally, you need to be aware that all of these questionnaires always find what they set out to find. These days, every second patient coming through the door says he's found some tests on the internet and he's pleased to say he's diagnosed himself with half a dozen different conditions and he needs lots of tablets. That is, they are biased in favor of seeing essentially normal behavior as abnormal. Add to that the fact that there is no difference between 'anxiety' and 'stress,' except that anxiety can be defined whereas 'stress' can't. Look at this explanation from the DASS21 questionnaire itself:

> The **Depression** scale has subscales assessing dysphoria, hopelessness, devaluation of life, self-deprecation, lack of interest/involvement, anhedonia and inertia.
> The **Anxiety** scale assesses autonomic arousal, skeletal muscle effects, situational anxiety and subjective experience of anxious affect.
> The **Stress** scale's subscales highlight levels of non-chronic arousal through difficulty relaxing, nervous arousal and being easily upset/agitated, irritable/over-reactive and impatient.

Depression is OK, sadness, apathy and despair are pretty clear. The other two scales are just clever ways of saying the same thing: anybody who thinks he can tell the difference between 'anxiety' and 'stress' is kidding himself. What is the difference between "autonomic arousal" and "nervous arousal"? None. The difference between "situational anxiety" and "being easily upset/agitated, irritable/over-reactive" etc? None. These are differences without a distinction. There is an important point here, the tendency for psychiatry (and psychology) to dress itself up in high-sounding but hollow jargon. You will often hear people talk about something called "clinical depression." There is no such thing. You're either depressed or you're not. Same goes for the DSM diagnosis "Major Depression." It's an absurdity, just because there is no such thing as "minor depression." I saw a patient last week who was given the diagnosis of "mild schizophrenia" by a professorial unit. Again, absurd: there's only one sort of schizophrenia, the serious sort (he wasn't schizophrenic in the slightest, he was severely anxious with regular bouts of sleep deprivation). The worst, of course, is so-called "Bipolar Affective Disorder II," which serves only to throw the elastic bipolar diagnosis over an ever-increasing proportion of the population (currently about 15.1%, according to three psychiatrists in Hong Kong).

Once diagnosed, people are put on drugs and once on drugs, they're hooked. But back to Adam.

In childhood, he was given two separate and distinct diagnoses, ADHD and Asperger's Syndrome. But: these are descriptive only, they have no explanatory value. They say what he does but do not say why he does it, there is no mention of a possible mechanism to cause his behaviour. Worse still, these diagnoses actually block explanation because they are assumed, on zero evidence, to be unassailably biological in nature. To start looking for "inner mechanisms" that could cause his observable behaviour would be seen as ridiculous: everybody knows you can't see anything at the molecular level. But there is an inner mechanism that can account for all his symptoms in both diagnoses, and then some: anxiety. Of all the symptoms of his alleged "conditions," there is nothing that cannot be explained either as anxiety itself or as the direct result of anxiety, such as depression.

And that is exactly how it panned out: when he was given specific treatment for anxiety, he responded rapidly and dramatically. One week after he was first seen, he was reviewed and the following were noted:

> Shaking: all but stopped.
> Fidgeting and restlessness: much better, able to watch TV shows.
> Sweating: 90% reduction.
> Heart rate: down from 110 to 72.
> Churning stomach: stopped, eating better, gained 3kg in one week.
> Shortness of breath: not noticed.
> Tightness in throat: gone.
> Stammer: much less, speaking clearly.
> Irritability: huge improvement.
> Shouting and arguing: None.
> *Et la pièce de résistance*, sexual performance: Very much improved, 5-7 minutes on the job instead of 60 seconds.

That is, one week's specific treatment of anxiety (total cost: $2.10) had cured his genetic diseases of the brain.

In the seventeen years since he had first been diagnosed with "ADHD and Asperger's," he had received stimulants (methyl phenidate) for the former and nothing for the latter, as there is no "treatment." All his appointments and drugs produced no tangible benefit. There is no reason to believe his life had been altered for better or for worse by the money spent on him, and plenty of reason to believe that he had had a dreadful time while all the adults were telling him he was weird. He's not weird: he's actually clever, very observant and funny. I always look forward to seeing him.

I have never once diagnosed ADHD, autism or Asperger's Syndrome. A friend of mine from university had twin boys who developed normally for fifteen months, then started to decline. Today, they are physically adults but are completely incapable of caring for themselves or leading an independent life. They have no language, they have to be led around by the hand, they cannot get a drink of water or make a sandwich, they are incontinent and cannot wash themselves, clean their teeth or change their clothes. The most extensive investigations have revealed absolutely nothing. That ghastly tragedy is autism. The absurd misrepresentations of Alan Turing in the film *The Imitation Game*, or of Michael Burry in *The Big Short*, are not. I have never seen a case of a person who announced he (rarely she) had previously been diagnosed as "ADHD" and/or "Asperger's" and/or "autism" who did not have the full anxiety syndrome. Moreover, not one of them had ever been assessed properly. They were asked "Do you fidget? Do you have trouble relating to people?" They were never asked "Why do you fidget? Why do you have trouble relating to people?"

In over forty years, I have commenced two people on stimulants, and then only very reluctantly. The first was an odd-looking ten year old boy whose mother and stepfather were fiercely insistent he "was ADHD" and demanded a trial of stimulants. As soon as they had the prescription, they disappeared and were not seen again (because it was initially prescribed by a psychiatrist, they would have been able to convince general practitioners to prescribe it). The second was a third year engineering student who was in dire danger of failing again and being expelled from the university for what he said was a medical inability to concentrate. Very reluctantly, he was given the prescription and did not return for six weeks. At his next appointment, he arrived with the prescription in his hand and sheepishly apologised for deliberately deceiving me. So much for ADHD.

Why am I anxious?

So far, we've looked at what it's like to be anxious, and how anxiety reinforces and maintains itself, entirely without the assistance of "chemical imbalances" of the brain. We still need to explain why it starts. Actually, we know why it starts, it's a normal part of human life. What we really need to explain is why it gets out of control.

Whether he (or she) likes it or not, every human on earth is hard-wired for anxiety. The essential brain centres that mediate anxiety are deep in the brain substance in the termporal regions and are intimately connected with all parts of the brain. Anxiety does not exist independently of all other mental functions. It is primitive, all-pervasive and immensely powerful. But 70-80% of the population are never much troubled by it. If they have a bout of anxiety, it settles and they go back to normal. Why then do the remaining 20-30% become disabled? Are they just 'weak characters,' or 'genetic inferiors' who will be bred out as genetic engineering is refined? Are they morally deficient, simply too lazy to make the effort of controlling themselves? I don't believe so. I genuinely do not believe anybody is anxious through choice. People can be anxious by mistake, but that's totally different. You cannot will yourself to be anxious, as in: "Ho hum, what a boring weekend, I think I'll have a panic attack to liven things up." You can only be anxious if you have genuinely seen a threat (even if nobody else sees it):

> A class of thirty 10yo boys is lined up at the jetty, all wearing their bathers (you may call them togs, or trunks, or swimmers, I don't mind). 29 of the boys are laughing and joking and looking forward to having a good time in the water. The last is pale, sweating and tremulous because, it emerges, he doesn't know how to swim and is too scared to tell the teacher for fear of being mocked by his classmates.

Like beauty, a threat is in the eye of the beholder, but that one is fairly simple.

Case 5.3: Samantha, student

> Samantha is a 22yo social work student who very reluctantly referred herself after she had self-diagnosed Asperger's syndrome by completing some on-line questionnaires. She attended with her mother. She lived with her parents who both worked, her father as an accountant and her mother as a optical assistant. An only child, she had attended a private school where she gained good marks but she had always been shy and reluctant to join in with the other girls. She attended a conventional church with her family but did not belong to any other social groups. She described mild to moderate anxiety symptoms which she generally tried to conceal but said it was becoming increasingly difficult. There was absolutely nothing of note in her background, except her description of her parents: after much hesitation and blushing, she described both of them as "terribly nice and caring but quiet." In fact, they were both socially anxious and led a withdrawn lifestyle with no more than superficial involvement with relatives or neighbours.
>
> At first, her mother said Samantha was a very quiet child who was perfectly content to stay at home and play with her dolls and her cat. It soon became clear that it was the parents who were quiet, shy and withdrawn. Whenever their daughter had said she didn't want to go to something, they immediately gave in. "Her first day at school was dreadful," the mother said. "She was so upset and crying because she had to leave us. I'm afraid I was too." This pattern had persisted throughout her schooling and her years at university. The parents never once pushed her to do anything; at the slightest hint of any worries, they kept her home.

Biological psychiatrists leap for joy when they see a case like this. Aha, they exclaim, that proves it's all genetic. In fact, it doesn't prove anything interesting. Samantha and her parents all speak English, eat the same food and go to the same church: is that genetic, too? Actually, the neurophysiologist, Eric Kandel, says it is. Even wearing a bow tie is genetic, he says. My father wore a tie every work day of his life. I never wear ties. No, the answer is much more prosaic: every child goes through anxious phases. Anxious parents can't train them out of it, partly because they don't recognise it as abnormal (because they are socially anxious themselves) and partly because they are too scared to upset their little darlings. At the first sign of a quivering lip, they give in and do whatever Junior wants. This is a perfectly rational explanation for why anxiety runs in families. We don't need to invoke unseen and unknown genes.

It gets a bit more complicated as there is often a close relationship between a parent and the first-born child of the opposite sex. It's unfortunately true that parents do have favourites, or that mothers do hang on to the last-born and baby her, more commonly him. First-born sons are heavily over-represented in the lists of high-achievers, and the explanation is psychological, not genetic. So parents don't have to be terrible people in order to produce anxious offspring, just anxious themselves.

Case 5.4: Karen, student

Karen is a 17yo student in her final year at a well-known private school. She lives with her parents in a fairly expensive suburb and has never gone without in her life. Over a period of four months, she has become distressed and agitated, with poor sleep and concentration. At first, her parents thought it was due to the pressure of her school work but then they realised it had started quite abruptly, at the beginning of the mid-year break.

Karen described more or less constant, low-grade anxiety with 2-3 "meltdowns" a week, i.e. bouts of intense agitation during which she was "frozen with fear, terrified that something terrible will happen." She had all the symptoms of anxiety but not a big range of specific fears. She had no fears of the natural world and had no trouble mixing with people. She had never feared making mistakes and was socially capable. However, she had recently developed intense fears of illness and disability, death and mental illness, and didn't want to be far from her parents.

Reluctantly, she revealed that at the end of term party, somebody had pressed her to drink a full bottle of cough mixture. She said it made her feel "out of it, really strange and scary," and it had taken her days to get over it. For about 36hrs, her heart was racing, she felt weak, unsteady, tremulous and dizzy, and was unable to eat or sleep. She was frightened she had done some sort of lasting damage to herself. This was the first thing she thought about in the morning ("What sort of day will I have? Am I getting better?") and the last at night. Whenever she thought about it, she started to become panicky, which she took as evidence of brain damage. She kept her symptoms to herself for several months before telling her mother, but didn't mention the cause.

Here, the thought "I have done something terrible, I may have caused permanent brain damage, I could easily go mad," is itself a terrifying thought. It produced the symptoms of anxiety, which are very similar to those of an overdose of a stimulant (phenylephrine, in this case). That is, her fear had become self-sustaining.

Case 5.5: Evan, unemployed

Evan is a 22yo unemployed man whose mother attended the interview with him. He complained of vomiting and anxiety which led to him giving up his degree course in IT, but no physical cause has ever been found. He lives with his family and is taking no medication although he was previously prescribed sertraline (Zoloft in the US), which he didn't like. At present, he feels miserable most of the time. He sleeps poorly and his appetite is erratic but he is gaining weight. He has little energy, interest or motivation and doesn't mix much. Physically, he does very little. His memory and concentration are patchy and he has trouble thinking clearly under pressure or making decisions. He feels low and miserable half the time and sometimes feels death would be a relief but is not actively suicidal. He never feels good but he has frequent bouts of agitation with many somatic symptoms of anxiety, secondary to a long list of social fears. He is highly self-conscious but not paranoid. He has been this way as long as he can remember. He saw a psychiatrist some years ago but wasn't happy with the treatment.

His family background was very unsettled as his father is a very bad-tempered man who was previously an alcoholic and they don't get on. His mother is more calm but "controlling." He has two younger brothers, both of whom appear to be in the same sort of trouble. He attended local state schools but was tall for his age and was often teased. He was very shy and didn't play sport as he was too self-conscious. During his final year at school, he gave up and stayed in his room, played computer games alone but he managed to pass his final exams. On leaving school, he studied a diploma in IT and then transferred to a degree course but had to give up because he couldn't go into the classrooms. He drinks very little, smokes a bit of weed at times but nothing else, doesn't gamble and has no police record.

He was unable to describe himself, which is very unusual and indicates poor self-perception. He agreed he is very anxious and bothered by guilt, shame and self-consciousness. He is assertive at home, which leads to arguments, but not anywhere else. He is wary of people and feels no need for company. He is untidy, impatient, sometimes holds grudges, and follows rules but he doesn't trust authority. He sees himself as "very quick-tempered," his intellect is "average" and his self-esteem is "rock bottom." The mental state showed a tall and overweight young man of stated age, dressed in clean plain casual clothes, with no visible tattoos, studs, scars or jewellery. He was wary and edgy and slow to settle. He was not very talkative and his mother tended to try to answer for him. He was tremulous and sweaty and not very happy but was able to laugh once or twice. He was not hostile or suspicious. There were no psychotic features and no signs of organic brain damage. He is probably of superior intellect but is educated below his potential.

As they say, the sins of the fathers shall be delivered onto the heads of the children, even for three generations. It's actually a lot more.

This is a very typical anxious personality, secondary to poor parenting and unhappy experiences at school. Tall boys who become shy and unassertive at school are often teased badly but nobody notices it. Typically, they become withdrawn and spend their time on computer games or, of course, they may discover drugs. Evan was anxious because he grew up in a violent and unpredictable atmosphere. His father was professionally-qualified but had lost his business due to drinking and gambling, and he now worked from home.

Evan had always lived in fear of his father's explosive and violent rages. When he pushed open the front gate after school, he never knew what mood his father would be in. Because he knew that if he ever got in trouble at school, he would get a belting when he got home, he didn't retaliate when he was teased or pushed around. His 19yo brother had discovered drugs early and had been thrown out of home at sixteen, which also terrified Evan as he was particularly scared of trouble with the police. He was petrified by the thought of going to prison.

Because his mother was with him, I didn't ask about his sexual interest. He later revealed he had very little interest and no sexual experience of any kind. He was far too anxious to talk to girls which was doubly tragic because before he had put on the weight, he had clearly been good-looking.

If you grow up in a violent and unpredictable atmosphere, you will be anxious just because the world is harsh, judgemental and you never know what's going to happen next. What about children who grow up in war zones, especially the ghastly civil wars which seem to be tearing up half the countries in the world? Everything says that they are indeed anxious, but a lot depends on the quality of the care they receive from their parents. Children who believe they are valued by somebody who is trying to look after them do much better than those who are thrown on their resources, such as orphaned or abandoned children. However, that's another story so we'll talk about wealthy, stable western societies (as wealthy, stable western societies much prefer to do).

Case 5.6: Tim, 29yo IT worker

Tim is a 29yo single man who recently resigned his job in IT in order to treat his "crippling social anxiety." He lives in shared accommodation and is taking no medication apart from asthma puffers, which he uses regularly. At present, he feels "pretty bad." His sleep is poor and he has little appetite, energy or interest. He is motivated only to fix these problems so he can get back to work. Socially, he is almost unable to mix and earlier in the year, was effectively housebound for about four months. His memory and concentration are mostly good but he has trouble thinking clearly under any sort of pressure. At work he has trouble making decisions as he is very fearful of making mistakes. His mood is now "not so bad," in that he feels low and miserable only half the time although it can still be "absolutely terrible." His is sick of life itself and feels death would be a relief but is not suicidal now although he has been for long periods in the past. The unhappiness is due to his anxiety and how it restricts his life.

He does not experience elevated moods but he suffers more or less constant, severe anxiety punctuated at least once a week by a full panic attack, which can last for hours on end. He has a long list of social fears, especially loneliness and death, but there were no paranoid ideas. He is very fussy and ritualistic and is bothered by repeated, intrusive ideas of doom but there were no formal obsessive-compulsive features. Physically he is well apart from the asthma. He has had no previous treatment apart from some antidepressants years ago.

His family background was simply bizarre. His father, a 62yo public servant, is "very weak but also over-bearing" and they never got on. His mother, who is in her 50s, was a kindergarten teacher but spent most of her time crippled by mental symptoms. She is "very, very controlling and emotionally manipulative," and he cut contact with them about five years ago. He has a younger sister who was studying when he left but he doesn't know what has become of her. Asked about schooling, he said he didn't go to school. Their mother was so scared of something going wrong that she wouldn't let them out of the house but she was also so disturbed that she didn't teach them herself: "They're weird, obsessive religious maniacs, completely crazy. We were locked in the house, running wild, no sport, no hobbies, no friends. I was forced to study music which I hated." His only social contact was with one or two children in his parents' little religious group but he never liked them. Not surprisingly, he had no sexual education of any sort.

At 16yrs, he decided he needed to go to school otherwise he would have no life. He enrolled in a technical college and managed to pass

Year 12. He later passed a degree in IT but he had a terrible time at university. He had no friends, no social life and was drinking heavily to control his anxiety about entering the lecture rooms. He graduated at 24yrs and has had two jobs since but said they were a torture: "I was in absolute crisis, non-functional, drinking to stay alive." Socially, he has always been single. For seven years, he has rented a room from a single woman twice his age but she appears to be quite severely disturbed herself. He has had practically no sexual experience (and certainly not with his landlady), no longer drinks or uses marijuana and has no police record.

He sees himself as having "a lot of potential." He is severely anxious and intensely bothered by guilt, shame and self-consciousness, but also prickly and assertive. He is either very wary of people or over-trusting, "desperate" for company but also unable to mix due to fear, and avoids any contact with authority. His temper is "mostly OK," his intellect is "a bit above average" and his self-esteem is "terrible." The mental state showed a lean but well-built chap of stated age, neatly dressed in casual clothes, with razor-cut hair and a Zappa moustache. He is of mixed race but speaks with a rich, almost public school accent. There were no visible tattoos, studs, scars or jewellery. He was tremulous and sweaty and apologised frequently. He was wary but keen to talk, unhappy but not hostile or suspicious. There were no psychotic features and he is clearly of superior intellect.

It is difficult to know how this could happen in this day and age but it does. It's almost as if his parents were in league against their children. Surely they understood that children need to socialise from very early? Apparently not, the Lord will provide or some such nonsense. And where were the welfare people who are paid to prevent this sort of abuse? Who knows, because Tim never had anything to do with them.

OK, you say, point taken. Children exposed to unpredictable, violent or otherwise mad households will grow up disturbed. What about all the people who say their lives have been changed by experiences as adults? Remember that for practically the whole of its history, psychiatry didn't believe life experiences could lead to mental disorders. They laughed at the idea that grief or guilt could drive people mad; everybody knows that all mental disorder is biological in nature, so what's all this psychology stuff? This case explains:

Case 5.7: Walter K, retired

I met Mr Walter K in 1984, when he was 89. He was a courtly old gentleman, dressed in an old-fashioned linen suit which hung loosely on his bony frame. Carefully placing his panama on his knees, he explained that his wife had recently died and, pressured by his daughter, he had applied for pension benefits relating to his military service—in the Great War.

In August 1914, Walter was a 19yo engineering student. Like all of his mates, he wanted to rush out and enlist but the lecturers convinced the class that they would be of much greater value to the Army after they finished their courses. At the end of the school year (November in the southern hemisphere), he went home to his family in a moderate-sized country town where his father owned and operated a large timber mill. Walter had grown up surrounded by machinery and his family had the first power tractor and trucks in the district. All the boys he had gone to school with, whose fathers worked in the mill, were enlisting so, after pleading with his parents, he was allowed to join them. Because of his education, he was quickly commissioned as a sub-lieutenant and was put in charge of a platoon with about thirty young men he had known all his life.

In June 1915, his regiment embarked for Europe. At first, they thought they would join the heroic battle raging in the Dardanelles but they didn't stop at Suez. Instead, their convoy went to England where they underwent further training as combat engineers. In November, they shipped to the Western Front in France. Twelve months later, Walter was repatriated and was discharged medically unfit for further service early in 1917. When I saw him, I had on my desk his entire service records, including his attestation papers from 1915, so I was able to check his memory for detail over nearly seventy years.

I took my normal history, emphasising his current mental function and the evolution of his symptoms. As is typical of the elderly, he was restrained and careful in his description of his symptoms but there was no doubt that, for many years, he had been quite seriously disabled by anxiety symptoms. For practically the whole of his adult life, he had suffered severe anxiety, with regular bouts in which he was essentially disabled for hours on end. From time to time, he became miserable but he fervently insisted he had never once contemplated suicide, until his wife died, that is. It was then he realised he could not manage by himself and he had no option but to apply for veterans' benefits.

The rest of the history followed and, before looking at his files, I asked why he had not previously applied for benefits as it was clear he had a compensable condition. Very reluctantly, he revealed that he had applied, in about 1920, 1930 and most recently in 1954. Each time, his application had been rejected on the basis that there was nothing wrong with him. Close to tears, he recalled how, at his last attempt, thirty years before, he had been ordered out as a fraud. As he made his way through the cavernous waiting area, crowded with much younger World War II veterans, the doctor shouted after him that, as an officer, Walter should have been too ashamed to come and claim benefits when he was perfectly fit. He went home and had hardly left the town until this trip to the city.

On July 1st, 1916, after the biggest artillery barrage in history, the British Army launched a massive attack on the German lines in the area of the Somme River. By evening that day, over twenty thousand troops were dead, mown down by the deeply entrenched machine guns that had survived the artillery. Undeterred, the British generals ordered their men to attack again, and again, with exactly the same results. On July 19th, they ordered an attack in the Australian sector, at Fromelles, to divert the Germans so they could press their attack. In two days, 5,500 Australian troops were slaughtered, as well as another 2,000 British tommies. Sub-Lt Walter K was there on that day.

Haltingly, and clearly gripped by the most terrible anguish, Walter told the story he had kept to himself for just on 68 years. On the morning of July 19th, a lovely summer day, as he recalled, he marshalled his men in their trenches to wait for the attack. At 9.00am, as the artillery barrage lifted, the first waves of troops were ordered over the parapet. As an engineering unit, Walter's troops were among the first. He was scheduled to go with the third wave, at about 9.10am. It was expected that they would storm across no-man's-land and take the German trenches with no difficulty. Walter had a periscope and was able to watch the first line of troops advancing. To his horror, he saw them begin to stumble and fall as heavy machine guns opened up along the German front. Shortly, a whistle blew and the next wave advanced, only to suffer the same fate before they had advanced fifty yards. Then it was Walter's turn. Even though his men couldn't see what was going on barely a stone's throw from where, trembling with excitement, they stood, Walter knew exactly what would happen when he blew his whistle. He didn't know what to do. If he didn't order his troops up, they could all be charged with failing to obey orders, desertion and, worst of all, cowardice.

His watch hand clicked around and, as in a dream, he blew his whistle and clambered up the trench wall, his troops eagerly following him. In a minute, the men he had known for years were tumbling to the ground, cut down by the remorseless fire from the German positions barely two hundred yards away. Somehow, he wasn't injured. With bullets flying around him, he fell into a shell hole which sheltered him and several other wounded men. He remained there for several hours until the firing died down, then he was able to help the injured men crawl back to their lines. For the next few days, his unit remained in position then the surviving troops were withdrawn. As one of the only officers able to walk, he was expected to care for his troops but it soon became clear that he was unable to function. A month later, he was evacuated to a base hospital where he was found to be "tremulous, pale, tachycardic, loss of weight, stammering, vague and confused." He was unable to sleep or eat so he was returned to England and, a few months later, shipped back to Australia for discharge.

Medically, Walter was a problem. He hadn't been injured in any way, not even a blow on the head, so he couldn't be deemed injured. The concept of shell shock was still being developed but he hadn't been blown up, so that couldn't apply. Eventually, he was given the new diagnosis DAH, Disordered Action of the Heart (known in the US as da Costa's Syndrome), and underneath was a more ominous abbreviation, LMF. Everybody knew what that meant: Lack of Moral Fibre. It meant weak, unmanly, not strong enough to serve in His Majesty's Imperial Forces. Discharged from service, profoundly humiliated and ashamed of his failure, he went home to his family. Two years later, he married the girl next door and, at her urging, applied for benefits. His records showed that the examining medical officer could find nothing wrong with him apart from a slight tremor and racing heart so he was sent home. He and his wife bought a small business in a little town nearby and there he remained for the next sixty years. In the main, she ran the business, tending the customers while he hid out the back, handling the orders and stock. In time, they had two children, and life seemed to settle. In the fullness of time, his father died so they leased the mill to his cousins and were able to live comfortably.

It was only when his wife died that he realised he was totally dependent on her. He could not manage alone but, without veterans' benefits, he could neither afford to enter a retirement home, nor could he manage to live close to other people. If he had benefits, he could live in his daughter's home and have a nurse call on him. His benefits were approved on the basis of what would now be called Post-Traumatic Stress Disorder and he went home again. About eighteen months later, I took a call from a lady who identified herself as Walter's daughter. He had just passed on, she said, and she wanted to express her immense gratitude that somebody had finally taken the time to listen to his story, a story that even she hadn't heard, and award him the benefits he deserved. Knowing that he had finally been recognised as a disabled veteran had taken a huge weight off his shoulders and she felt he had died, if not happy, then at least at peace.

What happened to Walter? How can a perfectly healthy and intelligent twenty year old be turned into a life-long invalid in the space of a few minutes? His documents showed that he was very fit when he enlisted. He had shone during his training and was well-regarded by his superiors and by his men. Scattered through his thin, seventy year old file were letters from some long-dead local worthies, including his family doctor. They swore that they had known him before his service but he was not the same person, nor was he the type to attempt to gain benefits dishonestly.

There's no point in trying to summarise the shameful history of attempts by the military and psychiatric professions to avoid grasping the nettle of the long-term effects of massive psychological trauma. Indeed, the very word 'trauma' is Greek. It had to be imported because English didn't have a word for the concept. After World War II, it was accepted that men could break down as a result of the stresses of battle but only weak men, men who really shouldn't have been in the front line in the first place. Real men take warfare in their stride, as all staff generals know. It was only after Vietnam that western psychiatry accepted the inevitable: pure psychological pressure can wreck the mental balance of even the best-trained and most disciplined troops. That hasn't stopped them trying to find a biological cause for it, of course, but it's all a waste of time. We know exactly what causes the chronic over-arousal and over-reactivity of the post-traumatic states, and it isn't biological.

The definition of an anxious person is *a person who reacts to neutral events in the environment as though they were a threat.* People who have been exposed to massive psychological stressors change, they are no longer the people they were. Two things have changed: their perception of the world and their perception of themselves. From living in a safe, predictable world where everything is ordered and predictable, their new world now seems chaotic and terrifying, full of danger and ready to explode or engulf them at any second. Something tapping at the window? In the old life, it was a branch but now it's somebody trying to break in. Something isn't where you thought you left it? Previously, you blamed the kids and got on with it but now, it's because somebody may have booby-trapped the house so you need to be totally alert and aware.

A person with a post-traumatic state moves to a stance of being ultra-alert to everything. Instead of ambling through a pleasant life, his over-aroused mind now sees risks everywhere. Because it is a healthy brain, it responds by sending the correct, alerting instructions to his body:

> Look out, watch that man. Don't relax, never let your guard down. Nothing is random, nothing is neutral or trivial or not worth worrying about, every sound and smell and movement has meaning, all of it bad. Everything has to be watched, every person, every movement could mean mortal danger so never drop your guard. Watch. Be aware. Be alert. Never let anybody close, that child could be a spy, that teenager has probably been indoctrinated, that woman could be carrying a weapon wrapped in her baby's blanket.

As Walter K showed, the crucial point is this *never stops.* Just because you have left the battlefield and gone home, doesn't mean your hyper-developed sense of danger will slowly fade away. Oh no, that would be far too easy. Walter's fear of the world burned brightly for seventy years, searing him relentlessly every moment of that time. We learn danger very much easier than we unlearn it. Of course. What would have happened to our humanoid ancestors, scampering around the veldt, if they forgot yesterday's lesson about where the leopard was hiding? But there's more to it than that, and it stems from the other major change in a traumatised person, his perception of himself.

Most people have never experienced a panic state. If you haven't, be grateful and hope it stays that way. And just remember, the main reason you haven't experienced a full-blown panic is luck. It is not due to your brains, or diligence, or strong character or faith or any such thing. Overwhelmingly, people who have never been seriously frightened think that it is due to their superior moral equipment but don't believe it. It was just your good luck that the bus didn't skid on the wet road and pin you against the wall, so don't be conceited. The people who are most at risk of developing a permanent anxiety state are those who have no idea what fear is, or how powerful it is. A person who is suddenly engulfed by massive fear learns something new: that he can't control his inner state. In a few seconds, he learns to fear his own mental state just because he never wants to go through that again. Thus, ever thereafter, at the first sign of a change in how he is feeling, he is hurtling toward panic:

> Am I going to lose control? Is this the one where I melt down totally? What if those people see me, what will they think of me? I have to get away, quick, before it gets too bad. Gimme that drink, get out of my way you fool, I'm in real danger.

But... the danger is within. Nobody else can see it, nobody can feel it or understand it. Something catches his attention, a movement, a slight sound or something that shouldn't be where it is. Previously, he would hardly have noticed it but now, constantly alert and scanning the environment for danger, he reacts as though it were a threat (the definition of anxiety). Instantly, his body and mind are thrown into high arousal. And just as fast, he realises he is losing control of his inner state, and he knows only too well where that ends: "I'm about to lose it again." That thought, instantaneous and compelling, is the mechanism of the perpetual post-traumatic state. The thought that he is about to panic is itself a terrifying thought, and immediately brings on the panic he didn't want. It is the ultimate self-fulfilling prophecy.

This is the trap: the traumatised person fears his own fear state, to the extent that he is now operating on a hair-trigger. His alarm system was once set to respond only to major events. Now it is set to react to the most trivial incident, just because he doesn't know if it will lead to melt-down. The more he fears his own fear state, the more likely it becomes that he will activate it inappropriately: The symptom we fear most is the symptom we create. As soon as his arousal shoots up, other terrifying ideas take over:

How long is this going to last? Can I survive this? What do people think of me? Is my brain damaged? Am I a weak character? Am I going mad? What's the point?

This state is self-reinforcing, self-perpetuating. A few lucky people can get out of it, most can't, which is why psychiatrists like to talk about the post-traumatic anxiety states being chemical in nature. Sure, there are chemical changes in the brain of a terrified person but they are the *mechanism* of his fear state, not the cause. His beliefs drive his fear, then the fear reinforces the beliefs.

Case 5.8: Allan F., Army sergeant

A 34yo career Army sergeant, Allan was referred for assessment of his mental state. He was in an elite unit and, until three years before, had performed conspicuously well. However, during his first deployment to a combat zone, he had developed severe mental symptoms. Despite his efforts to conceal his symptoms, his medical officer wondered whether he was fit for continued service on the basis of possible PTSD. He was living off-base in married quarters, although his partner and her 4yo daughter from a previous relationship had recently left him because of his outbursts. The presenting complaints are copied directly from my report to his medical officer:

Presenting complaints:

In general, he is feeling "no good, embarrassed, depressed, anxious and angry." With regard to vegetative functions and appetites, he has not been sleeping well. He goes to bed by about 10.00pm but takes up to 3hrs to get to sleep, then wakes often during the night until he gets up at 5.00am. He wasn't sure why he wakes, sometimes bad dreams but mostly due to worrying. He wakes feeling tired but doesn't sleep in on weekends or take naps by day. His appetite is "not so good" but his weight is steady, probably because he is not exercising. He has very little energy and his activity level is very low. He has not been doing PT lately or any other exercise. He has no interest or motivation, either at work or in his private life. Socially, he actively avoids people in his private life and at work. He is irritable and argumentative and spends time with just one friend who served with him in X. His sexual interest is low.

He feels his memory is patchy and he has trouble concentrating as his mind wanders. He is able to think clearly most of the time and can make decisions as required but, under the slightest pressure, he becomes confused and disorganised. The thought content is full of worries over what is happening to him, his career and future employment, his relationship etc. He has not experienced any significant disturbances of perception.

He described his mood as "terrible." He feels low and miserable about three quarters of the time. This is "pretty bad," meaning he feels sick of things as they are and feels he cannot go on like this. At present, he is not sick of life itself and there were no suicidal ideas but he has often felt this way over the past few years. He wasn't sure why he is so unhappy: "It's everything, work, home, stress, the lot." He is short of money but there were no other pressures in his life at present that would cause this mood. He has not experienced any bouts of abnormally elevated mood.

He has frequent bouts of intense agitation during which he feels he can't breathe and he has the sense his chest will explode. With these, he is shaky and sweaty, his stomach churns violently and he feels he may vomit. His heart races and his throat feels tight. He feels light-headed and dizzy and stumbles over his words. During these episodes, he has the feeling of the walls closing in or feeling trapped, and feels he has changed, he is not the same person. He is very angry and frightened and he yells and punches walls. He has to get away from whatever is troubling him before he can settle. He has about 5-6 attacks per day, each lasting half an hour or more. They are caused by minor upsets, friction with people, arguments or disputes of any kind, worrying about the future, and the sense that he has been abandoned in his role and career.

On questioning, he no longer feels safe in the dark and startles badly with sudden noises or movements or if anybody touches him unexpectedly. He is fearful of crowds, queues and public speaking. He can't use public transport and doesn't want anybody to come behind him. He quickly becomes agitated by interviews or tests of any sort, and especially by threats or criticism. Disputes or confrontation of any sort cause intense agitation and rage. He fears letting people down or any sort of trouble, loneliness, humiliation and disapproval. In particular, he fears failing at anything and is now becoming fearful of the idea of mental illness. He is immediately agitated by drunks or aggressive people and becomes irritable when he has to deal with authority.

When he is out, he has a very strong feeling that people, including acquaintances and strangers, are looking at him, talking behind his back and judging him. He has a strong feeling people will assail him in some way or are an actual danger to him. He feels he is being closely monitored at work but there was no sense of surveillance away from work. He has the feeling that certain people at work are plotting or conspiring against him, holding information back or spreading lies or stories to harm his career.

He has always been inclined to check doors, locks, keys etc carefully and often rechecks them if he doesn't feel sure he has done it. At night, he has to get up to check noises, and will then recheck every door and window in the house. He is very fussy about cleanliness, tidiness, order, punctuality and efficiency to the point of getting into arguments with people, especially at home. He has repetitive intrusive thoughts of betrayal and abandonment but there were no true obsessive-compulsive features. Physically, he has some low back pain and trouble with his knees and ankles but has not sought attention.

We needn't worry too much about his family background. Like 60% of recruits, he came from a broken family but it wasn't the worst I would have seen that day. During his schooling, he performed well in his classes and very well at sport. From about the age of eight, his heart was set on a military career. Even at school, there was no such thing as second best, he was a perfectionist for whom winning was everything. In high school, he often had two part-time jobs to help his mother support the younger children. As soon as he was of age, he enlisted in infantry and won several awards during his basic training. Very early, he was marked for rapid advancement. At the first opportunity, he applied for Special Forces, which is highly competitive but he blitzed the course. He was quickly promoted to sergeant and when the opportunity to deploy overseas arose, he grabbed it. This was what he had always wanted, he was going to show everybody what he was made of.

It didn't happen. Within a few days of arriving in the combat zone, he knew something was seriously wrong but he didn't dare tell anybody. They were scheduled to serve six months but these troops are watched very closely. After three months, he was called in for medical review and, to his utter devastation, was declared unfit and was sent home. He knew, and everybody else knew, that it meant "mentally unfit."

What happened? With Allan, we're not dealing with an ordinary man in the street who took a wrong turn and ended up in a war. He was a very tough, intelligent, highly-trained, diligent and capable man who had worked for nearly fifteen years for the chance to leap from a plane into a war zone. When he flew to an unnamed overseas destination three years before he was referred, Allan was mentally and physically perfectly fit. Even though everybody in his unit knew he was very tough, he was also known as a bit of a mother hen. He knew all his men very well and was genuinely concerned for their welfare. Nothing escaped his attention, nothing was ever left to chance. Nobody had ever seen him make a mistake or overlook something.

For Allan, embarking on the aircraft with his company, taking off and, a few hours later, crossing the coastline as they headed north was, as he said, "the peak experience, it doesn't get better." However, within two weeks of deploying, he was forced to admit that something was desperately wrong. Over the next month or so, as much as he fought against it, he knew he probably wasn't going to make it. His history tells all although it took him several sessions before he could reveal it.

Recent history:

It was a long flight from Australia. Most of the troops were keyed up and edgy but Allan was in a state almost of serenity. Quietly, calmly, he walked up and down the aisle, making sure everybody was OK, checking, watching, reassuring, missing nothing. They flew into a magnificent sunset and a few hours later, the order came to buckle up for descent. Allan had a window seat in front of the wing. The cabin lights were switched off and as they came lower, they saw the lights of the gigantic city spread out below them. The airport was almost in the middle of this huge lake of light.

Suddenly, all the lights went out. The city had completely disappeared. A moment later, anti-aircraft fire started, sending streams of tracer bullets arcing toward them. Several of the men yelled out that they were under attack. Perhaps there had been another coup? With a jolt that took his breath, it occurred to Allan that they were going to die. These glowing shells would rip up through the fragile floor of the aircraft, through the seats, tearing them apart and spattering their innards over the ceiling even as the aircraft began to plunge down. He had seen videos of crashed planes, even the charred bodies and he knew that, in a minute or two, that would happen to all of them. As these ghastly pictures tumbled through his mind, he felt gripped by a bizarre and totally alien feeling, something he had never felt in his entire life. He felt he was choking, that his chest was about to burst, that he was going to lose control of his bowels. For a long moment, he sat frozen, watching the shells rise lazily toward them then rush past, then he vomited.

Nothing happened. Five minutes later, the plane touched down and taxied to a distant part of the field. An officer walked past and laughed: "What's wrong, sarge, didn't you like the food?"

He tried to smile and say something but his voice sounded weak, barely a croak. His heart was pounding violently in his chest, his hands were sweaty and shaking and it seemed he was having some sort of heart attack. That scared him badly. Somehow he stood to get his gear but then the strangest thing happened. His legs wouldn't support him. His head swirling, he slumped into his seat while the privates he was supposed to be leading filed past, laughing and talking eagerly.

He was one of the last men off the plane. No sooner had his boots touched solid ground than the violent heaving started again. In front of his entire company, he vomited again and again until he was barely able to stand. As the men climbed into the waiting trucks, somebody led him to a jeep and helped him aboard.

Two hours later, they arrived at their temporary barracks. Driving through the warm night in the open vehicle, he had started to feel a bit better, or a little less awful. He had no idea what had happened, he could only put it down to some sort of air sickness or perhaps something he had eaten. He found his room, had a shower and collapsed into bed but, again for probably the first time in his life, he was unable to sleep. While he was brushing his teeth, he had noticed that his hands were still shaking. Every time he closed his eyes, he could see pictures of shattered bodies lying among smoking wreckage, or smashed and bloodied faces staring sightlessly past him. He must have slept a few hours but it was disturbed by vivid, twisted dreams.

Next day, they travelled out into the countryside of this alien country. He had dreamt of this for so long but everything seemed wrong. The colours and smells were lurid, everything was so crowded, the air was steamy and cloying, the traffic a nightmare. When they reached their destination, he was feeling a little more settled but everything seemed weird, almost bizarre; he had the sense of seeing and hearing everything as though through a tunnel, that he was not quite in contact. They were extremely busy so he put off seeing the MO re his attack of "gastro." A few days of orientation and then they went out on patrol. He found that by switching his mind off, by focusing precisely on what they were doing and not thinking of anything else, he could control the worst of his experiences but still, nothing felt right.

Over the next few weeks, he forced himself to function and gradually, he started to settle but he knew he wasn't normal. At the first sign of anything going wrong, even the slightest upset, it started again. His stomach threatened to dump on him, his hands shook, his heart thudded wildly in his chest and he felt he was about to choke. That was the worst, choking. He knew that a nice clean bullet wouldn't bother him but to choke to death? Even the very word filled him with dread. Actually, at that stage, he didn't know it was dread, all he knew was that he had almost lost control of himself at the airport and he was terrified that whatever it was would happen again.

The weeks passed, his platoon wasn't doing as well as some of the others. Once or twice he heard his men whispering behind his back, several times his lieutenant looked at him strangely or asked if he was feeling OK. He insisted he was, everything was fine, nothing to worry about, let's get on with the job. But inside, he knew that it wasn't fine. At thirty-one years of age, superbly fit and trained to a T, something inside had broken and he didn't know how to get it back.

Over the next few years, he did his best to get back to normal but clearly, it wasn't working. He knew his career was blighted, he felt cut off from everybody who had stayed the full tour and especially those who went back on their second trip. He was no longer the confidant of his young officers, but then he was moved to an admin post and his world fell apart. Still, he refused to accept there was anything wrong. When the routine medical checks came around, he lied his way through them. In his private life, he had formed a relationship with a school teacher who had a small child but this was not going well. He was tense and irritable and, the crowning insult, his sexual performance had dropped off, as they say. He began drinking and was getting into arguments at home, at work, at gym, at the shops and on the road. Once he was pulled over by police and was very lucky not to have been arrested. To his bitter humiliation, the younger of the cops was also a veteran who recognised his card and his unit and told him off in no uncertain terms. That pushed him into weeks of the blackest mood he had ever experienced and, for the first time, he understood why people blow their brains out.

Years later, choked and close to tears, he reminded me of the nursery rhyme, Humpty Dumpty:

> This stupid rhyme used to go through my head all the time. That's what had happened to me, I couldn't get it back together again. I'd crossed some line, something vital had broken and I was just a shell, going through the motions. Finally, they sent me to the MO and I was chucked in the broken toys bin. My first test and I broke. I have to live with this for the rest of my life. That's why I often wish it would be a short life. I can't live like this, but over and over, I ask myself, Why me? What did I do wrong? Where did I go wrong? That tortures me because I don't know. Can you tell me?

When he finally came to psychiatric attention, he had already been awarded the diagnosis of PTSD by a military psychologist, who certainly didn't have the history but filled in the blanks herself. That didn't help, because he knew that everybody in his unit knew that his problems had started before they had even landed in the war zone. How, he asked caustically, could it be PTSD? Perhaps it also means Pre-Traumatic Stress Disorder, formerly known as LMF, or weak character.

Allan was not an easy person to interview. He was clearly very intelligent but bitterly angry, full of self-hatred and barely-suppressed hostility to the military who were treating him like a diseased dog. The schoolteacher had left him for her fourth partner and wouldn't allow him to see the child he had helped raise for over two years. He had argued with the last few of his relatives who had any interest in him, even though he was still paying his mother's mortgage. He had no training or experience other than the military, and the thought of starting again at the bottom of the pile filled him with despair. Fortunately, his brief stint in a declared war zone qualified him for a small pension but it was barely enough for one man, certainly not enough for a family, even if he could convince somebody to join her life to such a hopeless case.

Alan had never experienced fear. He had not the faintest idea what the word meant and no idea how powerful it was. Of course, as a soldier, he had accepted that he stood a chance of getting killed but it didn't mean anything, it was purely an abstract consideration. It's like all the young blokes who buy motorbikes. They know that quite a lot of people who ride motorbikes get killed but not one of them considers that he will be the one to end up in a box.

It was also my feeling, but I would never have said it directly, that a lot of Alan's fear came from the knowledge that the men he secretly loved as his younger brothers would also die, and there was nothing he could do to stop it. He had always seen himself as tough, bullet-proof but here, slowly curving up the sky toward them was glowing proof that human flesh is very frail. That knowledge shattered his self-perception, flooding him with fear and he lost control. But later, it was the new awareness that he had totally lost control, that his body had secret weaknesses and he could not order himself back together again, that did the damage. That idea, that he wasn't superman after all, was absolutely terrifying to him; those few seconds destroyed a lifetime's self-delusory efforts.

Subsequently, anything that caused the slightest variation in his inner state sounded the alarm bells: *Is it happening again?* But that, of course, was itself a terrifying idea so it triggered the very response he didn't want. That is the essence of the anxiety state.

6   Anxiety and Human Nature

In the world of Western psychiatry in the 1950s and 60s, Sigmund Freud was king. Academic writers advanced their careers by mining the vast opus of his works for ever-more abstruse gems, or wrote arcane articles showing that everything Freud had said (and he said a lot) was absolutely right and he was the greatest genius in history. If you wanted to get ahead in this world, you memorized the Greats (Freud, Jones, Sullivan, Fenichel and all the rest), and hammered your clinical observations into the sharp outlines of psychoanalytic theory. Any bits that didn't fit were swept out with the rubbish (such as the anthropologists who found that, apart from neurotic upper-middle class urban intellectuals in the West, nothing Freud said was true).

One of his Big Ideas was that the essence of mothering was as a source of food. This even led one author, Karen Horney, to come up with the idea of a Good Breast and a Bad Breast. Don't ask me what it all meant, I thought it was Manichaean gibberish when I read it, but one psychologist who said she was wrong caught my attention. His name was Harry Harlow and he published a series of papers on the importance of the actual feel of a mother, or physical contact, rather than mere feeding alone.

In his experiments, baby rhesus monkeys were separated from their mothers at birth and raised in artificial environments. One of his earliest conclusions was that socialization with other little monkeys was terribly important for normal psychological development of the infant monkeys. Social deprivation early in life regularly produced the most severe defects of behaviour in adults. Another was that it didn't really matter who fed the babies as long as they felt right. He showed this by "surrogate mothers," comparing artificial models made of wire, with or without a sort of monkey face at the top, or the same models covered with terry towelling. Regardless of which model fed them, the baby monkeys much preferred the feel of the towelling mothers, and did better in adult life than those raised solely on the wire mothers. This was critically important: for the first time, there was solid evidence that fathers could be effective in raising normal children.

Since then, we have moved so far that we now talk of 'parenting' while 'mothering' is seen as something not quite right. So much for Freud's ideas.

Putting that aside, the research of Robert Sapolsky, a primatologist from New York who studied wild baboons in Kenya, was both highly original and highly ethical. Sapolsky has done a lot to publicise ethology (the study of wild populations in their natural environment), and a lot of his conclusions could almost be written about humans. His work shows that, based on field observations, there is something called "higher primate nature." All this says is that there are certain innate behavioural tendencies in higher primates, including humans, that, under normal conditions, exert an effect on what the animals do. It doesn't say what they *will* do, only what they are *likely* to do. From now on, I will talk about 'human nature,' but it should be understood that, in these crucial respects, we hardly differ from troops of baboons ambling around the East African savannah.

The first and most obvious principle is that we are social animals. An alien anthropologist would probably see this as the preeminent feature of humans. Overwhelmingly, we like to be surrounded by our own kind. We even build giant cities so we can stack ourselves on top of each other. The other side of the social coin is that we find isolation very frightening. If you want to break a person's will, put him in solitary confinement. If you want a punishment that goes on and on, exile him.

Being with our own kind is comforting but this trait doesn't stop there, it extends to xenophobia, or fear of the stranger. We feel secure surrounded by our own kind but we fear and hate "the other." This duality is the basis of tribalism. Not only do we form tightly-knit, homogenised groups where everybody has to follow the same set of rules, but we play up the differences with other groups, then use them to build walls of hostility. In hunter-gatherer societies, this forces tribes to move apart which reduces competition for food but all too often, the differences break into warfare. This is as true of small tribes such as team sports and religious groups as it is of mighty nation-states. It may sound contradictory, but fear of isolation is of critical importance in understanding social phobia.

This brings us to the next point of human nature. No sooner have we formed a group, tribe, clan, union, nation or whatever than the second principle comes into play: within the group, we form a dominance hierarchy. Somebody gets himself appointed chief and all the rest have to fall into line and serve him. I'm sure some clever evolutionary psychologist will argue that it has strong survival value for the species by preserving the best genes but that's a "just so" story, meaning it's the sort of thing that can't be disproven. We now know that our drive to form hierarchies has a powerful basis in physiology and we'll come back to it.

Third principle: we're territorial. In fact, we are very strongly territorial, intensely attached to familiar places and objects which we regard as extensions of our sense of selves. Within the tribe, sharing and reciprocal favours help build trust and strengthen the bonds but we don't like to share anything with strangers, unless they pay for it in one way or another. Territory doesn't just include land, it includes goods and chattels, the most important of which is sexual goods. The Big Chief has a harem, the poor go without. That's how humans like it (actually, that's how the man with the gun likes it; nobody worries what the helots think). Again, it may have something to do with preserving the best genes but first impressions suggest that the world's Big Chiefs don't come equipped with the best genes.

Next, we are creatures of habit and ritual. Repetition makes us feel better; reciting a familiar incantation or performing an ancient ritual, especially in times of distress, helps keep the fears at bay. The opposite is that in times of low anxiety, we are highly inquisitive and like to explore our surroundings, which includes ideas. In addition, we like to decorate things, including ourselves, and we use decoration to reinforce our sense of tribal identity and our place in the hierarchy. Also like baboons, we like to play; and we like to play-fight (we call it football) although often it's hard to tell where the play ends and the fighting starts. Unlike baboons, we have a strong sense of rhythm and melody: did you know that humans are the only animals that can march in step? And that marching in step produces definite physiological changes in both marchers and on-lookers? We'll come back to this point as it is very important.

Finally, we are aggressive. As animals, we are right up there among the most aggressive species ever to have walked the planet, so aggressive indeed that it may well be our undoing.

If we combine all these features—love of tribe and land, xenophobia, dominance, aggression, love of decoration, pomp and circumstance, more aggression—and add one secret ingredient, we get... that's right, armies. A newly-appointed Big Chief likes an army, it makes him feel more powerful because he knows he can pound the competition. But as soon as you have armies, they need something to do otherwise they cause mischief. For the chief, the easiest move is to fan the ever-smouldering embers of xenophobia and let his troops loose on his enemies, otherwise the troops might get bored and turn on him. Stripping away the propaganda and the self-justification shows that the only justification for armies is that everybody else has them but the problem is, they feel so good and so reassuring that nobody wants to take the first steps to do without one.

We can account for many of these elemental features using anxiety and the "secret ingredient" mentioned above. The social principle in human nature is driven by fear: fear of isolation, fear of ostracism and of exclusion because, in ancient times, isolation meant certain death. We can presume that the early proto-humans who *didn't* fear isolation didn't leave many descendents because they were the first to be hooked out of the gene pool by a passing proto-leopard. The successful breeders, the ones who left the most descendents, were the frightened and insecure ones who were scared of the dark, scared of strange noises and comforted by the feel and smell of their own kind. Granted, this is a "just so" evolutionary story but it has a lot of support from field experiments.

Now hold it, you say, surely social phobia just is the need to be isolated? How can fear of isolation lead to profound isolation? The answer is a two-step process. Disapproval, scorn, contempt or physical assault are scary in their own right just because they presage exclusion from the group. The insecure person quickly learns that by avoiding contact with people, he can avoid disapproval, so he retreats into self-imposed isolation. It may not be pleasant but it isn't as directly and immediately terrifying as facing a mob of people hurling abuse or rocks. The sequence is something like this:

1. If I go among those people, I may do something stupid and they will ridicule me;
2. Being ridiculed is terrifying because it means I'm not wanted, I'm less than human;
3. The thought of being terrified is itself a very scary thought;
4. When I'm scared, I'm much more likely to make mistakes;
5. If I make mistakes, they will ridicule me;
6. Therefore I'd better just stay home and pretend I'm happy collecting stamps.

It's essential to understand that a phobia does not arise as a single mental event, or gestalt; it is constructed from various cognitive elements in an ordered and comprehensible sequence. However, this sequence is very, very fast; a person can zip through those half dozen steps in the order of a few hundreds of milliseconds, to the point that all he knows is that if he goes out, it will be terrifying so he'd better not go out. Here is a prediction:

> When full Virtual Reality games and headsets arrive, the numbers of young people who stay in their bedrooms, sleeping by day and glued to their computers all night, will rise dramatically. Priests will rail against it; psychologists will call it an "epidemic of video games addiction" and demand government money to "treat" it; while psychiatrists will label them autistic or schizoid or ADHD or whatever, and put them on drugs. Then they will all get worse.

The further step is that hiding from people causes a poor self-perception, or low self-esteem:

1. I can't even talk to girls without stammering.
2. That makes me feel I'm useless and hopeless.
3. They must see I'm a total jerk.
4. I'd better not try to talk to them, I'll pretend I'm not interested, it's easier.

We are social animals. We need the sense of security (= absence of anxiety) that comes from being surrounded by our own and feeling wanted and valued as a member of the tribe. A person with very low self-approval is necessarily dependent on other people for approval, and is therefore immediately scared he isn't going to get it. For a person with low self-esteem who has to mix with people, the first thought is:

1. I have to mix with those people but they may not like me.
2. That's a very scary thought.
3. Oh dear, here I am feeling scared again.
4. The closer I get to them, the more scared I become.
5. Therefore I'd better move away.
6. Yes, that feels a bit better, I'd better not try that again. I'll just get used to being alone.

So he goes back to his room but, because he's just failed again, he feels even worse. After a while, the loneliness bites and he feels he needs to try again, but that also fails and his self-esteem gets worse.

The whole process is self-reinforcing or recursive: the outcome of last week's failed attempt to socialise becomes the starting point for today's attempt, which means each day is worse and the noose tightens. This is the mechanism of social phobia. All phobias follow this pattern, of fear causing failure which reinforces the fear. It is wholly a psychological process and has nothing to do with brain enzymes or genes. Phobias are complex *mental* mechanisms, assembled in a perfectly healthy brain. A phobia is in fact the brain doing precisely what five million years of evolution have programmed it to do, protect the genes, but it is a self-tightening noose.

The fear response has two components. The major hormone involved in the immediate fear process is adrenaline (epinephrine to some people). The psychological perception of a threat activates the peripheral adrenergic system via the adrenal medulla (which is itself part of the nervous system), resulting in immediate activation of the somatic fight-or-flight response (sympathetic response). However, because there are two parts to the response to a threat, we run into problems with that useless word 'stress.' There is an immediate reaction, commonly and probably accurately known as the "adrenaline response." This consists of the usual tremor, sweating, pounding heart, rapid breathing, churning stomach and so on. This response is activated by pure psychological events, such as the perception of a threat from a police car stopping outside your house, or looking up and not seeing your child, or the sudden realisation you've made a serious mistake and you'll lose your job.

There is also a much slower reaction involving the hormones of the other part of the adrenal glands, the cortex. These are true endocrine hormones, meaning chemicals secreted in one part of the body which travel via the bloodstream to exert their effect in a distal organ. The glucocorticoid hormones, or what we would normally call steroids, are immensely complicated in their effects. They act to suppress inflammation and facilitate repair, and are activated by a very wide range of biological "stressors," such as infections, burns, fractures and so on. However, if a person is subjected to protracted psychological threats, such as after disasters, in wars, prison, major losses and so on, this system is activated, probably as a protective mechanism. Thus, and regretably, the steroid hormones have come to be known as "stress hormones."

Over many years, there has been a great deal of research trying to find links between these hormones and mental disorder, hoping to show that disturbances in the hormones cause mental disorder, or to use the disturbances to diagnose it, or treat it, or something. It's gone nowhere. Part of the reason it has gone nowhere is because of the confusion created that miserable S-word: well over half a century ago, a writer in the *British Medical Journal* skewered it by pointing out that "Stress, in addition to being itself, is also the cause of itself, and the result of itself." That is, the word 'stress' is incapable of taking part in a scientific explanation.

The rest of the reason this research goes nowhere is the old problem of confusing cause and effect: the steroid hormones are a reaction to the psychological or physical stressor, not a cause. They mediate the body's response to the challenge, they are the mechanism of part of the "stress response" but they are not the response itself and they don't determine it.

Blind Freddy can see that you can't build a science on a circular definition but they tried, they spent fortunes trying and, for ideological reasons, they're still trying. Any person who uses the word 'stress' is using a word worn smooth by a billion loose tongues. Robert Sapolsky, for example, is obsessed with it. He assumes that other people know what he is talking about but it isn't true. Anybody who doesn't believe this can try a simple experiment: ask a dozen people, even psychiatrists, to define 'stress.' You will get at least two dozen, mostly circular and largely contradictory definitions.

Forget 'stress.' Anxiety is everything.

Now we can turn to the "secret ingredient" mentioned above. This is another hormone but this time, it's a 'feel good' hormone, probably the most powerful of all: Testosterone. To explain its role, we need to divert to, of all topics, ornithology, so sit back and we'll go through the story.

Since time immemorial, it's been known that the male gonads are essential to masculine behaviour. Farmers have always castrated excess stock to pacify them while for hundreds of years, boy sopranos were emasculated to preserve their ethereal voices (it wasn't banned in Italy until 1870). The pure hormone essential for those qualities was isolated in 1927 from animal testicles collected from the huge slaughter yards in Chicago. It was first synthesized and named in Europe in 1935, which earned its researchers the 1939 Nobel Prize in chemistry.

During the post-war period, large scale manufacture began and the complexity of its biochemistry soon emerged. Testosterone is extremely widespread in nature, with practically the same hormone appearing in most vertebrates, including mammals, birds and reptiles. We presume this indicates it appeared very early in the evolution of life.

In mammals, its physiology is complex and its effects widespread. It has a powerful anabolic or tissue-building effect, especially muscles and nerves. Behaviourally, it leads to increases in assertive and aggressive behaviour, in exploration, questing and challenging. A man who has been given extra testosterone will be more likely to perceive challenges to his esteem and to respond aggressively, and far less likely to try to avoid disputes. He will be much more assertive in trying to interest potential mates, in attracting and trying to dominate them and in seeing off the competition.

Now we get back to the birds. From the early 1970s, people studying breeding patterns in birds were able to analyse testosterone in their little subjects. An unexpected finding emerged, that testosterone levels in birds varied dramatically, much more so than in mammals. The great majority of birds have very distinct breeding seasons, tied mainly to the availability of food. In the non-breeding season, males of breeding age don't have much circulating testosterone, just enough to maintain their secondary sexual characteristics. With this basal level of the hormone, their colours are generally fairly dull and their behaviour is quiet and unobtrusive. With the first signs of the breeding season (increased daylight hours, rising water levels etc), testosterone levels rise and the birds start to show changes. Full breeding plumage emerges, and the gonads enlarge and begin to develop sperm (spermatogenesis).

A further rise comes from the challenge of seeing other cock birds in breeding plumage or hearing them calling, or seeing hens, which causes testosterone concentrations to jump to a third level. Full of vigour, the cock birds aggressively stake out a territory, doing everything they can to attract a mate and defend her against interlopers. If there are no challenges from other males, this doesn't happen, hence the name of this phenomenon, the Challenge Hypothesis. Once his mate is impregnated and brooding, testosterone levels remain high because he must guard against other cock birds intruding into his territory. When the chicks hatch, his level may drop as he takes part in feeding and protecting the chicks, or they may stay high, which is seen in species that try to steal hens and breed again.

That is, there are three distinct levels of testosterone: the quiescent level; a physiological rise driven by specific environmental changes; and the response to species-specific challenges, which maintains aggressive behaviour. In teleological terms, testosterone levels rise to allow him to perform the tasks confronting him.

The Challenge Hypothesis has been investigated and found in many species of animals including, not surprisingly, our own, *Homo sapiens.* In the 1950s and 60s, there had been many studies hoping to show that high testosterone levels equated with high levels of aggression, but they went nowhere. In humans, we now know that what counts is the psychological perception of a threat, which is largely personality-based, not biological. In essence, when a man perceives a challenge of any sort, his testosterone levels will rise to enable him to respond to it. *But,* with higher levels of the hormone in his blood, he is more likely to perceive further challenges, which leads to further rises and more aggression. If he wins the challenge, his levels go up again and thus he enters a dangerously destabilising cycle of aggression leading to challenges, leading to more hormone, leading to perceiving more challenges. Throughout, he will be sexually aggressive and demanding. Conversely, if he loses, his testosterone levels plummet. His aggression melts away, he feels glum and avoids confrontation and, of course, his sexual drive diminishes rapidly.

This has been shown in many different settings but the important point is that it is the sharp rise in the hormone in response to the perception of a challenge that gives him the burst of energy and confidence to face it and not run away. The perception doesn't have to be direct: simply expecting a challenge will do it. It can be any challenge: a sporting match, a debate or exam, an insult in a pub; a new girl in the office, handling a gun, riding a big horse, or driving a powerful sports car or any other big machine such as motorcycles, trucks, tanks, jets or big yachts.

The testosterone response is powerfully reinforced by being part of a group of bonded men such as wearing a uniform or having a common purpose like supporting a football team. It is boosted by stirring music, flags, carrying weapons, marching in step, by groups of cheering girls... In short, everything about armies is designed to boost testosterone levels in the troops, to make them more aggressive and more likely to respond aggressively to challenges:

> Soldiers parading in dress uniform are just humans in full breeding plumage, so why do we kill them?

In humans, the perception of a challenge is a psychological phenomenon through and through. Supporters of football teams get a blast of testosterone as their team runs onto the pitch. That's why they're supporters: jumping up and down, punching the air and singing rowdy songs with your mates feels better than staying home to weed the garden, wash the dog or, worse still, visit the in-laws. It feels good *just because* it causes a shot of testosterone. If their team wins, they get another boost and will start to look for fights. If they lose, they go home and watch the reruns to prove they were cheated. A team that believes they won fairly gets a bigger boost than a team that thinks they won only by luck. A team that feels they deserved to lose will have lower testosterone levels than a team that feels they were cheated.

This goes some way toward explaining the innate human drive to dominance hierarchies. Being on top feels much better than being at the bottom of the pecking order, just because being at a higher level in the hierarchy *causes* higher levels of testosterone, which feels physically, psychologically and sexually great. On the other hand, being a loser suppresses testosterone which feels miserable and sexually pathetic. A winner struts around in a state of sexual arousal while the loser slinks off and hides. A victorious army goes on a sexual rampage but, for the defeated troops, sex is the last thing on their minds.

Women, of course, are attracted to cheerfully confident winners because their own testosterone levels, although much lower than males, also respond to challenges in the same way. Every woman knows intuitively that a confident, sexually-assertive winner gives more and better sex than a brooding loser slumped sullenly at the kitchen table.

As you would expect, this effect reinforces social phobia in males: Why would a socially-anxious young man want to go out when all he can expect is misery and humiliation? By playing computer games while hiding in his room, he can gain some sense of winning, which gives him a slight boost of testosterone. A small boost is better than nothing. It's certainly better than venturing out into the real world where humiliation is guaranteed, because that always leads to further suppression of testosterone, and thus to ever-increasing misery. The essential point is that both victory and defeat are self-reinforcing, the mechanism being via testosterone secretion as part of the Challenge Hypothesis.

If we look at human behaviour from this point of view, practically everything we do can be seen in terms of competition to get on top and stay there. Politics, business, academia, religion, sport, houses, clothes and cars, physical appearance, wealth, war, crime and corruption, it seems it's all driven by testosterone. Forget the noble principles and the lofty or pious ambitions, forget the dispassionate search for knowledge or the perfect symphony or golf score, it's all about winning. It's all about getting on top and kicking away the ladder to make sure there's no competition. Winning gives great erections and pulls in lots of chicks. What was that song?

> Everybody loves a winner
> But when you lose, you lose alone (William Bell, a brilliant singer).

Of course, the thrust for naked power is discreetly hidden under platitudes about fairness, decency, democracy and all that jazz but, at base, it's all about winning. Are the powerful aware of this? Some are and for them, winning is its own justification. For the rest, as Kenneth Clarke said, they will sleep well:

They suffer from that most terrible of delusions, they believe themselves to be virtuous.

Institutional religion, for example, combines fear of the unknown, tribalism, decoration, ritual and the lust for power in an unholy mix. As we saw above:

> We are creatures of habit and ritual. Repetition makes us feel better; reciting a familiar incantation or performing an ancient ritual, especially in times of distress, helps keep the fears at bay.

It's been said that religion has four functions: explanation, inspiration, exhortation and consolation. *Explanation* doesn't need much explanation, every religion has its account of creation, or 'creation myth,' to explain to curious children why we're here. *Inspiration* makes us feel we're part of something bigger and better, while we're being *exhorted* to follow the rules, donate to the church building fund and not covet thy neighbour's wife. *Consolation* is designed to help distressed or grieving people feel this life isn't just random, that we're a little bit more special than ants.

I'm not sure why that's necessary, especially as the message is all too often perverted to mean "In this world, you're a nobody because that's what God intended for you but just keep working and you'll get your reward in the next world." Religions may start with noble intent (it's hard to beat the Sermon on the Mount) but it doesn't last. It's not long before the power-hungry realise what a gravy train it could be and take over. Indulgences, anyone?

Granted, this is not a very inspiring picture of human affairs. A lot of what we thought were positive drives are actually impelled by fear of the opposite, while many of our drives to achieve are barely-disguised urges to smash the competition into the ground and keep them there. But it's reality. Strip away the high-sounding speeches, the appeals to divine authority or patriotism, and a very great part of what we do becomes pointlessly stupid, destructive and wasteful. We humans are very clever creatures. We can design and build an ICBM to drop a thermonuclear bomb on a city on the far side of the world. We just haven't quite worked out whether we ought to be doing such things.

Let's look at two stories that illustrate some of these points. The first is tragic but he's slowly coming good.

Case 6.1: Nathan L, soldier

Nathan L, a 19yo soldier, was referred for psychiatric assessment as part of his discharge procedure following a severe injury to his right shoulder. He enlisted at eighteen and was initially extremely happy in the Army. However, on a combat training exercise one night, running in full kit with his rifle held firmly against his right shoulder, he fell face forward into a hole. The whole of his weight smashed on to his rifle butt. The shoulder was dislocated with extensive ligamentous tearing and he had months of conventional treatment without success so, nearly a year after the injury, he was booked for surgery. Following the operation, he could hardly move the shoulder and was unable to put on his uniform.

The first day he returned to work, he hurt the shoulder while dressing. He was supposed to be on part-time light duties but there was a mistake with his medical chits and his unit assumed that he was actually fit. He was ordered to take off his sling and join normal activities. When he said he couldn't, a senior officer screamed at him that there was nothing wrong with him, that he was malingering. The other troops heard this (as they were meant to) and soon began mocking him for being weak and making up his injuries. After a few months of what amounted to mental torture, he was scheduled for discharge.

When he was seen, he was so distressed that, at times, he could barely speak. He described difficulty sleeping, poor appetite, and no energy, interest or motivation. He didn't want to mix with anybody on base and had no sexual interest. His memory and concentration were poor and he had trouble thinking clearly, especially under any sort of pressure.

From his file:

> Nathan describes his mood as "hopeless." He feels low and miserable about 70% of the time, only feeling good when he can get away from the base. This is "pretty bad," meaning he is sick of things and sometimes of life itself. He has not had suicidal ideas but has had the feeling that if he could disappear, it would solve all his problems. This is all due to the shoulder injury and all that has happened since. The only time he feels good is when he is working on his car by himself and nobody bothers him.
>
> He has frequent bouts of intense agitation during which he is shaky and sweaty, his stomach churns and he often vomits froth. He is short of breath, with a tight, choking sensation deep in his throat and his mouth is dry. He feels light-headed and clumsy and he stumbles over his speech. With these bouts, he has the feeling of the walls closing in and he feels frightened and angry. Depending on what has caused it, he will either try to get away by himself or he loses control and starts yelling and swearing. While at work, he has 2-3 bouts a day but much less on weekends and had practically none when he was recently on leave. They usually last up to several hours each although sometimes they can go on for the rest of the day. They start early morning by the thought of going to work and dressing in his uniform, or by any friction at work. He is instantly inflamed if people make fun of him and "cracks it" if anybody implies that he is malingering.
>
> On questioning, he is fearful of water as he never learned to swim and still can't swim properly. He is very nervous about public speak-

ing, written tests and other paperwork. He immediately loses control with threats or criticism but he also fears letting people down, loneliness, humiliation and disapproval. In particular, he fears making mistakes or failing at anything, and he now feels he has failed at his military career. He is very frightened of disability and of death. He dislikes dealing with drunks (he doesn't drink). He is very uncomfortable near aggressive people and is apprehensive of anybody in authority.

At work, he has the very strong feeling that people are talking behind his back and judging him. If anybody laughs near him, he is sure they are laughing at him. He has a sense of danger directed at him, that people will "have a go" if they can: "Someone is always trying to take you down, they use their authority." He has a vague sense of being under surveillance, of being targeted for extra, punitive attention, and has a very strong feeling that people spread stories and lies about him. This is personal, targeted and malicious, and he is certain it is true, that he isn't imagining it as other people have confirmed it.

He checks doors, locks, keys, "everything, especially my car. I don't want anybody near my things." This is for security but he doesn't do it off-base. He is extremely fussy about cleanliness, tidiness, order, punctuality and efficiency: "I'm a real clean-freak, everything has to be spotless, a white glove freak." He is highly ritualistic in the way he cleans or arranges things. He experiences repeated intrusive thoughts but these relate to impending trouble and are not stereotyped. There were no true obsessive-compulsive features.

Personal background.

His family life was poor. After years of unhappiness, his parents had separated two years previously. His father, a carpenter, had developed a painful physical illness which meant he could hardly work but he was also mentally disturbed. He smoked a lot of marijuana and was "impossible, I've given up on him." He got on better with his mother but was unhappy with his younger brother. He had given his brother money to set up a small business but he was also smoking marijuana heavily and wasn't doing well.

Nathan attended local state schools to the age of 16yrs, passing only Year 10. His marks were quite good and he got on fairly well with the teachers but not very well with the other children. He was quite shy and nervous and was teased in his early years,. He didn't play a lot of sport but started body-building in high school. This made him feel a lot better but people still teased him over his teeth as they were very crooked. His main interest at school was playing guitar. He feels his home life was "average." On leaving school, he worked as a junior storeman for a furniture firm but the senior man left so, aged 16yrs, he was in put in charge of two older men. He enlisted at eighteen and was very happy with military life until he was injured. Socially, he has always been single but he has a girlfriend now. He doesn't drink, uses no illegal drugs, doesn't gamble and has no police record. Apart from his physical injuries, his general health is good.

After his humiliating return to work, things got worse. He was kept apart from the other men who soon made it clear they didn't want him to sit near them at meals etc. He was given trivial jobs to do and was eventually moved to the canteen where he had to serve the other men but wasn't allowed to talk to them. People often laughed when they saw him or made disparaging comments about him being weak. Quite often, he heard people calling out "Linga linga," which is slang for malingerer.

Because none of the men in the barracks would talk to him, he wanted to move off-base to stay with his girlfriend but his application was blocked for several months. One evening, he went to his car to find it had been "keyed," i.e. somebody had scraped right along the side of it with a sharp object, usually a key. This hurt him terribly. He felt he had been completely excluded from the unit, that nobody liked him or respected him, and nobody wanted anything to do with him:

> It was so bad, I couldn't look at anybody because I knew they despised me. On Friday nights, I'd hear them in the quarters, getting ready to go out for a night on the town. They were laughing and having a great time but none of them ever came to ask me if I wanted to go. They didn't want me. I'd hear them go out and then I'd be alone. That was so bad, sitting in my room, nobody to talk to. I'd always wanted to be in the military and now I'd failed. You've no idea how bad it is sitting in your room alone. Nineteen years old, a broken soldier, totally alone in the world, crippled, crying, just wanting to die.

The brutality of the military toward injured soldiers is a national disgrace—or it would be if it got out. It's actually a closely-guarded secret. The military ethos is built on the fantasy that real men are made of steel, that illness and pain and misery are frames of mind that can be banished by "right attitude." A real soldier is a totally disciplined machine, entirely free of emotional weakness, whose body is trained to perfection and who follows orders without a moment's hesitation. If a body is injured, then all its owner has to do is issue some more orders, the injury will miraculously heal and the soldier can rush off and rejoin his mates.

If he doesn't get back to fighting trim, it's because he isn't trying hard enough, he's a "weak character." All uninjured soldiers know that the way to deal with weak characters is to punish them. Pain and sickness, in their heroic estimation, are moral failings and everybody knows that the way to deal with moral failings is to force the weakling to find his moral strength and become one of them. If the injured man foolishly persists with his malingering, he should be punished more, and more, until he is forced out with the maximum contempt and brutality on the basis that he was a weakling who must have slipped into the military by false pretences. He has to be expelled before he infects other troops with his moral crime. That's why soldiers who panicked in battle were shot, it was contagious.

This is not a modern fad. During the Crimean War, British troops suffered severely from cholera. The commanding officers simply could not believe that a bit of diarrhoea could hurt a real man; anybody who collapsed from it or, god forbid, died, was malingering. There are stories of officers concealing their illness, then toppling off their horses dead, only to have the rest of their unit keep marching, leaving their bodies to rot by the roadside on the basis that that was all they were fit for.

The stupidity of this is blindingly obvious. First, anybody who has not experienced severe pain has not the faintest idea of what it feels like. Pain is a brute fact, it cannot be learned except by direct experience. People who have never experienced it are convinced there's nothing much to pain, just get a grip, grit your teeth and you'll get over it. Second, anybody who gets ahead in the military has never been injured, otherwise he wouldn't have got ahead, he would have been discharged as medically unfit. QED. Third, everybody who gets ahead is convinced he got where he is by virtue of his superior moral equipment, such as diligence, self-denial, hard work, grit and determination. They do not accept for one second that luck has anything to do with it. It was Nathan's bad luck that he was not half a metre to the right when he was running along being a good soldier, so he lost what would have been a rewarding and rewarded career.

Finally, an injured soldier who foolishly rejects all the chances he is given to recover and get back on the job must be expelled before his moral disease infects the others troops. From being "one of us," he is pushed aside and vilified as "the hated other." In as little as a few short weeks, he goes from being one of the tribe to worse than one of the enemy, he becomes a traitor. At least the enemy are honourable.

All this is based in the fundamental imperatives of higher primate nature. The military tribe is a small, tightly-bonded, closed circle with elaborate entry and initiation rites, whose only function is aggression. Within their tribe, they organise themselves into a rigid but highly competitive dominance hierarchy held in place by the overt threat of actual violence (a soldier cannot wake up one morning and say "This is ridiculous, I'm going home"). To distinguish themselves from their conspecifics, military tribesmen wear distinctive uniforms and other paraphernalia and engage in a variety of risky and essentially pointless activities to prove they are an elite. As an example, check Youtube for the daily flag-lowering ceremony at the Wagah border post on the Indo-Pakistani border.

Everything soldiers do, from the moment they wake each day until they collapse into bed at night, is designed to produce a powerful sense of masculine wellbeing, specifically by boosting testosterone secretion. All the shouting, marching up and down, stamping and saluting, slapping weapons; the flags, trumpets, medals and weapons; the thumping drums, roaring engines and explosions, the whole deal, has the single effect of making them feel great. That's what it is, that's what it does, that's what it's for.

Anything that doesn't make them feel great will be dropped. If they have the choice of doing something quietly with no fuss and drama, or using twice as much energy to do it with lots of shouting and marching to and fro, they will always choose the drama just because drama is exciting and stimulating; it *feels* better just because it selectively boosts testosterone. They call it *esprit de corps*, but we all know what it is.

It is estimated that, taking both the direct cost of the armies and the damage done by fighting, military activity around the world costs something of the order $14.5trillion a year, or one fifth of the world's entire GDP. That doesn't count all the people whose lives are ended or ruined forever by being blown up. That is a very, very great cost, and it's all because of that damned hormone.

Isolation is brutal but to be isolated while surrounded by people, to be hated and ostracised, is devastating. Most people can't endure it just because it is so frightening. It is frightening because we are social animals, meaning we are hard-wired to feel anxious unless surrounded by other humans. It's worse for a child.

Case 6.2: Gavin T, 29yo interstate truck driver.

This man requested a referral after he had suffered two severe panic attacks at work in a month. The second occurred when he was about to leave the depot at the other end of his route to head home. He was unable to get into his truck for three hours, which caused big problems with his schedule and he had been threatened with dismissal. He lived with his partner and their baby, her two children, and also had his other three children about one third of the time. The family were totally dependent on him working and he was very worried he would lose his job. He also had another weekend job to make ends meet. He was taking no medication but he had taken antidepressants on and off since age thirteen. Over the years, he had seen public psychiatric services who had given him the diagnosis of "borderline personality disorder." He didn't think they'd done much to help him although he added that he was scared of their reputation for locking people up and didn't trust them.

Presenting complaints:

"I'm questioning what I'm doing, why I'm here" (he meant alive, not seeing the psychiatrist). His sleep was poor as it was taking him two hours or more to settle each night. He woke feeling groggy but he was unable to sleep in on weekends. He was tending to overeat and had gained about 5kg in a year because he had no time to exercise. He had little energy and always seemed to feel tired. While his job was physically demanding when loading the trucks, he spent most of his time behind the wheel. He didn't have much interest or motivation and wasn't mixing with people. At work, he had been having trouble with one of the supervisors who was related to his ex-wife. He didn't have much sexual interest.

He feels his memory and concentration were reasonable but, under pressure, he had trouble thinking clearly and making decisions. At those times, he had the sense of too many thoughts tumbling through his head. The thought content was dominated by his endless family and money worries and how he could make things better. He had not had any disturbances of perception.

He described his mood as "guilty and worried." He felt he was not doing enough for everybody and was letting his partner and children down because he was either always working or tired. He felt low and miserable about half the time, sick of things but not sick of life itself although some mornings he had the feeling it would be easier if he didn't wake up. The unhappiness was due to constant worry and pressure, problems with access to his children, friction with the father of his partner's children, problems at work and so on: "Doesn't matter where I turn, there's problems. I just can't get anything right, always feel I'm a failure." When he was on the road, he felt a sense of relief and would start to sing along with the radio but it always faded as he got closer to the city and he became worried and gloomy.

The main problem was frequent bouts of intense agitation and irritability, during which he was shaky and sweaty, his heart raced and his stomach churned. He was short of breath, his mouth went dry and he felt tight in the throat and his voice quavered. He felt lightheaded and unsteady and tended to stumble over his words. He had the sense of the walls closing in and often felt he was different from other people. During these, he felt frightened and angry and sometimes started to yell and throw things but mostly tried to get away and keep it to himself. He was having 1-2 bouts a day lasting half an hour, mostly at work but also when he had to deal with his ex-wife. They were caused by friction with other people, especially if they didn't work properly, by any sort of pressure or too many worries. As a teenager, he had hurt himself during these moods by running into things or punching his head.

On questioning, he was fearful of crowds and queues and was very edgy with public speaking or any sort of attention. He became very agitated with interviews or appointments, with tests and exams to the point where he often withdrew at the last minute. He was fearful of meeting strangers and was immediately agitated by threats and criticism, and by arguments or disputes of any sort: "I always take it very personally." He hated saying No to people and went out of his way to avoid letting people down, causing trouble or giving offence. He was fearful of loneliness and disapproval and, in particular, of making mistakes or failing at anything. For years, he had feared developing a serious mental illness, and was frightened of blood and needles. He couldn't go near teenage gangs and was immediately agitated if he had to deal with aggressive people.

When he was out, he had the strong feeling of people looking at him and talking behind his back, judging or disparaging him. If anybody laughed near him, he felt they were laughing at him, especially at work. From time to time, he had the feeling he was under surveillance but it was usually related to friction with the supervisor at work who, he felt, reported back to his ex-wife (she knew him). Sometimes he felt this man was conspiring with others at work to make his job difficult. He had always been concerned about security and tended to recheck doors, locks, keys, etc at night. He was tidy but didn't think it was excessive. He often had intrusive thoughts of trouble but these were usually related to something going on around him. He doubted himself and had never felt secure in his life. Physically, he was well apart from intermittent low back pain.

He had had mental problems of one sort or another for most of his life. He saw a psychologist from about ten and was first prescribed antidepressants by a GP at age thirteen. He had been seen at public mental health services a number of times over the years but didn't trust them and generally didn't go back. His big concern was that they would realise how disturbed he was and put him in a locked ward.

Personal background:

He was born in a rural town but moved to a suburb on the outskirts of the city when he was aged nine, after his parents had separated because of his father's affairs. His father was aged 52yrs, and worked for another branch of the same company so they sometimes met at work. He was "pretty good" but they were not close. His mother was about the same age but she had moved back to the country so he didn't see her a lot. She was "very anxious and depressed" and they used to argue. When he was about thirteen, she remarried but he didn't have much to do with his stepfather who worked away. He had two younger sisters, one of whom was also anxious and depressed, but they lived interstate and he wasn't close to them. There was a much younger half-brother who didn't play any part in his life.

His schooling was interrupted by frequent moves but he was desperately unhappy throughout and left at sixteen, having barely passed Year 10. He was often in trouble from the teachers for not paying attention, which was why he was sent to the psychologist. He did not get on well with the other children as he was very shy and nervous and was teased and bullied through most of his schooling. He liked sport but was small for his age and didn't do very well. From about the age of twelve, he worked after school or helped his mother. His main recollection of his childhood was that nobody wanted him. He felt his father only saw him because he had to and wasn't interested. His mother was always busy with the younger children, especially after his half-brother was born, and he often felt she blamed him for everything wrong in her life.

On leaving school, he started an apprenticeship as a butcher but left as he was bullied by the older boys. He had had a variety of jobs, mostly driving, but he often changed jobs if he felt unwanted. Socially, he was married from 21-27yrs and had three children but this was poor and there were several separations. He had been with his current partner for about eighteen months and she had just had a baby. He drank moderately as he found alcohol calmed him. He had previously smoked a lot of marijuana and had tried other drugs but stopped when he separated. He didn't gamble and had no police record.

Self-assessment:

He saw himself as "a good person" but nervous and bothered by guilt, shame and self-consciousness. He had become very assertive, to the point of arguing, but for most of his life had been unable to stand up for himself. He was generally wary of people and not very social. He wasn't jealous but tended to hold grudges. He was tidy, patient, followed rules and got on fairly well with authority. His temper was "mostly placid," his intellect "average" and his self-esteem "low, no confidence at all."

Mental state:

The mental state showed a fit and solidly built chap of stated age, neatly presented in clean casual clothes. He was clean-shaven with trimmed hair, some tattoos and a couple of studs. He was cooperative and keen to talk but not anxious about the interview, and neither hostile nor suspicious. While he was unhappy, there were no psychotic features and he was of bright normal intellect.

With treatment, his anxiety settled and he felt he was managing his work and home life better. He revealed he had hurt himself a lot more and for a lot longer than he had originally said: "I hated myself at high school, everything was black but nobody knew what I was thinking. I had no friends, my old man wasn't interested in me, my cousins were losers, my mother was a mental wreck. I couldn't do anything right, I still can't. If I didn't have the kids, I wouldn't be here." He consistently returned to the theme of being unhappy with himself, a poor father and husband: "I don't like who I am, never have. I expect more of myself, never happy with what I've done. People say I'm a good father but I don't feel it. I do my work properly but the slackers all stick together and fill the boss' head with shit so I don't get any thanks."

Three points to consider. Firstly, people who go to the doctor and say "I'm depressed" will be given antidepressants but nobody will ever ask about causes. About 40% of men and somewhat less women will stop the drugs within six months either because of side effects (especially drowsiness, loss of sexual function and weight gain) or because the drugs don't work (even among those who persist, over 35% won't respond to anti-depressants). People who persist will usually be on them in the very long term, up to thirty years. Every time they try to stop, they will "relapse." Part of this is the direct withdrawal effect which comes from stopping a highly addictive psychoactive drug, and part of is because the drugs have done nothing to ameliorate the personality factors that caused the depression.

Gavin showed this very well: he hated himself. Marijuana made this a little less intolerable but that was all. He had taken antidepressants on and off for sixteen years but his personality was unchanged. His case gives the lie to the claim that depression is "caused by a chemical imbalance of the brain." It was actually caused by personality factors which had developed during his emotionally-deprived childhood. It may have been *mediated* by chemicals in the brain but this is entirely a different thing. Brain chemicals are the *mechanism* of depression, not the cause.

Second, it's not just adults who are aggressively competitive and hierar-chical, it starts in childhood. Bullying is part and parcel of children sorting themselves into dominance hierarchies, albeit a very destructive part. We would like to think that our little darlings' aggressive instincts are safely channelled into their class work, sport, arts and social groups but it doesn't happen. Bullies are kids who can't make it in the normal run of things, often because they're too insecure to run the risk of failing, so they get their kicks by picking on the small ones.

Actually, that's not quite true: they pick on the children who won't hit back. Tall boys are often bullied mercilessly, as are fat boys, and even fit and good-looking boys, but the common feature is that they are anxious and unassertive. They don't hit back. That is what attracts bullies and why it continues even if the child changes schools. The bullying will continue until the first bloodied nose, then it stops. Gavin learned this when he was about seventeen but he had never learned to manage his anger. It was either full on or full off, which didn't improve his self-esteem.

It is very difficult for a bullied child to get help. If they complain to the teachers, they will get more trouble in the playground. Often they don't dare tell their parents because that's where their insecurity started: aggressive parents. The only way to deal with it is for teachers to be extremely aware of it, to know that bullies are often very clever and manipulative, to keep the little darlings busy and to watch like hawks. But when I went to school, back in the dark ages, we never saw teachers during the breaks. It was a free-for-all. Some years after I left my high school, a boy who had been seriously bullied from Day One got his own back by setting fire to the school. They didn't believe him.

It's human nature to dominate, and bullying is just part of it. Trouble is, a lot of teachers, and doctors, and police and officers and government officials and so on are bullies. If a bullied person complains to them, guess what he gets back? Right first time.

Finally, the diagnosis of "borderline personality disorder" is an absurdity. For a start, it's such a stupid name. Not one of the people who uses it knows what it is borderline to (it's actually a psychoanalytic term meaning not fitting a single category but borderline to everything else). It is extremely loosely defined and is essentially just a measure of severity of disturbance and not a thing in itself. Finally, in practice it means only one thing: the psychiatrist didn't like the patient. Mostly, it's applied to people who insist on asking sticky questions that the psychiatrist can't answer and who aren't rich enough to make him think it's worthwhile putting up with the embarrassment of having a smart-arse patient who does dreadful things (like hurt themselves) and never gets better. I never use it but I see plenty of people who have been awarded the label on their travels through the psychiatry system. It's actually one of the psychiatric system's many ways of bullying patients

7

Anxiety –
Short and Long Term

The Freudian concept of mental disorder was that very early in life, severe conflicts generate intense emotions which can't be resolved. In order to survive, they have to be suppressed into the unconscious but they remain active and ever after exert a baleful influence on the individual's mental state. This model is no longer accepted; it has no basis in science and there is ample reason to believe that Freud actually fudged his evidence to suit his model. While the Freudian model made for great Hollywood, that's just not how the brain and mind work.

The modern approach is that there are no dark cisterns hidden in the depths of the mind, filled with seething emotions straining to break free; instead, we now say that emotions are generated on demand. Rather than cerebral cisterns, a better example would be a siren. If you switch it on, it makes a noise. Turn it off and the noise stops. The fact that it emits a loud noise doesn't imply that it has a great deal of loud noise stored in it. Instead, we say that the machine is generating the noise on demand. The same goes for human emotions, they are generated on demand.

The best model for emotion is humour: I see something funny and without further thought or deliberation, I start to laugh. I don't make a decision that it's funny; that decision is imposed upon me, you could say, and I am at the mercy of my sense of humour. That is, the emotion of humour is generated on demand by an interaction between a pre-existing set of beliefs and attitudes, and what I see or hear going on around me. It flares up, spills everywhere then dies down until next time. In between, I go back to my normal boring self. The fact that I laugh quite a lot doesn't mean I have big stores of "repressed humour" buried in the nether regions, nor that I have "unresolved humour" stored since childhood that is bursting to get out. That's not how it is.

Anger is the same. I see or hear about something bad happening. Without any attempt to analyse it rationally, anger flares and I react in the usual way. A while later, it has faded; nothing may have changed, it may be that nobody has taken the slightest notice of my tantrum but I will have calmed down. I may still resent what happened, I may be hoping to get even but I'm no longer showing or actually feeling angry.

A person will laugh a lot if he has a set of rules and attitudes that make him see a whole range of things as funny even though other people don't. One person's humour may be driven by seeing the rich, the powerful and the pretentious discomforted; other people may be scandalised by such irreverence. Similarly, another person's anger may be driven by seeing the rich and powerful taking advantage of the poor and weak but there are plenty of people who feel the poor deserve what they get in life, that helping them only encourages them in their wastrel ways.

Anxiety has to be seen as part of the same model: fear is an inherent, biologically-determined part of being an animal. It has a vital role to play in the individual and group economy, that of saving the genome. The machinery of anxiety, the body's alarm system, lies quiet until it is needed, then it fires into action. In an instant, it takes over every aspect of the individual's body and mind until it gets what it wants, security for the DNA. Granted, that is seeing it from a Darwinian perspective but human anxiety states are merely variations on an ancient biological theme present in all animals.

In daily life, we see two sorts of anxiety state. The first is the acute or short-term anxiety state as a reaction to a particular event while the second is the chronic or long-term, recurrent anxiety states, such as Melissa F, in Chapter 3 ('acute' means short-term; it doesn't say anything about severity). People sometimes talk of these as 'state anxiety' and 'trait anxiety.' The acute anxiety state or reaction, or what used to be called a stress reaction, is exactly what you experience after a bad fright. It doesn't matter what the cause or stressor is, the reaction is stereotyped. It has two components, physical and mental. Physically, an acutely anxious person is agitated and restless, she feels shaky and sweaty, her heart is racing and she feels short of breath. She may feel tight in the chest, with a dry mouth and a sense of tightness in the throat ("lump in the throat") which makes it difficult to talk or swallow. Her voice may quaver and she may stammer or stutter or stumble over her words. She may feel light-headed or unsteady on her feet, dizzy or clumsy.

The mental part of the fear response also has two components. The first is the actual emotion of fear or fright, the reaction to a threat, the chilling sense that something bad is happening. This ranges from the mildest apprehension all the way to abject terror. Remember that fear is always directed at the future, it's a warning that something bad is *about to happen*. You can't be scared of the past. The second mental component is the cognitive element. Our subject will probably have trouble thinking clearly, with the sense that there are too many thoughts tumbling through her head, or that her thoughts are jumbled and don't connect properly. Other people complain of the sense that their minds have gone completely blank. They can't focus on something without losing the thread, and they're distracted and forgetful. You may tell them something and a few minutes later, it's completely gone and they have little or no recollection of you saying it. People commonly complain of cognitive distortions, such as the sense of the walls closing in so that they feel they need to escape. Other people feel that the world is somehow different (derealisation) or that they have changed in themselves (depersonalisation) or are different from all other people (alienation).

The somatic and the cognitive symptoms of anxiety are more or less the same regardless of the cause. The only differences are the intensity and duration of the reaction. We can graph the acute anxiety reaction as arousal versus time, as we saw chapter 4. (See Fig. 4.2)

The anxiety reaction ranges from a mild apprehension that something isn't quite right, then intensifies to a sense of fear and foreboding, then dread until finally it reaches the level of overwhelming panic and terror. In this state, where the physiological arousal is so high that the person can't focus on anything and can't make sense of what is happening around her, it is impossible to eat or drink or, more ominously, to sleep. 24hrs of sleep deprivation has about the same effect on thinking as an alcohol level of 0.15mg%, i.e. dangerous if you have to do anything serious like drive a vehicle. In this state, people commonly misunderstand what is being said to them, or appear to understand only to forget within a few minutes. They have difficulties working things out or following plans or procedures and react badly to mistakes or misapprehensions.

Thirty hours of sleep deprivation is equivalent to about 0.25% blood alcohol. The subject will start to show visual disturbances, often the sense that solid things (walls, floors, carpets) are moving or shimmering as though their surfaces have turned to liquid. If the subject believes they have actually turned to liquid, her fear goes through the roof. At about the same time, she may start to see shadowy movements from the corner of the eye and will often jerk around, startled and worried by the experience. Severely agitated people can also hear odd sounds or misinterpret sounds or voices, especially seeing them as hostile or persecutory. They may form the idea that people are trying to hurt them although these beliefs are fleeting and will change almost by the minute. After 36hrs without sleep, they seem to start to dream while awake, acting as though seeing real people or animals and responding to them. This is dangerous, as they have now entered a self-sustaining phase of sleep deprivation, where the effects of lack of sleep are themselves terrifying and lead to further arousal, which blocks sleep. This is an acute, high-arousal psychotic state that should be treated by very rapid sedation.

There is a very important point here: orthodox psychiatry says the acutely psychotic person is agitated because he believes he is being persecuted or believes bizarre things are happening to him. That is, it says he was fine until these weird things started to take control of his mind. Get rid of his beliefs and the fear will settle. The biocognitive model turns this on its head: his terror is causing his bizarre experiences, and the experiences then cause the delusional beliefs which amplify the terror. Therefore, treatment in the biocognitive model is specifically directed at reducing the level of arousal through a number of approaches.

It is critically important to remember that if a calm person is having a profoundly frightening experience, he will react with a state of panic which seems perfectly reasonable in its context. If, however, a person has a second fright while still recovering from the first, his anxiety will *double from where it was*. That is, he will appear to be "over-reacting" to a minor stimulus (see Fig. 4.3). Because anxiety is cumulative, a rapid series of relatively minor frights can also induce a state of panic. That doesn't mean he is a weak character, or she is hysterical, or borderline or any of the myriad nasty expressions psychiatry uses on people it doesn't understand, it's a normal reaction that could happen to anybody. If it hasn't happened to you, be grateful, but if you don't believe it would happen to you, we can easily arrange a little experiment to convince you.

When a person presents in an acutely agitated state, it is important to work out just where she is on the Yerkes-Dodson curve (Fig. 4.1). A person who is still coherent will respond to minor tranquillisers (benzodiazepines such as diazepam) while anybody who complains of visual misperceptions will probably need sedating antipsychotic drugs, such as thioridazine or olanzapine. These should be reduced and stopped over a few days as it is critical not to mistake an acute, high-arousal psychotic state for a longer-term disorder and leave them on the drugs until they become addicted. That moves the problems to a new level.

Case 7.1: Justin T. 31yo mechanic.

While at work, Justin slipped on some grease and fell into an inspection pit, fracturing his right ankle. Almost immediately, things started to go wrong. At the hospital, somebody thought he smelled strange and wondered whether he had been drinking. The surgeon decided to treat it conservatively with a plaster cast and rest so he was sent home on crutches. However, the insurers saw the comment that he may have been drinking and, even though he bitterly denied it (he had been drenched with radiator coolant when he fell), they put his claim on hold pending investigations. This meant he could not get paid so he became irritable and was having trouble sleeping. After several weeks, his partner felt she could not manage him and their two small children so she insisted he go to stay with his parents on the far side of the city. This distressed him and his sleep deteriorated further.

A week later, somebody rang to say they thought a strange man had stayed at his house overnight. He became intensely agitated and drove to his home with his leg in a cast. His partner was out so he went inside and started drinking. When she arrived, he was drunk and angry so she called the police who dragged him away and put him in the lock-up overnight. They placed a domestic violence order on him, barring him from approaching his home or contacting his partner. Intensely agitated, he began ringing her as soon as he was released, with the result that he was arrested and taken back to the lock-up. By this stage, he was almost incoherent, shouting that the police were trying to kill him and threatening everybody, so they brought him to hospital.

When seen, he was intensely agitated and unable to sit in a chair. He insisted on pacing up and down, for which he needed his crutches but they had been removed by nursing staff as a safety measure. He was alternately angry and threatening or weepy, talking loudly but was difficult to follow. He was shaking violently, sweating and panting for breath. His heart was racing at about 120/min, his mouth and lips were cracked and dry and he was unsteady on his feet. He said his stomach was churning to the point where he had vomited, he was stammering and kept losing the thread of what he was saying. Mostly, he was ranting against the police, demanding to speak to his wife to find out what was going on, and angry at the hospital staff for not letting him go or call his wife. A junior medical officer, clearly frightened, had told him he would be detained in the security ward if he didn't cooperate, which made things worse.

He was given diazepam 10mg by mouth, his crutches were returned and he was taken outside to a quiet spot in the garden for a cup of tea and a cigarette. Gradually, he settled and began talking about what had happened to him. He had never had trouble with the police in his life and was terrified after he was shoved in the lock-up with drunks and deadbeats. In the middle of his night in the lock-up, completely unable to sleep, he had developed the idea that the insurance company would refuse to pay and he would lose his job through being imprisoned. While he was talking, a phone call to his wife revealed that the "strange man" was a cousin who had stayed one night on his way back home.

As Justin didn't want to stay in hospital, he was allowed to go to stay with his parents while his insurance claim was sorted out. A few days later, it was accepted and he received his back pay. Next day, he went home and remained well. A month later, when the fracture showed no signs of healing, he underwent surgery but there were no complications and he recovered well.

This is a typical case seen in the emergency department of any big hospital. Typically, a state of very high arousal follows an accumulation of pressures and upsets rather than a single incident.

I need to point out that the word 'stress' actually has no meaning in psychiatry. It apparently comes from a largely forgotten work by a Hungarian physician, Hans Selye (1907-82), who migrated to Canada early in his career. He was interested in the capacity of organisms to respond to various events, some noxious, some beneficial, but he had no neutral term to name the response. He decided to lift a term from engineering but because his English wasn't the best, he chose the wrong word. To engineers, the stressor is the external force applied to a structure while the internal response is known as the strain. Selye misnamed the internal response as "stress."

Ever since, the word "stress" has been misused freely by just about everybody for just about everything you can imagine, but mostly regarding mental life. It seems to have at least seven different meanings so the easiest thing would be to stop using it, except it is now cemented into psychiatry by the American term "post-traumatic stress disorder." This actually means "the disorder that comes on after a stressor of traumatic intensity." It *doesn't* mean that after an incident, there is some fluid-like thing called "stress" sloshing around inside the body and brain. That comes from a misconception of Freudian theory, the totally incorrect idea that if you are severely disturbed now, then something very severe must have happened to you in the past and you have to "get it out" before you can get better. In one word, that's rubbish. But back to "stress."

When somebody says "I'm terribly stressed," she means "I'm terribly anxious." As a matter of biology, this means that every system in her body has been switched to high alert. Her heart is thumping, her muscles are twitching, her lungs are inflating rapidly, the blood is coursing through her vital organs and her brain is highly active. You could say her body is firing on all cylinders, ready for whatever strenuous action is needed to save her genome. Physiologically-speaking, being highly aroused is very demanding of the body's reserves. A person who is anxious for several hours will report feeling completely exhausted and washed out. All too often, this is misinterpreted as a symptom of depression. We see this most often in people who are subjected to prolonged anxiety because of pressure in their work or home environments, protracted court cases, financial pressure, family illness, etc.

Case 7.2: Mrs Jenny M, 34yo teacher's aide.

This lady, the mother of two small children, worked only during school hours, although she had been off work for about three months. She was referred by her GP for assessment after two years' unsuccessful treatment of depression. The referring letter said: "She has treatment-resistant depression so I have warned her that you may decide she need admission to hospital for ECT." Jenny attended with her husband, a fairly grim-looking 32yo police officer. At the interview, she was neatly dressed and presented in quality casual clothing, with no visible tattoos, studs or scars. She had some gold jewellery, a neat hairdo, and was generally the picture of young middle-class respectability.

She gave a clear history of several years of feeling low and miserable, with poor sleep, and little energy, interest or motivation. Her appetite was poor but because she was taking antidepressants, she had gained about 22kg in weight, which caused her considerable distress. She didn't want to mix with people, and had no sexual interest at all. She had trouble concentrating and often felt she couldn't make decisions, so she left them all to her husband. She was preoccupied with the sense that she was a failure and felt guilty over not being able to do more for her children. She felt low and miserable most of the time, describing it as "overwhelming." She felt sick of things and said she couldn't go on as she was, that something had to change. Sometimes she felt sick of life itself and occasionally had had the idea that if she didn't wake up one day, it would be a relief. When an elderly relative suddenly died of a massive stroke, she was shocked to realise that she felt envious. She repeatedly insisted that she had no idea why she was depressed as there was nothing going wrong in her life. She said she never doubted what doctors had told her so many times, that it was a chemical imbalance of her brain.

Her husband said that when they were married, she was a very happy, physically active and outgoing person who loved a party. He believed she was very intelligent and responsible and an excellent mother. They had some money problems due to borrowing to finance some housing investments but he was sure they could work their way through it. Otherwise there was nothing going wrong in their lives. He was obviously concerned but was definitely not keen on the idea of her going to a mental hospital, especially if it involved ECT. He had met psychologists through his work and was very dismissive of their techniques. However, he accepted that depression is a disease just like any other and curing it would involve some sort of medical treatment, although he wasn't sure what as the drugs hadn't worked. For himself, he worked long hours, he was studying for promotion and also went to gym five times a week to indulge his hobby of body-building.

Her history did not reveal anything of note. She came from a good middle-class family in a middle-class suburb and attended a respectable girls' church school. As a child, she was cheerful and popular, very sporty and a school prefect. She got on well with everybody, had plenty of friends and relatives who adored her, and was always very social and helpful. On leaving school, she started training as a dental nurse but found she didn't like it so she began working as a teacher's aide and had continued with it. She drank very little alcohol, didn't smoke, used no illegal drugs, didn't gamble and, of course, had no police record. Physically, she had always been healthy.

She denied any significant anxiety symptoms and had only a few minor fears, such as snakes and letting people down. There were no signs of excessive self-consciousness, no paranoid ideas and she was tidy and organised without being obsessional. All in all, she was just a capable and happy person. She gave no history of mental or personal difficulties prior to about three years after they were married, when she was pregnant with the second child. She felt she became depressed after the baby was born but she declined drugs and slowly came back to normal. However, the depression returned a year or so later and she had never recovered.

Over the next two weeks, she settled and was asked about returning to work. She agreed, the school offered her light duties and she began the program. Everything seemed to be going well but after two weeks, she presented in a state of great agitation, crying uncontrollably. She insisted she was seriously depressed and would have to accept admission and ECT. This time, it was clear she was shaky, sweaty, light-headed and unable to eat. Her heart was racing, she couldn't think or speak properly and was unable to sleep—all the symptoms she had studiously denied at her initial assessment. Under fairly firm questioning, she revealed that as the day of her return to work approached, she became increasingly agitated over the thought that she would not be able to manage, that she would fail and lose her job, that the family finances would collapse, they would be bankrupted, her husband would lose his job, the marriage would fail and they would be destitute. Her terror was a real and living thing. She genuinely believed that they were facing total ruin if she didn't get back to work immediately but she knew she couldn't do it.

The picture that unfolded was of slowly accumulating pressures in a person who had never suffered any adversity in her life. She firmly believed that everybody should be able to cope with life if they had Right Attitude. She believed the *Women's Weekly* image of the radiantly cheerful and capable young mother who worked almost to the day she delivered and never fussed over anything. In fact, she had suffered badly from morning sickness but she diligently ironed her husband's uniforms even though the smell of the detergent made her ill. Just when the second baby was born, a cousin's marriage fell apart and she took it on herself to bring them together again.

This didn't work and she gained the impression her cousin blamed her, leading to an intense sense of guilt and failure. Pressures kept adding: her husband had trouble at work, some tenants damaged their rental property, her eldest child developed asthma, on and on. Through it all, she tried to cope by working harder and harder until she began having trouble sleeping.

She insisted her husband had time off to go fishing with his mates but she took no time off herself. One day, she burst into tears at work and was seen by the school nurse who, after one minute, announced she was seriously depressed. The nurse took her to see her GP, a family friend, who agreed with the diagnosis and prescribed an antidepressant.

Yes, she was depressed but the primary problem was her carefully concealed anxiety over failing. She was working herself to exhaustion, driven by a need to cope with everything that life threw her way. When it was suggested to her that her husband could iron his own uniforms, she was horrified: he worked hard, she said, he needed his time to himself, she should be able to cope; her mother, her sister, her cousins and all her friends coped so she should be able to as well. Fear of failure, of not measuring up to some vague, totally unrealistic vision of the Good Mother had pushed her into a severe state of anxiety, which eventually led to depression. All she had to do was learn to say "No, you can do it yourself," and she was over the worst of it. Antidepressants, of course, don't teach people how to assert themselves.

There are a couple of important points in this vignette, which is quite a common presentation. First, the most common cause of a persistent or recurrent depressive state is an unsuspected anxiety state. The reason it is unsuspected is because nobody asks. Psychiatrists ask about depressive symptoms but as soon as they find them, they stop, they don't enquire further. This is because modern psychiatry says that the mere fact of depression is enough: it's biological, it doesn't actually have a cause so there's no point looking for one. I disagree: to me, depression is a reaction to life events. Sometimes those events are in the outside world, sometimes they are wholly in the inner world; some are in the present, some are in the past but if you want to know what they are, you must look for them. Grief is a clearly defined state which has the same symptoms as depression, yet we accept that it has a psychological cause. If an unhappy person doesn't give a clear history of a serious loss, then psychiatrists say he must have a biological disease of the brain. But the only reason they say he hasn't experienced a serious loss is because they didn't bother to ask.

In Jenny's case, she had experienced years of unremitting anxiety which she felt she had to conceal. She never once said to anybody, especially her husband and her mother, that she was struggling to manage two small children, a husband on shift work who often had to work overtime with no warning, her own job, the house, their finances and maintain a busy social life. It wore her down. Over time, she became increasingly anxious, an endless whirlwind of trying harder to cope combined with her fear of failing until she fell in a heap. Hugely distressed, she started to believe she was a failure as a mother, wife, friend and worker; that if this was all she could look forward to, she may as well be dead and her family would be better off without her. That state we call "depression" but the *cause* of her depresssive state was chronic anxiety. If the cause is not addressed, the effect won't go away. Drugs don't deal with psychological causes, hence (and our second point) the concept of 'treatment-resistant depression.'

Sometimes it's a bit difficult being a psychiatrist because everybody likes to make fun of us. But sometimes we invite it, and the expression 'treatment-resistant depression' is a good example. The term comes from general medicine, probably from the notion of 'antibiotic-resistant infections.' If a physician is treating a severe infection but the patient fails to respond, the first thing to do is make sure the bug is sensitive to the antibiotics. Increasingly, we find that bacteria which once responded to the antibiotic have become resistant, and that explains why the patient remains ill. Our treatment failed just because it was the wrong treatment for that patient at that time. It may still work for other people but it didn't work for him.

But psychiatrists are in a difficult position. They want to be seen as "real doctors," part of the medical mainstream, complete with lots of biology-talk, drugs and procedures like ECT. They don't want to be seen to be messing around with feelings or mental pain or any of that other squishy subjective stuff, they want something hard, objective, verifiable, deterministic and so on. Their theory says depression is biological; they have a group of drugs called antidepressants; give a depressed patient the drugs and he should get better. But very often they don't. OK, don't worry, we know there's nothing wrong with our approach just because there can't be. We *believe* in the biological causation of depression. If our treatment doesn't work, we have an escape route, we can always *blame the patient*. We can say he doesn't have an ordinary type of depression, he has in fact a 'treatment-resistant depression.' This is actually a dumb person's idea of how a clever person would explain the fact that a patient doesn't get better.

You see what they've done, they've taken half the concept of antibiotic resistance, the face-saving half, and left the effective bit behind. That's the bit that says "Oh dear, we gave him the wrong treatment." But psychiatrists will not accept that they gave the wrong treatment, because that would call their whole model into question. In this respect, they're like the physicians of yesteryear whose treatment consisted solely of bleeding their patients. If the patient didn't get better, as George Washington didn't (malaria doesn't respond to bleeding), it wasn't that the treatment was wrong, it was that he didn't get enough, so they had to give more. As you know, Gen. Washington died of exsanguination. They bled him to death: for him, more most definitely meant worse. But his physicians wouldn't, couldn't, admit the failure of their model. Why not? Because they had nothing else. If they couldn't bleed people, they had nothing and they were out of a job.

So be it with modern psychiatrists. If a patient fails to get better, it's not their fault, it's not that they gave the wrong treatment for his condition, it's that they didn't give enough. So he gets more drugs, and more again, and then ECT, then ECT and drugs, and still more drugs. A recent paper from the US on deaths caused by drug treatment of depression showed, firstly, that from 2000-14, deaths from drug treatment of depression rose 135% while the US population rose only 15%. This means drug-related deaths rose 900% faster than they should have (actually, we would really like them to have gone down). Second, the researchers found no less than 45 different drugs were being used to "treat" depression (they didn't count ECT or TCS). If that isn't therapeutic desperation, I don't know what is. Surely it would occur to a sensible doctor that if depression doesn't respond to all those chemicals, then maybe, just maybe, there's something wrong with the entire approach? But like Washington's determined physicians, they don't have anything else. Mental disorder is either biology, they mutter nervously, or we're out of a job.

The third point in Jenny's case is this: The fact that she was depressed as an adult tells us nothing about the quality of her childhood. Let's go back to the point about the lack of a relationship between early life events and adult mental state:

> That comes from a misconception of Freudian theory, the totally incorrect idea that if you are severely disturbed now, then something very severe must have happened to you in the past and you have to "get it out" before you can get better.

Months later, I learned that this lady had been referred to a psychologist who was absolutely convinced that all mental disorder in women meant that they had experienced a very severe "trauma" in childhood. The more severe the mental disorder, the more severe the traumatic event must have been. Because Jenny's condition was very severe, she must have experienced the most severe of all traumatic events, sexual abuse. Because she couldn't recall any, that meant it must have been so severe that she had totally repressed it and she would need prolonged (and very expensive) psychological treatment to get it all out. When the psychologist told her she must have been abused, Jenny was appalled and denied it. This convinced the psychologist she was on the right track, which made Jenny even more distressed. I'm satisfied that there was no such event in her childhood, that her adult mental disorder was due to a long series of events, none of which amounted to very much but which together had a devastating effect.

In Jenny's case, there was definitely nothing untoward in her childhood. She freely and wistfully said that she'd had a wonderful life until she became depressed. She'd had no childhood trauma. This is exactly the sort of case that biological psychiatrists like to use as proof that the notion of psychological causation in mental disorder is completely off the mark. But they are using Freudian concepts of psychological causation as their model and Freud's concepts, as we now know, are all wrong. And why should they not be? He formulated them about 130 years ago, using the then-standard model of causation in science, hydrodynamics. That model says that if there is an intense pressure now, it must have been caused by an intense event in the past. Today, we no longer believe that. We understand that people can become seriously anxious as adults with no known adverse events *just because* anxiety is self-reinforcing.

The informational approach is that, over time, tiny errors can amplify to produce catastrophic results. Machines or structures can shake themselves to bits; a small exposure to a toxin can accumulate in the food chain to produce fatal results in the peak predators; a tiny error in a network can eventually bring the whole show crashing to a halt; and a fault in a small part of the international financial markets can lead to a Global Financial Crisis. There is even a name for this idea, Chaos Theory, which has bred the trope that the flap of a butterfly wing in the Amazon can eventually cause a violent hurricane to smash into Florida. I must admit that I don't think much of Chaos Theory, which seems to be little more than a few elementary mathematical truths dressed up with some fancy jargon (Strange Attractors, anyone?). However, one of those elementary truths, the notion of a recursive function, has widespread application in modern science. We'll define a recursive function then explain it.

In maths, a recursive function is a recurrent function (or mathematical operation) that uses the outcome of its first iteration as the starting point of its second iteration. That is, we perform some sort of sum or algebraic operation to get an answer; we then use that answer to do the sum again, and again and again, ad infinitum. By this means, it amplifies itself. A practical example is when, each time a pendulum swings, we give it a tiny tap. Each time, it will swing a little bit further until eventually, it will swing right over the top. It's the same principle as when a wheel on a car is slightly out of balance. This causes abnormal wear, which leads to more pronounced imbalance, which causes more wear and more imbalance until one day, the tyre blows up and the car crashes. The fact that the car crashed doesn't mean somebody put a bomb in it. The accident could have been prevented with a 5gm weight on the wheel to balance it. The concept of a minor reaction reverberating and amplifying through time is critical to this model of mental disorder.

It's also central to a lot of general medicine. The body can absorb a lot of punishment until one day, it starts to run out of reserves, then it quickly starts to fail. This is how alcohol wreaks its damage. The liver is a very powerful organ and can absorb massive punishment from alcohol but slowly, it loses its capacity to regenerate after drinking binges. One day, it crosses the point of no return in that it fails to replace the tissue that was damaged during last night's binge. With each subsequent night on the grog, there is further loss of hepatic tissue, and so the discrepancy widens exponentially until the organ starts to shrink. This is also true of alcoholic brain damage and, in fact, is true of all living systems.

Jenny's problem was that she didn't realise (or didn't want to accept) that humans have limits. She was brought up to believe that in order to succeed, all you needed was Right Attitude. Winners have Right Attitude, and Right Attitude Always Wins. You can see the corollary to this, of course, and it's hopelessly wrong: that if you don't win, you obviously don't have Right Attitude, which is a moral failing. The next step, which she had long believed, was that if you lose, you must have had Bad Attitude all along. She had never really thought this, of course, but she knew it intuitively, just as you know intuitively that a Green Great Dragon is wrong. Her intuitive (or unconscious) belief was very powerful and essentially controlled her life. She could not admit she was struggling. She kept piling work on her shoulders until her knees were giving way. Unfortunately, her response was not to dump some of the work and have a break but to work harder. And harder. Until one day, she woke up and thought "I can't face the day. If this is all I can expect from life, I may as well be dead."

So where does anxiety fit in this? The thought that she couldn't cope caused stirrings of almost subliminal anxiety, and she automatically moved in the opposite direction. She couldn't allow herself to fail because if she did, it meant she was morally weak, a bad person. This went straight back to her schooling in a religious school: throughout her life, she was driven by guilt. The thought of failure frightened her and drove her beyond her limits. This attitude is very widespread, although generally more so in men than women.

Jenny's policeman husband had a very serious case of Winners Have Right Attitude, which she knew intuitively, and she feared his disapproval. He was a bit different, in that he believed firmly that only he had Right Attitude and would never fail, while everybody else on earth was weak and it didn't worry or surprise him if they failed. Despite his tough appearance, he was actually a very caring chap. If his wife had ever said to him "I'm too tired, you'll have to iron your own uniforms," he would willingly have done so, and not just because it proved she was weak, but because he wanted to help. However, she repeatedly rebuffed his offers to help until he eventually stopped offering. Then she felt guilty about resenting him going on his fishing trips, which made her feel worse. The point is that not all mentally-disturbed adults have had bad childhoods. Some didn't, but the seeds of their own destruction are deep in their personalities. And here is an important point: until they break down, they can't and won't be considered to have a personality disorder.

On the other hand, people can become seriously anxious because of dreadful childhoods but if there's no sex, everybody loses interest, as the next case shows.

Case 7.3. Liam C. A life of anxiety.

Liam was 29yrs old when he was referred for treatment of "agoraphobia and mood swings from low to hyperactivity." He was living with his partner and their 2yo daughter but because of his mental symptoms, he hadn't worked for about eight years. He was taking no medication at the time but had been referred to a psychologist who suggested he needed to see a psychiatrist for antidepressants. At the appointed time, he crept into the room, a picture of abject and rather smelly misery several sizes too small for his rumpled old clothes.

Presenting complaints:

He said that in general, he was feeling "pretty terrible." His sleep was very poor as he was unable to sleep early and often didn't go to bed until about 3.00 or 4.00am, but even then, it could take him several hours to get to sleep. Sometimes he had no sleep at all but he tried to avoid taking naps by day. The delay in sleep was caused by "...my head, I can't turn it off." His appetite was "terrible" and although he weighed 57kg (meaning his BMI was about 18, or severely underweight), he had been down to 50kg at different times. He said he had no energy at all, his level of activity was "none," and his interest and motivation were both "zero." Socially, he never mixed with people, which was normal for him, but his sexual interest was "mostly OK."

He felt his memory was patchy but his concentration was "horrible." He didn't drive as he became so agitated that he had never been able to pass the test. He had trouble making decisions and delayed them where possible. Mostly, he was unable to think clearly, saying he had a "ping-pong" brain, i.e. his thoughts were all over the place and he often had the feeling of too many thoughts cramming into his head. The thought content was preoccupied by worries including his elder daughter, money and providing for his family. There were no disturbances of perception.

He described his mood as "crap." He felt low and miserable most of the time and was "almost suicidal." He was sick of things as they were but was not sick of life itself although he often felt that death would be a relief. He had been suicidal in the past and had taken overdoses of carbamazepine (a fairly toxic anticonvulsant, trade ame Tegretol). The unhappiness was due to "traumatic events that keep repeating themselves, everything always going wrong." He did not have any additional pressures such as court cases etc.

Sometimes he felt good but this was very unpredictable and didn't last long. He simply felt good and tended to talk more but he didn't do anything unusual, and certainly didn't spend money. However, these episodes were rare as he suffered more or less constant agitation: "I'm always on edge, people make me flinch, they startle me for fun because I always jump." When agitated, he felt shaky, sweaty and short of breath. His mouth was dry, he felt tight in the throat and he had trouble speaking. His stomach churned and he was unable to eat, which was why he could never gain weight. He had the feeling that the world was different. During these bouts, he felt frightened and angry and tended to yell and bang things or get into arguments so his only way of dealing with the agitation was to get away by himself, which was difficult in their flat.

He was having several bouts per week but they lasted all day or even several days on end and he was rarely free of agitation. It was caused by having to go out or dealing with people, especially officials, but also anybody who looked threatening.

On questioning, he was very frightened of cars and accidents and never felt safe walking on the street. He feared heights, confined spaces and sudden noises or being touched unexpectedly. He was frightened of weapons, such as firearms and knives, but unusually, his only animal fears were horses and cows. Most of his fears were social in nature, including crowds, queues, public speaking, and interviews or appointments. He panicked before any sort of test or exam, which was why he did not have his driver's licence. He was frightened of public transport and of meeting strangers or using phones. He feared threats and criticism, arguments and disputes of any sort, even if they didn't involve him, as well as confrontation or saying No to people. He hated letting people down, causing trouble or giving offence and went out of his way to avoid it but, all too often, this made matters worse. He was very frightened of loneliness, humiliation and disapproval, and of making mistakes or failing at anything. He was scared of drunks and junkies, teenage gangs and any aggressive people.

Whenever he left the house, he had a strong feeling that people were looking at him and talking about him, or judging him. This was so strong that he often had to go home again. If anybody laughed near him, he felt they were laughing at him. He had a feeling of danger directed at him, and often felt he was being watched or under surveillance. He had the feeling that his former partner was conspiring against him to make his life miserable, e.g. by denying access to his daughter.

He always checked doors, locks, keys etc. for security but he was not fussy about cleanliness, tidiness, order or punctuality. He had no rituals but he had recurrent thoughts of danger or something going wrong but these were not stereotyped and depended on where he was or what he was doing. Physically, he was healthy.

He said that these symptoms had been present "forever." He had seen a psychologist who diagnosed bipolar disorder and PTSD and recommended antidepressants but he'd had no other treatment.

Personal background:

Liam was born and raised in a depressed regional city. His parents separated when he was aged four and he was raised by his mother. His father, who was then in his late 40s, had been a process worker but he was a very bad-tempered alcoholic and Liam had nothing to do with him. His mother was aged 42, which meant she was 14 when Liam was born. She lived in a small rural town but had never worked. He said she was injured years ago and used a wheelchair but he didn't believe there was much wrong with her. She had always used drugs and gambled. He described her as "selfish" and recalled that, as a child, he had to do a lot of the housework and look after his younger half-siblings because she was incapable. After his father left, his mother quickly found another partner and had a further three children. This man was "extremely paranoid, violent and abusive, always on speed and grog... He hated my guts." One of his half-brothers is "much worse than me, really mental" and they have no contact. One has an apprenticeship but is also anxious and uses drugs. His sister lives with their mother and is very disturbed but he had very little contact with her.

During his childhood, the family moved repeatedly and he went to 21 different schools, finally leaving at age 18 but he had passed only Year 10. He did well in maths but his marks were patchy in other subjects, depending on how he got on with the teachers. He wasn't in much trouble as he was very quiet but, because of the chaos at home, he often didn't get his homework done on time. He didn't get on with the other children at all. He was very shy and nervous and was often teased until he flew into rages. Most of the time, nobody would speak to him and he had no friends. He didn't play sport, partly because he was so small but also because he was so shy that he walked away and went home. He couldn't recall any interests he had had during his schooling. At different times, he was sent to stay with his maternal grandparents and was a bit happier with them but school was no different. At age eleven, he was briefly in care.

On leaving school, he went to stay with his father and found some part-time work in shops but his father was extremely bad-tempered and finally forced him to leave. For the next three years, he lived on the streets "...because of my head" but he wasn't drinking or using drugs. Sometimes he found some work in shops or stores but he never lasted long because he was so easily agitated and walked out. Socially, he was in a relationship from 20-22yrs and had one child, now aged nine, but the mother was very disturbed and had repeated affairs. She now denies access to his daughter, which troubles him greatly. He has been with his present partner four years and they have one child. He doesn't drink, uses no illegal drugs, doesn't gamble and has a minor juvenile police record. His general health is reasonable but he is very unfit.

Self-assessment:

> *How do you see yourself as a person?*
> Scum.
> *That's it?*
> Always been.

He sees himself as intensely nervous and bothered by guilt, shame and self-consciousness. Normally, he tries to avoid any conflict with people but if he can't, he becomes prickly and over-assertive to the point of arguing. He is impatient and very mistrustful of people, and actively avoids company. He is jealous and insecure but doesn't hold grudges. Most of the time, he follows rules but he is wary of authority and avoids trouble by keeping his head down. He sees his temper as "bad," his intellect as "pretty good" but his self-esteem is "terrible, never been any different."

Mental state examination:

The mental state showed a painfully thin and very youthful looking chap of about average height, dressed in old and rumpled, loose dark clothes. He was unshaven and his teeth were seriously eroded. There were no visible tattoos, studs, scars or jewellery. He moved warily, and actively avoided eye contact. He spoke freely and seemed relieved to be able to talk. He was unhappy but not anxious about the interview, and neither hostile nor suspicious. There were no psychotic features and nothing to indicate an organic impairment of brain function. He appeared to be of superior intellectual ability (two weeks later, brief IQ testing showed a score of 140).

It seems Liam was given antidepressants at some stage but there was no attempt to deal with his anxiety. When psychiatrists (and psychologists, and nurses and counsellors) hear the word 'suicidal,' they stop asking questions: Break out the antidepressants! Bring up the ECT machine! But if a person is suicidal, you owe it to him to ask why. The *fact* that somebody is suicidal is the beginning of the enquiry, not the end.

One of the greatest philosophers of the nineteenth century was a misanthropic German named Arthur Schopenhauer. He was so miserable that while he was still a student, his mother, writing to him to describe the brutal occupation of Weimar after the battle of Jena, said:

> I could tell you things that would make your hair stand on end but I refrain, for I know how you love to brood over human misery in any case.

He never had any doubts about himself. Much later, he said of his philosophical colleagues:

I should like to see the man who could boast of a more miserable set of contemporaries than mine.

Schopenhauer gave a version of what is called The Principle of Sufficient Reason, which says that nothing happens without sufficient cause; or everything that happens has a cause. In the case of mental events, the "sufficient cause" is a prior mental event. If a person has a mental event called "feeling suicidal," then it needs a prior mental explanation, not a biological explanation (I should point out that no credible philosopher believes it is possible to give a biological explanation of suicidal ideas).

In the case of suicidal ideas, if you discover that the person has suffered severe anxiety for years and has decided that an anxious life is not worth living, you have found the "sufficient prior mental explanation" of the suicidal ideas. The anxiety must therefore be treated. Stands to reason.

If psychiatry is governed by common sense and not by dogma, it's really quite simple.

PART III –
How Not to be Anxious

8 Avoidance and Denial

People who think that anxiety is just a matter of neurotic, middle class self-indulgence need to remember two facts. First, it is extremely common, at all levels of society. At any one time, at least 15% of the population are significantly affected by anxiety. It affects male and female, young and old, rich and poor, smart and not so smart, well-behaved and naughty, without fear or favour. Second, it has to be taken seriously. In Australia, anxiety is the most common cause of early retirement from the Commonwealth Public Service, and I'm sure it's true in other countries. The natural history of an untreated anxiety state is that it is likely to intensify with the passage of time. It is most definitely not a case of "Oh, just stop worrying, you'll get over it." The question then becomes: If all these people are suffering, and their lives are steadily getting worse, how do they manage it? What can they do about it?

The next few chapters start with this fundamental principle: Anxiety is intolerable, so sufferers must do something to calm it. In this, they have no choice because anxiety intensifies until they do something. In practice, because of its nature as the fight or flight response, there are only three possible means of resolving it. First, *run away* from the threat. There are plenty of people who resolve their fears of frogs, heights or darkness by avoiding them. Scared of frogs? That's easy, just keep away from wet places. In the north of Australia, where frogs enjoy living in sewers and regularly swim up into your toilet bowl, that's not so easy. I heard of one man who, after having had a bit too much to drink, had to go to the toilet. Suddenly, there was a dreadful shriek followed a moment later by a gunshot and the sound of falling glass. Expecting the worst, his family ran to see what had happened. They found him leaning drunkenly against the door, shaking and trembling as he pointed his rifle at the pile of shattered china. "There was a bloody frog in there," he slurred, as though that explained all.

That's a bit extreme but if you're scared of heights, just stay on the ground. Scared of the dark? Leave a light on. Scared of people? Aha, here we run into trouble. It isn't quite so easy to avoid people. In an earlier chapter, I mentioned a student who hid in his flat for four years (I've just been in touch with him, he's now studying the course he wanted). Another stayed in his bedroom for six years, only venturing out late at night when he knew everybody would be asleep. In one word, this form of self-management is called *avoidance*, but there's also a variant of avoidance called *distraction,* which is very important. We'll also mention *denial,* which leads to a great deal of wasted effort.

Second possible resolution: *Start a fight.* There are certainly plenty of people who follow this path. They may not always fight physically, but you will see them in meetings, sports games, minor disputes between neighbours and workers etc., where they quickly become intensely and inappropriately agitated and can't let the matter rest. This is very common and we'll come back to it.

Third, use *chemicals* to suppress the anxiety response. Get drunk. Get high. Get smashed, hammered, kippered, stoked, spaced out, wrecked or wasted, or whatever. A wide and ever-growing variety of chemicals will suppress the anxiety response. That wouldn't matter so much except practically all of them are physically and psychologically addictive, with serious long-term side-effects, which does matter.

Finally, all of the above. Some people do what they can to avoid their anxieties but if they can't, they get drunk, get into fights and blame their parents.

Avoidance

We'll start with simple avoidance. Mostly, it's very easy to avoid your anxieties. Enter a monastery. Get a job as a lighthouse-keeper. Come to Australia and get a job as a boundary rider or a dogger (the man who catches dingoes) on a remote cattle station. Get a hobby that nobody else is interested in. Don't talk to anybody. Don't accept invitations to parties, weddings, birthdays, funerals etc; avoid conferences, don't join clubs, a-a-and... (drum roll) ...take up computer games. In fact, since the internet arrived, hardly anybody enters monasteries, keeps lighthouses, rides boundaries or writes sonnets in Sanskrit. Even stamp collecting has gone into a decline. All you have to do is sit up all night, playing fantasy games under a false name and sleep all day. Then you can persuade yourself you're not a misfit and you do actually have a rich and busy life. Being a serious gamer means never having to explain why you have no sex life.

I have a patient now, a 24yo university student, who very reluctantly revealed that he had clocked up 12,000 hours on a online game called DotA. That tally didn't include the other games that he didn't record. Twelve thousand hours will give you two university degrees. Needless to say, at twenty-four, he is still stuck in second year, which he should have passed at nineteen. All because of severe social anxiety. What was that expression? Oh yes, here it is: "On the internet, nobody knows you're a dog."

If you link up as StarWarrior286 and talk hip on the chat rooms, nobody knows you're a social cripple, but it's not funny. He has wasted five years that will not come back. I tell avoidant young people: "These are supposed to be the best years of your life so you'd better get organised and start enjoying them." (DotA stands for *Defence of the Ancients*, which is as puerile as it sounds but its owners are fabulously wealthy).

Case 8.1: Classic avoidance.

Rudolph K. is a 42yo single doctoral-level student who receives a disability pension for psychiatric problems. He studies part-time in a course quite as abstruse as Sanskrit sonnets. During the week, he lives in a small flat near the university while on weekends, he travels by bus to stay with his elderly father in a distant, outlying suburb. He has had ten years of private psychiatric treatment, including several admissions to hospital, but could no longer afford the fees. When referred, he was taking four prescribed drugs:

> Olanzapine 20mg per day (an antipsychotic);
> Valproate 1000mg (anticonvulsant, used as "mood stabiliser");
> Desvenlafaxine 100mg (antidepressant); and
> Mirtazepine 45mg (antidepressant).

Rudolph is very tall and very thin, with long fingers, thick spectacles and long, lank hair (medical students reading this might like to consider a spot diagnosis). His clothes are clean but old-fashioned and mismatched, and he has no adornment such as tattoos, studs, scars or jewellery. Despite being born here, he has a faint foreign accent and a very stilted, almost dysfluent style of speech, as though he scans everything he says—which he does.

He said he was referred because he was having trouble sleeping and with trusting people. Questioning showed that he goes to bed at about 8.30pm but is often still awake at 4.00am. He gets up at 7.30am to get to school, and feels tired and groggy throughout the day. His appetite is adequate and he has enough energy to get through his day. As he doesn't drive, he gets his exercise walking around the university or when he visits his father. He feels his levels of interest and motivation are high but he has little social life: "I find it difficult to relate to people, I'm not talkative." Of his sexual interest, he said he has no interest or experience at all as he is "asexual." His memory and concentration are quite patchy and he has trouble thinking clearly or making decisions, especially under any sort of pressure. Of his thought content, he said: "I often wonder if I'm in contact with reality, but then what's reality?"

He described his mood as "OK but could be better." He feels low and miserable about half the time but it has been very much worse in the past. This mood is bearable although he isn't sure why it keeps happening. Sometimes he feels "a bit hyped up, sort of a nervous tension" but it doesn't last long and he never does anything unusual. His main problem is frequent bouts of agitation, during which he shakes and starts to sweat, his heart races and he feels very unsettled in the stomach. He tends to sigh and gasp for air, his mouth is dry, his voice quavers and he is likely to stammer and lose his words. He feels unsteady on his feet, with a "pent up" feeling of irritability and apprehension. His way of dealing with them is to withdraw from contact with people and keep to himself until they settle. He has 2-3 bouts a day, lasting half to one hour each. They are brought on by minor upsets, delays or friction with people: "I think that most of the time, I live in an alternative reality to other people."

On questioning, he startles badly with sudden noises or being touched unexpectedly, and is scared of spiders and cockroaches. He fears public speaking, appointments and interviews, tests and exams, and meeting strangers or using telephones. He is immediately agitated by any sort of threat or criticism, by arguments, disputes and confrontation or by having to say No to anybody. He fears letting people down, causing trouble or giving offence of any sort. Even though he hardly mixes with people, he is frightened of loneliness and of humiliation or disapproval. In particular, he fears making mistakes or failing at anything. He is edgy when he has to go to the dentist or sees police. He is frightened of teenage gangs, drunks and black men or any aggressive-looking people. He keeps his distance from anybody in authority.

When he goes out, he has a strong feeling of people looking at him, talking behind his back and judging him. If anybody laughs, he feels they are laughing at him. He has a vague sense that people may be a danger to him. When asked whether he has the feeling people are watching him or he is under surveillance, he said he has had dealings with intelligence services and is very aware that things are not what they seem to be. He is wary of using telephones although he added he doesn't believe he is actually under surveillance. Of conspiracies, he replied: "I strongly believe some people have lied to me in the past but there's no pattern to this." He has a strong need to check and recheck doors, locks, keys etc. because he forgets, "double and triple recheck" (obsessional doubting, as in "can I be sure?"). He is fussy about punctuality and efficiency but there were no true obsessive-compulsive features.

He said he has been this way all his life, "very anxious in high school," and first saw a psychiatrist at age nineteen. The next year, he was diagnosed as suffering bipolar affective disorder and had since been in private hospitals four times.

His family background was unsettled as his parents, who were married overseas and were in their forties when he was born, separated when he was aged five. From then until age 17yrs, he was raised by his mother, who worked as a clerk. She was "seriously mentally ill, anxious, paranoid, aggressive and maybe sociopathic." She has not spoken to him for the past 25yrs because he moved out. His father worked most of his life in a secluded job in the public service. He is "domineering, protective, over-bearing and distant" but they get on tolerably well. Rudolph was an only child and they have no other relatives in the country.

He attended local Catholic schools to age seventeen, passing Year 12 with good marks. He said he got on very well with the teachers as he was "quiet and obedient." However, he didn't get on with the other children as he was very shy, nervous and insecure and mixed only with a small group of similarly-afflicted boys. He was often teased and bullied so he spent his lunch hours in the library studying religion and science. Because he went to stay with his father on weekends, he didn't play sport but he wouldn't have known what to do anyway. His home life with his mother was very unpleasant. She would never allow him to visit anybody or have friends around, even if he'd had any. She was aggressive so he moved out as soon as he finished school, and she hasn't returned his calls since.

At eighteen, he went interstate to study science, living in a small guest house run by nuns. He had no social life apart from the other, equally conservative and religious people in the house. In his second year, he was referred to a psychiatrist. Somehow he passed his degree but he has never worked. He was given a disability pension at age 21 and has led a marginal life since, studying part-time and involved in a number of esoteric religious groups. He has studied early church history and Middle East history and languages. This led to a contact from intelligence services but he fearfully declined their offer and became even more mistrustful. Socially, he has always been single and has had no sexual experience. He doesn't drink, uses no illegal drugs, doesn't gamble and has no police record.

Asked to describe himself, he smiled uneasily: "I'm lop-sided, I'm all intellect." He sees himself as very nervous, unassertive and intensely bothered by guilt, shame and self-consciousness. He is mistrustful and a "loner" who follows rules and keeps a low profile around authority. His temper is "very mild," his intellect "very high" and his self-esteem is "below average, 3-4 of 10."

The mental state showed a tall and very thin man with longish, straggly hair who looked younger than his years. He had heavy spectacles and drab, plain old clothes. He moved stiffly and had a generally awkward and uncomfortable demeanor. Initially, he was guarded and wooden but he slowly relaxed and was able to smile a little by the end of the interview.

This is a classic example of what used to be called a schizoid personality, meaning a serious impairment of interpersonal relationships due to an inability to relate to non-family figures; a preoccupation with solitary and highly intellectual pursuits; and an inability to gain pleasure from non-cerebral life such as physical and sexual activity. The end result was a sad and lonely life. Nowadays, this constellation would attract the diagnosis of Asperger's Syndrome, which is said to be part of the "autistic spectrum." In this respect, psychiatry is like the old joke about the economics exams: they ask the same questions each year but change the answers.

We can be crystal-clear on one point: Rudolph is not and never has been "bipolar," regardless of how it is defined. His primary problem is anxiety; it's primary because it started first, in early childhood, and because it leads to, explains and dominates everything else about him. Partly, he is frightened of people because he doesn't have the faintest clue how to deal with them, and because so many of his early experiences with people involved him getting hurt. Long ago, he found the easiest way to deal with people was not to deal with them, so he withdrew into his head and there he remains to this day.

For the other part, he is frightened of people because he has no self-esteem. A person with no self-esteem is reliant on other people for approval but as soon as you rely on other people for something, you will start to fear you may not get it. He is frightened of loneliness so he has to make contact with people, but he fears them and he fears their disapproval. The end result is that he hovers on the edge of society, not really part of it but not truly out of it. He shows what is known as approach-avoidance anxiety. As he said, "...most of the time, I live in an alternative reality to other people." Granted, he has been quite seriously depressed at different stages but who wouldn't be? It doesn't require any great insight to work out that his existence has been utterly miserable for at least 41 of his 42 years.

The problem is that if you label a person as a schizoid personality, all you're actually saying is "Oh, that's just him, that's how he is," with the unstated rider, "...and there's nothing anybody can do about it." In fact, there is plenty that can be done about it but that relies on a proper assessment, which he'd never had. Psychiatrists simply found the depressive symptoms, looked at him and decided he was a bit of a spook, and that was that. Goodnight Rudolph.

The same thing applies to the label "bipolar." The problem we have today is that what is now known as Bipolar Affective Disorder hardly existed forty years ago. When I started my training, there was a condition called manic-depressive psychosis, much the same condition as Emil

Kraepelin had named eighty years before. It was rare: manic-depressive psychosis occurred in no more than one to two people per thousand population (0.1-0.2% incidence) but because they tended to go in and out of hospitals rapidly (rapidly compared with anybody with a diagnosis of schizophrenia, because they usually went in once and didn't come out), they accounted for a relatively large number of admissions. However, in 1980, the American DSM-III was released, which dramatically widened the diagnostic criteria for what had been renamed as Bipolar Affective Disorder (BAD). By 1983, in a book called *The Broken Brain*, the former editor of the *American Journal of Psychiatry*, Nancy Andreasson, said BAD was 1.0% of the population, a 5-10 times increase. In 2004, a former president of the American Psychiatric Association, Lewis Judd, said it was 5% of the population. In about 2010, Phillip Mitchell, professor of psychiatry at Sydney University, said it was 11%, and the latest figure I have seen says it is just over 15% of the population.

Now let's take stock of what's going on. On the one hand, everybody who deals in BAD says it is a genetic disease of the brain with a high heritability. On the other, we are asked to believe that the incidence of this genetic disease of the brain has increased no less than 150 times, or 15,000%, in one generation. That's not genetics as I understand it. Something is wrong, and I think I know what it is. First, I can state emphatically that, forty years ago, Rudolph K. would *not* have been diagnosed manic-depressive. Granted, he was depressed from time to time, and yes, sometimes he showed agitation, but the operative term was "psychosis." Even though he sometimes feels "out of it," Rudolph has never once been psychotic. Manic-depressives were the maddest people of all, they were truly manic. They were full of huge ideas, grand schemes and claimed to be bosom-buddies with everybody who counted. They couldn't sleep or eat as they were too busy running around, panting, laughing and babbling about how they were going to fix every problem in the world though love. They tore their clothes off and ran down the street, shrieking with laughter and grabbing passers-by where you don't normally grab strangers. If they weren't rapidly sedated, they could die of dehydration.

The problem comes from DSM-III, which said the diagnosis can be made even if the patient has never been in hospital, and if he has been agitated or restless or unable to sleep properly for as little as three days. Effectively, that means all of us. If we debase the word 'mania' to mean what we used to call 'just a bit agitated,' then everybody who has had a glum period after a bit of an upset is Bipolar. Thus relabelled, they are then put on large doses of highly addictive psychoactive drugs which seriously affect brain function, producing a host of dangerous side effects. Then their real problems start. Once people start these drugs, they can never get off them. If they try, they get a severe withdrawal state (in order to avoid the connotations of addiction, this is now known by the terribly precious expression 'discontinuation syndrome'). But the most important factor is that their original problems are never broached, as Rudi's weren't, throughout their long and increasingly unhappy careers as psychiatric patients.

In brief, the current "epidemic" of bipolar disorder is caused by a very widespread, active process of rediagnosing anxious people as sufferers of a genetic disease that requires lifelong drugs, drugs which *themselves* cause severe mental disturbances. Up to 15% of people who are prescribed SSRI antidepressants will experience a bout of intense agitation, with poor sleep, scattered thinking, poor concentration etc. They are then relabeled "bipolar" on the basis that the drugs "unmasked a bipolar tendency," which will require lifelong treatment with ever-increasing doses of ever-stronger drugs. This is false: it is not a matter of the drugs "unmasking a bipolar tendency," it is a matter of the drugs predictably inducing a very unpleasant side-effect called akathisia, a sense of irritation and restlessness in the limbs. Akathisia is the reason people who have recently been prescribed antidepressants suddenly kill themselves, or others.

There should be no doubt in anybody's mind that relabelling people with drug side effects is not an accident but is part of the specific program of the Academic Psychiatry—Big Pharma axis. DSM5, the latest version of biological psychiatry's approach to mental disorder, says that a manic reaction to starting an antidepressant is sufficient to give a diagnosis of bipolar disorder (DSM5, pages 124 and 133; it also applies to stopping them, see pp 712-14). A person can present with a minor bout of the miseries; he will then be prescribed an antidepressant. If he reacts by becoming agitated, he will be rediagnosed as bipolar. He will then be put on much larger doses of very powerful psychoactive drugs for life, on the basis the antidepressant "exposed a bipolar diathesis" (a fancy word for tendency). This is absurd: he would not have experienced the drug reaction without taking the drug. It's like saying alcohol exposes a "staggering and slurred speech diathesis."

So we now have the ridiculous position where biological psychiatry is conducting massive studies, called Genome Wide Association Studies or GWAS, to find tiny genetic variations in people with a particular diagnosis. If anything is found, the researchers immediately ring up the nearest TV station and get themselves a slot on the evening news so they can announce they have found "The Cause of ___" (fill in the blank). Thus, a minor genetic variation is taken as proof of the biological cause, but when people are given drugs and react differently, that is NOT taken as evidence of genetic variation in their capacity to metabolise the drug. In philosophy, there is a name for this little ploy: *Avez votre gâteau et mangez-le aussi.* It means "having your cake and eating it too," or trying to run a bet both ways. Genes are said to be the cause of a condition, which means drug treatment, but genes are *not* taken as the cause of a bad reaction to the drugs used to treat the condition. In fact, no GWAS has ever found anything interesting in psychiatry, although that doesn't stop academics spending untold millions on these studies.

But back to Rudolph, who demonstrates two points about modern psychiatry. First, nobody takes a history beyond "Are you depressed?" If they did, they would have realised that he had a very good reason to be depressed, namely, his life was being wrecked by anxiety. Second, he was then given drugs, because that's all modern psychiatry knows, but when they did nothing for his underlying problem, his condition was reformulated so that it was his problem rather than psychiatry's:

> "He's depressed; we gave him antidepressants; he didn't get better but he shows signs of agitation so he must be bipolar; therefore he needs lots more drugs."

This shifts responsibility for the failure of treatment from the psychiatrist to the patient and justifies more of the same treatment. There is no mention of the possibility that the psychiatric management may have been inadequate or just plain wrong. This is the critical point: the psychiatrist is never wrong. We will come back to this point but we'll look at one example now. In Queensland, if a patient is diagnosed as depressed, he does not have the right to refuse treatment. For example, if he is told he needs ECT, he may feel that it isn't a good idea, or that he isn't that depressed, or he can't afford the time off work, or whatever, it makes no difference. If the psychiatrist rules that the patient has "unreasonably refused treatment," he can be detained and given it regardless of his wishes. As you can guess, nobody has ever defined "reasonable refusal of treatment." If treatment is refused, it is *ipso facto* unreasonable, so you'll get what the psychiatrist has decided is good for you. You'll get it, good and hard, as Henry Mencken used to say.

But we're talking about avoidance. Avoidance isn't quite the same as being house-bound, even though the net effect may be the same. A house-bound person wants to go out but knows he can't. If he tries, he is disabled by anxiety and has no choice but to retreat to safety. An avoidant person also can't go out but he chooses not to try, he invents excuses as to why he doesn't need to go out. He occupies himself or arranges his life in such a way as to give the impression he's happily engaged in something so interesting that he doesn't have time for ordinary life. One 42yo single man with two degrees has never managed to hold a job because of his anxiety, so he gets by with short-term or contract jobs separated by long breaks. His hobby is collecting and restoring old engines, which requires him to go to farm clearance sales in remote towns and takes all his spare time. That way, he never has to mix with people longer than a few minutes and he always has a good reason to get in his car and drive away.

If you don't want to talk to anyone, you can always become a photographer. A 56yo man spends every moment he is not at work on his hobby of photographing... spiders. A lot of this is at night so he wanders off into the bush with a torch and his camera and doesn't have to talk to anybody. By day, he is too busy sorting his photos to talk to anybody. If you can't handle people, you can devote yourself to animals and everybody will praise you for your devotion but nobody will guess your motive. Cat ladies, young men who collect snakes, horsey girls, all these and many others may in fact be disabled by social anxiety, and are using the animals to avoid engaging in normal life. If, however, you're allergic to animals, you can always throw yourself into an obsessive sports program such as body-building or marathon running. If you're pushing up steel or pounding the pavement, nobody will ever bother you in case you ask them to join in. People find niches for themselves that reduce their social anxiety, and reduce the embarrassment of having to explain themselves. Endlessly working on a novel or thesis, breeding rare fish or delicate exotic birds, making model sailing ships, making a garden of black flowers... anything that you have to do by yourself and is likely to put off all but the morbidly curious.

There's another form of avoidance that manages to slip under the radar. In the old days, if you didn't feel like going to a party, you could always have one of your swooning attacks. However, these days, the general standard of health is a lot better than it used to be, and if you keep complaining you're too ill or weak to go out, somebody will drag you to see a doctor who is likely to say it's all in your mind and put you on nasty drugs. But there is one way you can avoid real life by being sick without running the risk of being unmasked or labelled a malingerer, and that's to go to hospital.

Thus, if you're normally anxious and insecure but you don't want anybody to know, then every so often, the strain of pretending to be normal will wear you down. Life will get a bit much for you and you'll feel the need for a break but normal people don't need breaks, so you're stuck in a jam. You can't ring your niece and say you don't feel up to going to her wedding, that's against the rules, but if you've been admitted to hospital with a physical illness, you can legitimately cancel. And what better than a physical illness of the brain, such as the invisible disease of depression?

Unfortunately, this doesn't work with public mental hospitals. Their attitude is that anybody who wants to come into hospital must be a malingerer and must therefore be sent away, whereas anybody who doesn't want to come in is insightless and therefore has to be dragged in by the police for "unreasonably refusing treatment." But it does work with private hospitals, it works a treat because that's how they make their money.

Case 8.2: Harry L, 60yrs.

Harry is a retired man who had a small business in a distant country town but had to close it because of depression (that's his depression, not the economy's). He is now sustained on insurance payments, which also fund his private health insurance. Over the years, he has had about 22 admissions to private hospitals for "treatment-resistant depression." He has been prescribed at least 30 different drugs as well as ECT and a new form of treatment called transcranial magnetic stimulation. He moved to the city to be closer to relatives and immediately asked to be referred to a psychiatrist. At his first appointment, he came through the door plaintively announcing that he suffered severe clinical depression confirmed by Professors X and Y and he felt the need to go to hospital.

The history showed a truly ghastly childhood in a tiny town coincidently not far from where I went to school; I had no doubt he was telling the truth. I also believed him when he complained: "What's this got to do with it? I've been seeing psychiatrists for over 30 years but nobody ever asked me about my parents or what it was like at school." He was shy and anxious in primary school, a social disaster in high school and a complete misfit as a young man. His first marriage happened because he had danced with a girl at a country dance. A few months later, she told him she was pregnant and he was the father. With tears and snot running down his face, he blubbered: "I don't even remember it happening but she said it was me so there was nothing I could do. There was no choice in those days, I had to marry her. And if you knew her brothers, you'd know why." That lasted ten desperately miserable years; he has since found that the child wasn't his but the other two were. He remarried a very brisk and enterprising widow and they worked hard to build a small business but his mental state was always fragile.

For as long as he can remember, he has been crippled by anxiety. He has a full book of anxiety symptoms and a seemingly endless list of social fears. His life is a torture from the moment he wakes until he can slip into his study at night and look over his collections of dried wildflowers. He is only ever at peace wandering through the bush collecting specimens and preparing them. The rest of his life is an endless strain of trying to cope without letting anybody see he is anxious, because (remember this) he firmly believes anxiety is a moral failing. Every now and then, it all gets too much and he retreats to hospital for a bit of TLC (tender loving care). Of course the private hospitals love to see him, his insurance company pays for all the frills. How much? Probably close to $3million over his lifetime. Has he enjoyed his many admissions? Yes. Has hospital done him any good? No.

Every year or so, he goes into hospital severely anxious and worn down by normal life. While he is in hospital, his wife deals with everything and has it all sorted so that he can come home to a clean slate, as it were. When everything is neat and tidy, he is discharged with a bag of new drugs, a little more chirpy but still severely anxious, and nothing changes. In no time, he is making a mess of things again, just because he's severely anxious but he doesn't want anybody to know, so he tries to make all the decisions and won't listen to advice.

The moral of this story is that private hospitals are an excellent cover for anxious people to avoid facing their reality. Having trouble in your marriage? Tell the doctor you're depressed. He'll tell your family you've got a chemical imbalance of the brain and you need six weeks of intensive ECT so everybody had better be nice to you. There is a collusion between doctor and patient to avoid dealing with the anxiety. There are overtones of the late Thomas Szasz in this. Szasz said there is no such thing as mental disorder, that anybody who claims to have mental symptoms is just pretending. The psychiatrist, he said, is also party to the fraud because he pretends that he believes the patient when he has to know from his medical training that the very idea of mental symptoms is rubbish.

Thomas Szasz was completely wrong: mental disorder is a very real thing, but he almost had a point. The psychiatrist is obsessed with depression, which he believes is a brain disease; he therefore doesn't ask the patient about anxiety. The patient knows perfectly well that he or she is anxious but believes it is a moral failing and doesn't want to talk about it. When the psychiatrist mumbles something vague about chemical imbalances of the brain (about which he actually knows less than nothing), the patient eagerly grabs it. Now he has the perfect excuse to avoid an intolerably painful life: "I'm sick," he tells his wife, "the doctor said so. In fact, I'm so sick that I have to go into hospital for ECT. I won't be able to go to your sister's third wedding and it will probably affect my memory again but gosh, I don't have any choice, do I?"

For Gary and many people like him, losing chunks of your memory is far preferable to admitting the moral failing of being an anxious person. And the memories were all horrible, anyway: he knew perfectly well he hadn't got that girl pregnant but it was better to marry her than admit he was so frightened he hadn't been able to perform and she had mocked him cruelly.

Case 8.3: Avoidance at the extreme.

When Kallym V was referred, he was 22yrs of age and had spent the last six years, a quarter of his life, in his bedroom. During that time, he had had no contact with his family. He came out for perhaps an hour or two a day, after his flatmates had gone to work, then spent the rest of the day asleep. Sometimes he went a week without showering or shaving. He had been taking desvenlafaxine 200mg per day for about eight years (this is a very large dose of a powerful and highly addictive antidepressant) and also used diazepam so that he could go to the shops. He mentioned that he had taken 20mg of diazepam to get to the appointment.

Presenting complaints:

He said he was "super low, suicidal and super anxious." His sleep was very poor. He was spending up to 18hrs a day lying in or on his bed. He slept from about 9.00am to 5.00pm and was awake all night ("I'm nocturnal"). His appetite was poor and he rarely ate more than one meal a day, mostly junk food because it was easier, but his weight was steady. He had very little energy and got practically no physical exercise at all. He had very little interest in things and no motivation to do anything, but due to lack of money and his anxiety, there was practically nothing he could do. Socially, he hardly mixed with anybody. Until just recently, he had not spoken to his family for years and he almost never saw or spoke to his two flatmates. Of his sexual interest, he said: "I can't be bothered."

His memory was reasonable but he said his concentration was poor, adding that he was diagnosed as suffering ADHD as a child. He could focus on computer games but had never been able to get his driver's licence. Mostly, he could think reasonably clearly but not under any pressure. He hardly made any decisions because there were none to make. The thought content was "nothing, I try to keep my mind blank. I only think about the games." There were no disturbances of perception.

He described his mood as "hopeless." He was low and miserable most of the time, usually sick of life itself and mostly felt that death would be a relief. In the past, he had often been suicidal. He felt the unhappiness was due to his early life experiences. Apart from his seriously distorted lifestyle and having no money, there was nothing else going on in his life. He never felt good but he had regular and severe bouts of agitation. These came on with a "hot rush," and he felt shaky, sweaty, short of breath and sick in the stomach. His heart raced, his mouth was dry, he felt tight in the throat and unable to speak, and was dizzy and light-headed. He had the feeling of the walls closing in but mainly felt "out of it, out of place, alienated like I don't belong here."

Even with his severely restricted life, he was having one or two bouts a day, lasting an hour or two each, but if he had to go out, he became agitated as soon as he woke that morning and it lasted until after he got home again. The anxiety was due to dealing with people or worrying about his life or future.

On questioning, he had a huge list of fears, including confined spaces or open spaces such as streets. He startled if anybody touched him and was scared of deep water, snakes, spiders and cockroaches. However, most of his fears were social in nature, including crowds, queues, public speaking and public transport. He feared interviews and appointments, meeting strangers, threats and criticism. He was fearful of disputes and saying No to people, letting people down, humiliation and disapproval. In particular, he feared making mistakes or failing at anything, but only if somebody was watching. He was frightened of hospitals, dentists, blood and needles. He feared any aggressive-looking people such as bikies or teenage gangs and was frightened of drunks. He had the strong feeling people were looking at him and talking behind his back, and of being judged. If anybody laughed near him, he felt they were laughing at him, but there were no frank paranoid ideas. There were no obsessive-compulsive features. Physically, he suffered frequent headaches.

He had been this way as long as he could remember. He first saw psychologists at age fifteen and had seen a psychiatrist who prescribed methylphenidate (for ADHD) and the antidepressant. There was no other treatment and he stopped seeing the psychologists after a few years.

Personal background:

He had lived most of his life in the same suburb. His parents separated when he was aged fourteen but their marriage had always been poor and they rarely spoke to each other except to argue. His father, who was about fifty, was a business manager but they had had no contact since Kallym was seventeen: "He was cold and distant, very critical, very domineering. We got into a fight. He slapped me because I hadn't set the table right so I hit back." His mother was aged 48yrs and worked part-time in a local business. After six years, he had recently resumed contact and she had convinced him he needed psychiatric treatment. He didn't get on with her at all: "She's very inappropriate, acts like a teenager, totally messed in the head, bipolar. She used to walk around the house in clothes from the sex shop." They had never got on. Before the separation, he said, she would often start screaming at him and go on for an hour.

He had an older half-brother of 25yrs who lived with their father and worked but he was "...like me, problems with depression and anxiety." A sister of nineteen lived with the mother but she was "very shy and anxious" and had been diagnosed with "pseudoseizures." He had practically no contact with any of his family. He wasn't sure of any formal history of mental disorder but his mother often drank quite heavily and he thought his brother smoked a lot of weed.

He passed Year 12 at school but his marks were barely average. He didn't get on with the teachers: "I was always in trouble for fighting and never paid attention." He didn't get on with the other children: "I was soft, I was bullied for several years in high school until I learned to hit back." However, he liked athletics and did well at it. Academically, he took the easy courses but he couldn't study, not least because his home was often in uproar due to his mother's moods. On leaving school, he had some casual work in stores but he was smoking marijuana heavily and was making money by dealing in it. However, he gave it up after it caused a psychotic episode. This left him seriously anxious and he stopped going out. He had always been single and didn't have much sexual experience. He rarely drank alcohol but he knew that it calmed him. Over the years, he had become addicted to tramadol which took most of his money because he had to pay other people to get it for him. He had no police record.

Self-assessment:

"I'm a failure." He saw himself as intensely nervous and highly self-conscious. He was mostly unassertive but if people annoyed him, he was likely to explode in temper. He was very mistrustful and not social at all; he was untidy, impatient, very resentful and used to be jealous. Often he broke rules just to show he could. He was very mistrustful and resentful of authority. However, he saw his temper as "even." His intellect was "a bit below average" while his self-esteem was "pretty low."

Mental state examination:

The mental state showed a pale, lightly-built and youthful chap of average height, dressed in drab casual clothes. He had a crew cut and no visible tattoos, studs, scars or jewellery. He was edgy and wary and sometimes struggled to speak. He was unhappy but was able to laugh a bit. He was not hostile or suspicious. There were no psychotic features and he was probably of superior intellect.

This is avoidance with a vengeance. This is not what used to be called "...a schizoid personality, meaning a serious impairment of interpersonal relationships due to an inability to relate to non-family figures; a pre-occupation with solitary and highly intellectual pursuits; and an inability to gain pleasure from normal daily activities such as physical and sexual activity." He certainly had a serious impairment of interpersonal relation-ships but it started with and extended to his highly dysfunctional family as well. He had always been shy and nervous. Apart from sport at school, he had no choice but to amuse himself (people can be solitary through choice or because it is the lesser of two evils) although because of his anxiety, he couldn't gain pleasure from anything. However, having said that, I am sure there would be plenty of psychiatrists who would look no further than his sad and lonely life and give him the schizoid label or, more likely these days, "autism spectrum disorder," if not frank autism.

He is not schizoid or autistic. Anxiety accounts for all the disturbance throughout his life. It accounts for his shyness as a child and being bullied. It accounts for his difficulty paying attention in his classes and with studying in high school. It accounts for his sudden outbursts of rage when goaded, which led to the fighting, which led to further trouble. It accounts for him smoking too much marijuana, which led to a brief psychotic episode, and then his withdrawal from life. It accounts for his inability to hold jobs or maintain any sort of social life, his inability to relate to non-family figures and develop friendships and eventually sexual relationships, his addiction to the narcotic, his depression and finally, his suicidal ideas: "If all I can look forward to is another 20yrs like this, then I may as well end it now. It's perfectly logical." It gives the lie to the notion that mental disorders are totally distinct and unrelated categories of illness. The only justification for that idea lies in biological psychiatry, which wanted to find a range of discrete mental disorders and relate them all directly to errors in the genome. It will never happen.

Denial

In psychology, denial means refusing to accept an unpleasant truth. The idea has been around a long time: nearly four hundred years ago, the philosopher, Rene Descartes, said:

> Good sense is the most fairly distributed thing in the world; for everyone thinks himself so well-supplied with it, that even those who are hardest to satisfy in every other way do not usually desire more of it than they already have.

That is, even the most difficult person likes to believe he is reasonable. Anxiety is a bit different in that a lot of anxious people have trouble accepting their problem just because they see it as a moral failing. This is more common in men, who tend to flip their anxiety into rage, but we'll talk about them in another chapter.

Case 8.4: Mrs Elizabeth C. 64yo single woman.

Not many people will try to remain in total denial of any problems in their lives although it certainly does happen. Part of their denial is that they won't come for assessment or, if they are dragged in, they become angry and defensive. Elizabeth has lived alone for eighteen years since her husband abruptly left her for another woman. She has one daughter who constantly worries about her because she has swelling of her ankles and is quite breathless. She has no social life and won't go to see her doctor or dentist. Her diet is poor as she rarely eats fresh fruit or vegetables and the daughter is sure that most of the meat she takes to her mother goes to her pair of very fat cats.

Mrs C. was clearly agitated even though she hadn't had to wait for her appointment. She couldn't decide whether she wanted her daughter in the room or not, agreed at first then changed her mind and wanted her to leave. She said there was nothing wrong with her, her daughter was over-reacting, her legs were perhaps a bit swollen but it was due to the way she had been sitting and she expected it would go away soon enough.

What's your sleep like?
There's nothing wrong with my sleep, I get quite enough.
What time do you go to bed?
I go to bed when I'm tired, I don't have to get up in the morning so I don't look at the clock.
What time do you wake, then?
When the sun's up, I don't know, I don't look at the time.
When you wake, how do you feel?
I'm OK. I don't see what this is all about.
It's to check on your health. Your daughter's worried about you.
She shouldn't be, she's always worrying about something.
Well, do you have naps in the day time?
I suppose I do sometimes, I don't really know.
And your appetite, what's that like?
Same as always, I suppose.
What's your weight doing?
What do you mean?
Are you gaining weight, or losing it or is it steady?
I don't know, I'm sure it's the same it's always been.
Your shoes seem very tight.
My what? (tucks feet under chair) I'm sure they're... the same.
Do you have enough energy to get through the day?
Yes, I'm sure I do, I don't have to do much.
And your level of physical activity, what's that like?
Activity? I'm busy, I've got plenty to do.
No, do you exercise? Do you walk?
I get enough exercise looking after myself. Is this really necessary?
It's to make sure you're alright. People who live alone are at risk, you know. So you don't belong to the local walking group, for example?
I don't need to. And I wouldn't want to mix with all those old people anyway.
They're very active, they have a good time. And your level of interest in things, what's that like?
I'm sure I am, it's the same as ever. I don't know why you're going on, anybody would think I'm mental the questions you ask.

When this happens, you know you're in for the long haul. Just dig in and don't respond to provocations because all she wants is an excuse to walk out the door. She was, of course, seriously anxious but she couldn't bring herself to admit she hadn't coped since her husband had suddenly decamped. She had always been very dependent on him but one day, he got sick of it and ran off with a barmaid. That was profoundly humiliating for her; she tried to tell people it hadn't bothered her but it devastated her.

A lot of people deny their anxiety by insisting there is nothing wrong with them mentally but they have a physical illness which interferes with their lives. They are not easy to deal with as they almost always see anxiety as a moral failing and angrily resist the diagnosis. Neither of the next two cases was impressed with being told they were anxious and didn't come back. These are the letters I sent to their GPs.

Case 8.5: Mrs Yvonne K.

Thank you for referring this 49yo case worker who loudly insisted she wanted "to be tested for autism and ADHD." She lives with her partner, her two sons, a fostered niece and her partner's mother but she is the only person in the house who works. She has had many antidepressants and other psychiatric drugs over the past thirty years but they were no help. She said both sons are "ADHD and ASD," and two nephews are "autistic," as was their father before he committed suicide. She was keen to talk but it was soon clear that she didn't like the way the interview was going, meaning she couldn't control it.

At present, she doesn't feel very good. Her sleep and appetite are very erratic but her weight is steady. She has little energy, interest or motivation and doesn't mix much socially. Her memory and concentration are a bit patchy and she often has trouble thinking clearly. She feels low and miserable about a quarter of the time and is often sick of things and would like a big change but is not suicidal. She wasn't sure why this happens. She almost never feels happy as she suffers more or less constant physical agitation with many somatic symptoms of anxiety, mainly manifest as irritability. She has a long list of fears and is very self-conscious. She is very fussy and ritualistic, which causes arguments, and has recurrent thoughts of trouble but there were no true obsessive-compulsive features. She has been this way all her life.

Her family background was very unsettled. Her father was very strict and bad-tempered while her mother was severely anxious and depressed. Her parents argued ceaselessly until they separated about five years ago. She has an older sister, a kindergarten teacher, who is "very OCD and controlling," and a younger brother, a parole officer, who is "very unstable" and they don't speak. There is a lot of mental disturbance on both sides of the family. Her schooling was disturbed as she was shy and nervous but she enjoyed sport and dancing. On leaving school, she worked in shops until she completed her certificate at age 40yrs. Socially, she had a 25yr de facto relationship, with three children, but he was very domineering. She has been with her current partner four years but the atmosphere at home isn't good. She doesn't drink, smokes a bit of weed, doesn't gamble and has no police record.

She sees herself as nervous, unassertive and bothered by guilt, She is overtrusting, excessively tidy, impatient and not very social. She feels her intellect is a bit above average but her self-esteem is "pretty low." The mental state showed a healthy woman of stated age with elaborately dyed hair and tattoos, dressed in clean casual clothes. She was loud and intrusive and given to bursts of cheerful laughter. She was not anxious, depressed, hostile or suspicious. There were no psychotic features and she is of bright normal intellect, if not superior. This is a classic anxious personality but it was clear that she resented the idea that somebody could question her self-diagnosis and wasn't prepared to prescribe the drugs she felt she needed, amphetamines. I don't think she will return.

When people come through the door, loudly announcing that they "are ADHD and ASD," I get that sinking feeling. You just know it isn't going to go well, that they will resent answering all the questions and they probably won't be back. The next patient had been corresponding with an interstate psychiatrist who had diagnosed him without seeing him and without an interview. This is my letter to his GP.

Case 8.6: Trevor W.

Thank you for referring this 39yo unemployed man whom I saw with his gay partner. He complained of "severe akathisia and tardive dyskinesia" for two years. He has been taking sertraline (anti-depressant) since age 15yrs but has been unable to stop it. Whenever he has tried, he becomes agitated and irritable. Two years ago, he was prescribed an antibiotic whereupon his agitation suddenly got much worse. He is now essentially disabled and unable to work. He has been in touch with a psychiatrist who diagnosed these conditions remotely but I haven't seen the case notes. The interview did not go smoothly as it was obvious that he was reluctant to attend. He constantly tried to control and direct the interview, repeating dozens of times that he knows what is wrong with him and just wants somebody to give him the treatment he wants.

At present, he feels "terrible." He sleeps erratically and his appetite is reasonable but he has gained 5kg in a year. He has very little energy and gets next to no exercise. His levels of interest are low and although he is keen to work, he can't due to the agitation. He has no social life and little sexual interest. His memory and concentration are a bit patchy. He has trouble thinking clearly as he becomes flustered under any sort of pressure and can't make decisions. The thought content is dominated by concerns over his health. There were no disturbances of perception.

He described his mood as "frustrated." He is low and miserable most of the time, "overwhelming," meaning sick of things as they are, with occasional ideas that death would be preferable to this gloomy existence. He never feels good but he has frequent bouts of intense agitation. The symptoms were difficult to extract as he wanted to attribute all of them to his 'neurological conditions,' whereas they are in fact classic symptoms of anxiety. He has a full list of anxiety symptoms, secondary to a very long list of social fears. He quickly and unconvincingly denied any and all paranoid symptoms and obsessive-compulsive features.

Physically, he described a wide range of odd twitching, writhing and jerking spasms affecting the whole of his body at different times. He didn't like describing them but attributed all of them to the drugs acting on different parts of his brain ("I get spasms due to low dopamine in the midbrain and my heart races because of excess adrenaline caused by serotonin deficiency").

He was first prescribed sertraline at age 15yrs because of what sounded like a panicky reaction to his first experience of marijuana. Things seemed to settle a little but ten years later, when he tried to stop the drug, he couldn't. He described a range of odd physical and cognitive symptoms, some of which are only seen in psychotic states except there was no evidence of psychosis. The dose was increased and he remained on this, able to function, until he was prescribed an antibiotic two years ago. Within a few days, he became more agitated, with twitching movements so he went to a private hospital where he was given a powerful antiemetic. This made him worse and he hasn't been back to work since. He has seen a number of doctors but feels it hasn't helped.

His family background in a small rural town was very unsettled as his parents separated when he was five because of his mother's severe mental disorder. She died last year, apparently from a drug reaction, which has terrified him. He was raised by his father, a very quiet and submissive man, but said the stepmother was "emotionally abusive." He has an older brother who works as a sheep shearing contractor and is "outgoing." There were several younger step-siblings but he said they bullied him and he has nothing to do with them. He attended local schools to age 17yrs, passing Year 11 with average marks, but he was shy at school and was only interested in music and drama. He didn't play sport and his home life was "terrible." By the end of Year 11, he was miserable at home and desperate to get away so he took a job in a small business owned by a much older gay man who offered him a room. He met his present partner, a truck driver, soon after and moved out amidst "a most frightful scene." He doesn't drink, uses no drugs, doesn't gamble and has no police record.

He sees himself as "easy-going and caring," somewhat nervous, unassertive and bothered by self-consciousness. He is "very wary" of people but said gets on well with authority. He sees his temper as even, his intellect as "pretty good," but his self-esteem is not strong. The mental state showed an overweight man of stated age in clean drab clothes, with no visible tattoos, studs, scars or jewellery. He was wary from the beginning, constantly trying to control the interview and impose his self-diagnosis. He was talkative, defensive, edgy and moved in short bursts, twisting his arms or fidgeting but did not show classic tardive dyskinesia. He was guarded and unhappy but there were no psychotic features. He is of average intellect.

I have no doubt that the primary problem is anxiety but he wouldn't have a bar of it. After lengthy discussion, I gave him some reading material on treatment of anxiety as this is the only treatment worth trying. He was intensely suspicious but didn't have any suggestions as to alternative treatments. I doubt he will return.

He didn't.

The history showed that he had been anxious all his life due to his totally miserable upbringing. As is quite common among anxious teenagers, the first time he tried marijuana he had a bad reaction which made him more anxious. The antidepressant partially suppressed his anxiety but sertraline is addictive and when he tried to stop it, he developed withdrawal symptoms, which made him more panicky. The antibiotic can cause allergic reactions so it's possible that's what happened to him and he panicked again. His movements were not akathisia or dyskinesia but were repetitive and faded out if he was distracted. There are a few films of soldiers after World War I showing their movements and I have seen the same movements in veterans with severe post-traumatic anxiety. However, a diagnosis of anxiety was the last thing on his mind. By diligent searching, he had found the interstate psychiatrist who ordered a vast array of blood, enzymic and genetic tests, including heavy metals in his hair. He confidently diagnosed the patient without seeing his movements.

These sorts of cases are very difficult. Orthodox psychiatrists insist their drugs don't cause any serious side effects. If a person becomes agitated on them, it isn't due to the drugs, it's due to the "disease," for which the treatment is, of course, more drugs. As a business model, this is unbeatable.

Final case of denial, another example of self-diagnosis. When people start setting too many conditions, you know it isn't going to end well. At least I warned the GP he may not come back.

Case 8.7: Norman J, 44yo mechanic.

This 44yo man announced at the outset that he is "Asperger's, ASD and autistic and not coping but I wanted to see a female psychologist, not a male psychiatrist." He lives with his wife and step-son and is taking no medication. At present, he feels "overwhelmed," which is code for anxious. He works shifts so his sleep is disturbed but he gets enough. He has little energy but keeps himself active. He doesn't have much interest or motivation, avoids company and has little sexual interest. His memory and concentration are good but he has trouble thinking clearly as he becomes flustered under pressure and avoids decisions. His mood is "worn-out, flat, deflated, apathetic" but he insisted he is not miserable. He does not experience elevated moods but he has frequent bouts of feeling agitated and restless with many somatic symptoms of anxiety. He has a long list of fears, mainly social in nature, and is highly self-conscious, which he believes is "paranoia." He is obsessional, fussy and ritualistic with frequent intrusive thoughts of impending trouble. He has been this way all his life but has never had treatment.

His family background in a working class family was unsettled. His father, a carpenter, was very strict but he got on well with his mother. He was the youngest of five children and said the older ones often pushed him around. One sister is an alcoholic and one brother is addicted to narcotics. They all appear to be quite seriously anxious and he has little contact with them. He didn't do well at school as he was nervous and loud. He didn't play sport and his home life was unhappy. On leaving school, he trained as a mechanic and has always worked. He has recently started his own business and is doing reasonably well. Socially, he married at age 31yrs and has had two children, as well as caring for his wife's first child. He drinks very little, uses no drugs, doesn't gamble and has no police record.

He sees himself as "law-abiding." He agreed he is nervous, unassertive and bothered by guilt, shame and self-consciousness. He is mistrustful, impatient and quick-tempered. His intellect is "fairly high" but his self-esteem is "fairly low." The mental state showed an obese man of stated age with studs and drab, floppy clothing. He was wary, defensive and attempted to control the interview. There were no psychotic features and he is probably of superior intellect.

This is personality-based anxiety but nobody wants to be "anxious" as they see it as a moral failing. They would much rather be "Asperger's" as it licences their social inadequacies. We will try standard treatment but he was not keen so he may not return.

He was another who didn't return. The non-return rate among public patients (as mine are) is fairly high by comparison with other private practices. If people don't attend their appointments with the trend-setting psychiatrists in the wealthy end of town, they find a large bill waiting for them when they get home. But their patients are more reliable anyway, they are unlikely to forget, or get drunk and sleep in, or get arrested for fighting. This may tend to bias my results a little as people who do well are more likely to come back. However, if you look at any trial of psychiatric drugs, they exclude people who don't finish the course of drugs, although they never tell you why they didn't. The assumption is that they're unreliable and don't really need drugs but it is equally feasible that they dropped out because the drugs weren't working, or made them worse due to side effects.

The issue here was that he didn't want to be seen as an anxious person. People of his social background are unlikely to be comfortable with the idea that they are anxious because, almost invariably, they see it as a personal weakness, a sign of moral failure. They much prefer the idea that they "have" a "disease of the brain," because that takes the responsibility off them: "Of course I'm not scared of crowds, it's just that I've got this pesky chemical imbalance in my brain that won't let me go in crowds. But I'm not scared, perish the thought."

That's why they can't get better.

9 Distraction

One way of not being troubled by problems is to distract yourself on to something more agreeable. Sometimes they will go away but other problems may not be so amenable and may engulf you. It is generally a good idea to ignore all the myriad little aches and twinges that happen in your body each day, rather than get anxious about them. For 99.9% of them, that is the treatment of choice but it is not a good idea to ignore a traffic summons, or what looks like a snake disappearing into your garage just because it makes you anxious. You may be able to distract yourself by watching the football match but it will probably come back. However, for a lot of people, distraction is their preferred option, just because they don't know what else to do. Again, the problem is made much worse by the widespread attitude that says "All anxiety is a sign of a weak character."

Distraction is the process of diverting attention from a threat or unpleasant event to a less noxious event. Politicians do it all the time, diverting attention from some problem at home by picking an argument with a neighbouring country (preferably smaller, poorer and full of foreigners). A full account of distraction would probably require a small library so we can only hint at a couple of examples. In general, it's fair to say that anybody who does anything, regardless of its nature, sufficient to earn the label "compulsive" or "addiction" is almost certainly driven by anxiety. Drugs, as in drugs of addiction, we'll do later. Let's start with a common problem; later, we'll see that it isn't an addiction after all, just a distraction.

Case 9.1: Gambling as distraction from anxiety.

Scott B, aged 34yrs, has a problem. In fact, he has two problems. He has the problem he's had for several years, and he has the problem of what to do when his wife hears of Problem No. 1. He gambles, and soon she's going to find out that the money she thought was going to the mortgage is actually being fed into poker machines when he's supposed to be at work. He thinks he's lost about $150,000 in four years but he isn't sure as he doesn't dare add it up. What he is sure of is that he can't borrow any more, his many credit cards are at the limit and his plumbing business is about to go down the gurgler. A picture of abject misery, he sits in my office dressed in dusty work clothes, head down, wiping an occasional tear, barely able to speak. He would kill himself, he says, but his wife's brother-in-law committed suicide about five years ago and he couldn't do it to her.

He comes from an ordinary working-class family in a country town, left school at 16 to start his apprenticeship, completed his training with no delays, employed for a few years then started on his own. Things were going well, married at 27, two small children, everything should be fine. Except he gambles. Why does he gamble?

"Doc, if I knew that, I wouldn't be sitting here today. I do not know. I know it's bad, I know I tell lies about it, I know it's wrecking my kids' lives and yet I'm driven to it. I can't keep away, it's like an addiction."

At present, he sleeps badly, he has little appetite or energy, he isn't exercising, he has no interest or motivation and he doesn't want to mix with people. He feels sick all the time and has no sexual interest, which is most unusual for him. His memory and concentration are patchy at times but with an effort, he can focus on jobs. If things are quiet, he can think clearly but under any sort of pressure, he quickly becomes confused and flustered. At present, he is consumed by worry over what will happen, such as losing their house. His biggest fear is his wife leaving him and not seeing the children. As he says this, he shudders, grips his head and begins to cry in fear.

He feels low and miserable practically all of the time, "real bad, suicidal," but he feels totally trapped as suicide is not an option. He feels unbearably guilty and useless, a worthless human who needs to be dragged outside and flogged to bring him to his senses. In his ordinary life, meaning at work or home, he tries to be cheerful but in fact, he is constantly nervous. He has frequent bouts of intense agitation, with shaking, sweating, churning stomach and a violent pounding of his heart. He is short of breath, can hardly speak and feels dizzy and clumsy. Sometimes he actually vomits, such as after any sort of confrontation with people.

Most days, he has 2-3 bouts of agitation, lasting half to one hour, but lately, even getting ready for work causes it as he knows there will be arguments with angry clients or creditors. He has a huge list of social fears, mainly related to how he is performing and how people are judging him. He is highly self-conscious, easily embarrassed and tends to blush and stammer when people look at him. There are no paranoid ideas and he is normally quite a tidy person but recently he hasn't been paying attention to detail.

Quite often, on the way to work, the thought of what the day holds for him is so terrible that he has the urge to jerk the wheel and smash into a big truck. Most days, he gives in and drives to a hotel or a TAB (gambling franchise) shop and starts gambling. He never feels good except when he's gambling, then he feels a sort of serenity, a calmness that he has never experienced in his life and can't get anywhere else.

How do you feel when you decide to turn off the road to work and go to the TAB?

I feel an amazing sense of relief, all the fear just melts away and I'm sort of on Cloud 9.

Does it last?

As long as I'm sitting there looking at those spinning wheels and hearing that brain-dead music, I feel as though the rest of the world doesn't exist. There's just me and the machine, nothing else in the universe. It's the only time I feel calm, the only time I feel like a human being.

What happens when it's time to go home.

Ah mate, you've got no idea. It's as though somebody pressed a button and all the walls fell down, the light flooded in and everybody's looking at me, pointing and laughing. That's the time when if I had a gun, I'd put it here and pull the trigger. That's the worst. I have to go home and tell lies and cover up and pretend everything's fine. Then I can't sleep.

So gambling feels good?

That's all that ever feels good.

Because there's no fear?

Because there's no fear.

You do understand, don't you, that if you can switch your fear off in the casino, you can switch if off everywhere?

If I knew how to do that, I'd be over the moon. But it won't happen so... So what can I do?

There was nothing in his family background to produce a severe state of anxiety, no traumas, no separations, no drunken father or wicked stepmother, no drugs or lascivious uncles. His was a perfectly ordinary childhood in a medium-sized country town with lots for boys to do. At school, he was an average student; he played sport competently but was not outstanding; he helped in his father's business from about twelve and could drive trucks, tractors and loaders by thirteen; he started to learn the guitar and was good with animals. He didn't smoke or drink, he had plenty of friends and relatives. Everybody liked him although everybody knew that he was rather shy and needed encouragement. If he had stayed in his home town, his life would probably have continued much the same but, at eighteen, he transferred his apprenticeship to a city firm and left home. Suddenly, things started to go very wrong.

He found driving around the city scary, the crowds intimidating, the distant relatives he was staying with were not very friendly and their son kept badgering him to smoke marijuana. The first day on his new job, he was nervous, far more nervous than he had ever been in his life. He knew he had to make a success of his move, that he couldn't go home with his tail between his legs. During his second week, he was given a job he had never seen before. Rather than tell anybody he didn't know what to do, he did his best but made a mess of it; the supervisor angrily told him off in front of the other men. Ten minutes later, he vomited and was sent home. The night was a torture. He had no sleep, then had to get up and go to work. The next night, he decided he had to return to his family. Having made that decision allowed him to get through to the weekend.

On the Friday, he hung around until practically everybody had gone, left a note for one of the men and ran to his car, which was already packed. Half-way to his home, he stopped in abject fear and vomited violently. Sitting in the dark, alone on the remote road, he had his first thoughts of suicide. An hour later, he turned around and went back to the city. Early Monday, he got to work early, put his tools back and destroyed the note but it wasn't long before he discovered gambling. Very quickly, he found that he could focus on the spinning icons and not think about work, social life, or anything. He knew that while he was playing the game, nobody would speak to him or bother him, that he could comfortably sit four or five hours, alone and unbothered, and the tension faded. Soon it happened that simply making the decision to go gambling would be enough to start to calm him. Knowing that he could go to the casino at night got him through the day. Weekends were best as he could sleep in, have a leisurely time cleaning his flat then get ready and drive to the TAB. Normally, he went to a different place each day so that he didn't meet the same people or get known by the staff.

In no time, gambling became his life. As long as he was sitting at the table, he had no thoughts of the real world. It really ceased to exist for him. However, as soon as he had to leave, and especially get ready for work, the anxiety flared up. He lived in fear of what could go wrong, of making mistakes, of being seen as incompetent, of having to talk to people or interact socially. At first, he played only the cheapest machines but gradually, he began to increase his stakes, which meant his losses mounted. Before long, he was trapped in that familiar spiral, of trying to recover his losses, then of borrowing money to cover his losses, then of borrowing more to cover his borrowings. It was at that point he knew he had to get some sort of help or he would go completely mad.

There are so many ways people can distract themselves from trouble but it all goes back to the nature of anxiety as a general threat warning. If I see a threat coming at me, I *must* react with arousal, that is the nature of humans. If the threat I see just is anxiety itself, or its effects, then I am caught in a trap of being scared of my own anxiety, which makes me anxious. Anxious people fear their own mental state. They know they cannot control it, that it's a raging beast which, once aroused, will drag them hither and thither. It's as though the beast which was designed to protect them is trampling them underfoot. They're saying: "If X happens, I believe I will be anxious." But for them, that thought, of being anxious, is in and of itself a terrifying thought. It's no different from somebody saying "If X happens, I will be in the most serious trouble." That is in and of itself a terrifying thought. A thought of something terrifying about to happen must cause intense fear, so simply having the thought causes the fear they didn't want: "I'm terrified of being terrified, which makes me terrified, because I can't control my terror and don't know when it will stop."

But it works the other way, too. An anxious person will often say "If I get to X, or see Y, or do Z, I know I'll be fine, I will know there's no danger and I'll just settle down." They know from experience that the anxiety will go away, so that knowledge or belief immediately starts to dampen their fear. The expectation that the dreadful feeling will abate produces just that effect. This is important in a large number of conditions, and is the basis of the placebo effect.

If you work in the emergency department of a big hospital, you get rather tired of the people brought in by ambulance who are clearly panicking. You give them an injection of water, tell them "There there, dear, you'll be fine, don't worry," or "OK mate, she's apples, you can go home," and they immediately start to settle down. They settle because they think something in the injection is going to control their mental state because they know they can't control it, so that's good enough. This doesn't just work on panic, it works on other states as well. We'll mention some of them as we go.

Far and away the most common form of distraction is the major health problem in the developed world, obesity. While some people may eat for fun, or greed, or because it's there, anybody who is technically obese (BMI>30) by age eighteen is almost certainly anxious. Oddly enough, when listing causes of obesity, Wikipedia hardly mentions psychological factors (one passing reference to the word 'stress' in relation to obesity in the poor). For anxious people, finding, preparing and eating food gives them something to focus on instead of dwelling on their inner distress. What the women's magazines now call "comfort eating" is actually anxious eating. There is no such thing as a "sugar addiction" but there is such a thing as using food to reduce anxiety.

The solitary runner or the compulsive body-builder is generally driven by anxiety. If anything goes wrong and he (or she) can't exercise, then the sudden upwelling of anxiety can be volcanic. They will tell themselves that the agitation is caused by not exercising, that they need those endorphins, but it's the other way around. Exercise relieves their normal anxiety, rather than not exercising producing an abnormal agitation. Again, it is not an "addiction" in any sense of the word. It is simply that they have learned to focus on the exercises, thus suppressing their worries and concerns for the time they are there. Quite often, it is the only time they feel reasonable. The agitation will start to rise again within a few hours. They will say: "Aha, I feel my endorphins wearing off, I need another dose," but endorphins have nothing to do with it (actually, nobody has any real idea of what these mysterious chemicals do).

Promiscuity in women is closely linked to high interpersonal anxiety and low self-esteem and has to be seen as part of an abnormal personality. The same thing in men, known as satyriasis, is an urgent need to seduce any and every woman in sight, and the more remote or higher in status, the better. Again, these people are seriously insecure socially but they often cover it with bluster or bravado. Simply being engaged in "the hunt" distracts them from their social insecurity and gives them something better to think or talk about than their inability to function as an independent adult. People who cover themselves in tattoos, or studs, or dress in a bizarre manner, are very often concealing high levels of social anxiety. They are able to relate to the world as "the tattooed man" or "the feral woman" because this restricts the extent of their social intercourse, giving it a structure and thereby reducing interpersonal anxiety.

What else? Spending, of course, a great way of distracting oneself but these days a person who overspends and then suffers anxiety and guilt over the bill is more likely to be labelled as bipolar disorder. Meditation is a time-honoured way of reducing anxiety simply by making the mind go blank, by deliberately "removing all distractions," i.e. by making distraction the goal. I can do the same thing staring at water waiting for the fish to bite; it feels good at the time but all benefit has worn off by the start of work the next day (true meditation is a much more active process than simply turning into a vegetable for half an hour every day).

Among anxious or unhappy teenagers, sleep is a very successful way of distracting oneself from the "stress of modern life." Many people report that as soon as they pull the sheets over their head, the outside world ceases to exist.

Finally, we need to mention what is now delicately termed "deliberate self-harm," formerly known as cutting. Cutters are male or female, and they start in early adolescence. Mostly, they use a very sharp instrument such as a razor or even a scalpel blade, because these don't hurt much and are unlikely to get infected. They describe a rising sense of tension and inner agitation from some cause or other, which builds up and up until they feel they're about to go mad. They solve this by inflicting a series of fairly superficial lacerations on the forearm or thigh, mostly parallel and often in the scars of previous cuts so that nobody can tell how many they have done. As soon as the blood starts to flow, the tension starts to dissipate. Some will say "I feel as though I'm releasing a sort of poison," but mostly they gain a perverse satisfaction from doing something that most people regard as abhorrent. It gives them a sense of control in a world that is largely hostile or indifferent to their distress.

Case 9.2: Eating as distraction.

William McK. is a 44yo single carpenter employed as a building sites inspector by the local council. He lives alone in a small rented flat, drives a battered old car and wears anything he can buy that fits. That isn't easy, as he is 175cm tall, weighs 165kg (BMI 54, dangerously overweight), and has three credit cards sitting on the limit with not a penny to his name. He has been working 28yrs, he doesn't drink, smoke, gamble or use drugs, he never takes holidays, doesn't own a boat, dog, motorbike, racehorse, plane or shares in a goldmine. He doesn't have a girlfriend, his elderly parents live on a farm interstate but he rarely goes to see them as he can't fit in an aircraft seat. He doesn't belong to any clubs or organisations of any sort, and doesn't go to church, football, brothels, casinos or séances, yet he is completely broke. In fact, he doesn't do anything but it takes all his time and money.

Bill presents as morbidly obese, dressed in loose, rumpled and mismatched clothes, but he bustles around the place and chats loudly and cheerily to the receptionist with a jolly smile and lots of belly-shaking chuckles.

Presenting complaints.

In general, he feels he is "trying to make the best of it." He sleeps heavily and his appetite is "ravenous." He doesn't have much energy and has been in trouble at work as he can't walk up steep slopes, climb ladders or squeeze into confined spaces. He never gets any physical exercise apart from walking up the flight of stairs to his flat once or twice a day. He has practically no interest in things and rarely gets around to tasks such as cleaning his flat or his car. Every few weeks, he takes all his clothes and linen to a laundromat, dumps it in the machine and washes it, producing a tangled mess. He has no social interest but said he gets on well with people at work as he tries to keep a bright face. He has little sexual interest and has no sexual experience whatsoever.

His memory and concentration are good and he is able to study building regulations or specifications etc with no difficulty. If he is not under any pressure, he can think clearly and make decisions but he quickly becomes flustered and confused if there is a deadline or if people are watching him working. The thought content is dominated by worries over his finances and his future if he loses his job. There were no disturbances of perception.

He describes his mood as "pretty flat and dismal." He feels low and miserable a lot of the time although it is much less when he is at work because he is a bit of a joker and likes to make people laugh. He has never been suicidal although lately he has been wondering about the point of life. From time to time, he feels good such as when he leaves the city to drive to his parents' place for a weekend. He likes being on the road even though he knows he should get a new car but the driver's seat on this one has been crushed into shape over the years and he doesn't like the seats in modern cars. That apart, he doesn't get much fun. He watches comedies at night but on thinking about it, he rarely does more than give a bit of a chuckle. Apart from being fat, lonely, bored and broke, he can't imagine why he is unhappy.

Asked if he thought he was a nervous person, he said he didn't think so. He gets on well with people at work and isn't scared of heights, rats or snakes. Or police, he adds with a chuckle. He was then questioned directly about the somatic symptoms of anxiety but blithely denied all of them.

So you never get shaky or sweaty? Your heart never races or your stomach churns?

No, I can go to meetings and I regularly have to give talks at seminars. I'm pretty cool at all that.

Right, so if you don't drink or gamble or do drugs, where does all your money go?

Actually, that's a bit of a problem. I have to eat. As you can see.

I would have thought you didn't have to eat for a year or two. So are you saying you spend all your money on food?

Actually... yes.

Why?

Why?

That's what I said, why.

Well I get hypoglycaemic attacks and I've got to eat. It's physiological, the doctors have sorted it out.

What do you mean, hypoglycaemic attacks? That's exceedingly rare if you're not on insulin, and it can be fixed. What happens?

At this point, he starts to sweat and his jolly fat man's smile slowly congeals: Well you know, I start to feel dizzy and out of it and I've got to eat.

And if you don't?

I'll get worse. And worse.

What sort of worse? Do you mean shaking and your heart racing?

Yes, that's it, and I may even vomit.

I see, and when does this happen? At work or at home?

That's funny you should ask, it's worse at home. I'm always busy at work and I drink lots of soft drinks.

With lots of sugar. So what happens when you're driving home?

Well that's it, I don't eat while I'm driving and my blood sugar starts to go down. That's what hypoglycaemia means, you know.

Thank you, I actually passed physiology. So why don't you drink while you're driving?

Actually I do but it doesn't seem to work. The closer I get to home, the worse it gets so I have to stop at a shop and get something to eat.

OK, so you get home, then what happens?

I make my dinner.

You eat. And then what happens?

I watch a bit of TV.

And then?

And then it starts again.

What starts again?

The hypoglycaemia.

By this stage, he is clearly not the same happy chappy. The smile has completely gone, he is dripping sweat, he has to keep wiping his face and hands and he is looking at his watch.

Don't worry about the time, Mr McK, time means nothing in a mental hospital. And don't give me a diagnosis, just describe exactly what you experience.

Um, I'm not... I mean...?

Do you get shaky? Hold your hand out now. Right, so what's that due to? An earthquake?

But that's hypoglycaemia, that's what it does.

I'm the doctor, thank you. That's a tremor, there are a thousand causes of tremor and hypoglycaemia would be about number 926. OK, with your attacks, do you get short of breath? Dizzy? Dry mouth? Stumble over your speech? Sense of the walls closing in or the world seems different? Right, that's thirteen out of thirteen. And with these attacks, how do you feel inside?

Terrible.

Like now?

Yes, how did you know?

I've got eyes. What sort of terrible?

Like... something bad is about to happen. That's what hypoglycaemia does, you know, it affects the amygdala... I've got a very dry mouth, could I have a drink of water?

Later. What sort of bad?

Bad, I don't know, maybe I'll faint or have a heart attack. I'm always scared of having a stroke, my grandmother died of a stroke.

So you're scared during these attacks?

Oh yes, absolutely terrified.

Why is it worse at home?

I'm scared I'll have a turn and nobody will find me, and I'll die of thirst or something... (starts to cry) ...It's so lonely, I just don't know what to do. So frightening.

So you eat? And that's where your money goes?

I'm so sorry, you must think I'm such a weak person but it's the only thing that stops it. The hypoglycaemia...

You don't have hypoglycaemia. This is a perfect description of a panic attack. The symptoms are practically the same, that's why you can't diagnose yourself. So let's go through the list of fears, shall we?

Do you mind if I have a drink of water first?

No, you can wait. Answer the questions first.

Have you ever been told you're... quite a... hard doctor?

Every day. OK, so in your ordinary daily life, is there anything you're frankly scared of, like heights, confined spaces, wide open spaces? Sudden noises, being touched unexpectedly, thunder and lightning, electricity...?

It emerges that he is crippled by social anxiety. His family were farmers on a property at the end of a road. He had one much older sister but there were no children in their area so he was lonely. At school, he was fat, clumsy and shy. Even though he was in the same school for eleven years, he had no close friends. He didn't belong to any groups or play sport, his family kept to themselves and he was frightened of his sister until she married and left. If he was invited to birthday parties, he found a reason not to go but his own birthdays were a torture as his mother always invited half his class. When he left school, he managed to complete his apprenticeship as a carpenter with a neighbour's son but it was an unhappy time. As soon as he gained his ticket, he began work with the local council and later trained as a building inspector. At about 25, he moved to an outlying suburb of the city and worked for the council. He had never had any sort of social life. He was reasonably comfortable at work because he went in and out of the office all day and he didn't have to make major decisions. He reported on projects but his manager decided what should be done.

Bill was utterly incapable of talking to people on a social level. He could keep up a few minutes of jovial banter but then he would look at his watch, give a hearty laugh and say he had to rush off. He was always rushing off but he never had anywhere to go. His little flat was a trap. He could hear his neighbours coming and going, car doors slamming or people calling up to their friends from the parking area but nobody ever called him. As soon as he left the office to go home, he would start to become frightened and that was the signal to eat. When he had finished his evening meal, he would watch some TV, have something else to eat then go to bed but weekends were a nightmare. Friday night he ate and ate until he toppled into bed. The next 48hrs, he was in a state of high agitation and spent his time either eating or planning where to go to get food. He knew he shouldn't eat so much and tried to hold back but the agitation built up and up.

As soon as he made the decision to get food, he started to feel better. He always took his time about going out, perhaps have a shower and find some clean clothes, then sit down and work out what he needed. He didn't like fast food places as they were too quick and he never ordered in advance. He much preferred to go to a Chinese restaurant where they cooked each order, or fish-and-chip shops, because they took longer and he could sit there, happily talking to the owners while they made his order. He always ordered two meals, he explained, because he didn't want to have go out again but in reality, he didn't want anybody to know he was eating alone. He would then take the food home and carefully eat every last bit of it. Then it was time to clean up but he didn't like taking food containers to the bin by day because people knew he lived alone and they would see how much he ate. Quite often, he would take his rubbish to work and put it in the bins at the back of his building.

After he had eaten, he would watch an hour or two of TV or perhaps have a sleep, then it would start again. Within an hour, he would have to give in and start the ritual again. On a weekend day, he would do this four or five times, eating enough in one day for half a dozen people. At first, he hated himself for it but then somebody told him he may be suffering from hypoglycaemia, which made him feel better. Months later, he admitted that secretly, he knew it wasn't true, that his "symptoms" were the same as he had felt at school before going to a party.

He was incapable of talking to women because he knew they would despise him; couldn't talk to straight men in case they thought he was a fag; couldn't talk to gay men in case they thought he was one of them; couldn't talk to children in case anybody thought he was a paedophile, or the children wouldn't want to talk to him because he was fat and weird... on and on, an interminable nightmare. As he was driving home, his fears started as a dread of the loneliness of his nights and pointless weekends but, as his agitation built up, they quickly morphed into a fear of having a heart attack or stroke. He was very frightened of pain, illness and disability, of mental illness and, in particular, of dying alone. That terrified him but he couldn't tell anybody. His only solace was food. As soon as he made the decision to get something to eat, he had a purpose, he had a reason to be out of his flat and driving somewhere, and he felt better. This was the key to convincing him that he wasn't having hypoglycaemic attacks as they don't get better just because you've made the decision to get something to eat.

Always beware of people who self-diagnose. Almost invariably, they find something that will account for their symptoms while saving them the embarrassment of admitting they're anxious. Anxiety is everywhere. Look at this little example.

Case 9.3: Drugs as a distraction from anxiety.

A 25yo man was addicted to morphine and was on a controlled reducing program as part of his probation terms. One day, he arrived in a state of intense agitation, saying somebody had stolen his drugs and he was already in a severe withdrawal state. As he had done this before and I strongly suspected he was partying on his drugs, he was told he would have to wait three days until the next lot were due. He began to wail and blubber pathetically, shaking and sweating, complaining of violent abdominal pains, runny nose, nightmares, vomiting and etc. After listening to this for a few minutes, I reached for my script pad and wrote his name. Immediately, he began to settle. The tears dried, the tremor abated and so on.

"Oh you're such a good doctor," he panted gratefully, "so understanding. I'm so lucky to see you, I always feel better just from knowing I can see you."

"Really? So what's happened to your bellyache?"

"Funny you should ask, but it's going away."

The shaking and sweating was settling, the runny nose had dried with his tears, and it was clear his "withdrawal" symptoms were simply severe anxiety. Which was the reason he had become addicted to morphine in the first place.

"So you're feeling pretty good now?"

"Yes," he said with a beatific smile, "it's because I know there's somebody who understands, not like the drug clinic, they treat me like a criminal."

"Well you are a criminal but if you feel better from simply looking at a script pad, you're not addicted, you're just a panic merchant. You don't need these at all."

With a flourish, I tore the script and threw it in the bin. Immediately, the wailing and pleading and shaking and snot began again. Five minutes later, I wrote another script and the same thing happened. It stopped his "withdrawal" symptoms like turning off a tap. Three times in thirty minutes, we went through the same routine until he left with just enough drugs for the weekend. I would have thought that 95% of his so-called withdrawal symptoms were pure panic but he, like all addicts, would not accept it. They refuse to admit they're anxious, which is why they get addicted in the first place.

Case 9.4: Crime as a distraction from anxiety.

A case from my work in prisons, years ago, shows how powerful and pervasive anxiety is. We'll call him Brian.

When Brian was sentenced to six years for what the newspapers had been calling a "reign of crime," he was aged 28yrs. I saw him for a pre-sentence report but he was very guarded and gave little information so I couldn't say much. My interest was sparked when I saw how intelligent he was. I mentioned this to some of the prison officers who agreed and pointed out that he was actually the nephew of a well-known professor in my medical school.

A week later, I was asked to see him as he had cut his wrists with a blade he had somehow smuggled in. He was quite tall and well-built, good-looking, with dark wavy hair and very dark eyes. He spoke quietly with a public school accent and an extensive vocabulary. The first session was spent trying to make contact with him but he was very wary because he thought he may be transferred to the mental hospital.

Over the next few sessions, he began to talk about his background in one of the city's better known academic families. Yes, he lived in an expensive suburb and went to a very good school; yes, he played sport very well; yes, he had had every opportunity thrown his way. So what went wrong? Nothing, he replied distantly, perhaps I'm just a loser.

Over a couple of weeks, he revealed an unhappy childhood. His ex-military father was away a lot with his work but was strict when he was home while his mother was busy with her own career as well as pushing her elder two children to achieve at the family's usual stratospheric level (ig emerged that she was locked in a competition with her brother, the professor). She didn't have much time to worry about her youngest and, she later revealed, didn't want anybody to think she was babying him. This was in the days before the epidemics of ADHD, ASD and whatever so he was largely left to his own devices.

Throughout high school, his marks deteriorated slowly but he scraped into university and decided to study archeology. There isn't much call for archeologists in Australia (essentially, none) so only the very best stand even a remote chance of a job. Because he started smoking marijuana and took up gambling, he wasn't anywhere near the best. Before long, he was in financial trouble so he dropped out and found casual work. Because of arguments at home, he moved out but he never stayed anywhere for long. His family provided some money but he needed more and more to pay his gambling debts.

At some stage, he went to see a woman he knew to see if he could borrow some money. She refused and threw him out; angered, he went home and brooded on his misery. After a while, he decided to break into her house and steal some valuables he had seen. To his surprise, it was easy but he was cautious and hid the goods in a nearby park. Sure enough, the police arrived to question him; he stood back and let them in. They found nothing and he was later able to pay his debts. Some time later, he was in trouble again so he started breaking into houses on a regular basis. He was clever but most importantly, he worked totally alone. Hardly anybody knew where he was living and he never told anybody what he was doing. He found a comfortable day job, gave up drugs, bought himself a car and kept a low profile. He had a string of women he could visit if he wanted but he never let them into his life. By night, he played poker quite successfully and every few months, he did a bust. Why? Why did he lead this peculiar double life when he had everything that anybody could want?

Mystified, I presented his case at an academic meeting.

"He's a psychopath," the assembled psychiatrists snorted. "That's what psychopaths do, that's what psychopaths are. Does anybody have an interesting case to present?"

But there had to be more to it. I went back to work and continued seeing him, trying to untangle his motivation. And slowly it came.

As a child, growing up in the shadow of his older siblings, he was quite shy and nervous. He was convinced he could never achieve at their level, could never satisfy his increasingly critical and demanding parents who had used all their tolerance by the time he was born. In his teenage years, his insecurity became much worse. By the time of his final year of school, he was barely able to enter the classrooms for fear of making a mistake or looking stupid. He gave up his sport, stopped music lessons and spent most of his time in his room reading ancient history. At university, he was more or less crippled by fear of failure, of humiliation, of making a mistake or causing offence. He started smoking marijuana, which helped but it was expensive so he began gambling.

By his early twenties, he had largely withdrawn from his family but nobody seemed to notice or say much, they were all too busy with their own careers. Gambling was the only time he felt calm. He knew that if he kept calm and watched the cards and the players, he could do well, especially if the other players were drinking. But then he discovered crime. It was the same thing. As soon as he made the decision to rob the woman's house, he felt perfectly calm. All his tension disappeared, channelled into preparing for the job. Even though he was working, he needed to maintain a complete double life and, for the first time in his life, it stopped bothering him. He stopped worrying about being alone and accepted it as necessary to his plans.

If he felt any tension, he explained it away as the reasonable response to what he was planning. He no longer felt ashamed of his reticence but saw it as essential. Instead of worrying that nobody seemed to know where he lived and nobody bothered to call him or drop in, he was pleased. Instead of being an anxious and insecure worker in a boring job, he became a calm and self-contained man on a mission.

For a week or two after he had done a job, he was edgy and worried that he may have made a mistake or left some evidence but that gradually settled. For the next month or so, he was cheerful and able to get on with people but then the anxiety started again. It wasn't long before he was back to where he started. After several weeks of worry, he would then make the decision to do another job and very quickly, his anxiety disappeared. He became steely calm, he organised everything carefully, built an elaborate cover, got in touch with friends, kept his life in order and resumed contact with his family. This cyclical pattern went on for several years until he was arrested and convicted. He pleaded guilty to a dozen charges but it was clear there were a lot more.

It took him a long time to understand that if he could switch his anxiety off in order to plan and execute a robbery, he could also do it for ordinary life. If he could stop worrying about what people were thinking for an hour, he could stop forever. At the base of his social anxiety was terrible self-esteem based in a deep-seated fear that he wasn't good enough, that if people got close, they would see he was weak and insecure and not a man, and they wouldn't want to know him. Essentially, he believed he was unlovable. His way of dealing with it was to take himself off the social market, just as a spy does. He was acting, of course, but if you can act calm, you really are calm.

I've met plenty of murderers but never a true serial murderer or serial rapist. I strongly suspect the same thing happens with them. Something drives them, and anxiety is the only emotion that has that power.

Case 9.5: Jenny M. Cutting as distraction from anxiety.

I met my first cutter in my first year of psychiatry. Jenny was a single woman aged 34yrs who was admitted one night after threatening suicide. I saw her early the next morning and took her history. It was grotesque. She had been abandoned as a child and spent most of her early life in institutions where she was routinely abused sexually, by older children and by staff, men and women. This was many years ago, long before it became clear how common sexual abuse of children really is, and it took a lot for her to talk about it. At age seventeen, she was admitted to the psychiatric hospital, the first of many times, where she was given large doses of drugs and eventually had over a hundred ECT.

When she was aged 29yrs, the government had a change of policy. All the people who had previously been locked in secure hospitals because they were too disturbed to be released were suddenly deemed fit to fend for themselves and were pushed into the community. Needless to say, most of them couldn't fend for themselves. Jenny was one that didn't. She drifted around, sometimes working as a prostitute, other times kept by dreadful men who abused her in every possible way. She drank, fought, used drugs, went to prison, cut her wrists, went to mental hospitals, in an endless cycle of distress and disturbance. In between, she cut herself. With a shrug, she pulled up her sleeves to show hundreds of symmetrical scars on her arms. There were many more on each thigh and on her chest and abdomen.

At the ward round, I described all this to the consultant but he was very dismissive. Cutters, he said, were selfish nuisances who distracted psychiatry from its real job of looking after the mentally ill. They chose to cut themselves, psychiatry had nothing to offer them and the best thing was to show her the door. That wasn't very helpful so I went to the library to see what I could find. There was nothing. I found an article on two men who had amputated their penises but they were clearly psychotic, whereas Jenny wasn't. An American journal of psychoanalysis gave some bizarre formulation of why people cut themselves but it didn't make any sense to me so I went back to ask her what was happening. When I reached our ward, the place was in uproar. Jenny had been found in the toilet, carefully removing the stitches from the lacerations on her forearms. Half the staff wanted to throw her out and the rest wanted to send her to the mental hospital so I sat down with her to try to find out what was going on. For nearly half an hour, she sat staring out the window, smoking, and said nothing.

Finally, she turned with a quivering sneer: "Why are you wasting your time on me?" she demanded in a strangled voice. "Go and see some sick people, everybody knows there's nothing wrong with me" (I've left the swearing out, it gets a bit repetitious).

She was shaking and breathing rapidly and I could see her pulse beating wildly in her throat. Clearly, she was terrified. Very slowly, she began to calm down and described how she lived in a state of more or less constant fear, of what she didn't really know, except several times a day it started to spin out of control. She did everything she could to control it, starting with getting right away from people (very difficult in a psychiatry ward), drinking or smoking weed (ditto), arguing or getting into fights, finding men for casual sex or, if this didn't work and the nervous tension was building up and up to screaming point, giving in and finding a knife. As soon as she decided to cut herself, the terrible tension started to fade. With a knife or razor hidden in her pocket, she would walk around until she found a quiet place, then sit down and slowly begin the ritual of cutting. As the blood started to flow, the feverish tension faded like air going out of a balloon. Entranced, she would watch as the blade slid through her skin, then start the next one, and the next. She had no idea how many times she had done this, at least ten times a year on and off for nearly twenty years. Each time she inflicts up to fifty cuts, but she mostly does them in old scars so it didn't look quite so bad. It still looked pretty bad.

If she didn't cut herself, what would happen?

"I'll go completely stark staring mad. I'd have to kill myself, I couldn't live with that terrible tension."

Routine interview showed that she experienced every symptom of anxiety in the book (at that stage of my career, I was still paying attention to books) and a whole lot more that weren't there. She was constantly nervous; she couldn't relax even in the toilet because she was listening for somebody to come stamping in and hammer on the door, demanding to know why she was taking so long or maybe to walk in and demand sex. Even sex didn't work because she expected the man to start hitting her, or the woman to abuse her. The only time she felt relief was when the blade began its bloody dance over her arms. She was frightened of the natural world because she had grown up in institutions and had no experience of going to the beach or to a park, or walking through the bush, but her main fears were of the human world. There was nothing that didn't frighten her. In fact, she wasn't a bad person. She didn't hurt people, she stole only when she had to, she hated fighting but became so agitated under pressure than she would lash out in order to escape. She lived in terror and this is what controlled her.

I saw her on and off for some years as she would often find where I was working and come in when things were getting too difficult. Needless to say, I had no idea what to do as I hadn't yet grasped the concept of a self-reinforcing model of anxiety. She said that talking helped her so I sat and listened. Eventually, she decided that if she had a baby, she would feel a lot better so that's what she did. The welfare people put up a bit of a battle, arguing that she wasn't a fit mother, but the court accepted that they couldn't make that decision until she had shown she was unfit. After that, I moved into prisons and lost contact with her. It wasn't a very big city, I knew most people in the psychiatric scene so if anything had gone badly wrong, I would have known.

This story illustrates a very important concept: the notion that high anxiety is intolerable. People have to find some way of reducing it or they will go mad. Or kill themselves.

Compulsive comics.

Years ago, I saw a 16yo boy who had made a fairly determined attempt on his life. His family was from eastern Europe, with all the neuroses that Freud turned into theatre. It turned out he was one of the most intelligent people I've ever met but high intelligence can be a problem in psychotherapy. As Garrison Keillor says, "High intelligence is like a four

wheel drive vehicle. It lets you get stuck in much more interesting places."
He did fairly well, then the family moved interstate but, very unusually, he
gave me a parting gift (psychiatrists don't get many gifts). It was a coffee
mug with a picture of clowns in a psychotherapy group. One of them says
"How come I'm the only one who's laughing on the inside?"

There's a time to be serious and a time to laugh but people who can't
stop making jokes, who can't be serious, are very often driven by social
anxiety. It's their way of controlling a scary world, keep it laughing. They
learn very early in life that if somebody's laughing, he can't punch your
head in so they keep up a barrage of silly puns, gags, noises, giggles and
guffaws. Generally, compulsive jokesters can't stand silence, it worries them
because they don't know what people are thinking or plotting, so they
wreck the moment with idiotic comments, farts or belches. The trouble is,
they also can't tell anybody when they're in trouble. Their way of dealing
with trouble is to intensify the jokes, to become increasingly histrionic in the
hope that the trouble will somehow just go away. When, suddenly, the jokes
no longer work and the fear breaks through, they will burst into tears
saying "I just don't know what's wrong with me. Everything is fine in my
life but this silly crying just keeps happening, it's so embarrassing." Then,
with a superhuman effort, they put on a huge smile, wipe away the tears
and change the subject.

A compulsive comic is at serious risk of getting a diagnosis of manic-
depressive psychosis, or bipolar disorder in modern parlance. It that
happens, he'll be put on huge doses of drugs and then he won't have much
to laugh about. And one day, everybody will be astounded to learn that he
has killed himself: "My god, whoever would have guessed? It just seems so
out of character." That's because he made sure that nobody knew his real
character. The comedian that everybody saw was a façade, a persona in the
classic sense of the masks that actors wore in dramas (hence our word
personality). Forced laughter drives me nuts, all I can hear is the anxiety
under it.

Pseudo-addictions.

If you ask somebody "Why do you always do that?" and he replies
"Because I'm addicted" or "Because of my compulsions," he hasn't
answered the question. The expressions "an addiction" or "a compulsion"
are not explanatory, they are descriptions masquerading as an explanation,
essentially just another way of saying the same thing as "Because I always
do it."

If it's a physical addiction to a drug, then the answer to the question
"Why do you keep taking that stuff?" is "To avoid withdrawals." That we
understand; drugs cause major changes in brain chemistry but if the drug is
stopped, the brain starts to revert to normal. The process of reversion is
experienced as very unpleasant symptoms which can be reversed by the

same drug or something very close to it. That doesn't mean the drugs have to be similar chemicals, only that they work on the same brain enzyme systems.

A behaviour, however, is not in the same category or order of things. If you ask "Why do you always do that?" it explains nothing to be told "Oh, that's my OCD." In fact, these types of answers are not intended to be explan-atory, they are designed to stop further questions. Any driven or obsessive behaviour can be explained, but it needs a psychological explanation. This topic is so big that it needs a chapter of its own.

10

Obsessions and Compulsions

One of the less-attractive features of the internet is the ever-present, all-knowing Dr Google, who offers infinite knowledge for nothing. These days, anybody can self-diagnose using the endless array of tests that pop up at the click of a mouse. Feeling a little glum? Click here and learn that you too have "clinical depression," so go and see your doctor. Who, of course, will give you tablets. But don't take my word for it, try it yourself. In no time, you can complete a dozen different questionnaires on very professional web-sites that will give you fifteen separate diagnoses, if not more. Coincidentally, all of them will tell you which drugs you need. Then you can march into your doctor's office and announce: "I'm ADHD," or "I'm autistic," or "I'm major depression." But most common of all is "My boyfriend is sooo OCD and I'm totally over it."

There is a huge problem with the expression 'obsessive-compulsive,' which our friends at DSM have been compounding for the past four decades. Let's look at two vignettes to illustrate it.

Case 10.1: Carmel B

Carmel B is a 24yo single woman who lives with her parents and her younger brother. Her mother attended the interview with her but said very little. Carmel is enrolled in a social work course but hasn't passed any units for two years and, it emerges, hasn't been to any classes for over eight months. She presents as attractive, neatly-dressed, bright and cheerful and well-spoken. She had made the appointment, she said with an endearing smile, because her OCD was getting a bit out of control. She wasn't convinced she needed to see a psychiatrist as she had been prescribed antidepressants in the past but they caused weight gain. Instead, she would like some strategies so she could get back to normal life, or perhaps a referral to a psychologist for CBT.

Presenting complaints.

In general, she said with a bright smile, she was feeling "fine." Her appetite was "fine" and her weight steady. Her levels of energy were "fine." (*By this stage of the interview, an alarm is ringing*). She was interested in things in general and was motivated to get back to studying. Socially, she had friends and was getting on well with people. Her memory and concentration were both "fine," she could think clearly and was able to make decisions. The thought content was concerned with "getting everything done" and she denied all disturbances of perception.

She described her mood as "fine" and she did not feel low or miserable. This didn't seem right so she was asked to repeat herself. With a slight furrowing of the brow and one finger reflectively touching her quizzical smile, she considered the question then announced cheerfully that no, she never had been low and miserable, she had nothing to be low and miserable about, did she? In fact, she said, warming to the interview, she had been feeling very well with the pleasant spring weather we'd been having. And no, she never felt excessively good and certainly didn't do anything untoward like overspend or act frivolously. She didn't get anxious, there were no somatic symptoms of anxiety, or perhaps if she saw snake she may feel a little apprehensive but otherwise she never felt panicky. Detailed questioning revealed no fears; specifically, she politely but very firmly denied fears of dirt, contamination or disorder. She had no paranoid ideas and was not self-conscious, but she did have OCD so if I could just give her a few or those strategies, she'd be on her way and not be any trouble.

With a slight frown, she insisted that "her OCD" wasn't too bad, it was just a matter of tidying things, cleaning the house but certainly not out of control. Excuse me? Oh well, yes, perhaps she did wash her hands a bit. How much? Oh, just a bit, you know how it is when you're cleaning the house, you need to wash your hands every now and then.

Clearly, this was going nowhere so it was time to try another approach:

Why are you cleaning the house?

With a look of politely amused surprise, she pointed out that houses need to be cleaned.

How long do you spend cleaning the house?

Oh, a while.

How long do you spend cleaning your room?

Really, she said, shaking her head, is this entirely necessary? It takes time to clean a room, everybody knows that.

Exactly how long did you spend cleaning your room yesterday?

With a look of somewhere between pain and annoyance, she looked to her mother but she had her head down and didn't react.

How long? I want to know exactly how long you spent cleaning your room yesterday.

After much more verbal sparring, she finally conceded that she spent sixteen hours tidying, arranging, dusting and rearranging her room. She didn't get time to start on the toilet but she would surely get to it tomorrow, it was another sixteen hour job.

One toilet. Sixteen hours. Are you serious? Do you have a life?

She didn't answer but stared beseechingly at her silent mother. After a minute, a tear ran down her face. She whispered reproachingly at her mother, who replied: "You promised me you would tell the truth."

The truth was very simple. This woman had no life whatsoever. She hardly went out of the house and often stayed in her room for days on end. She spent the entire time cleaning and arranging things. She didn't come out for buckets of water or to change the mop, as you or I might do if we were spring-cleaning a room; instead, she stayed in the room all day, carefully taking her collections of ornaments and gewgaws off each shelf, studiously arranging them in a line on another shelf, checking them all with a tape measure, carefully wiping the shelf then putting them back where they came from—only to start again as she couldn't be sure if she followed the correct order in moving them. This went on all day, day after day, week after week, without end. From the corridor, her mother could hear her moving around but she wouldn't come out by day.

What do you do when you have to go to the toilet?

With a little laugh and a toss of the head, she dismisses the question: Oh, I manage.

How do you manage?

I beg your pardon?

I said, How do you manage? I want to know how you can go 14hrs without needing to go to the toilet?

Without looking up, her mother says: "She doesn't drink."

Oh, that's a good idea, you'll get kidney stones. Do you know how painful kidney stones are?

She's already had two.

Great. So what do you do when you need to open your bowels?

A look of immense distaste crossed her face, as though she had opened a cupboard and found a fresh turd.

I said, What do you do... Forget it, we know what you do. You take tablets. Codeine?

"Lomotil," muttered her mother.

This isn't getting better, is it? Now you'll probably get diverticulitis, which is both painful and dangerous. But why don't you go to the toilet when you shower?

I have to wash the bathroom first but...

"She doesn't shower."

I see. So you have a fetish for cleanliness but you don't shower, is that right?

After a great deal of to and fro, she revealed she often goes three weeks without showering because she has to finish cleaning the bathroom and toilet before she can shower, but somebody always uses them first so she has to start again. What did her father think of all this? It turned out he didn't know. He worked away three weeks in four but when he came home, she kept out of sight.

Personal background.

Her family background, on her estimation, was fine. Both her parents arrived in the country as refugees but their children were born in Australia. They had no other relatives here although her mother's parents visited occasionally. Her father had a small transport business; he was "OK" and they got on "fine." Her mother managed the orders and did the books for the business from home; she was "nice and caring" and they too got on "fine." The younger brother was studying psychology and was "fine," as was their relationship. They'd gone to church girls school throughout, no problems at school, not shy or nervous but didn't play sport, more interested in music and singing in the chapel choir, home life.... Home life?

I said, What was your home life like?

Again she smoothed her skirt and, with a smile, glanced out the window. "Yes," she finally says, "home life was fine."

What does that mean?

You know, no problems.

If there were no problems, why are you seeing a psychiatrist?

That stumped her. She muttered and smiled and quickly changed the subject back to education. Started social work but took a break...

Why did you take a break?

Oh... I just... felt like a change.

A change? And you sit in your room all day, unwashed and scrubbing things that don't need scrubbing? Was this when you saw the psychologist?

She glanced accusingly at her mother, who kept her head down. "How do you know about that?"

You said so. You said strategies.

Oh... yes. But not for long.

I'm sure. So you dropped out because you had a breakdown, is that it?

I wouldn't call it... a breakdown.

Well, what would you call it?

It was just... nothing much, I was fine.

> *Can we just be sensible for a bit? People do not drop out of their courses because they're having a good time. So what did your family say when you dropped out? Let's start with your father. By the way, how long since you actually layed eyes on him?*
>
> Turned out she hadn't seen him for about eight weeks, which was pretty normal. But what did he say when she told him she had dropped out? Er, it's like... she hadn't actually told him.
>
> *I don't believe this. Why haven't you told him?*
>
> Oh, I will, I'll get around to it, it's just that I haven't seen him.
>
> *I don't believe you. You already said he uses the toilet and bathroom so you have to clean them again, and now you say you don't see him? He's not a ghost, ghosts don't need to poo. OK, so you're avoiding him, is that it? But time's up for today, we'll continue next week.*

Weeks and months went by, and her story eked out by dribs and drabs. Her father had a foul temper, she had always been terrified of him and her way of dealing with him was to keep out of sight. Starting in high school, she stayed in her room studying but by her final years, she was staying there even when he wasn't home. If her mother asked why, she flew into a temper and stormed off, shouting tearfully that nobody understood her. The rituals began about then so by second year of university, she was more or less trapped by the need to clean things. It took a year of intense pressure for her to reveal that in high school, she only felt safe in her room as her father would never go in it. When he was home, she started cleaning things as an excuse for not going out but this gradually intensified until she felt frightened if she left the room, then at the thought of needing to go out. The only way she felt calm was slowly, meticulously cleaning things. If she made a mistake, she had to start again as it would bother her until she gave in. And this is the essence of compulsions:

> If I don't do X, I will feel bad.
> I'm scared of feeling bad, so I'll give in and do it.

However, what they don't realise is that the bad feeling *just is* fear, i.e. they are scared of their own fear state.

A compulsion is a repetitive action or fragment of an action that the person must carry out, even though she knows it is absurd or unnecessary, just because failing to do it will result in ever-increasing agitation until she gives in. An obsession is a repetitive idea or fragment of an idea that the person must observe, which she knows to be absurd or pointless, but which she is incapable of resisting. Obsessions and compulsions are driven by fear.

In Carmel's case, she was not being entirely dishonest when she said she didn't experience fear; the only reason she didn't was because she always gave in and did exactly as her ever-expanding lists of obsessions and compulsions demanded. In fact, she had a most severe anxiety state: at the slightest threat to her routines, she dissolved in uncontrollable fear. That's why obsessive-compulsive disorder was always known as obsessive-compulsive neurosis and it is correctly classed as one of the anxiety states. However, what is now known as obsessive-compulsive personality disorder is wrongly named. It used to be known as the anankastic personality. Note that I didn't say 'anankastic personality disorder,' because an anankastic personality just is a disordered personality:

> 'You're a classic anal-retentive,' he says, 'tirelessly absorbed by minutiae, anankastic in the extreme – it's lucky you have me to deal with the broad sweep of things, to do the abstract thinking' (Will Self: *Mono-Cellular* in *The Quantity Theory of Insanity*).

Anal retentive, anankastic, obsessive-compulsive: let's leave the jargon aside and look at the reality but first, what was the alarm bell about? Any person who repeatedly answers "fine" to questions is lying. It's possible that they don't actually know they're lying but it's still lying.

Case 10.2: Michael B, 43yo anankastic Army sergeant.

Until he arrived, I didn't know Michael was in the Army. His referral was from a civilian GP and he had registered using his Medicare number, but everything about him screamed 'military.' He was sitting in the waiting room dressed in spotless sports clothes, receding hair trimmed, a neat moustache, feet and knees together, hands resting on a folder on his lap and staring straight ahead. Scrupulously polite, he jumped to his feet, followed me into the office, gave a slight bow as he carefully shook hands and kept calling me 'sir.' He immediately opened his file and began a prepared speech about his problems, all the while laying documents neatly on the desk, carefully nudging them into line as he spoke. His voice was precise, clear and sincere and he was startled when I interrupted and began taking the history my way.

This raises an important point about the process of taking a history. When I see newly-trained psychiatrists or medical students taking a psychiatric history today, they mostly let the patients talk about whatever takes their fancy. The history rambles on here and there, with a few questions about interesting bits but otherwise, it is what they now call "undirected." While the patient prattles on, the psychiatrist either scribbles a few words on a card, or takes reams of scrawled notes with no format. I routinely see insurance and legal reports prepared by this method. They're useless. They often have headings but everything is jumbled. There will be material from the history under "mental state examination," current problems under "personal development," unrelated physical symptoms under "recent history" and so on. Then, after ten or twelve pages of turgid prose larded with jargon, a diagnosis pops up with no clue as to how it was reached.

I recently spent half a day commenting on a legal report consisting of 20 pages (loosely typed, extra wide margins, double-spaced) of what was essentially incoherent nonsense. On the last page, we suddenly learned that the subject was the perpetrator in "Factitious disorder imposed on another," more commonly known as "Münchhausen Syndrome by Proxy," and was thus unsuitable to have custody of the children. This is very scary because a great deal hangs on psychiatric assessments. People can be locked up for indeterminate periods and denied practically every known human right just on the say-so of psychiatrists who, all too often, don't know how to take a history. Lawyers and courts, unfortunately, are hugely impressed by psychiatry and almost invariably defer to the "expert opinion" even when it is manifestly tripe.

A psychiatric history has to be directed. There is a lot to cover and it has to be covered fairly and impartially; allowing the patient to prattle on will produce only a flood of irrelevant dross, tears and recriminations—and self-justification. Almost invariably, it will not get to the crucial points of what is actually wrong in the patient's life. They don't want to talk about it, it's too painful, or embarrassing or it doesn't put them in a good light. Remember that people writing autobiographies rarely have it in mind to write a critical appraisal of their subject. This is also true of undirected psychiatric histories: undirected psychiatry is about as effective as undirected surgery. Sgt Michael B was a perfect example. He wanted to take control of the interview from the outset, because that's what he was used to doing. He said he needed an objective assessment of his mental state for court, but his idea of objective and mine were poles apart (fortunately, the courts and I agree on this point).

We needn't go through his history in great detail; his second wife had recently left him, denying him access to his children on the basis of his "mental disorder." His first marriage had lasted ten years and left him destitute; his 22yo son was on methamphetamine while his 20yo daughter was an aggressive, heavily-tattooed and -bestudded political lesbian with a green mohawk haircut. His account of his childhood was sparse; left to his own devices, he would not have mentioned it. But he was left to my devices, not his. When you're in my office, I'm in charge and yes, we will talk about your home life and your school days, I don't care whether you keep trying to dismiss it as "nothing much."

In fact, it was very much. He was raised on a small farm in an isolated area (that always sets alarms ringing), the eldest of four children; his father was a Vietnam vet (more alarms) who drank all day and smoked barrow-loads of weed. His only brother was killed in a dumb accident on the farm for which Michael felt overwhelmingly guilty (it wasn't his fault; his guilt was that he hadn't taken his brother with him that day so he got up to mischief with the tractor); one sister had become wealthy from her serial marriages to rich men and wouldn't talk to any of them from her mansion on the Gold Coast while the other was a tramp. All par for the course, more or less what you expect in the military. What was important was his way of dealing with all of this: to freeze inside.

Starting in early childhood, he had an overwhelming sense of responsibility for everything. If anything went wrong, he was immediately blamed by his father and belted. By the time he enlisted, he had worked out that if he worked exceedingly hard, took total responsibility for everything and didn't rest until everything was spotless, he could actually get people to approve of him. He sailed through recruit training, picking up several prizes for best recruit, best shot etc, and was clearly destined for great things. At twenty, as do so many soldiers from deprived backgrounds, he married. She was eighteen, his first, he reluctantly admitted, as he had been too shy. With the proceeds from his first deployment to a combat zone, he gave her full responsibility to decide when and how they should be married, even though the costs she ran up cleaned him out.

On his fourth overseas tour, he got the letter he had been dreading, that his wife was having an affairt. A bitter divorce ensued, he was deemed depressed by a military psychologist and put on drugs, which he hated, not least because it was used to prove he was mentally unfit to have custody. Somehow, he got off the drugs, forced himself back on course and back to gym, gained his third stripe and finally met another girl who seemed everything the first was not. She may have been but it didn't last, she was a spendthrift and a social butterfly. For her, looking good and being seen were more important than mere housework.

By the time their youngest child was three, Michael was doing all the housework and childcare but he didn't mind. He was determined the marriage would succeed and the children would not go through what he had survived as a child, or his older children had endured. Needless to say, it didn't work. She finally found someone more exciting, pushed Michael out, brought in the new man and applied for his children and all his assets. All this is unremarkable: for every disturbed or unstable man, there's a disturbed or unstable woman and all too often, they find each other. It's called assortative mating.

Once again, Michael found himself being assessed by psychologists; once again, too dumb to tell lies, he told them that yes, sometimes life did seem pretty tasteless; no, he had never contemplated suicide but yes, if he dropped down from a heart attack, it wouldn't bother him as long as the children were OK. Alarmed, the psychologist notified the military police, Michael was dragged off to a mental hospital, drugged, labelled and spat out, minus his home and family and facing discharge on the basis of chronic mental disorder. He wanted a psychiatric report to counter all the various reports floating around that said he was severely mentally ill and thus a danger to his wife and children and unfit for service.

In a case like this, it is vital to follow a standard format for taking the history because he will not volunteer anything unless specifically asked.

First, he's male; men generally don't like to be seen as complaining as it's a sign of weakness. Second, he's military, and they hate being seen as weak because weak = unmanly, and unmanly = effeminate and probably a repressed fag to boot. Finally, he has a very powerful interest in presenting himself in the best possible light. Even if he wanted to spill the beans, he would probably not be able to.

The history revealed that he was pretty unhappy but not suicidal; his sense that death would be a relief from all this stuff was not anywhere near being suicidal. It also showed that he had a long list of social fears, what we call performance fears, how he was performing and how people were judging him. He had an intense fear of disapproval, which powered his intense need to be perfect and to be perfectly in control at all times. His need to dominate and control led directly to his marital disasters but his humorlessness contributed. Everything was controlled, ordered, neat and done by the book at all times. If the book says the children should be put on solids at six months but not before, that's what happened. If the book says soldiers should march 40km in nine hours with full packs, that's what happened, even if it was over 40C. He had to be up at 4.30am to go to gym so, regardless of what was on TV, lights had to go out at 8.30pm. Bills were to be paid in strict order of priority, not when she got around to it, and hiding bills from him invited a torrent of moral criticism.

Actually, he learned that from the wreckage of his first marriage, don't cut loose with criticism. In those days, if anything went wrong, he would start yelling and tell everybody to get out while he fixed it. He didn't recognise this as panic but that's what it was, the fear of loss of control. The male pattern is to flip panic into rage. For the second marriage, if he found an unauthorised bill, he took it, paid it and spent several days in teeth-grinding silence until he had got over it. What did he have to get over? Not so much treachery or deceit as idle flippancy, irresponsibility or just dumb-headed carelessness. Carelessness he couldn't handle, it was probably the ultimate moral crime.

Carelessness costs lives, isn't that what they tell you? Does that remind you of something? Perhaps your brother's death?

For the first time, his adamantine self-control cracks. Biting his lip, clearly unable to speak, he stares at the name neatly stencilled on his folder while tears force themselves out. For a minute, he sits unmoving, then he rubs his face and blows his nose loudly:

"I can't get over the guilt," he says in a strangled whisper. "Twenty-seven years, and I can't get over the guilt."

But if I hadn't pressed him to give a proper history, he would certainly not have mentioned his brother.

The anankastic or obsessional personality is about control. It is about controlling the chaotic and dangerous outside world in order to gain peace in the inner world. Everything has to be done by the rule book, a place for everything and everything in its place. Nothing is left to chance because something could go wrong. His fear is that he will be blamed and he will have no way of defending himself. Chance leads to chaos and chaos is terrifying, either the terrifying and brutally punitive outer world or the inner tempest of his own, barely repressed emotions, he doesn't clearly distinguish them. Anankastia. The word is Greek, as you can guess, but I'm not sure how it ended up in psychiatry. In grammar, there is an anankastic conditional: *If you want this, first you must do that.* It's about abiding by rules, about deferring pleasure or rewards, about working before playing but since there's always work to do, well, play never quite happens. Ultimately, it gets to the point where if it feels good, it must be immoral. For the rigid obsessional personality, the only good is perfection. Sex, of course, is loss of control, weakness, self-indulgence and must be carefully rationed.

Don't get me wrong, the rigid obsessional personality isn't all bad. If you have a rigid obsessional surgeon, be grateful: nothing will be left to chance. If you need an operation, don't fall for the glittering, high society A-list surgeon whom everybody is talking about, head for the boring plodders. Of course, if there's nothing much wrong with you that a nice expensive operation can't give you something to talk about, then go for glitter, you have nothing to lose but your wallet. Obsessional means obsessed with rules and procedure. Obsessionals run the country; they keep everything ticking over because nobody else can be bothered checking to see if there's fuel in the engine, the electricity bill was paid or there's water for the dog. They raise children by the book, make sure they have their injections on time, have every text book ready for the first day of school, shoes polished, shirts starched, ties in order. If the children have a party, everything will be organised, places for everybody, cut the cake at 2.50pm, games start at 3.05 and continue for 35 minutes until it's time to go home, no pushing, wait your turn.

An obsessional young man joins the government, a bank or insurance company, a big mining company or, especially, the military. They like big organisations, they feel secure knowing there is a very large rule book to follow. In very short order, he is recognised as a "responsible type" and is quickly steered toward extra duties, which he acquits admirably without a murmur of protest. Overtime and late shifts are his specialty; when the office goes out for a boozy Christmas lunch, he will be at his desk answering phones, keeping the show on the road. He's promoted, sent to training courses (at which he does very well; not for him staying up late drinking and then sleeping through the next day and, horror of horrors, none of the bedroom hopping that goes on). Soon, he has his own department and is marked for greater things. Somewhere along the line, he takes time off to get married, probably to a shy young thing from Accounts, and a couple of picture book children appear. All is fine. But then the cracks appear.

At home, his marriage is struggling because The Other Half is getting sick of being ordered around and not permitted to take the kids off to DreamWorld in mid-week because her sister is visiting from Goanna Creek. At work, he is passed over for promotion and becomes silently embittered. He can't understand it, he has all the certificates and experience anybody could want yet they gave the job to that young bloke from another section. But this is the point: an obsessional attention to detail will quickly get you to middle levels of responsibility but then you hit your limit. If you want to leave the ranks of middle management and get to junior executive level, you need do more than just memorise the rule book. You need flare, panache, intuition and, above all, the ability to sell yourself. But for obsessionals, that's impossible. They have made conformity and rule-abiding into more than just a career, it's a lifestyle, a political choice, even a religion, but they cannot break it. Leopards can't change their spots, nor rigid obsessionals kick the traces and rush joyfully into the sunset because there are no rules for it. As for self-publicity, forget it. They have a rule against self-indulgence.

So by age forty-five, our once golden-haired boy has become a pudgy, balding and embittered middle manager who sees no prospects ahead. Worse, all these bright young things who have never known the firm hand of self-discipline are scooting past him; above all, women. Oh my god, how galling, passed over for a woman. At home, in the house he worked so hard to pay for, his wife is sick of him always working and has built a life of her own while his children only talk to him to say they need more money or a good lawyer, or money for a good lawyer. There are different ways he can handle this. If he is inclined to anger, he will stamp around the place, full of bile, constantly finding fault with everybody and everything. If he is a bit on the nervous side, what we call an anxious obsessional, he gets panicky and lies awake at night worrying about everything. Very soon, he will start to complain of stomach trouble so off he goes to see the physician for a gastroscopy. Which shows nothing but he is given a complex diet for Irritable Bowel Syndrome which keeps him busy but doesn't stop the problem.

He can, of course, have a few drinks to calm down, where a few quickly becomes a few too many, which soon leads to its own problems. He may feel it's his health letting him down, so he starts consulting our old friend, Dr Google, and quickly decides he has every ailment he reads about, which causes more panic. If he has always been inclined to see conspiracies around him, well now he has all the evidence he needs to prove that people at work are conspiring against him. And, of course, he'll get depressed. Naturally enough, he won't say that, he'll let somebody tell him that yes, this is depression, you've got it pretty bad but don't worry, it's a chemical imbalance of the brain so take these tablets and don't believe anything you read about them causing weight gain or wrecking what's left of your sex life, just press on and come back in a month.

In a month, he will be back, no better and feeling pretty sluggish and unable to concentrate but don't worry, double the dose and come back in a month. A month later, fatter and no better, he comes in mournfully. OK, says the doctor, why don't we add these nifty mood stabilisers, they're just the trick. Some months later, steadily getting worse, he agrees to a trip to hospital where they take one look at his wallet and decide he needs the electrical treatment. That's ECT. He panics. Years ago, he saw something called *The Cuckoo's Nest*...? No, the nice staff say, that was prehistory. Nowadays, ECT is so refined you'll hardly know you've had it. So he signs on the dotted line and gets his shocks, but he knows he's had it because he's stopped worrying. In fact, he can't remember what he was worrying about. Greatly encouraged, he thanks the staff, pays his bill ("Well, I suppose if you want the best, you have to pay for it") and goes home and back to work.

A few months later, he's back again, mournful, dejected, apologetic that he didn't seem to pick up properly, secretly resentful; perhaps he should have some more of that ECT? Obsessionals love ECT, it's the ultimate proof that their disorder is biological, not moral, it gives them oblivion, and it punishes them for being weak-willed.

The obsessional, anankastic or obsessive-compulsive personality is common. They present in a myriad ways but it all gets back to the same core symptoms of fear, misery and a sense of being isolated and unwanted in a harsh and punitive world. Which is how they grew up. They don't want to talk about their childhoods, they believe real men should be able to pull themselves together and get over all that self-pity stuff but, of course, they can't get better until they do talk about it.

True Obsessive-Compulsive Disorder is quite different. More often female, they are completely dominated by their rituals, very often to the exclusion of a normal life. A 52yo single school teacher collected every bit of paper that came her way, from junk mail to shopping dockets, and put them in boxes to sort later. She was finally convinced to dump most of it but that took nearly two years. She had to go through each magazine to see if there was something important in it, or she had left something in it that people could use to harm her, such as her credit card number. When at last she reported that she had cleaned her house, it added up to 360 large boxes, or about 5000kg of rubbish. Her fear was that she might miss something, or lose something, or the tax department wouldn't believe her, she had no real idea. All she knew was that if she didn't put the stuff in the box, she wouldn't be able to sleep that night for worrying about it.

Obsessional cleaning is driven by fear. Some people fear catching a disease, other people fear spreading one, so they scrub and clean and wash and sterilise, except it never quite seems convincing so they start again. Then they have to do it by a ritual in case they make a mistake, then they do it twice to make sure, and so it spreads to take control of their lives. Anxiety cannot be contained by a behaviour, or a ritual, or a drug. It is the most pervasive and powerful of emotions just because it acts back on itself to reinforce itself.

Do people get over fear spontaneously? Some may, but most don't. It has to be tackled directly, but very often, that is the last thing they want. By telling them they have no control over their fear, that it's a brain disease, orthodox psychiatry reinforces their sense of helplessness and makes things worse. People become trapped in a merry-go-round of drugs, more drugs, admission to hospital, ECT, psychologists, CBT, DBT, ACT, hypnosis, meditation, mindfulness training, and so on. None of it works because it doesn't get to the core of the problem, which is a set of self-reinforcing beliefs driven by fear.

11

Drugs

"The desire to take medicine is perhaps the greatest feature that distinguishes man from animals."
Sir William Osler, 1st Baronet (1849-1919).

How big is the international drug and alcohol industry? Needless to say, nobody knows for sure but suggested figures are something like $360 billion a year for illegal drugs. The US alcohol industry alone is worth about $525 billion a year, meaning the international industry is several times larger. In all, we are talking about something like 3.5% of total world GDP. That doesn't include the damage these substances do; if we tried to factor those costs in, it would treble the figures.

Of all the drugs we consume, the bulk are drugs to control anxiety, more even than drugs to relieve pain. This is not just because drugs that control anxiety are necessarily addictive, but because overwhelming anxiety is both extremely common and intolerable. The single most common drug humans use, alcohol, is probably the most specific and most effective anti-anxiety drug available, and also the most destructive. It's not just in the Western world: in 1982, I surveyed a tiny rural village in the far south of Thailand and found that 11% of the men over eighteen were alcoholics. This was in a culture which strongly disapproves of drinking. They made their own arak from palm sugar; it was so strong it could easily catch fire. In post-Soviet Russia, alcoholism is driving the life span of men down to Third World levels. 25% of Russian men die before age 55yrs, compared with 7% in the UK, and alcohol is the biggest factor.

Any person who starts steady drinking under eighteen almost certainly requires treatment for anxiety. That's what they are doing, self-medicating with the most effective drug available. Even those who drink because of "social pressure" are simply saying "I can't say No, it makes me too anxious so I give in."

All opiates, both legal (morphine, codeine, oxycodone, fentanyl, etc) and illegal (such as heroin), are very powerful anti-anxiety drugs. They are of limited value as analgesics. With the possible exception of codeine for bone pain, you can still feel the pain, it's just that you don't care about it. That can be worse, because pain tells you what your body needs to know. Ignoring it is dangerous. There is a very large industry developing, manufacturing and marketing legal opiates but up to 90% of them are taken either for the purpose of reducing anxiety and/or treating the addiction that inevitably follows. In the US, 19,000 people a year die from the synthetic opiate oxycodone, more than heroin and cocaine combined, and more than from breast cancer. They are mostly poorly-educated, unemployed rural people. From 2007-12, the 1.84 million people in the state of West Virginia, one of the poorest in the Union, consumed no less than 780million doses of narcotics, or 433 doses for every man, woman and child. A single pharmacy in a town of 400 people sold 9million opiate tablets in just under two years. Three drug distributors made over $17billion from their share of this flood of drugs, which resulted in at least 2,000 deaths. Sued by the state attorney-general, they settled out of court. The most recent figures show that the wave of opiate addiction in the US has increased by 400% in the past six years, and is costing the nation over $500billion a year.

Like all other legal opiates, oxycodone was initially marketed as non-addictive. There's no truth in it: all opiates are addictive, partly because of their direct effect on brain chemistry (i.e. they induce a 'chemical imbalance of the brain') and partly because the anxiety that led to the addiction hasn't gone anywhere. When you sober up, it's still there, just as nasty as before but now worse because of the withdrawal effects. Illegal opiates, especially heroin, are often more dangerous because users have no idea of the purity of the stuff. Dealers typically 'cut' it, using anything from carb soda to caustic to cement dust, so surviving heroin users often end up with amputated limbs from wrecking their arteries.

The area where I live in Australia, the south-east of Queensland, doesn't have such a big opiate problem because it's the national centre for methamphetamine production and abuse. Ice, as it's called, is everywhere. I see four or five people a week who have been using the stuff. Why? They all say the same thing:

> I feel great on amphetamines, I'm ten feet tall and bullet-proof. I can do anything, go anywhere, talk to anybody. I've got confidence oozing out of every pore. That's why I like them, that's why I can't keep away.

That is, with ice, they don't feel anxious. All stimulants are extremely powerful anti-anxiety drugs although they have a wide range of other effects and aren't as specific as alcohol. They're the drug of choice for losers, drop-outs and sad cases, the bereft, the hopeless and the pathetic. Perhaps you could make a case for sipping a cognac with a cigarette in one hand being the essence of cool, but there's nothing cool about being an ice addict. Being on ice means a short, shitty life.

Marijuana is also good for anxiety but it's probably not as specific as the others. Perhaps it isn't as much fun because most people drift off, they don't want to fight or cause trouble. Should it be legalised? I've seen a lot of people who have smoked an awful lot of marijuana in their lives and they aren't in the same state as people who have had a life time of booze, or opiates, or ice. For a start, they're alive. Can it precipitate a psychotic state? I believe so. Acute panic states are not uncommon in naive smokers who get an overdose while paranoid states, with or without hallucinations, are fairly common in long-term, heavy smokers. If they stop the drugs, the paranoid ideas go away with little or no assistance from antipsychotic drugs but if they start smoking again, it all comes back.

Remember that all the rehab programs in the world will fail if they don't address the underlying anxiety that drove the user to start in the first place. It's not that difficult to get people off the drugs but keeping them off is another thing. We see this in the Alcoholics Anonymous model, where formerly addicted people go to meetings, usually several times a week, to confess. And confess. For decades. Some people are happy with this and as long as they get their weekly or even daily fix of impassioned confessional, they can struggle through life. However, they know only too well they are but a momentary slip away from oblivion and don't dare relax their guard; "Once a drunk, always a drunk," as they say. That is because the original problem that drove them to drink, anxiety, is not touched by confession. Guilt-ridden pleading doesn't do anything for anxiety, so until they turn and face that demon, they need to keep rushing to their meetings, beating their breasts and confessing. It works for some people, not for others.

That will do on the nasty drugs for self-medication of anxiety. Now we can turn to the really nasty drugs for anxiety, psychiatric drugs. But where to start? A good place is the general practitioner's surgery. After decades of brainwashing by Big Pharma, all medical practitioners now think that the correct response to a touch of the jitters, or the weepies, or the glums or off your food or aches and pains, or not happy at work, school or home, or loss of sexual interest, whatever, is to take a happy pill. There is a very large literature on this now so I won't repeat it but the real question is: How did it come about?

A book by two sociologists, Allan Horwitz and Jerome Wakefield, called *The Loss of Sadness: How psychiatry transformed normal sorrow into depressive illness* (2007), is a detailed account of how Big Pharma and its friends in academic psychiatry abolished common-or-garden sadness by convincing everybody it's actually a terrible disease called Depression. In the old days, if somebody felt sad or upset, everybody rallied around and was nice to them until they got back on their feet. Nowadays, they are rushed off to see their doctor who prescribes an antidepressant, then out into the arms of the "grief counsellors" or "trauma counsellors" who are hanging around like ambulance chasers, waiting to scoop them up. The problem is, the drugs are no good. How do we know? Because in 1991, 1% of adults in Australia took antidepressants. Now it's about 10%, yet the suicide rate keeps going up and up. It's now at a 28yr peak. That is, the more antidepressants we take, the more people kill themselves. Remember that in the original study by Doll and Hill in 1948, tobacco was first shown to be the cause of lung cancer on less evidence than this.

The drug companies will say the high suicide rate proves that people aren't taking enough antidepressants, they need more. Perhaps, but the rate of bad reactions to drugs used in depression, including suicides, just keeps rising. Between 2000-14 in the US, where no less than 13% of adults take antidepressants, the numbers of "serious outcomes" (including suicide and homicide) to drugs used to treat depression rose by 225%. In that time, the population increased by just under 15%, meaning adverse drug effects rose 1500% higher than they should have been. Clearly, something is very wrong: people are supposed to get better by taking drugs, but these figures show things are rapidly getting worse, and it's costing us a lot of money. The problem lies in what we are told about depression, and what we are told about psychiatric drugs.

First, the commonest cause by far of chronic or recurrent depression is an unsuspected anxiety state. The reason it is unsuspected is because nobody takes a proper history. Giving depressed people antidepressants may relieve some of their symptoms but it does nothing for the underlying anxiety problems. As soon as they try to stop the drugs, the anxiety problem comes roaring back. Second, practically every study designed to show the effect of antidepressants is very short, mostly six to eight weeks, yet we find people are routinely taking these drugs for 25yrs or more. The reason is that they can't get off them. Every time they try to stop, they quickly get worse. Before antidepressants came on the scene, depression was nowhere near as common as it is now. Sure, people became depressed but they got better in 4-8months and it was rare for them to have more than a few bouts.

Aha, says mainstream psychiatry, that proves that depression is a chronic, life-long illness of the brain that requires permanent treatment, just like diabetes or hypertension. No, it doesn't. It shows that the drugs are highly addictive and practically every attempt to stop them, especially abruptly, will inevitably result in a severe, prolonged and very scary withdrawal reaction. Naturally enough, the withdrawal state will be relieved by resuming the drugs, which is not the same as saying they relieve a lifelong illness. If an alcohol-dependent person stops his drug abruptly, he will certainly experience a severe, prolonged and very scary withdrawal reaction which can be relieved by a dose of alcohol. That does *not* say he has a "chemical imbalance of the brain cured by alcohol." It is the case that all psychiatric drugs, and not just the benzodiazepine group (valium, etc.), meet every definition of 'addictive.' They are *highly addictive drugs*, with a huge range of serious side effects. They should not be prescribed willy-nilly for people who are simply feeling out of sorts.

Although the drug companies fought it bitterly, it is now accepted that in the first few weeks after they are started or stopped, antidepressants cause a sudden spike in suicidal ideas and impulses. This is especially the case in children and adolescents. Peter Gotzsche, who is head of the Nordic Cochrane Centre in Copenhagen, says they are dangerous and should not be prescribed for children under any circumstances. In his book, *Deadly Psychiatry and Organised Denial* (2015), he details this in a very readable form. Psychiatric drugs, especially antidepressants, are also found in the bodies of practically every mass murderer in the US. In particular, sudden and apparently pointless crimes of violence in previously normal people are associated with changes in psychiatric drugs, either starting, increasing, reducing or stopping them. They are seriously dangerous drugs. I believe general practitioners should not be permitted to prescribe them, but I'd also add that most psychiatrists wildly over-prescribe them. Most psychiatrists give antidepressants to about 80% of more of their patients. In my practice, I see about 250 new cases a year. I would not start antidepressants more than two or three times a year, and then for short periods only. If I can manage that in my solo, working class practice, so can every other psychiatrist on earth.

Third, antidepressants aren't actually very effective (if they are so effective, why do people need to take them for life?). If you give 100 depressed people placebos (sugar pills), about 55 of them will get better. If you give another matched group antidepressants, about 64 will get better *but* they will suffer a huge raft of side effects. If, however, you give the control group what are called active placebos, i.e. a mix of harmless drugs that cause a bit of dry mouth or constipation and some drowsiness, the "success" rate of the active placebo approaches that of the antidepressants. But it's the side effects of psychotropic drugs that you have to watch. Beside powerful, long-lasting addictions, the side effects include drowsiness and poor coordination; slow reaction time; constipation and dry mouth; massive weight gain; loss of libido and, in men, impotence and loss of ejaculation; and a particularly nasty set of muscular side effects. Of these, the most common, in perhaps 60% of all people taking the drugs, is an intensely unpleasant sense of muscle tension called akathisia. This is experienced as an inability to sit or stand still (it's also Greek, for 'I can't sit down'). Patients hate this, as these comments culled from the internet show:

> Akathisia for me was an anxiety so intense and deep seated I thought I was losing my mind. I also had an inner restlessness that made me want to keep moving, keep moving...

I was just extraordinarily restless. Not in the sense that I had to get up and go do something, but in the sense that it was distressing to stay still in the same position too long. You know how if you sit in the same position for too long, after a while your joints/muscles/whatever get uncomfortable and you have to get up and stretch or walk around or at least change positions? It was like that, only a million times worse, and it happened every 30 seconds. I had to keep moving, or my brain and body just would not shut up about how it was not OK to stay still.

...the most severe anxiety-kinda feeling EVER. Panic attacks are bad—that feeling is worse. Nobody ever called it akathisia when I experienced it on *Effexor* (venlafaxine, antidepressant). It got chalked up to anxiety and "histrionic behaviour"... I could not stop moving, I felt like if I did my body would explode.... For me it also comes with a feeling of rage—I needed to scream almost as much as I need to move. I think it's just a product of the desperation I felt, though—at times I would also cry uncontrollably (but did not feel sad).

(Akathisia was) like I HAD to move, but the *Abilify* (aripiprazole, antipsychotic) had made me fatigued as well so I was in this horrible in-between state that was driving me insane. My doc said that people have actually killed themselves over it because they couldn't describe what was going on with them and get so upset and frustrated they kill themselves. I could NOT get comfortable anywhere, no matter what. I had trouble sleeping, I couldn't stop moving, I needed to move.

I am just coming down off severe akathesia from *Remeron* (mirtazepine, antidepressant). I was pacing back and forth and up and down stairs from 5am to midnight two days ago. It felt like I'd had 18 shots of espresso. Worst experience of my life. Emotionally, I flipped back and forth from extreme anxiety (just want to die because the world is ending and you're losing your mind simultaneously) to a giddy, silly, hypomanic-type mood.

When I had it the first time, it was mainly physical. I had no idea what it was and my psychiatrist said it was mania. It wasn't though. It was sit down, stand up, try to lie down, pop back up, pace, sit etc. Once I shoved myself around the living room on an office chair with loud music on. I recommend that. That would have been *Seroquel* or *Abilify* or both (quetiapine and aripiprazole, antipsychotics). Next time it was *Abilify* withdrawal/ discontinuation and it was more mental, as in dread, grim, doom, and the the constant refrain in my head "I can't take this another minute." By then I knew what it was, not that it helped anyway.

It is often described as "torture" and when non-psychotic people are given these drugs, this is what they remember. About 25yrs ago, a psychiatrist convinced a number of perfectly healthy people to take a single dose of the antipsychotic drug, risperidone. One of them was Richard Bentall, a well-known research psychologist. He described it as an appalling and frightening experience, mostly due to the akathisia. Almost certainly, it is this sense of insane agitation that causes people to make sudden, unexpected attempts on their lives, very often successful because nobody was expecting it, or murder. A psychiatrist I know had to fly to the UK but he can't sleep on planes so he took 50mg or chlorpromazine (*Largactil, Thorazine*). He got no sleep on the flight but couldn't wake for two days after it. He described it as the worst experience of his life and swore he would never repeat it. In those days, people were routinely given up to 1200mg of chlorpromazine a day.

In 2006 in North Carolina, David Crespi, a perfectly respectable manager in his forties, was prescribed a cocktail of antidepressants and other drugs for what was essentially an anxiety problem. Shortly after, and without the slightest prior indication, he murdered his twin five year old daughters by stabbing them to death. The drugs have to be implicated, especially as this is just one of an ever-increasing list of inexplicable crimes and suicides associated with psychotropic drugs. David Carmichael of Canada had a similar experience, murdering his eleven year old son a few weeks after he started an antidepressant. However, it is all but impossible to get modern psychiatrists to take it seriously. If a patient is commenced on a drug and reports feeling agitated, he will be given more and more drugs in every increasing doses, as David Crespi was. Orthodox psychiatrists simply do not believe that their drugs can possibly make things worse.

There is a variant of akathisia which comes on while taking the drugs, either when the dose is increasing or decreasing, but which persists for many months or years after it has stopped. I have a 21yo male patient at present who has this form. He was using methamphetamine from age 14yrs and developed a paranoid psychotic state which persisted after he stopped the amphetamines. He is quite small, perhaps 62kg. He was prescribed the antipsychotic drug, quetiapine (*Seroquel*), but soon became agitated, so the dose was increased. And increased. Eventually, he was taking 900mg per day, a very large dose for somebody his size. Two years after it was stopped, he is still unable to sit or stand still for more than about two seconds. He moves constantly, jerking and twitching to the point that he has trouble walking down stairs. It has improved slightly with treatment but it may last for the rest of his life.

Almost invariably, people who develop akathisia are *not* seen as having a predictable side effect of a powerful psychoactive drug. Instead, they are labelled "mentally ill" and are given bigger doses, then more and more drugs, until they are barely able to move but the inner torment continues unabated. In general, psychiatrists do not accept that their drugs have significant side effects. If anything goes wrong or a patient complains about drug effects, it's not the drug that caused it but the patient's *disease*. What he needs is more of the same but for most of these side effects, the correct management is reducing the drug, not increasing it.

Another severe side effect is called tardive dyskinesia, which simply means a movement disorder that comes on fairly late. It consists of a variety of involuntary movements affecting the hands and legs but especially the lips, jaw and tongue. I see a 42yo woman who is affected after about eight years on antidepressants and quetiapine (Seroquel). Was she ever psychotic? No, that has never been an issue. She was prescribed a large dose of quetiapine, 400mg each night, which is a dose for schizophrenia, because she couldn't sleep. Why could she not sleep? Because she had this awful, crawling itching tension in her legs that made her want to keep moving, otherwise known as akathisia. She now shows a variety of quite grotesque smacking, licking and chewing movements of her mouth and tongue, and sinuous writhing or jerking of her hands and limbs. Tardive dyskinesia has been known for a long time: it was well-known in the early 1970s, but was thought to be more likely to affect older people. Now, as more and more people take increasing numbers of psychotropic drugs in ever larger doses for longer and longer, it is becoming more common and affecting younger people. There is no treatment.

Let's go back to the one of the most common side effects of these drugs, repression of sex life. This is very real. Practically all psychiatric drugs have a powerful inhibitory effect on libido or sexual interest in men and women. This is possibly via their effect in increasing the hormone prolactin, but that's not important. They have further effects on men, by causing impotence (inability to gain or maintain an erection), anorgasmia (loss of sensation of orgasm) and failure of ejaculation. This is a direct, drug-related effect. It starts within a day or two of commencing the drugs, is profound, does not wear off while they are taken, and can last long after the drugs are stopped, sometimes years. All psychiatric drugs can do it although some are worse than others.

The best figures available for Australia suggest that, in men, there will be one successful suicide in about every two hundred cases of depression. Let's assume that antidepressants are fairly effective (not a very good assumption, as we have seen) and will relieve 130 of those cases of depression, thereby preventing any possible suicides in those men. This suggests they can prevent, at most, one suicide in every three hundred treated cases of male depression. If you were to take any three hundred depressed younger men, a highly significant risk group for suicide, and tell them they should all have antidepressants in order to stop one suicide, they may agree that it's a fair deal. But then you give them the list of side effects:

> "OK fellows, there's three hundred of you and if we do nothing, it's likely that one of you will be dead by the end of the year. So we're going to put all of you on antidepressants to keep that one bloke

alive. Unfortunately, at least 298 of you will lose most or all of your sexual function. You won't be interested, you won't be able to get it up, it will feel about as exciting as sucking your finger and tough luck if you wanted a child, it probably won't happen. By the way, once you start antidepressants, it's very difficult to stop them so you may need to take them for life. Even if you do manage to get off them, there's no guarantee John Thomas will come back to life so some of you will be permanently asexual. But it's not all bad, think of all the money you'll save on nappies. And as you'll soon find out, antidepressants commonly cause massive weight gain so you probably won't be able to see your willie again. This means that because you won't get reminders from seeing it, you'll adjust to life as a eunuch without too much anguish."

I know exactly what they would say:

"You're for real? Well you can stick your drugs right up your arse, we'll take our chances."

And why shouldn't they? Wrecking people's lives on the off-chance it may save somebody else's life is ethically unjustifiable.

If you tell people the side effects of psychiatric drugs before prescribing them, as I do, 95-98% will refuse to take them. The remaining few per cent will take them because they want the oblivion the drugs promise. However, all too often they find they have swapped one sort of inner torture for another, which has a lot to do with why so many people who are taking antidepressants and other psychiatric drugs commit suicide.

Aggression

It's not called the 'flight or fight response' for nothing. Fear and rage arise from essentially the same physiological basis. What scares you may infuriate me, and vice versa. Or what scares me today may incense me tomorrow. Your response to a particular event, or thought, or reminder etc. depends on the high-speed interaction of dozens, if not hundreds of mental variables, so it's all a bit unpredictable. But plenty of people habitually flip their fear into anger, using aggression to 'boil off' their agitation. The only problem is that it usually makes things very much worse. It's fair to say that anybody who is habitually angry or aggressive has an underlying anxiety state, and will respond to standard treatment. A lot of people like being angry so they may not thank you for it, but they'll respond.

It's also fair to say that angry people rarely volunteer for treatment. Very few of them see that they have a problem, it's always somebody else's fault. If and when they arrive at the psychiatrist's office, it's usually because they're in trouble of some sort. Mostly, it's serious. An aggressive person will inevitably be labelled a psychopath but remember: Every psychopath has a story to tell. Most of their stories aren't pleasant. People become psychopaths for a reason, called surviving. It is the psychiatrist's job to find that reason, not to pass judgement.

Case 12.1: Brendan McC, failed criminal.

Brendan McC is a 31yo single unemployed man, recently released from prison for a botched armed robbery of a chemist shop. Just before closing time or a rainy night, he ran inside with a stocking over his head, reached into his bag and found he had forgotten his knife. In the drama, he grabbed a packet of oral contraceptives and ran out, only to slip on the wet street and twist his ankle badly. The chemist's assistant followed him at some distance as he hobbled up the street, and called the police who found him hiding behind a rubbish bin in the rain, crying (people sometimes accuse me of exaggerating but I don't need to).

When he was referred, he was taking pregabalin 600mg per day for nerve pain from a head injury (*Lyrica*, anticonvulsant used for neurogenic pain); tramadol 400mg per day (narcotic) for back pain; and quetiapine 300mg (*Seroquel*, antipsychotic) at night, commenced in the prison as a hypnotic. He was also taking *Suboxone*, a mixture of the narcotic buprenorphine and the narcotic antagonist, naloxone, as a reduction program for his narcotic addiction. Just before he was released from prison, he had been found to be positive for Hepatitis C, which he had acquired in prison from using dirty needles.

Presenting complaints:

In general, he was feeling terrible. His sleep was poor. He went to bed by about 8.30pm but, even with the quetiapine, was taking about two hours to get to sleep. His sleep was broken by bad dreams and he often woke in a panic. He finally woke at about 5.00am feeling very groggy from the tablets. His appetite was poor but he had gained about 30kg in 18months from the quetiapine. He had very little energy, interest or motivation and was physically inactive. He had no social life, he didn't want to see anybody as he couldn't mix, and had no sexual interest or performance.

His memory and concentration were very poor and he had trouble thinking clearly, becoming confused under even slight pressure, including interviews. He had trouble making decisions and almost always put them off, which made things worse. Most of the time, he wasn't sure what he was thinking about, usually all the troubles in his life. There were no disturbances of perception apart from bad dreams that persisted after he woke at night.

He described his mood as "really bad, hopeless." He was feeling low and miserable practically all of the time but quickly added that he was not suicidal: "I'm pro living life but I'm living it sadly." The unhappiness was due to feeling sick from the hepatitis and groggy all the time from the tablets and ceaseless worry about going back to prison. He never experienced bouts of elevated mood. Asked about bouts of agitation, he began to cry, saying that he was constantly in fear while in prison. When agitated, he was shaky, sweaty and his heart raced wildly. His stomach churned and he was likely to vomit. He was short of breath, his mouth was dry and he stammered and couldn't get his words out. He felt light-headed and his head went blank and he was unable to think or make decisions. He had the feeling of walls closing in and feeling trapped, and that he was some-how different from everybody else. He was having several bouts like this each week but it later became clear he was having half a dozen or more per day, lasting an hour each. When agitated, he would either start screaming and threatening people around him, although he very rarely got into fights, or he would run off to hide and start crying.

Asked what frightened him, he replied: "People." He was scared of the dark, confined spaces and also had what he said was a phobia of masks and mannequins. He was frightened in crowds and standing in queues and was completely unable to speak in public, including in court, so he usually pleaded guilty to get out of the place. In prison, he often wouldn't eat as he couldn't stand in the queue for his meals. He was very fearful of appointments and interviews, any tests or exams, and of meeting strangers. If anybody threatened him or gave any sort of criticism, he was instantly infuriated unless it was police or prison officers, when he would become so agitated he would start to cry. If there were any sort of argument or dispute nearby, he had to get away otherwise he would become agitated and get involved, usually to his detriment. He couldn't say No to people without feeling intensely guilty, and either gave in or became enraged. He hated letting people down, causing trouble or giving offence, except when he was screaming at people. He was very frightened of loneliness, humiliation and disapproval, and was terrified of making mistakes or failing at anything. He feared going crazy and getting locked up, and was very frightened of police and anybody in authority, drunks, junkies, and any aggressive people.

When he was out among people, he had the very strong feeling that people were looking at him and talking behind his back, judging him and generally disapproving. If anybody laughed near him, he felt they were laughing at him. He often felt in danger or that people were picking on him, including police and prison officers, to amuse themselves. He had a strong sense of people watching him and spying on him, that he was under surveillance, and often worried that his phone was bugged to find evidence that he was dealing in drugs. He had a vague sense of people plotting or conspiring about him, spreading lies and stories and holding information back. There were no obsessive-compulsive features.

Physically, he was obese, with pitting oedema reaching to both knees. He had an infected home-made tattoo on his left leg and his right ankle was splinted.

Personal background:

His family life was terrible. He was born and raised in a country town. His father had been diagnosed as a chronic paranoid schizophrenic but he drank heavily and used a lot of amphetamines and other drugs. He dealt in drugs and had a long police record. He was exceptionally violent, such as once chasing his children with a loaded shotgun. His mother also drank but she worked as a barmaid so she was away most nights and weekends. He was sure she was "on the job" for the truckies. He was the youngest of three children. He had an older sister whom he described as a "drug-fucked whore and liar" and a brother whom he thought worked in a distant mining town and had nothing to do with the family. He hadn't seen any of them for about fifteen years. Brendan's parents separated when he was aged 13yrs. The next year, he ran away and lived on the streets until he first went to prison at eighteen.

He went to school until age 13yrs, when his parents separated and his mother didn't try to make him go. He passed only Year 8 but his marks were "hopeless." He didn't get on with anybody. Quite proudly, he said he made it his goal to make a teacher cry every day. He didn't get on with the other children as he was very shy and nervous and was always fighting. He didn't play any sport and couldn't recall any interests. From about age ten, he was smoking marijuana and selling it to high school children. He missed a lot of school as he was always in trouble but welfare were never involved. Often, he left school and went to a weir not far from his home to smoke but there were "a lot of weirdos" there. He said he was once sexually assaulted by a policeman who had found him in the bush by the weir. By age sixteen, he was fully enmeshed in the squalid end of the drug scene and by eighteen, he was in prison. He had a long record of drug-related offences, generally at the minor and dumb end of the scale. He said he had had two children by a drug-user but had lost contact with them while in prison.

Self-assessment:

He described himself as "nervous, awkward, a mess." He was generally withdrawn and unassertive until pushed, then he exploded in rage. He was intensely bothered by guilt, shame and self-consciousness and was highly suspicious and mistrustful of people. He was very impatient and excessively tidy, which regularly caused friction when he had to live with other men. He could not mix with people but hated being alone, was intensely jealous of any friends or girlfriends and never forgave an insult. He could follow rules in prison but generally looked for ways around them. He didn't trust anybody in authority but generally tried to keep the peace. He said his temper was "not very bad," his intellect was "capable" but his self-esteem was "real low."

Mental state examination:

The mental state showed an overweight but still fairly fit looking chap of stated age, of average height and with surprisingly small and delicate hands. He had wavy light brown hair, blue eyes and was generally quite good-looking but was covered in tattoos, including some on his face. He was wary and guarded, agitated and unhappy and was weepy several times, pleading for assistance. There were no psychotic features and he appeared to be of bright normal intellectual ability.

He was what we would once have called an "inadequate psychopathic personality." Every psychopath has a history but they won't volunteer it. The core of his disorder was his abysmally poor self-esteem, which led to the explosive interpersonal anxiety, which he tried to control with drugs.

The next two vignettes are cases I saw this week. These are the unedited letters I sent to the referring doctors. The first had been diagnosed as "bipolar disorder" and had been prescribed a range of antipsychotic and anticonvulsant drugs, which he hated because they caused massive weight gain and ruined his sex life.

Case 12.2: David L, aged 38yrs.

Thank you for referring this 38yo unemployed pensioner who is presently homeless and living in a shed on his cousin's property. Some years ago, he was diagnosed with "bipolar disorder and others" and is still taking quetiapine 300mg. In general, he feels very poor. His sleep is solid with the tablets but he wakes feeling groggy and hungover. His appetite is excessive and he feels unable to stop eating. He is gaining weight as he has little energy and doesn't exercise. He has very little interest or motivation, doesn't want to mix with people and has practically no sexual interest. He feels his memory and concentration are patchy, and he has trouble thinking clearly as he becomes intensely agitated under the slightest pressure. He feels low and miserable most of the time but is not suicidal. He never experiences elevated moods but he has frequent bouts of intense agitation, with many somatic symptoms of anxiety, during which he yells, throws things and gets into fights. He has an extremely long list of fears, mainly social in nature, and is self-conscious but not frankly paranoid. He has been this way all his life and has been prescribed a variety of drugs but feels they haven't helped.

His family background in rural areas was very poor. His parents separated when he was aged 13yrs as his father drank heavily and was very bad-tempered. His mother is nervous and bad-tempered and has taken tablets for years. He has two younger siblings who appear to be doing reasonably well in life but they don't have much to do with him. He did very poorly at school and was smoking weed and drinking from age 13yrs. He was always in trouble for fighting at school and at home. At 14yrs, he left home and hung around, dealing in dope and later using amphetamines and heroin. At 18, he was injured in a accident in which his only friend, the driver, was killed but he still feels very guilty about this. Because of his mental symptoms, he has hardly ever worked in his life. He had a de facto relationship from 23-37yrs and has two children but he has lost contact with them. He drinks erratically, uses methamphetamine intermittently, and had a long police record.

His self-assessment indicated severe difficulties with anxiety, trust and jealousy. He said he doesn't get on with authority, is bad-tempered, of limited intellect and has no self-esteem. The mental state showed an overweight, stocky chap of stated age with old acne scars and many tattoos. He was in clean casual clothes and was generally wary, edgy and defensive. There were no psychotic features and he is of dull average intellect.

His list of fears was: confined spaces; sudden noises and being touched unexpectedly; firearms and knives; big dogs, snakes, spiders, scorpions, centipedes etc; crowds, queues, public speaking; tests and exams; public transport, meeting strangers and talking on phones; threats, criticism, arguments, disputes, confrontation and saying No to people; letting people down, causing trouble and giving offence; loneliness, humiliation and disapproval; making mistakes and failing at anything (his worst fears); illness, disability, death and mental illness; hospitals and dentists; police, military personnel; coloured people or foreigners of any sort; bikies, drunks, junkies, teenage gangs and all aggressive people or anybody in authority.

What this means is that he can hardly move from his bed without bumping into something that will terrify him and provoke another attack of panic. He does not suffer "bipolar disorder" but his anxious personality disorder generates frequent bouts of agitation, interspersed with bouts of depression. Depression is a reaction to life events, and he had enough adverse life events to keep anybody depressed.

I do not know why people who have never shown psychotic symptoms are put on antipsychotics but it seems to be de rigueur in public mental health systems, especially in prisons (it may have something to do with the fact that patients and prisoners who sleep heavily cause less trouble). The quetiapine meant that this man had no energy but also had an insatiable appetite, leading to massive weight gain. He sat around the place, bored and unable to do anything due to being hungover, with no sexual function, eating and gaining weight, which reduced his desire to exercise, made him more self-conscious and miserable, more withdrawn, and therefore led the psychiatrist to prescribe more drugs that cause weight gain. The whole thing is self-reinforcing.

Case 12.3: Brett L, aged 28yrs.

Thank you for referring this 28yo single unemployed man who was recently released from prison and is scared of being sent back as he has pending trafficking charges. While in prison, he was seen by forensic mental health services but was not prescribed medication, which is most unusual for them. At present, he feels very bad, with poor sleep, loss of appetite, energy, interest and motivation, and no sexual interest. He has trouble thinking clearly as mostly he has too many thoughts tumbling through his head. He feels low and miserable most of the time, with some suicidal ideas, and never feels good. The main problem is severe anxiety with frequent bouts of intense agitation, secondary to a very long list of social fears. He is highly self-conscious, and decidedly paranoid about police and junkies, although this has settled somewhat since he stopped using methamphetamine. He has been this way most of his life but has not had any sort of regular treatment.

HIs family background was poor. His father was a bad-tempered, gambling pothead and they have no contact, while his mother was seriously disabled by anxiety. He is the youngest of five siblings, several of whom are using drugs. He passed only Year 10 at school and was often in trouble so he wagged school because he was "too anxious." He didn't get on with anybody and his home life was miserable. From about 16yrs, he was using and dealing in weed. He has had a number of jobs, mainly removals, but lost his job last year for "attitude" and can't handle job interviews in order to get another. Socially, he has always been single but he has a girlfriend, currently in prison on a drug charge. Until recently, he was drinking a litre of spirits a night then began using ice. He used to gamble a lot but, surprisingly, he has only a minor police record.

He sees himself as "no good, can't even look in a mirror." He is intensely nervous, prickly, and bothered by guilt and self-consciousness. He is highly mistrustful, impatient, jealous and can't mix with people unless intoxicated. His temper is "real bad," his intellect is "average" and his self-esteem is "real shit." The mental state showed a fairly tall, overweight chap in drab clothes and with many tattoos. He was distressed and agitated and close to tears. He was neither hostile nor suspicious and showed no psychotic features. He appears to be of average intellect but is educated below his potential.

Brett's list of fears included: confined spaces; firearms; crowds, queues and public speaking; interviews and appointments, tests and exams; public transport and meeting strangers; threats and criticism, arguments and disputes; saying No to people; letting people down, causing trouble or giving offence; loneliness and humiliation; making mistakes or failing at anything; death and mental illness; hospitals, especially psychiatric hospitals; police and military; drunks, gangs and aggressive people. He felt he could manage authority reasonably well by being polite. In his appointments, he is always polite and distant but clearly in a hurry to get out of the room and go home.

As always, high performance anxiety is related to low self-esteem. The problem is: terrible childhood leads to anxious personality, which leads to drug and alcohol abuse, violent outbursts and criminality. These are the men who commit suicide early. They are not the people who are engaged by orthodox psychiatry, which can't get beyond the fact that they're naughty, tattooed, smelly and not courteous. But that's a matter of psychiatry's endless problem with narcissism. Its own narcissism.

Don't make the mistake of thinking that aggression is purely a male indulgence. There are almost as many aggressive women out there as men, but they tend to be more subtle. This one wasn't, as the letter to her GP shows.

Case 12.4: Kerryn B.

Thank you for referring this 30yo single mother who said her family and friends want her assessed because of her bad temper and "mood swings." She attended with her younger half-brother who confirmed her story. She has previously seen a psychologist but is taking no medication. At present, she feels reasonable but her sleep is quite erratic. Her appetite is steady and she is physically active but her levels of interest and motivation vary greatly, depending on how she is feeling. Socially, she doesn't mix well. She has no real problems with memory and concentration but often has trouble thinking clearly as she becomes flustered in company. She tends to avoid decisions or make them very impulsively, then regret them.

She feels low and miserable about half the time and sometimes feels death would be a relief but is not actively suicidal. She has brief bouts of feeling good when she is cheerful and talkative but these last minutes, not hours. The main problem is frequent bouts of intense agitation with many somatic symptoms of anxiety, secondary to a long list of social fears. After even trivial upsets, she becomes very angry, yells and throws things. These moods last for hours each day, sometimes extending for days on end. She is highly self-conscious and worries that an ex-partner spreads lies about her but there were no other paranoid ideas. There were no obsessive-compulsive features. She has been this way all her life but feels things are steadily getting worse.

Her family background was very unsettled as her parents separated when she was seven. She was raised by her mother, a severely disturbed alcoholic who had streams of violent, drunken men in her life. Fortunately, her father kept regular contact with her and he remains supportive. She has a 32yo brother who is professionally qualified but he tends to keep his distance from the family. There were numerous half- and step-siblings along the way, most of whom are in various sorts of trouble although the young man who attended with her works as a miner and presented very well. She didn't do well at school as she was smoking marijuana early and often wagged school. Because her mother was usually drunk, she exerted no restraint at home and Kerryn did as she pleased. She left school at age 16yrs, having passed only Year 10. Since then she had a variety of unskilled jobs but she usually leaves as she gets bored. She has had half a dozen relationships and three children by different men but their fathers keep in touch. She used methamphetamine on and off for 11yrs and tends to drink in binges. She has a police record for assault and the police have taken a number of domestic violence orders against her.

She sees herself as "bubbly and erratic." She feels she is nervous, unassertive and bothered by guilt and self-consciousness. She is overtrusting but also very jealous, untidy, impatient and very bad-tempered. She likes company but argues with "anybody" and holds grudges. Her intellect is "a bit above average" and her self-esteem is "below average." The mental state showed a fit and healthy young woman, neatly dressed in office-type clothing (she had come from a job interview) with a generally abrupt and masculine manner. She was talkative and not anxious, depressed, hostile or suspicious. There were no psychotic features and she is of superior intellect, meaning she is educated well-below her limits.

Kerryn had a huge list of performance fears, meaning she was easily agitated by how she was performing and how people were judging her. As is common with people raised in chaotic households, she was rigidly obsessional and demanding in her attention to cleanliness, tidiness, order, punctuality and efficiency, which caused endless arguments. Whenever she became aroused, she would start screaming and punch into the nearest man, which meant that they didn't stick around long, unless they were police who were never terribly impressed by her pugilism.

Case 12.5: Dr Cory V, aged 34yrs.

This man would never have seen a psychiatrist without the most intense pressure. A medical practitioner, he was referred for assessment by his medical defence lawyer after his ex-wife complained to the Medical Board that he was "psychotic and dangerous." They had separated about eighteen months before and were locked in a bitter divorce case. He was working full-time in a solo practice in a small country town and was not taking any medication.

His appearance was quite striking. He was Eurasian, of above average height and of lean, muscular build, with olive complexion and neatly trimmed dark hair and beard. He was dressed in carefully pressed office clothing with polished shoes. From the moment he entered the room, he conveyed an air of barely repressed menace. He was tense and unsmiling, his dark eyes very alert and observant, and sat on his chair as though ready to spring into action. It was nearly half an hour before he allowed himself to glance out the window. He spoke precisely with an extensive vocabulary but with a common accent, swearing as a normal part of speech, which is how the military speak. Because that's what he was, ex-Army.

Parts of his history are taken directly from the report to his solicitors. If it sounds vaguely familiar, it is because of the close parallels with Sgt Michael B in Chapter 10. The syndrome is very familiar to anybody who deals with country people.

Presenting complaints.

In general, he feels terrible. With regard to vegetative functions and appetites, he sleeps very poorly. He rarely goes to bed before about 2.30am as he feels wide awake until then. He gets to sleep in half an hour but has to wake at 6.00am to go to work. While on holiday, he has been sleeping for an extra hour or two at most. He sleeps solidly but is bothered by frequent bad dreams, mostly relating to experiences during military service. Often, he wakes drenched in sweat. He wakes with an alarm, feeling tired and washed out, but doesn't take naps by day. His appetite is quite poor and he has lost a little weight recently. He has little energy and his activity level is now low. He goes to gym and spends half an hour on a basic routine but does very little else. He doesn't play sport or take any other regular exercise. He has little interest either in his private life or at work and has no motivation to do things. In his private life, he actively avoids social contact with people while at work, he says as little as possible and doesn't mix with the other staff. His sexual interest is quite poor.

He feels his memory is reasonable but he has trouble concentrating in that his mind wanders from his tasks. Where possible, he delays decisions as he doubts his ability to make correct choices. This is now becoming normal for him although he doesn't like it. He has trouble thinking clearly in that he becomes confused and flustered under any sort of pressure or when he is feeling irritable. The thought content is dominated by his many worries, including a fear of sleeping, and his irritability at home and at work. There were no true disturbances of perception although if he has to move in a crowd, he starts to feel somebody may be armed and about to attack him. Specifically, there were no first rank symptoms of psychosis or other disturbances of contact with reality.

He described his mood as "bad." He feels low and miserable most of the time. At present, this is "pretty bad" meaning he is sick of things as they are and feels the need for a major change in life but he is not sick of life itself. He was quick to emphasise that he is not suicidal. While on holiday recently, he felt a lot worse and reluctantly admitted that suicidal ideas had bothered him so he was relieved to get back to work. The unhappiness is due to his inability to control his irritability. He has not experienced any bouts of elevated mood.

He experiences frequent bouts of intense agitation during which his heart races violently, he has an unpleasant "butterflies" sensation in the stomach, his palms are sweaty and he may shake a little in his hands. He is short of breath and a little light-headed, and has a tight sensation in his throat. He may stammer and has trouble expressing himself. He feels the walls are closing in and he feels trapped and has to get away. During these attacks, he feels frightened and angry. Depending on where he is, he either goes completely quiet and doesn't talk to anybody, or he will try to get away by himself and keep quiet until it passes. If there is nobody around, he may yell and punch or kick things. He has four to five bouts a day, mostly lasting about fifteen minutes but if he is unable to escape, they can last several hours. These prolonged bouts of agitation leave him feeling completely exhausted and hopeless and he often feels he would be better off dead than endure them. They are caused by minor upsets or pressures, by crowds or by the smell of smoke or putrefaction. In particular, he is agitated by any official dealings, such as with the Medical Board or the divorce case.

On questioning, he never feels safe in the city, and is fearful of crowds, queues and public speaking. He avoids public transport or aircraft because he feels trapped and is bothered by the crowds. He is quickly agitated by arguments or disputes, and by the thought of letting people down, causing trouble or giving offence. He is fearful of loneliness, humiliation and disapproval but, most of all, by making mistakes or failing at anything, even if nobody else knows about it. He is frightened by the thought of illness, disability and being dependent on people, and fears mental illness. He is becoming increasingly fearful of people with power or authority, such as police or the Medical Board.

When he is out, he has a very strong sense that people are looking at him and talking behind his back, spreading gossip. This includes all people who know him but also complete strangers, and is strong enough to make him stop what he is doing and go home. He has a very strong sense of people judging him and a strong sense of danger directed at him, especially by his ex-wife's family and friends. He has the strong feeling that they have him under some sort of surveillance and he is quite sure that she conspires with various relatives and people such as lawyers or health officials to push him into killing himself. He has an intense sense of stigma over being labelled mentally disordered, and worries how medical people criticise any colleague who admits to mental problems.

He constantly checks doors, locks, keys, or his phone, wallet and other belongings and will repeat it even if he knows he has just done it. At work, he is renowned for his fastidious approach to every problem, no matter how small. He is very fussy about cleanliness, tidiness, order, punctuality and efficiency. This regularly gets him into arguments as he expects everybody else to keep to his standards. This was a major problem in the marriage. He is ritualistic in the way he likes things ordered and becomes very annoyed if any of his belongings are moved. He has constant intrusive thoughts of needing to check things and is aware that his thoughts of danger are unrealistic but he cannot resist them. Physically, he is healthy but feels tired and run down.

At this stage, he pointed out that his mental symptoms were accepted as due to military service, which I knew anyway, but he had refused psychiatric treatment because he feared he would be detained and given ECT against his will. Even though his accepted disability was "Adjustment Disorder with Anxious and Depressed Mood, Borderline Personality Disorder," he was referred to a PTSD course run by a well-known A-list psychiatrist at a prodigiously expensive private hospital. This was planned for five weeks but he didn't finish the first day. Asked what had happened, he gazed blankly into space for a long moment, grinding his teeth and clenching his fists, then launched into a bitter tirade against psychiatrists. After a minute, sweaty, pale and trembling, he paused for breath and stared at me in utter contempt:

> "So I suppose I've just fucked my career, have I? You're probably shitting yourself, reaching for the alarm button, calling your goons to get me banged up with all the fucking loonies in that shitheap hospital."

I explained that I don't have an alarm button in my office, there were no security guards, that the door was unlocked and he was free to leave and come back another time if he wished.

> "Yeah?" he sneered. "And then you'll charge me double to pay for your new Mercedes."
>
> "Your medical defence fund is paying but it's a set fee regardless of how long it takes. And I drive a ten year old diesel Patrol."
>
> "What sorta dumb fucker are you," he scoffed in real disgust, "driving a shitheap like that? Alright, let's get on with the pantomime but I'll tell you now, I will not go into a fucking nuthouse, private or public. And don't ever, ever make the mistake of signing one of those orders to give me ECT. I know it fucks your memory but I won't forget that."
>
> "I hardly ever admit people to hospital and I don't use ECT. I'm here to work with you, not against you, but my report has to be neutral."
>
> "Well that's a fucking change, did you fail shrink school? Sorry, I take that back. Let's get on with it."

Recent History.

He married at the age of twenty-three, while still in his final year as a medical student. His wife was a year older and had just completed her training as a physiotherapist. She came from a well-known and wealthy city family whereas he was a poor student from the far north, living in a room under a friend's house and supporting himself by working as a security guard at nightclubs. They moved into a city unit owned by her family but almost from the beginning, the marriage was tempestuous. In the first twelve months, his wife left him several times to go back to her family.

By the time he was twenty-five, they had two children. He was working very long hours in the hospitals as he wanted to specialise in surgery but he wasn't earning much. His wife insisted on opening her own practice, which they couldn't afford, so she borrowed a large sum of money without telling him. She had absolutely no business sense and the bank closed the practice within the year. The only way he could survive financially was by enlisting in the Army, which meant he could not continue with specialist training. Over the next six years, he served overseas twice, not least because he desperately needed the extra money.

Gradually, it emerged that his wife was having affairs, sometimes two at once, and it was quite possible that the second child wasn't his but he refused genetic testing. He became more and more agitated, arguing ferociously with anybody and everybody, especially with her family who openly wanted her to leave him. Eventually, he was referred to a psychiatrist for assessment of his suitability for military service. After what he insisted was a twenty minute interview, he was given the two diagnoses and was quickly discharged. Bitterly angry, blackly depressed and completely isolated, he saw no option but to take over a country practice as the quickest way to make some money and get out of his financial hole. His wife refused to leave the city. Funded by her family, she went to a large and expensive law firm who launched a flood of legal suits which he couldn't possibly defend as he had no money.

One of the suits alleged that he was severely mentally ill and included quotes from his military medical file, which he had made sure she had never seen. Enraged, he rang the law firm and accused them of stealing his file. It was his good luck that he spoke to a very junior lawyer, who mistakenly told him that his wife had provided the reports. Next time his wife called, which she did regularly to demand this or that, he accused her of using one of her many military boyfriends to access his file and threatened mayhem if she tried anything like that again. Apparently on advice from her lawyers, she reported him to the Medical Board as "psychotic, delusional, paranoid and dangerous." Two months later, he came into my office like a hunted animal.

Family background:

He was born in the far north of the state and raised on a small farm in the foothills on the outskirts of a sugar town. His father, a disabled Vietnam veteran, had died some years before after a lifetime of heavy drinking and drug use. His mother, who was from Chiengmai in northern Thailand, had worked as a barmaid most of his life so she was rarely home at night. The farm was only about 30 acres so it wasn't enough to support them and they mainly survived on his father's military pension. He always knew that his mother sent money back to her family in Thailand, which caused ferocious arguments. His father was about forty when he was born and was in chronic pain from a back injury. He couldn't do much on the land so the house and property were very run down. He spent most of his time sitting on the veranda, drinking the beer he brewed or smoking the marijuana he grew and listening to the races.

What was he like as a person?
He was an evil shit. None of us went to his funeral, I don't know if anybody did.
Your mother?
She was overseas. She was always flitting back and forth. She got the land, it was worth quite a lot of money by then so she could go home and live like a queen.
Was he bad-tempered?
Ah mate, you got no idea. He was the most foul-tempered shit you can imagine. We were all absolutely terrified of him. He used to belt the living shit out of me. It wasn't as if you could run away, he'd pretend he'd forgotten, he'd wait until you had to come inside and then he'd strike. We all lived in fear. It might be days later, you'd be having breakfast and then he'd come up behind and grab you. I think he did forget, he was always shitfaced on something, then he'd see you and suddenly remember he owed you a belting and so you'd get it. He used to get morphine from his GP like you'd give out acid drops, they were all around the house, you'd find bottles of them everywhere. And benzos, all the addictive ones, he had them as well. I know he sold half of them to the neighbors. He had all this money coming in from drugs and dope but we never had a penny to our names.
And your mother, what was she like?
She was never there. She was leaving as we were getting home from school, she'd be home long after we went to bed. She always worked weekends, it was good money.

Did she protect you? Was she any help?

No. Nothing. I don't know why... I mean, I don't want to talk about it. What's done is done, it is as it is. OK, I always knew she was only there because she wanted the land. She was twenty years younger, only nineteen when I was born. She wouldn't do anything or say anything that he could use in a divorce. She got the money in the end, it was the most important thing in her life, nothing mattered to her but that.

Not her children?

Definitely not her children.

Cory was the eldest of four children. There were two sisters after him, then his younger brother. From about the age of nine, he looked after them. He gave them their meals at night, washed up, made sure they had their baths and went to bed, all without upsetting their father who was propped stuporose in front of the television in the next room. In the early days, his mother made breakfast and got them off to school but as the years went by, he took over that as she got home very late and slept in.

But what was she actually like as a person?

I can't really say, she was more like a servant who came and went. She wasn't a mother to us. I'm not saying she was bad, she was just nothing. I'd say she was terrified of my father, she just tried to live her life around him. It's as though we were somebody else's children, like she was the housekeeper he employed after his real wife had died.

She's from Chiengmai? They're very good looking people.

You know that? She is, she was. Quite tall for an Asian, she looked after herself, spent a fortune on makeup and her hair, hours getting ready for work.

So what did they think of her when she opened the bar each night?

It was a small town, what do you think they thought? She was on the job, I'm sure, she often got home at dawn.

Are you in contact with her?

Every now and then, when she wants something.

So what happened with your wedding, did they come?

You've got to be joking, they weren't invited. None of my family were there, the in-laws would have chucked them out if they'd shown up. What a joke, one day I'll be able to laugh about that.

That's pretty strange, surely your in-laws would understand that the bridal party includes the groom's parents?

They understood that perfectly but the women made up the invitation list, I didn't see it until just before and they weren't on it. I just sort of accepted that that's how it was. It was my punishment for daring to marry her, I suppose. Actually, it was just the start of my punishment, a warm-up, you could say.

His home life was dreadful. From about the age of ten, he started to take the beltings for his younger siblings, say if one of them broke something, he would tell his father he had done it rather than listen to their screams. One day when he was about fifteen, his younger brother let the chickens out. In a drunken rage, his father ordered them to catch the chickens and then stand against the wall of the shed. A few minutes later, he staggered down with his rifle and pointed it at them, demanding to know who had done it. With his sisters and brothers screaming in terror, he told his father he had done it and took the flogging although at first, he thought his father would shoot him.

Throughout all of this, he studied because he knew he had to pass his final year in order to escape that town. At the end of Year 12, he gained excellent results and was offered a place at university. As soon as his father saw the letter of acceptance, he tore it to shreds then grabbed his son by the shirt and threatened to kill him if he ever left. Enraged and terrified, Cory punched him to the ground and kicked him, breaking several of his ribs. He quickly threw his clothes and books into a bag, hugged the children, jumped into the car and drove off, never to return.

> *You've never been back?*
> No way. I would never set foot on that place again but he said he'd kill me if he ever saw me again. I believe he would have tried.
> *And the little ones? What happened to them?*
> For a long moment, he stared out the window, biting his lip, then shook his head forlornly. "That tortured me," he said quietly. "I don't know why I bring this up. I felt I had totally abandoned them, betrayed them. The guilt. You have no idea..."
> *Is this why you don't want to lose your children?*
> Slowly, he began to cry. Eventually, he forced himself upright and rubbed his face. "I don't think I ever thought about it like that," he replied faintly, "but it's true. I can see their faces now as I got into that ute and drove off. I can't abandon my children."

At a time when students couldn't borrow to cover their costs, Cory put himself through medical school. For six years, he worked all day, every day, either studying or earning money. When he wasn't working, he went to gym but in all those years, he had very little social life and made few friends.

> *You didn't drink or go to parties?*
> I couldn't afford it, anyway, I'm ALDH neg (sensitive to alcohol). I don't like the grog, I saw what it did to my old man but I would never let my guard down.
> *So you lived a very abstemious life?*
> No way, I could screw anything on two legs in that hospital.
> *So how come you ended up with your ex-wife?*

You want me to take my shirt off? I was the hot stud of the year so she couldn't allow any of her friends to get in first.

It's not enough that one should win, one's friends must lose as well. Vidal, I think. So why didn't it work?

Oh Christ, how long have we got? The short version is that she was a rich idiot, daddy's spoilt girl who had never heard the word No until she met me. Trouble is, I eventually gave in and let her buy an engagement ring, because I couldn't have afforded a ring-pull from a beer can. Then she thought that meant she owned me, I had to follow along, two steps behind like the Duke of Edinburgh, and perform on cue. She didn't believe that when I told her to clean up the fucking mess she'd left in the bathroom, that's what I meant. It would still be there next evening when I got back from work and I'd go mad. Way I was brought up, if I left a spot in that shitheap house we lived in, I was flogged. And I mean flogged, I don't mean a couple of whacks over the head. If I look at mess, or disorder, or waste or stupidity, I go into orbit. So she was wasteful, messy, disorganised and stupid. And dishonest, which sends me completely insane, she'd tell dumb little lies. My mother told lies, she never stopped, she'd blame me for something and I'd cop it. But if I questioned her, my wife, if I said, That's not what you said last week, she'd tell more lies to cover her lies. And more. And this is how her family operate. They all tell lies all the time, it's normal to them. Apparently it's normal all through their rich world, that's what the rich do. Fuck I hate them, it really got to the stage where I wanted to kill some of them. Don't write that down.

Your father wanted to kill, too.

Must be contagious. Or genetic.

It sounds as though she scared you.

She fucking did, how did you know that? She scared me witless all the time, she spent money like there was no tomorrow. I lived in fear of being bankrupted, of losing everything, of being on the street again... Or my children having to live in a dungeon under somebody's house. I'd be sitting in the hospital at night, waiting for her to call, waiting, waiting, like I used to wait for my mother to come home. I'd ring but she never answered. I knew she was rooting men in my bed... I don't want to talk about it.

Sounds as though you need to. Another day, when you're ready. How do you see yourself as a person?

I'd like to say, dedicated, devoted, caring, considerate. Hard-working, diligent, all that sort of stuff but in truth, I think I'm turning into my old man.

Would you say you're a nervous person?

I don't want to but... Yes, very nervous. I get sick, I vomit, I can't eat or sleep or think.

Would you say you're able to stand up for yourself or you get pushed around?

Oh fuck yes, I stand up for myself. I wish I didn't but I can't help it. Once that agitation starts, it's all over, just get the men with the buckets to mop up the blood.

You get into fights?

Not now but I used to, somebody so much as looked at me and I'd have him by the throat. They nearly kicked me out of medical school a couple of times. But I'm getting old, now I'm more concerned to protect my hands. Maybe I'll take up shooting.

You were never charged?

No, I was too quick.

Would you say you're easily bothered by guilt?

You're fucking joking, I was born in guilt. I live, breathe and fart guilt.

A sense of shame?

Same, always, can't look people in the eye.

And self-consciousness?

Yes, very. I can't handle the slightest blemish on my skin, my clothes have to be perfect. If I thought somebody was criticising me, I'd either smack him in the mouth or crawl out, hoping nobody noticed. Or both.

What about your marriage? Weren't they criticising you?

Don't start on the disaster we call my marriage. I could hear them nattering behind in the pews during the service. The priest looked up a couple of times to warn them. Pity I didn't listen to them but there you are.

Would you say you trust people readily enough, or you're wary of people?

I don't trust any living soul. The dead I could possibly trust if I really had to.

Animals?

I love animals. And kids. I trust them, totally.

And you've said you're tidy and organised.

To a fault. At least my old man taught me something.

Taught you to fear. Patient or impatient?

Impatient. And intolerant. And demanding and organised. And right. Add that to my list of faults, I'm never wrong.

Would you say you're a social person or you can get by without people?

In the main, people mean nothing to me. I don't trust them, I don't like them, they bore me and irritate the guts out of me. They're stupid, selfish, dumb, greedy and dishonest.

And you're not?

Er, I've been pretty stupid, I can't avoid that one.

But you're a physician, that means you deal with people all day.

They're sick. I know they need me and they won't hurt me. It'll be different tomorrow when they get better but today, I have nothing to fear from them.

Are you inclined to be jealous?

Shit, why did you ask this? Of ordinary people, no, they don't mean enough to me to bother being jealous about them but my wife? The mother of my children? She said I'm pathologically jealous but that's because she was fucking everything in trousers that passed our door. Are you jealous if you get angry because your wife is gobbing the entire battalion? OK, put me down as jealous. Except I'm not now, I really don't give a cold fuck who she's fucking. If you'll excuse the metaphor.

Are you inclined to hold grudges?

Oh yes, I hold grudges. Like the bikies, I don't get angry, I get even. Except I do get angry although I wish I didn't.

How do you rate your temper?

Incandescent.

How do you rate your intellect?

99th percentile, according to military psych.

Last question. How do you rate your self-esteem?

"Shit. None, negative, full of self-loathing and hatred. So," he sneered, slipping into a coarse rural accent, "whaddayer make o' that clusterfuck? You still gonna let me outuvere or you gonna lock me up?"

There is a close relationship between self-esteem and interpersonal anxiety. We are social animals, we need to feel part of a group or tribe. The signal that we are accepted in the tribe is approval, the sense that "They like me, they approve of me so I have nothing to worry about." However, as we all know, social approval is a fickle thing—here today, gone tomorrow. We need something more secure to carry us over the rough patches, and that comes from self-approval, the sense of being worthwhile as a person, also known as self-esteem.

At the core of personality lies the concept of self-esteem, the sense of being something of worth or value. This is the foundation of life as an effective person. Each day, we must get out of bed and put our feet on something solid. Without that, there is no traction, no efficacy; we stumble and flail and fall in a heap. Mentally, that "something solid" is the sense of self-worth. If you have it, your day is off to a good start but a person with no sense of self-worth is in serious trouble as he is dependent on other people for approval. Problem is, the moment you depend on other people for something vital, you are automatically scared you're not going to get it. Every time you deal with another person, your anxiety rises but, equally automatically, so does the chance of making a mistake. If you make a mistake, down goes the approval and up goes your fear. It is inevitable, a law of nature. The whole point of poor self-esteem is that it is self-reinforcing, it makes itself worse.

People with solid self-esteem simply don't get this. For them, life is effortless: you want something, you work toward it and, sure as night follows day, you will get it. They don't understand how difficult life is for people whose every minute is tortured by fear and self-doubt.

Poor parenting leads to poor self-esteem. It has nothing to do with wealth or poverty, brains or beauty. Children can survive disasters if they know their parents are there for them and they are loved and valued. But a child in a palace who is treated like a dog will grow up fearing and hating the world and himself.

Poor self-esteem leads to fear. The problem for the individual is how to manage it, how to stop it erupting out of control. Above all, it is how to conceal it so that others don't see it and make fun of the sufferer. Humans love to hate but for every human who hates, there is a human who is hated. To be hated as one of a group isn't nice but it is bearable, people draw strength from each other. But to be hated as the outcast is torture beyond belief, torture beyond endurance.

Poor self-esteem leads to fear. Fear leads to self-hatred and despair. That's why the peace of death is preferable.

PART IV –
Severe Mental Disorders and Treatment

13

Severe Mental Disorder

As I've mentioned, modern psychiatry relies on what is called the categorical model of mental disorder, the idea that the different clinical pictures of mental disorder are separate and distinct categories. That is, a person who is depressed has a completely separate and distinct "illness" from somebody who is anxious or another who hears voices. The reasoning behind this is part of the so-called biological model of mental disorder, which says each and every discernible mental disorder is caused by a separate and distinct brain disorder. In modern terms, it is believed that the brain disorder is some sort of defect of neurotransmission, originating at the enzymic level of the synapse or junction between neurons in the brain. The cause of this defect is assumed to be a genetic error, either inherited or a mutation.

The whole rationale of the categorical system of classification of mental disorders is that the surface picture, the clinical syndromes as we see them (depression, phobias, psychosis etc.) will map directly and uniquely down to the genome: for each discrete clinical syndrome, there will one discrete genetic defect producing one specific "chemical imbalance." The great hope behind this, of course, is that there will be one drug to correct each alleged chemical imbalance. What you think or feel, or you hope or believe, is irrelevant; all that counts is your genome. That would make psychiatry very easy: Just fill in this questionnaire, tot up your scores and press the button to get your prescription. Better still, don't come into our nice office, weeping and wailing about what a shit life you've had, have this blood test and we'll tell you what you are and send your prescription by post. Have a nice day and don't forget to pay your bill.

This is the vision of the vast drug industry that has psychiatry clamped in its maw and is racing headlong down the deterministic rabbit hole. It has been called a "mindless" psychiatry, meaning there is no place in a scientific psychiatry for the nebulous "mind." In fact, it's mindless because you'd have to be short of a few clues to believe it. If, for example, you feel very glum over the current state of world politics, that's not because you have liberal leanings, it's because you have a chemical defect of the brain. But wait a moment: if I support a particular political party, or religion, or football team, is that also a matter of chemicals? What about patriotism, aesthetics, art, fashion, taste in music and so on? Are they all just chemicals? I'm afraid so, says the true biological psychiatrist, one day, science will show that everything we once believed was of a mental (non-physical) nature is just chemicals bumping in the dark.

Of course, that won't apply to *his* politics, *his* religion, *his* football team, and so on. It would also mean that his belief in the biological nature of mind is itself a biological state, probably a mutation because not so long ago, everybody believed minds were spiritual.

We can discard this notion. There is not and never will be a genuinely reductionist model of mind, mental disorder, personality or personality disorder. What is called biological reductionism, or the drive to reduce mental events to biological events, arose because nobody could solve the mind-body problem. This ancient riddle says that if mind and body are so profoundly different, how does information get from the body to the mind, and instructions get back again. In another book, I will argue that the mind is, in fact, just an informational space generated by the brain's switching properties. That way, because the body traffics in information all the time, there is no disjunction between mind and body. Information can zoom back and forth without having to cross a boundary.

People sometimes object, arguing that each informational state is directly the result of a different brain state, so it's biological after all. Not so: the biological state is just the *mechanism* of the informational state, not the informational state itself. Biological events *carry* and *process* information but they are not *themselves* information. Each mental event is in fact an informational state, and the cause of each informational state is necessarily a prior informational state. Thus, the cause of a mental event, even a disturbed mental event, is a prior mental event, not a biological event.

That's fairly obvious with "minor" disorders such as anxiety (even though I believe anxiety is anything but minor) but it's also true of depression. Anxiety is a reaction to a specific class of life events, threats. What we call depression is a reaction to another specific class of life events, losses. Sometimes losses are out there in the real world, sometimes they are private; some relate to the past, others to the present and still others are reactions to our perception of the future. But what about the "serious mental illnesses," the psychotic disorders, such as schizophrenia or bipolar affective disorder? For orthodox psychiatrists, the notion that these conditions could be psychological in nature is so implausible as to be laughable. They simply can't imagine it. However, in science, it is important not to mistake the limits to one's imagination for a natural limit to the universe:

There are more things in heaven and earth, Horatio,
Than are dreamt of in your philosophy.

I have outlined a case for the psychogenicity of schizophrenia in one of my earlier books. Briefly, people enter a state of self-sustaining hyperarousal in which their perception of themselves and of the universe is grotesquely distorted by the rules of psychophysiology. However, this state is intolerably distressing, so they have to change their understanding of the natural order of things in order to make sense of their bizarre experiences. That is, in order to reduce their distress, they start to believe things which, to the rest of us in our normal states of arousal, are impossible. It is therefore possible, although certainly very difficult, to treat schizophrenia by psychotherapy. Trouble is, whenever anybody with this diagnosis gets better by psychotherapy, the orthodox psychiatrists laugh and say: "That just proves he wasn't schizophrenic after all." As I've said before, alone among all physicians, the psychiatrist is never wrong.

In this chapter, I want to look at what is known as "bipolar affective disorder," a major, lifelong mental disorder characterised by severe swings in mood. As mentioned in Chapter 8, there is a very, very big problem with this diagnosis. When I started my psychiatric training, many years ago, what was then called manic-depressive psychosis was rare. The incidence was estimated at 0.1-0.2% of the population, meaning one or two people per thousand. However, their episodes of disturbance were brief, mostly of the order of months or even weeks, so they went in and out of hospital fairly regularly. This meant that while they were only a small proportion of the people in the hospitals, they made up something like half of all admissions to mental hospitals.

Starting in 1980, under the influence of the system of diagnosis in the American DSM-III, the diagnostic criteria were substantially loosened. This meant that more and more people were diagnosed as suffering bipolar disorder and put on major drugs. Over the next thirty years, an allegedly genetic illness has gone from one person per thousand to, believe it or not, 150 per thousand. That's an explosion of about 15,000% in one generation. That's not genetic disorders as I understand them.

Clearly, something is wrong. My case is that what is happening is nothing more than relabelling. Specifically, personality disorder, which psychiatry can't treat, is being relabelled as "bipolar affective disorder." Once that diagnosis is made, it inevitably follows that these people must be put on drugs. Because the drugs are highly addictive, anybody who starts them will probably take them for life. This ploy leads to a relentless increase in the numbers of people taking drugs which, of course, guarantees an income for the ever-expanding mental health industry. Needless to say, it is also hugely profitable for drug companies, which means they have lots more money to award to their favourite psychiatrists, the ones who happen to be expanding the diagnosis of bipolar disorder.

Is there any evidence for this? Certainly, but it's indirect as the only way of confirming this would be to have a major, long-term prospective study using specially-trained psychiatrists who are not beholden to the DSM approach. These days, they hardly exist as, in order to get through the training, trainees are required to prove they wholeheartedly accept the DSM system. The indirect evidence comes from massive increases in the rate of prescription of antidepressant and antipsychotic drugs over the past 20yrs. In Australia in 1991, 1% of the adult population was taking antidepressants. By 2014, it was 10%. It is simply not feasible to claim that the incidence of this condition rose 1000% in one generation. Nor is it feasible to suggest that medical practitioners in 1991 couldn't diagnose depression. The only possible explanation is that because the diagnostic guidelines have been loosened, they are given to more and more people, but once the drugs are started, they can't be stopped. It is now common to find people who have been taking antidepressants for 25 years or more, even though there have been no long-term studies to show that they do anything other than cause weight gain and diabetes.

Similarly, from 2000-14, antipsychotic prescriptions in Australia rose 217% while the population increased by about 22%, i.e. the drugs were being prescribed nearly ten times as much as could be expected. From 2008-2011, sales of quetiapine alone rose 87%. These drugs are *not* going to people who would previously have been diagnosed schizophrenic. In fact, people are now far more likely to be taking the combination of antipsychotics and antidepressants, even when they have never been psychotic and the primary problem is not depression. These are the unfortunate individuals who have been labelled "bipolar," who have been put on large doses of powerful psychoactive drugs and who, every time they try to stop them, suffer severe withdrawal symptoms. These symptoms are then attributed to "a recurrence of the original illness" and the sufferer is given still more drugs in larger doses, thereby compounding the problem. It is not uncommon to see people taking five or six separate psychotropic drugs. In the US, people are often prescribed seven or eight different drugs in the very long term, meaning decades.

The problem here is that these drugs don't seem to lead to any improvement in life quality or life span. As the numbers of people taking psychiatric drugs rises, so too does the number of people on disability pensions for psychiatric reasons. At the same time, the suicide rate in Australia has recently hit a 25yr peak. More ominously, it is now clear that people taking psychiatric drugs in the long to very long term will die, on average, nineteen year younger than their undrugged peers. In the US, that figure is 25 years. That is, the drugs that people are given to save their lives actually shorten life. I don't believe that's a good bargain, especially for those people who were given the drugs against their will.

Mainstream psychiatry will say that these figures are irrelevant, that they are properly giving the drugs to correctly-diagnosed people in order to prevent severe mental disorder. My case is that the diagnoses are generally wrong, the drugs are inappropriate, and they cause more mental and physical problems than they solve. As usual, the intellectual culprits are the biological model of mental disorder, which is incapable of admitting psychological causes to mental problems, and our old favourite, psychiatrists who don't take proper histories. We'll look at two cases who were diagnosed elsewhere with "rapid-cycling bipolar affective disorder."

Case 13.1: Charles W.

Charles W. is a 43yo lecturer in English, author and actor who had been admitted to a public mental hospital five months previously. Prior to that, he had been attending a private psychiatrist for several years who had diagnosed "rapid cycling bipolar disorder." Charles was prescribed a range of drugs including valproate, antidepressants and antipsychotics but did not respond and became suicidally depressed. While in hospital, he was given quetiapine 300mg per day (antipsychotic) and mirtazepine 45mg (antidepresssant). He had also been given four ECT. He was advised he should take lithium but he declined and asked for a second opinion.

He hadn't worked for about six months since he had been involved in organising a big drama festival. He lived with his partner, an artist, while his 8yo daughter from a previous marriage stayed with them during school holidays.

Presenting complaints.

When seen, he said he was still suffering "big depressive episodes" although he had been worse. He was sleeping very heavily because of the drugs and was tired and sluggish all day. His appetite had increased dramatically with the drugs and he was gaining weight. He had very little energy and was mostly unable to exercise due to lethargy. He had very little interest in his work or his drama, was not mixing socially and had practically no sexual interest. Since the ECT, his memory had been poor and he could barely concentrate on tasks, including reading and writing. He was having trouble thinking clearly due to "racing thoughts" and did not feel capable of making decisions. The thought content was "all over the place, really paranoid... angry and resentful at what (the hospital) did to me." There were no disturbances of perception.

He described his mood as "low and vulnerable, no confidence." He was feeling low and miserable about one third of the time, although it had been up to 90% of the time: "I'm sick of all this, sick of life, be better for everybody if I just dropped dead." He wasn't actively suicidal although he had been before and during the hospital admission. He wasn't sure why this was happening but said none of it was new.

He described bouts of feeling "elevated, high, optimistic, keen to work." He tended to take on extra work during these bouts but he knew they were not right: "I feel high, I'm irritable, sexual, aggressive and picking fights with people, over the top." These bouts were usually fairly brief and at that stage, he hadn't had one for a year or more. At the first interview, he was unable to explain them.

He also suffered frequent bouts of intense agitation, with shaking, sweating, churning stomach and racing heart. During them, he felt short of breath, dizzy and light-headed. He felt a sense of "...dread, like something bad will happen" and was restless, irritable and unable to settle. Without the drugs, he normally had three or four bouts per week but under prolonged pressure such as his divorce case or before a major performance, they could last days on end. During these periods, he had great difficulty sleeping and was so agitated by day that he could barely focus his thoughts. He was very irritable and didn't want to deal with people. Sometimes, these would end in a bout of depression. His "normal" bouts of agitation were caused by work pressure, dealing with people, minor upsets etc.

On direct questioning, he was "paranoid" about darkness. If he heard anything at night, he had to get up to check, which meant he rarely slept through the night. He was "very anxious and agitated" by public speaking, interviews, meetings and meeting strangers, all of which were a large part of his work. He was instantly agitated by threats and criticism (which also came with the job), or by disputes or confrontation of any sort. He hated letting people down, causing trouble or giving offence, and could not say No to people, which led him to take on too much work. He feared disapproval and, in particular, making mistakes or failing at anything. He feared mental illness, hospitals, needles and blood. He was nervous around drunks and aggressive people and was quite fearful of authority.

Whenever he went out, he had a strong sense of people looking at him and talking behind his back. He had a very strong sense of people watching him critically and judging him. He had a vague sense of people conspiring against him at work but said this had actually happened before and was quite common in the arts but there were no consistent paranoid symptoms. He was very conscious of security and was constantly worried that something was about to go wrong. He was full of self-doubt, especially relating to his work, but there were no true obsessive-compulsive features.

Recent history.

These problems had been present in this form at least ten years, probably longer. He had originally trained as a social worker and worked in drugs and alcohol in a rural area. He began suffering repeated and increasingly severe bouts of depression so he saw a psychiatrist who prescribed antidepressants. Eventually, he had to leave the job and retrained in drama and literature, which he had always liked, but feels he never got better. When his marriage ended, he became much worse and finally went to see another psychiatrist who diagnosed bipolar disorder and prescribed antidepressants, anticonvulsants and antipsychotic drugs. The drugs were "slightly helpful" but his mental state remained poor, with recurrent bouts of depression and suicidal ideas. After a protracted period of work pressure, he was admitted to hospital in a suicidal state and had ECT but, because of its effect on his memory, he felt it made him much worse.

Personal background.

His family background was very unsettled as his parents separated when he was ten, after which he mainly lived with his father, a prison officer. He described his father as "...absent, a thief and a professional cheat, lazy and bad-tempered." If his father wasn't at work or out trying to get money from somebody, he spent days in bed and wouldn't talk: "He embezzled from charities and was sexually inappropriate." He had refused contact with his father for many years. His mother was "always lost in her own stuff, had affairs with the neighbour, depressed since childhood and saw the same psychiatrist for 25 years. She was overly reliant on me, definite role-reversal, and drank too much." When he went to see his daughter, he had to stay with his mother, which he hated as she complained non-stop about how everybody had let her down. He had a younger brother who was also seeing a psychiatrist because he was "unpredictable, a terrible temper and very depressed." His mother's father was an alcoholic and was diagnosed as manic-depressive but there was considerable disturbance on both sides of the family.

At school, he was shy and nervous and was often teased and bullied, to the extent that he stayed away from school or moved to another. He liked English, art and drama but didn't do well in his classes as he feels he was depressed through most of his high school years: "I couldn't take my friends home but mostly I didn't have any friends. It was terrible." On leaving school, he was out of work for a year, then managed to get into social work. As a student, he worked part-time in a drop-in centre in the worst part of town, counselling alcoholics and drug users, but he graduated with a substantial debt from his education. He met his wife and they moved around with his jobs but the marriage was never good. He now feels she was very abusive of him but at the time, he was tortured by anxiety and guilt as he blamed himself for everything that went wrong. They found the deposit to buy a house but not long after, his mental state was so poor that they separated. There was a protracted custody dispute but he finally had to give in because he was feeling so bad. He was in and out of work and had a three year relationship which he described as "really unhealthy." He had been with his current partner about three years.

In the past, he drank heavily in binges, mainly driven by his need for relief from his mental trouble. He had smoked marijuana on and off most of his adult life but was aware it made him "paranoid." He didn't gamble and had no police record.

Self assessment.

Asked to describe himself as a person, he just shook his head blankly. Prompted, he said he was "always a worrier, always agitated." He was prickly and excessively assertive, often impatient, and intensely bothered by guilt, shame and self-consciousness. He was wary of people and had trouble mixing but he didn't like being alone. He was inclined to be jealous and didn't get on well with authority: "I get agitated and angry, I don't trust them." He saw his temper as "not too bad" and his intellect as "pretty bright" but his self-esteem was "low, don't like myself, not going anywhere."

Mental state examination.

The mental state showed a somewhat overweight chap of average height, dressed in clean plain clothes, with some tattoos and a chunky Indian wooden necklet. He sat slumped in his chair, staring dully at the floor, talking in a slow monotone, giving brief and lifeless answers to questions and volunteering very little. He was intensely preoccupied with how bad he was feeling, low, miserable and despairing but not suicidal. He was not anxious, hostile or suspicious. There were no psychotic features and, despite the difficulties of communication, he was clearly of superior intellect.

Asked what he thought his problem was, he replied that he believed he has bipolar disorder. He wasn't sure why, partly heredity, partly work and social pressures such as the custody disputes over his daughter. He wasn't sure what he wanted as treatment, something more holistic than drugs. He was still very angry over the ECT as he had been heavily drugged when he was told he needed it and even though he signed consent, it was not in any sense 'informed consent.'

We can agree that when he was seen, Charles was quite seriously depressed. Nobody would dispute that he showed a long-standing pattern of mental disturbance characterised by recurrent bouts of depression punctuated by intermittent bouts of feeling "high, active, over the top." Likewise, there wouldn't be much argument that he would meet the current criteria for bipolar affective disorder. As he had already had about six years of conventional treatment, including ECT while admitted to hospital, and his mental state was, if anything, slowly getting worse, we can further agree that treatment of his mental disorder had roundly failed. This raises a very important point: What do we do when conventional treatment fails?

Without going through the history of medicine over the past few thousand years, we can state that when a patient fails to respond to their treatment, the almost invariable response of physicians is to give him more. More of the same. Double it up. Stronger, harder, deeper until the patient either recovers or he succumbs, as Gen. George Washington did. As a reminder, the standard treatment Washington received from his physicians was bleeding. When, after a bit of light bleeding, he didn't get better, they bled him again, and again and again, until they bled him to death. It never occurred to them that there may have been something wrong with their model of illness, they couldn't bring themselves to look at that possibility. They had invested so much of themselves in the idea of therapeutic exsanguination that they would rather kill someone than consider they may be wrong.

This is exactly the position modern psychiatry finds itself in. I can't name an influential figure in mainstream psychiatry who would be prepared to question whether the mantra "drugs, drugs and more drugs" may be flawed. Patients are given drugs; if they don't get better, the doses are doubled; if still they don't improve, they are given more drugs, extra drugs, quadruple doses, heroic doses (I should point out that the term 'heroic' refers to the person prescribing them, not to the poor stiff who gets them); if they steadfastly refuse to cooperate by smiling gratefully, they can be forced into hospital, drugged against their will and given ECT. In the old days, as you saw in Chapter 2, they could even get their brains cut.

Charles W didn't get better with conventional treatment for his bipolar disorder so they gave him ECT. He says it damaged his memory and his capacity to write. Older readers may recall the Nobel-winning author, Ernest Hemingway, who also suffered ups and downs. When he didn't get better from treatment that would now make us shudder, they gave him ECT. He was not entirely grateful. A few days after a course of 20 ECT, Hemingway said bitterly:

> What these shock doctors don't know is about writers and such things as remorse and contrition and what they do to them... What is the sense of ruining my head and erasing my memory, which is my capital, and putting me out of business? It was a brilliant cure but we lost the patient.

Two days later, he blew his brains out with a shotgun. That's ingratitude.

In today's general medicine, if the patient fails to get better, physicians first reconsider the treatment, then reconsider the diagnosis. They are endlessly alert for some novel way of looking at the problem or a new approach to treatment. But not psychiatry: if the treatment fails, they try it again. Only in psychiatry do we find physicians doing the same thing twice and expecting a different outcome (Einstein's definition of madness, as many will know). The reason is very simple: psychiatrists have spent the last forty years painting themselves into a biological corner, so many years contemptuously dismissing mentalist explanations as "pseudoscience" that they are now incapable of considering alternatives. So many careers, so many fortunes, so many professorial egos have been built on the biological foundation that any major change in psychiatric theorising will not come from them. In fact, we are rapidly reaching the point of no return, the point where psychiatry's professional memory of psychological concepts in mental disorder and the skills to deal with them are on the verge of dying out.

But back to Charles W. After about six years of treatment, costing perhaps $100,000 in all, this ingrate failed to get better. It is therefore fair and reasonable to suggest that either the diagnosis was wrong, or the treatment was wrong. But the diagnosis was made according to conventional standards, specifically the DSM-IV-R and then DSM-5, so how could it be wrong? However, the people applying those standards, and the standards themselves, studiously overlooked a very important part of this man's life, the severe anxiety that had plagued him since early childhood. They assumed that his recurrent depression and bouts of excitement were necessarily *sui generis*, a condition unto itself. That is, they believed that naming his disorder as "bipolar affective disorder" didn't just define it, but explained it as well. But it doesn't. There is an old rule in the philosophy of language that says you can't nominate an entity and define it in the same illocutionary act. That is, you can't point to something and name it, and expect that naming it will also explain what it is, as in:

> "What's that?"
> "It's a triantewobbegong."
> "What's a triantewobbegong?"
> "That is."
> "Ah, I see."

However, that rule assumes you know nothing else about the thing. In psychiatry, it is assumed that naming something will also define it *just because* of the background information that every psychiatrist has gained as a result of his training, that by naming it, you will automatically know everything there is to know about it:

> Student: "What's that?"
> Psychiatrist: "That's bipolar affective disorder."
> S: "And what's bipolar affective disorder?"
> P: "Please tell me."

S: "I'd say it's a genetically-determined disease of the brain with no demonstrable physical basis causing a chemical imbalance at synaptic level that manifests as mental disturbance and which can only be treated by means of drugs to correct the chemical imbalance or, if that fails, other physical methods such as ECT or brain stimulation."

P: "So you know everything about it, after all. Excellent work, young man, now this next patient has schizophrenia. Tell me what that is."

S: "I'd say it's a genetically-determined disease of the brain with no demonstrable physical basis causing a chemical imbalance at synaptic level that manifests as mental disturbance and which can only be treated by means of drugs to correct the chemical imbalance or, if that fails, other physical methods such as ECT or brain stimulation."

P: "Wonderful. And what about this man with depression, what's that?"

S: "I'd say it's a genetically-determined disease of the brain with no demonstrable physical basis causing a chemical imbalance at synaptic level that manifests as mental disturbance and which can only be treated by means of drugs to correct the chemical imbalance or, if that fails, other physical methods such as ECT or brain stimulation."

P: "Truly amazing. Please accept this diploma that shows you know all there is to know about mental disorder with no questions left unanswered."

As you see, this is the generic explanation for all things mental. But: an explanation, such as "chemical imbalance of the brain," which is offered to explain everything, actually explains nothing. It gives the impression of an explanation but it is a pseudo-explanation; in reality, nothing more than self-deception. Compare this with Molière's "dormitive principle":

> The learned doctors ask me why one sleeps after opium. I explain that in opium there resides a dormitive principle, and they are well satisfied with my explanation.

The remedy is simplicity itself: If the treatment fails, reconsider the diagnosis and/or the treatment. In Charles' case, the diagnosis was wrong, and therefore the treatment was inevitably wrong. That's not to say he didn't suffer recurrent bouts of depression and agitation because he did; but the *assumption* that it was *sui generis* was wrong. He gave the very clearest history of severe, personality-based anxiety going back to childhood. Why should his anxiety not have caused his recurrent depression and agitation? In the first place, depression is the response to a loss: If severe, untreated anxiety causes recurrent losses, such as jobs, marriage and finally self-

Severe Mental Disorders and Treatment

worth, then surely, and in every sense of that complex word 'cause,' it is fair to say his anxiety *caused* his depression? I submit that it is actually very fair to say that; that it makes perfect sense and thereby amounts to a causal explanation; and that only a person ideologically committed to a biological causation of depression would fail to see it. In this approach, would it not also follow that treating the anxiety would, in the ordinary course of events, prevent further depression? In fact, that's what happened but it's another story.

In the second place, agitation is agitation. As described in DSM-5, the symptoms of anxiety are all but indistinguishable from those of a manic or hypomanic episode in bipolar disorder. For the criteria for mania and hypomania, we turn to page 124 of the 2013 edition of DSM-5 (see Fig. 13.1). Criteria for anxiety are given on pages 189-190 and again under social phobia on pages 202-203 (to my mind, their description of anxiety is grossly inadequate but we'll let that pass).

Symptom	Mania	Hypo-mania	Anxiety
Irritability	Yes	Yes	Yes
Disturbed sleep	Yes	Yes	Yes
Talkative or pressure to keep talking	Yes	Yes	Yes
Subjective experience that thoughts are racing	Yes	Yes	Yes
Distractibility, poor concentration	Yes	Yes	Yes
Psychomotor agitation	Yes	Yes	Yes
Impairs social or occupational function	Yes	Yes	Yes
Risky or impulsive behavior	Yes	Yes	Yes

Figure 13.1: DSM-5 Criteria for Anxiety

That is, anybody who presents in a state of considerable agitation, *regardless of the cause*, is very likely to be given a diagnosis of hypomania. This is much more likely if there is no obvious cause for the anxiety which, in the case of personality-based anxiety, there is not (that's what personality-based means: independent of the environment). I emphasise the cause because modern psychiatry doesn't believe in psychological causes. If you present in this state, say because your spouse has disappeared with the children, you're very likely to get the diagnosis, especially if you're big, male and don't tolerate fools.

Anybody given a diagnosis of hypomania will be given drugs. That's axiomatic. The drugs will not do anything to alleviate the anxiety, just because they are not anxiolytics. No psychological treatment of the anxiety will be offered. We know that the natural history of untreated anxiety states is that they intensify with the passage of time. Anybody who deteriorates while taking psychiatric drugs will be given more and more, but he will not be able to stop them without suffering severe withdrawals symptoms. Psychiatrists do not believe their drugs cause withdrawal symptoms (although they are now gingerly accepting the precious term 'discontinuation syndrome'). A person who takes these drugs in the long term is likely to die young. Whatever you do, don't rock up to a hospital late at night in an agitated and irritable frame of mind.

According to DSM-5, pages 124-125, anybody who develops such a state of agitation during treatment with an antidepressant or during ECT is not suffering a side-effect of the treatment. instead, he is manifesting a true manic or hypomanic attack and is therefore properly diagnosed as suffering bipolar affective disorder type I, for which long-term treatment is required (there is a qualification but it's irrelevant because nobody takes any notice of it). The treatment will almost certainly include antidepressants, which caused the agitation in the first place. Antidepressants can cause the severe side-effect known as akathisia, an intensely unpleasant sense of inner restlessness or itching agitation in the limbs, which drives people to distraction (see Chapter 11 for descriptions by patients).

Be warned: if you develop akathisia while taking these drugs, you are highly likely to be diagnosed as bipolar and put on more drugs. This is because psychiatrists adamantly refuse to accept that their treatment is worse than the disease. But that's a fine psychiatric tradition, it's always been the case. People who were given camphor to induce seizures begged and pleaded not to be forced to take it but they were held down and injected just the same—it was all for their own good. If they got angry and lashed out, that proved they needed more.

Once more, we'll return to Charles. His agitation was purely personality-based. He had very poor self-esteem, meaning he had an intense need to please people and was very frightened of offending them. He could not say No, he kept accepting work but if anybody mistreated him and he became angry, he kept it to himself and suffered agonies of guilt. His anxiety kept him awake, wore him out, wrecked his jobs, wrecked his friendships, his marriage and made him drink. He suffered endless anxiety over dealing with people, over speaking or performing in public, his writing, everything. He was tortured by guilt over separating from his daughter, convinced he had somehow damaged her, and feared that her mother would somehow block his access, as she regularly threatened to do.

In his position as organiser of the drama festival, he had to deal with some truly impossible people who, at the slightest hint their work may not make the short list for the Nobel Prize this year, either flew into volcanic rages or slumped into depression, got drunk and cut their wrists, for all of which Charles blamed himself. At the same time, he needed to hide his distress from people who knew him, including prospective partners, because he believed that was putting burdens on them, which increased the guilt and agitation, and so his difficulties compounded.

If forty years of such life is not reasonable grounds for depression, I don't know what is. But what about his 'hypomanic episodes'? A very large part of it was pure anxiety but also he had bouts when he actually felt better which, if you ask carefully, you will find is common in anxiety. For whatever reason, the sufferer wakes one morning feeling reasonable, or something works out, or somebody thanks them or does them a good turn. Suddenly, they feel the world isn't quite so horrible and they aren't quite so hopeless. They get excited, dust off a bunch of old plans, ring friends they've been ignoring, lash out to buy that new dress or take the holiday they were too scared to book... all of which is grist to the psychiatrist's hypomania mill. But that's not madness, it's still normal. A truly manic person is clearly insane but an anxious person having a good day is not mad, everything he says and does makes perfect sense—*within the context of his anxious personality*. But if the psychiatrist hasn't done a personality assessment, which none of them do, then he won't know that, he won't have the context (he will reply that his 'science of mental disorder' is context-free but we know that's false).

The bad news for the anxious person having a good day is that, sooner rather than later, something will go wrong, the anxiety will flood back and he will crash. In no time, he is sinking into despair, convinced he's hopeless and useless and the world would be better off without him. That's called depression, but it is a reasonable reaction to once more learning the bitter lesson that anxiety is the gift that keeps on giving. It doesn't go away, it merely bides its time. We'll revisit Charles in Chapter 15, on treatment, but first, let's look at another case of "rapid-cycling bipolar affective disorder."

Case 13.2: Jeremy V aged 28.

Jeremy is an Air Force police corporal who injured his back in a fall at work. Six months after the injury, he underwent surgery for intractable pain and rapidly-developing nerve damage but the operation (laminectomy) was only partially successful. Despite being in constant pain, he managed to get back to work, doing his best to conceal his disabilty because he didn't want to lose his career. Over the next few years, he became increasingly disturbed and was drinking heavily so he was finally sent to a psychiatrist who diagnosed bipolar affective disorder. In fact, he dumped no less than ten separate diagnoses on young Jeremy's unsuspecting head, thus:

- Bipolar Affective Disorder
- Major Depressive Disorder

- Alcohol Abuse
- Generalized Anxiety Disorder
- Panic Disorder
- Agoraphobia
- Adjustment Disorder
- Obsessive-Compulsive Personality Disorder
- Avoidant Personality Disorder and, of course....
- Borderline Personality Disorder.

He was prescribed olanzapine 5-10mg at night (antipsychotic); paroxetine 60mg a day (antidepressant; a large dose) and lorazepam 7.5mg per day (a large dose of a highly addictive tranquilliser). Jeremy managed to stop drinking but felt the drugs were making him worse so he requested a second opinion.

At the time of referral, he was living with his wife and their infant daughter. He had been off work for over two months and was very worried about being discharged medically unfit. He was in the final year of a degree course but he knew that, without an income, he wouldn't be able to finish his studies. His wife was also studying and was dependent on his income to continue.

Presenting complaints.

At the first interview, he was edgy, wary and talkative. He said he was feeling "extremely agitated, anxiety through the roof and depressed on and off." His sleep was quite erratic. He tried to go to bed early, about 8.30pm as he always went to gym before work. He got to sleep without much trouble but woke several times most nights, sometimes due to pain, others for no reason. He woke at 4.30am when the baby awoke and, despite his pain, went to gym. He didn't take naps by day. His appetite was also erratic and he tended to eat in binges when he was agitated. He had been gaining weight rapidly since he started the tablets. Depending on how he was feeling, his levels of energy varied dramatically, from good down to none at all. His activity level was quite high as he was on his feet at work and spent 6hrs or more in the gym each week following a strenuous program.

He had little interest in his work but, in his private life, developed "addictions" to different things: "I feel driven, more than driven." Since his exams two months before, he had immersed himself in writing a novel. At home, his motivation to get things done was "routine" and he was keen to get back to work: "I change at work, I become a copper." Socially, he was actively avoiding company as he needed alcohol to be able to mix with people. He hadn't had much contact with people from work but didn't feel the need. His sexual interest was very erratic, varying from "beyond too much, down to none at all." He said this was normal for him.

He had the feeling his memory for small details was a bit patchy but nobody commented while, at work, he had a reputation for his ability to recall detail. His concentration was generally poor but he blamed the drugs. When asked whether he felt able to make decisions, he didn't answer. His thinking was "all over the place" and was almost obsessively focused on his novel, "to use all the thoughts in my head." There were no disturbances of perception.

He described his mood as "a mess." He was feeling low and miserable about half the time, "sick of things but not suicidal" although he had been when he was first referred to the previous psychiatrist. The unhappiness was due to "always feeling anxious," the back injury, the threat of medical discharge, money worries and family problems. He experienced bouts of feeling good but couldn't say whether it was normal: "I don't know what natural is, I get lots of ideas and start writing. I think about changing careers, I'm more confident and able to talk to people, I can get things done because the anxiety is down." During these bouts, he slept better and was sexually more active but he didn't spend to excess or do anything risky. These moods were very erratic; he might have several good days but wasn't sure why: "I feel relaxed, I get happy and more confident." However, before long, he would wake feeling tired or lacking energy, or his pain would be worse and then he would quickly deteriorate: "That's when I tend to gamble and drink. And I do dumb things like ride my motorbike drunk."

Asked whether he had bouts of feeling agitated, he replied: "I'm constantly agitated, it's almost unbearable." During these, he was shaky and sweaty, his heart raced and his stomach churned. He was unable to eat and sometimes vomited or he had to rush to the toilet with loose bowels. He felt tight in the throat, his voice quavered and he was likely to stammer. He was short of breath, his mouth was dry and he felt light-headed and clumsy. He had the sense of everything closing in: "I feel different in myself, everything's coming at me and I can't organise my thoughts." With these bouts, he felt frightened and angry at himself. He used to yell and argue but now tried to get away and take a tablet to calm down.

The bouts of agitation started as he was getting ready for work: "Thinking of the day, putting on my uniform, driving to work, having to deal with those people... I can't face it, I get so anxious." It tended to settle once he got to work and started on his duties but would flare up at the slightest pressure. On questioning, he feared confined spaces and the thought of being locked up. He was frightened by crowds and standing in queues with people close behind him. He hated public speaking, appointments and interviews, tests and exams because he became so agitated beforehand. He was fearful on public transport and before meeting strangers. He became very agitated with threats or criticism of any sort, even if he wasn't sure it had actually happened. He had to avoid disputes and couldn't say No to people. He was fearful of confrontation, letting people down, causing trouble or giving offence. He feared humiliation and disapproval and, in particular, making mistakes or failing at anything. Since his injury and the operation, he had become very fearful of disability. He didn't like hospitals and had feared authority until just recently.

When he was out of his house, he had a strong sense of people looking at him, talking behind his back and judging him. He had a sense that people were likely to be a danger but thought his back injury had a lot to do with that as he was aware he couldn't defend himself. He was fussy about order, punctuality and efficiency and liked doing things according to a routine but there were no true obsessive-compulsive features.

Physically, he had low back pain with persistent right-sided sciatica. This was made worse by exercise, by standing or sitting long periods or driving, especially in low'slung cars. A lot of his work involved exercise, standing or sitting for long periods and driving patrol vehicles.

Recent history.

The mental symptoms had been present his "whole life, to some degree." He recalled that at fifteen, he was suicidal. He enlisted at 23 and was doing well until he hurt his back. Post-operatively, he was prescribed a nerve stabilising drug (pregabalin) which also seemed to settle the anxiety somewhat. More recently, everything had been going wrong. There were changes at work, extra pressures, his wife and his parents didn't get on and the baby wasn't sleeping: "I wasn't dealing with things so I started drinking."

Personal background.

His family background was very unstable although his parents were still together. His father, who was aged 58yrs, had a small electronics business which he ran from home: "He was a useless father, an alcoholic, he never spoke except to criticise." His paternal grandfather came from Europe in the late 1940s and it seemed likely he was a member of the SS but he died when Jeremy was very young. His mother, who was aged about 56yrs, had worked in shops until she developed severe arthritis: "She's very loving but she can't handle any stress at all. She breaks down and cries, she's not strong." He had a younger brother who worked in IT. He had separated from his wife and lived with their parents: "He's like me, always depressed but not so severe." While his father was one of eleven children, they had very little contact with his many relatives although he could easily find them because of their distinctive surname. Several of his six uncles were alcoholics and he understood that many of his forty or so cousins had drug and alcohol or other mental problems and criminal records.

He attended local state schools to age 17yrs, passing Year 12. His record was very patchy. He was extremely shy and nervous and for years, he truanted rather than face the other students. His marks were poor until Year 12 when he realised he had to do better, so he worked hard and passed the year quite well. He didn't get on well with the teachers or the other children: "I was a loner, I didn't talk." He was often teased or bullied which led to fights or he would run away from school. For several years, he hardly attended. He left home in the morning, walked quickly to a park and climbed into the huge fig trees to hide in their dense foliage. Until his final year, he had no interest in school apart from sport, which he did very well. On the football field, he had no fears but the rest of his life was a torture. His home life was poor: "It was a big mess, lot of drinking... I was drinking from thirteen. My mother used to buy it for me." From sixteen, he was very active in body-building and later in martial arts. On leaving school, he had unskilled jobs while he waited to study. After a year, he began studying but was too unsettled and left the course. Because of his size and martial arts training, he worked in security for several years, then he enlisted and resumed his course part-time.

During his teenage years, he had several relationships before he met his wife at twenty: "She was really mixed up, as crazy as me." He drank erratically, often in binges when agitated, and was likely to gamble at the same time. At those times, he was often promiscuous. His normal intake was ten cans of full-strength beer or nothing. He used no illegal drugs and had no police record. Apart from his back injury, his general health was good.

Self-assessment.

Asked to describe himself, he didn't respond. He agreed he is severely anxious and intensely self-conscious, but not greatly bothered by a sense of guilt or shame. In dealing with people, he was very assertive to the point of arguing, and generally impatient "...but not with losers, I can handle them without losing my temper. I have a problem with idiots in authority." He was quite mistrustful of people but liked company although he was usually too agitated to mix, which led to drinking: "I can't relax with people so I drink. I have to be the life of the party or not there at all." He said he was not inclined to jealousy and didn't hold grudges. He had no trouble following rules and got on "superficially very well" with authority.

He saw his temper as "not good," his intellect as "smart and very creative" while his self-esteem was "not good."

Mental state examination.

The mental state showed a big and well-developed man of stated age, in neat clean casual clothing and with a trim, military appearance. He had several large professional tattoos on his arms and chest but no studs, scars or jewellery. He was clearly anxious and tremulous, and religiously avoided eye contact. He spoke clearly and well but tended to give brief, self-deprecatory laughs. In the main, he was generally guarded, preoccupied and pensive. He was unhappy but not overtly depressed, and neither hostile nor suspicious. There were no psychotic features and he was of superior to very superior intellect.

Once again, we find the picture of severe, life-long, personality-based anxiety presenting as alternating bouts of agitation and depression. That is, severe anxiety *mimics* the manic-depressive or bipolar picture, but it is not thereby the "real thing" (whatever that is). How can we be sure? Because they don't get better. Complicating matters, Jeremy presented a common diagnostic problem, in that he was remarkably adept at concealing how he was feeling. His teenage years were a disaster but luckily, he learned that if he threw himself into tasks, he could control his anxiety by controlling what people were thinking. If he decided to make people laugh, he was the life of the party although he had to drink to do it. Even then, he never relaxed, never took his eyes off his audience. At work, he worked harder than anybody, not least because he didn't waste time chatting to people or spreading gossip, which he hated. He spent 60-90 minutes in gym each morning before work but he didn't speak to anybody. So when he saw the first psychiatrist, he didn't reveal half of the material in this account. For example, the psychiatrist recorded that Jeremy had "no adverse childhood experiences." Later, he admitted that it was probably lucky he had kept quiet otherwise he would have been locked up. For the psychiatrist seeing a man with such a high level of disturbance, the very absence of "adverse childhood experiences" (the result of a poor history-taking technique) left the puzzled shrink little option but to believe it must be biological.

It's clear that a model of mental disorder is necessary in order to understand what is going on with this man, otherwise his history is just a jumble of essentially unrelated facts. That is, we need a sort of mental framework on which to hang all the observations. What, for example, is the relationship between a big boy of fifteen years who hides in the trees in the local park and a 26yo man who, between his bouts of depression, can keep a whole party laughing? A body-builder who has bouts of drinking at dangerous levels? Are they even related? The purpose of a model of mental disorder is to provide such a framework. My case is that personality-based anxiety is the common factor. It's often said that the child is the father of the man, which means that the structure of the adult personality is formed in the experiences of the child.

Starting in early childhood, and firmly entrenched by the age of fifteen, his every experience of the world convinced him it is punitive and unforgiving, that humans are deliberately cruel and hurtful. His parenting was a disaster, school was worse and the world terrified him, or rather, the human world, as he felt no danger perched high in the trees. Like all humans, he needed approval to confirm the sense of belonging to the tribe but it never arrived. Very early, he came to live in fear that every contact with a human would be hurtful so he kept away. Simply approaching people provoked the fear that he would be hurt but, lacking any support or assistance from the adults in his life, he had to find his own ways of dealing with his anxiety. When he felt good, he was able to control people but it didn't last. Anxiety explains all of this.

But, I hear you object, you said that the biological psychiatrists' attempts to explain all mental problems as a "chemical imbalance of the brain" amount to a pseudo-explanation. That is, a universal explanation explains nothing. By saying that anxiety underlies everything, aren't you lurching perilously close to pseudo-explanation yourself?

Not quite. I'm not saying that anxiety underlies everything, but it certainly is the basis of a lot of troubling things. Remember that, because of its recursive properties, its capacity to reinforce itself, anxiety is the most powerful human emotion. Unlike all other emotions, anxiety doesn't fade away just because you're tired or hungry or cold or in pain. It builds up and up until you give in and do what it wants. In psychiatry, its significance lies in what people do to *reduce* their anxiety, how they handle it and how they try to conceal it. Some people withdraw from life, others throw themselves into work, or drinking, or marathons, or aggression or drugs or sex or crime or medical tests or pills and so on. Jeremy used study, obsessive body-build-ing, drinking, hard work, sex, frenetic partying and periods of withdrawal, one after the other or even all at once, to control his intense fear of people looking down on him. What counts is this: what was the mental mechanism that generated the anxiety that dominated his life? That's not hard to find, he made that quite clear: "People. I'm terrified of people. I need their approval but at the same time, I despise them and I hate myself for wanting them to like me."

This is the essence of the concept of personality disorder, the ceaseless inner and outer conflict that comes from a mess of contradictory beliefs and drives. On the one hand, as he said, he needs approval. The reason is he has no self-approval, no self-esteem. He grew up in an atmosphere of endless disapproval from his very seriously disturbed father, who was himself the product of a brutal and domineering man. Minute to minute from the earliest age, Jeremy expected to be criticized for everything he did. Nothing he did was ever good enough, every move he made, every breath he took, exposed him to the risk of biting scorn and disapproval. The more his father drank, the more critical he became, pouring bile on his small son's head at the very time when children most need praise and encouragement.

By the time he started school, Jeremy was already nervous. Later, he recalled his first day at school, holding tight to a tree and screaming in fear while the teacher tried to drag him into the classroom. Even though he was quite big for his age and clearly intelligent, he was quickly marked as hesitant and unlikely to push himself forward. He was an easy mark for anybody who felt the need to push somebody around in order to make himself look bigger. If anybody teased him, he was gripped by anxiety of what might happen. Mostly, he felt he didn't have the right to stand up for himself or that if he did, more trouble would come, so he withdrew and the teasing got worse. Occasionally, he lashed out, which caused more trouble. This is what happens: a small defect early in life is magnified and amplified by circumstances. By fifteen, the boy was seriously disabled by anxiety and depression and almost completely lacking in any social skills.

Why did he go down this particular path? Why, for example, didn't he fight back when he was bullied? The answer is that some children do, and some don't. It depends entirely on the circumstances but whatever the child does is designed to reduce the intolerable emotion, anxiety. In Jeremy's case, he did his best not to get into trouble at school as he knew it would mean more trouble at home. Verbally more fluent boys often turn into the class clown, using their intellect to make jokes to deflect attention from the fact that they have fallen behind and can't bring themselves to admit it. The next child, equally clever, may decide that offence is the best form of defence. Each of the following cases had been diagnosed as bipolar:

> If anybody ever picked on me at school, I'd go completely mad and attack everybody in sight. I don't know how many teachers I belted into. I was suspended every week and expelled from three schools. I left school at fourteen because none of the schools in town would take me. If you'd seen me then, you would have locked me up and thrown away the key. Then I found alcohol so life seemed a bit better but inside, I was getting worse and worse (Andrew, aged 17).

> I was a thief from the beginning. I'd steal from my mother's purse and buy lollies to give to the other kids so I could say they were my friends. I was so lonely, I know that now, they'd take the lollies but nobody wanted to talk to me. Walking to school by myself was the pits, everybody knew my old man was inside and my mother was the truckies' moll. But going home was the worst because the tough kids would say they were going to get me and I'd get a flogging so I'd be pissing myself and just run home at afternoon break. When I got home, my old woman would be on my case so I'd lie and say I got top in the test and the teacher let me go home early. And it just went

on from there, lying and stealing, stealing and lying. I just kept getting myself into more and more trouble (Callym, aged 26).

I don't know how it started. I remember people said I was shy and I'd grow out of it but I didn't. By twelve, when I started high school, I couldn't look at anybody. If the teachers criticised me, I'd burst into tears. The other girls got sick of it, they called me the teacher's pet. Girls can be terribly catty. When we moved here and I went to the state high school, I thought I'd die. I had no idea how to talk to boys, I'd never had anything to do with them. They'd make fun of me and laugh at me and all I could do was sit there and blush but inside, I was crying. I couldn't say anything at home. My father is a senior public servant, he hates criticism but he's very critical, always angry and suspicious. He didn't believe us, he always takes things as a personal attack, I could never talk to him. My mother is very anxious but compassionate, she gets worked up and it's hard to try to tell her anything. It just got worse and worse. Somehow I passed Year 12 and was accepted at university but I had to leave in my second year. I was seriously depressed by this stage so they put me on all those drugs. They wanted to put me in hospital but my father refused, he said there was no mental disorder in our family. Later, when I was put in the security ward, he wouldn't speak to me. I was so ashamed, that's why I was suicidal but I couldn't tell the staff (Bronwyn, aged 27).

This is the central point of anxiety: anxiety is not a state, it is an evolving dynamic process, steadily reinforcing itself as life's circumstances unfold. Anxiety says only: I perceive a threat. At eleven, coming home to find your mother drunk is a major threat. Having your father look over your shoulder and sneer at your essay is a threat. Having to recite a poem in front of the class is a threat because it could go wrong, and it is more likely to go wrong when the child is anxious about it going wrong. We're social animals, approval is affirmation that we belong to the tribe so approval becomes more important than oxygen. Out there on the veldt a million years ago, being cast out of the tribe meant certain death. A mechanism evolved to prevent people wandering off into the darkness, a sense of fear when isolated and its converse, a sense of peace and reassurance when surrounded by other hominids, happily picking each other's fleas.

Anxiety starts small and builds up, it spreads to engulf more and more of your life until, one day, there seems no chance it will ever be any different. At that point, the mood changes, the last glimmers of hope die and despair takes over: "I'm hopeless, I'm useless. All these other people can cope with school or work, they can handle parties and sport, they don't fall apart with a baby or get drunk every time somebody says something critical. I'm the loser they always said I am, there's no hope for me. If this is all I can look forward to, I may as well end it now."

That mood we call depression, but sadness is a realistic response to life events, it is not a disease. If the depression is caused by an unseen and unsuspected anxiety state, which the sufferer may be trying to hide, or may not even recognise, then we are set for a cyclical pattern of ups and downs. My experience, from taking standardised and very detailed histories from every patient I see, is that serious anxiety is almost never recognised by conventional psychiatry. The overwhelming majority of patients who are now given the diagnosis of Bipolar Affective Disorder would not have been given that label forty or even thirty years ago. Orthodox psychiatry cannot deal with anxiety, and it cannot deal with personality disorder. The idea of an anxious personality disorder, therefore, is too difficult to comprehend so these people, about 15% of the population, had to be relabeled to bring them back into reach of mainstream psychiatry. Otherwise psychiatrists would have had very little to do and would have lost a large part of their justification.

14 The Dynamic Model

One of the big problems facing economists today is that they can't agree on what a model of an economy should look like. Is it a steady state machine, quietly rolling along under its own momentum and just needing a gentle touch on the throttle or the brake to keep it in equilibrium? Or is the economy a form of barely controlled chaos, a vastly complex monstrosity with 7.2 billion parts that nobody understands, constantly picking itself up after a disaster only to tumble into another as panicky corrections are applied? Are humans completely rational actors, calmly and maturely going about their business of building a better future for each other, or are they a bunch of aggressively selfish, short-sighted, self-deluding and ultimately self-destructive nitwits who shouldn't be allowed near the controls? Time will tell; but if it's the latter, we're in serious trouble.

As it happens, the equilibrium or steady state approach isn't far from the economic model employed by central bankers around the world. A bit too much inflation creeping into the system? OK, let's pump the interest rates up a bit, that'll squeeze it out and restore the equilibrium. Later, as the inflation drops, so too the interest rates are eased down again, carefully maintaining the balance. Not enough growth? Pump a bit of liquidity into the system, it'll soon pick it up again.

Orthodox psychiatry isn't far off this gloomy picture as it relies on what could be called an equilibrium or steady state model of mental life. Remember, of course, that it's an exceedingly restricted model, it has nothing to do with cognitive function, only with emotions. The general notion is that, emotionally speaking, we cruise along through life, perhaps a bit like a jet airliner cruising high across the ocean. The pilot sits in his comfortable seat, calmly watching the instruments. Seems like we're drifting lower, says the co-pilot. OK, says the pilot, a touch on the elevators and we rise back to the proper altitude. A bit of a cross-wind pushing us to the port? No worries, a touch on the starboard rudder and we'll soon be back on course.

It's all rather similar to basic general medicine. Blood pressure too high? Here's something to lower it. Blood sugar a bit high? Try a jab of insulin, that'll soon bring it down. Too much inflammation? An anti-inflammatory will clear it, but if it hurts, there's always narcotics to neutralise the pain. The goal is to restore the inner equilibrium which nature has foolishly unsettled. In psychiatry, the model is similar. Patient getting a bit too excited? OK, give him something to calm him and send him on his way. Next patient getting a bit depressed? A touch of the old antidepressant will soon have him bubbling along happily but if not, a whisper of electricity through his brain will do the trick. Unstable moods? Give him a mood stabiliser. He hears voices? Give him a drug to dampen hallucinations. It's all designed to restore inner harmony so the mental patient can get back on his bike and pedal happily into the sunset. Why does the inner harmony get deranged in the first place? Well, that's genes for you.

The mental model we are using here is completely different. It's a dynamic model of many interacting mental modules, a hugely complex and dimly-understood machine that has to work synchronously at very high speed within very narrow limits of tolerance, otherwise the whole thing starts to spin apart. In ordinary daily life, we don't have any inkling of this. Everything seems to work together and we just go about our affairs, completely unaware of how fine the tolerances of mental function are. You could say the same about your liver. The liver is an amazing organ, very large as organs go, structurally highly intricate and equipped with the devil's own array of powerful enzyme systems. As long as it works as it's meant to, you won't even know it's there but it works awfully hard 24/7 to keep you in ignorance.

The human mind eclipses the liver in complexity and conceptually, by factors of millions of times, but as long as it works smoothly, you don't know a bit of it. But it doesn't take much to make it start to break down. Some bad news and suddenly, we're intensely agitated, making mistakes and blaming everybody around us. Fortunately, after a while, everything seems to settle down as the mind corrects itself and adjusts to its new reality and we just get on with life. However, and crucially, mental distress isn't always self-correcting. Only minor disturbances to mental balance right themselves; as we drift further from the calm centre where everything works smoothly, errors amplify and disturbances begin to reinforce themselves, and so the problem rapidly spins out of control. Mental life is a very dynamic process; nothing is ever still. The whole of mental life is endlessly moving, changing, evolving, interacting. A sudden pressure here can result in something flying off over there, or a relatively minor event today can uncover an unsuspected weakness from the distant past which rapidly amplifies into chaos.

In general, it would be fair to say that single minor upsets are usually self-correcting while major blows are more likely to self-reinforce and cause further trouble (of course, we label an incident 'minor' when it doesn't lead to major repercussions, so that isn't as clever as it seems). At the same time, and just as it can in engineering, a minor upset repeated over time can amplify itself, perhaps even leading to complete breakdown. A good example is the Tacoma Narrows Bridge shaking itself apart in a steady breeze in 1940 (you can see it on Youtube). In that dynamic sense, mental disorder is very similar but, under the influence of the static or equilibrium model, modern psychiatry very often takes a *temporary* reaction to a stressor as evidence of a *permanent, genetic* brain defect that must be corrected—by *permanent* drugging. That is, because orthodox psychiatrists are looking for certain symptoms, they detect a false signal and react accordingly. If you want to put it bluntly, even though the patient actually has a temporary, self-correcting state of mind, they rush to label him permanently mad because of some "genetic defect" and put him on drugs. Esssentially, they don't believe in "temporary, self-correcting states of mind," only permanent, irreversible impairments of brain. Because psychiatric drugs induce changes in brain biochemistry, if the patient wasn't mad before he started their treatment, he soon will be.

We have seen examples where severe, persisting anxiety causes depression. The orthodox approach is that anxiety is a minor problem that couldn't possibly cause anything so devastating as depression, so it can be ignored ("the worried well"). The depression is "treated," either with drugs or physical methods such as ECT, and in due course, it goes away. Everybody's happy. The patient pays his bill and goes home. Strangely enough, before long, he's back again, in exactly the same state so he gets double doses, more drugs, more ECT, and so the familiar cycle of the "revolving hospital door" starts again.

Look at this case: an intelligent, 37yo man first broke down while studying philosophy. Since then, he has had something like 25 admissions to hospital, averaging six weeks each, or about three years in hospital at a total cost of something like $1.65million. He is regarded as seriously disturbed, with "rapid cycling bipolar disorder and treatment resistant schizoaffective disorder." At no point in his long career as a professional mental patient has anybody recognised, let alone treated, his glaringly obvious anxiety state. The reason, as he bluntly says, is that nobody has asked him about it. That's a lot of taxpayers' money to spend, and a lot of years of his life to waste, just because his doctrinaire psychiatrists didn't bother taking, or didn't know how to take, a proper history. They were beguiled by the 'false signals' generated by his severe anxiety and drug use: one swallow doesn't make a summer, and one auditory hallucination or whacky belief in a sleep-deprived state, drug-befuddled state doesn't make schizophrenia.

These days, the problem of bad psychiatry is made much worse by illegal drugs. For a seriously anxious person, ordinary daily life is almost intolerable so, all too often, he finds drugs. If he finds stimulants, he's in trouble because stimulants can cause transient psychotic reactions. If he ends up in a hospital with what would otherwise be a transient psychotic reaction to drugs, he will be labelled schizophrenic and put on an involuntary treatment order. Then his life really goes bad.

Case 14.1: Kevin G, 31yo single, unemployed man.

Kevin lives with his disabled father in their own home in a country town. He hasn't worked for about five years but he is deemed his father's carer so he gets extra benefits and doesn't have to look for work. He has requested a second opinion as, four months previously, he was diagnosed schizophrenic and was placed on an involuntary treatment order. He is now receiving monthly injections of an antipsychotic drug but he doesn't like its effects and wants it stopped. Kevin wasn't easy to interview because, quite often, he doesn't appear to be listening. Other times, he blurts out an answer a question before it's finished or he answers a different question. For example, if asked "Where did you go to school?" he may reply "I hated it."

Presenting complaints:

At present, he said, he feels "mostly anxious." He sleeps excessively, from 14-16hrs a day, and is sluggish when he awakens. He has gained weight since the drug started and has very little energy, so he isn't doing much at all. He has no interest or motivation and struggles to get anything done around the house. Socially, he doesn't want to mix with people, which is not normal for him, and he has no sexual interest at all, also not normal. His memory and concentration are both "hazy" and he has trouble thinking clearly or making decisions as his mind feels "fuzzy." The thought content is dominated by worrying about his predicament with mental health services. There were no disturbances of perception, meaning no hallucinations or abnormal beliefs. Specifically, there were none of what are known as first rank symptoms of schizophrenia, which are mostly voices talking to or about the patient.

He described his mood as "drained." He doesn't feel actually low and miserable; he has in the past and knows what it means but at present, he feels "flat, glum," and is not suicidal. He doesn't experience elevated moods but he also never actually feels good. He described frequent bouts of agitation, with a number of somatic symptoms of anxiety, including shaking, racing heart and a tendency to stammer. He wasn't sure about other symptoms as he seemed to be having trouble deciding what was present before the psychiatric drugs and what came on after. However, he described a long list of fears, mainly social in nature and present as long as he could remember. He said he is "agoraphobic" and has always been frightened of crowds, queues and public speaking. He is fearful of appointments and interviews, and tests and exams of any sort. Asked what he would experience if he had to give a talk to a group of people, he immediately lists all the standard symptoms of anxiety. He is frightened of disputes or arguments, confrontation of any sort and saying No to people. He hates letting people down, causing trouble or giving offence, and will always put himself out rather than upset anybody. He fears making mistakes or failing at anything, and death and mental illness. He fears groups of aggressive men, especially Aboriginals, and is frightened of authority.

He has always had a feeling of people looking at him and talking behind his back or judging him. He has a vague sense of being under surveillance, perhaps by the government, because of some "really dumb things" he had done earlier in the year. He doesn't feel in danger from them but has the idea they are possibly keeping an eye on him "...just to make sure, but I could probably be convinced they aren't." However, he has a very strong sense of hostility and danger directed at him by a man called Phil, one of the local heavies, a part-Aboriginal man in a bikie group who sells drugs. When Kevin has to go out, he always makes sure he goes out early morning and doesn't go anywhere Phil is likely to be. There are no obsessive-compulsive features and he is physically well.

Here we run into a common problem. If he doesn't have any symptoms of schizophrenia, he can't be detained and forced to take injections of anti-psychotic drugs against his will. However, we can be sure that the hospital will say the reason he doesn't have any symptoms is because of their drugs. If, somehow, he manages to stop them, it is highly likely that he will become intensely agitated as a withdrawal effect. The hospital will say, "Ah, but that's his genetic illness breaking through again as soon as the drugs wore off so let's start them again." Thus, you see their steady state model of mental disorder at work. It could equally be that the drugs are highly addictive and if he stops them, he will go into a state of intense agitation which prevents him sleeping. Soon, as a result of sleep deprivation, he will start to hallucinate or develop crazy ideas. However, mainstream psychiatrists don't believe their drugs are addictive. How do we know? Partly because they say so but partly because they keep handing them out like sweets. In Chap. 13, Jeremy was prescribed lorazepam without any advice whatsoever that it is about as addictive as morphine, but its withdrawal effects last at least six times as long and are terrifying.

So the steady state or equilibrium model of mental disorder can't lose. If you take the drugs and don't have symptoms, you need more drugs. If, however, you don't take them, you will certainly need more to feed your addiction. In its effect, it is a self-fulfilling prophecy, which makes it non-scientific. But why was Kevin given them in the first place? Why was he diagnosed schizophrenic at age 31yrs when it is normally diagnosed in much younger men? Its classic name, dementia praecox, means precocious dementia, specifically adolescence. This is where it becomes problematic because Kevin's odd way of talking works against him. We will change the pattern this time and look at his background before his recent history.

Personal background:

He has lived practically all his life in rural areas. His parents separated when he was about three and he was raised by his mother until he was six but he had no contact with his father for the next ten years. His mother is aged about fifty but he doesn't know much about her. He said she was "always grumpy" and he recalled they squabbled a lot. She had another partner who didn't want him so, at six, his mother sent him to live with his older half-sister's father for about six years and he rarely saw her. He said this was terrible as the man was extremely bad-tempered and he was often abused and hit. He recalled that if he did anything wrong, he was belted and locked in a room by himself for hours on end.

When he was twelve, his half-sister committed suicide over sexual abuse by her father and an uncle so he was sent back to live with his mother whom he hardly knew. However, he didn't get on with his mother's new partner so at about fifteen, he went to stay with his father, who by this time had been disabled by a back injury at work. His father is now aged about 55yrs and worked as a mill hand until he was injured. He bought his house with the settlement money following his injury. Kevin describes him as "OK, pretty grumpy, complains all the time." Kevin has to do all the housework and keep the garden tidy. His father drinks at times but he smokes marijuana every day, allegedly for pain. Kevin buys it from Phil, about $100 a week (10gm), and they share. Kevin has a much younger maternal half-brother but hardly knows him. His mother had three children by three different men but his father had only the one child.

His schooling was disrupted by frequent moves. He left school at age 16yrs, after passing Year 10 with fairly poor marks. He said he often wagged school as he was very shy and nervous. If anybody teased him or pushed him around, he would run away and hide for several days. He was very quiet in class and didn't get into trouble except for not doing his homework. He didn't get on with the other children as he was "very withdrawn" and hardly had any friends except at sport. He was quite good at football and the sports sessions were about the only time of week he enjoyed. On leaving school, he found seasonal work picking fruit or other unskilled jobs. He worked in the meatworks for a while but found the work too strenuous and didn't get on with the other men. He hasn't worked for five years.

Socially, he has practically no life. He has always been single, has never had a girlfriend and has had no sexual experience at all. He has no hobbies or practical or social interests, doesn't study and reads only fantasy or sensational material on the internet. He spends his time doing the bit of housework or shopping, or watching a bit of TV but mostly on the internet. He drinks very little but has smoked marijuana daily since about age 13yrs, except when he was given the injections, the combination made him feel very scared so he stopped it. About five years ago, before he moved to stay with his father, he was living in the city and smoking a lot of marijuana. He became nervous and his flatmate suggested he should see somebody. He saw mental health services once but didn't go back. He has tried a few other drugs over the years but nothing regular until earlier in the year when he started using methamphetamine. He doesn't gamble and has a minor police record for possession. He feels his general health is good with no chronic illnesses.

Self-assessment.

Asked how he sees himself, he replies: "Unimportant." He feels he is very nervous and is intensely bothered by guilt, shame and self-consciousness. He is unassertive and submissive, over-patient and over-trusting but also wary in dealing with people. He is not very social, not inclined to be jealous and rarely holds grudges. He is fairly untidy but mostly follows rules and keeps a low profile around authority. He sees his temper as "mild," his intellect as "pretty dumb, always making stupid decisions," and his self-esteem is "pretty low, not much of a person, no good at anything."

Mental state examination.

The mental state showed a fit-looking chap of about his stated age, of about 180cm and 80kg. He was dressed in clean but drab old casual clothes, with longish untidy hair and a thin, untidy beard. There were no visible tattoos, studs, scars or jewellery. He was hesitant and apologetic, and tended to give impulsive answers to questions, often fading out before ending as though losing interest in answering. His answers were generally vague, approximate or disorganised. He was slightly tremulous and uncertain, but not depressed, hostile or suspicious. There were no psychotic features and, despite his poor education, he is at least of bright normal intellect, probably superior.

This is the person who presented at the hospital a few months previously and was labelled 'schizophrenic.' They knew nothing about him at the time, of course, they were simply going on the symptoms he presented. Their records also showed that when he was discharged, they still didn't have any idea of him as a person. This is because, to them, he wasn't a person, he was a biological specimen. However, he was at all times a person, one with a history, a mental life and a future. Trouble is, by the beginning of 2017, his history was boring, lonely and miserable, his future seemed to be more of the same stretching endlessly forward, and his mental life was rapidly becoming desperate. One day in summer, when Kevin went to get some more marijuana, Phil suggested he should try amphetamines, which is the sort of thing drug dealers do. Having tried them once years before, he agreed. In no time, he was feeling excited and adventurous. He became engrossed in various conspiracies on the internet and was sure that the country was going to the dogs. He began writing his ideas on what was wrong and how it should be fixed, but he was sufficiently clever to see that every standard remedy would be blocked by vested interests.

His history becomes garbled now as, under the influence of amphetamines, he began posting material on Facebook and various other sites. Somewhere, he decided that the only way to fix the country's many problems would be to install a benevolent dictator but, being a fantasist and a bit of a traditionalist, he thought a king would be better than an all-powerful president. He wrote a long and detailed program for a king that would lead to a golden future but it seemed a bit pointless, so he rewrote it as a letter to the Queen, nominating himself as a suitable candidate for the crown and posted it on the internet. At about the same time, a girl he had known from years before told him that Phil had raped her. Full of the righteous rage of methamphetamine, he strode up to one of Phil's cousins and told him that if Phil ever did anything like that again, he, Kevin, would sort him out good and proper.

A day or two later, he ran out of drugs. In the grips of the "let down," he suddenly realised the gravity of what he had done and panicked. For several days, he stayed at home, terrified of what might happen if he showed his face at Phil's place but aware that he couldn't survive without the drugs. The marijuana ran out, his normally grumpy father began complaining angrily of pain and life got much worse. For several days, Kevin was unable to sleep. Finally, in a state he called "total melt-down," he managed to get himself to the local hospital and plead for help. Overwhelmingly distressed, he told them that the local bikie gang was after him and that he had written to the Queen asking to be crowned king. How much they understood we don't know because, even at best, Kevin isn't the clearest speaker. Distraught, confused, sleep-deprived, terrified and withdrawing from drugs, an interviewer who didn't speak his local argot could possibly feel he was thought-disordered. Now it gets complicated.

The psychiatric staff were new to the country. It would be fair to say that they had barely the faintest clue of modern urban Aboriginal culture, specifically that if you threaten one member of a family group, you threaten the lot. Because of his drug-fuelled threat, Kevin actually was in danger of a fairly serious flogging. His long and self-indulgent letter to the Queen, which the hospital didn't see but were convinced was *ipso facto* delusional grandiosity, was not delusional. It was the sort of thing a lonely fantasist might write late at night to convince himself he wasn't a total dead loss and may even be of benefit to society. It was excessively courteous, apologised for his presumption and set out a program of social, economic and environmental renewal that would appeal to a bright, lonely chap with a Year 10 education, living in a small country town, who could see problems wherever he looked but had no idea how to rectify them. It was not thought-disordered but was couched in the sort of flowery nonsense that made Walter Scott a wealthy knight (before he went broke). But: Kevin broke one of the most fundamental rules of life on the lower rungs of society: never tell a person in power anything he may use against you. Give the police your name, address and date of birth and nothing else.

Same goes for psychiatrists, who want to diagnose people with biological illnesses because they believe that's what psychiatrists do. That is, they responded inappropriately to the false signals Kevin's drug-fuelled grandiosity, his fear and his sleep deprivation were generating. They thought that one fearful idea that he might get a flogging was necessarily a paranoid delusion of persecution, and that what he had written to make himself feel better was a conviction that he ought to be crowned king. In his missive, he doesn't actually say that should happen, only that it would probably be good fun and he promised not to abuse power like everybody else.

From the psychiatric point of view, there is a general principle involved, one which actually goes back a long way: *Primum non nocere*. First, do no harm. The principle is simple: A person is not to be diagnosed psychotic unless and until it is unavoidably true. People should not be diagnosed psychotic on the off-chance that they may be. However, we immediately run into a major problem: in public practice, psychiatrists are driven almost entirely by a fear of what may go wrong if they *don't* diagnose somebody as seriously mentally ill: "If I don't label him schizophrenic and something goes wrong, where will that leave me?" In trouble, they all know that. Angry letters from relatives, a "Please explain" from the director of psychiatry, the coroner's court, the evening news, damages and, who knows, dismissal. For psychiatrists who are in the country on a restricted visa, being dismissed could mean the visa being cancelled.

So for a young foreign psychiatrist working alone in a rural centre late at night, there are very, very powerful reasons to overdiagnose rather than run the many potentially catastrophic risks of underdiagnosing. Once the distressed person is labelled, he can be wrestled to the ground, injected and put in the security ward. That way, if anything goes wrong, the psychiatrist will be fully covered. For a private psychiatrist, there are also potentially serious risks attached to underdiagnosing, including angry relatives, police enquiries, coroner's court, damages... It's all too scary. Far better to go to the most serious diagnosis and stick with it because nobody can argue, nobody will argue. It is easy to say a person is schizophrenic, far more difficult to prove that he's not. And, of course, it pays so much better, let's not forget that. Psychiatrists are paid far more to see people indefinitely than they are to send them home.

That is, the entire edifice of modern biological psychiatry is biased toward making major diagnoses, thereby depriving the patient of practically all his human rights and committing him to a form of "treatment" that will substantially shorten his life, just because it is safer for everybody else and, who knows, maybe even more profitable. The bias starts early, with psychiatrists trained in a gravely restricted ideology of mental disorder; most of whom can't take a proper history because they believe it's irrelevant; who are steeped in the doctrine of "cover your arse;" who have a wildly exaggerated (delusional?) view of the efficacy of their "treatment" and who simply don't believe it can actually do harm. Medically, failing to treat is regarded as a very much worse sin than over-treating because the drugs are harmless, after all.

Thus, we have the bizarre state where a person can be dragged into hospital and drugged or shocked against his will in order to forestall the dire danger of "mental deterioration" or even the illusory "reputational damage." The fact that the treatment may be worse than the "disease" doesn't penetrate. For example, people maintained on long-term antipsychotic drugs gain huge amounts of weight, smoke heavily, don't exercise, develop diabetes and high blood pressure (the so-called metabolic syndrome). Unsurprisingly, they die young. All this happens because psychiatry doesn't understand that for a sad and lonely virginal loser in a rural backwater, with no job, no assets, no friends and no hope, dreaming of all the good you could do as king may be more interesting than sitting in your room wondering whether the light fitting would support a noose.

Actually, it gets worse: I have heard of several cases where psychiatrists warned patients and their families that if the patient didn't take his drugs, he would suffer brain damage as a direct result of the psychotic process. Needless to say, this scares the families witless. There is no evidence for this claim; it is an urban myth.

While we're talking about trying to practice psychiatry in a foreign language and culture, I have done that so I know just how difficult it is. In 1981, I spent a year at Prince of Songkla University in Haadyai, Southern Thailand. Even though I could speak, read and write Thai, I would never have been able to discern the subtleties of speech and manner that the medical students immediately sensed in the patients. It was exceedingly difficult. Based on that experience, I would say it is almost impossible to practice anything other than the most elementary psychiatry using a second language.

Mainstream psychiatrists, however, will jovially disagree. It's easy, they chuckle, all you have to do is ask whether he's hearing voices, then Bob's your uncle, stick him on the drugs. But a "biological psychiatry" just is the most elementary psychiatry.

Case 14.2: Valerie S, 56yo unemployed teacher.

This lady was referred by her general practitioner in a small town about 250km from the city. She was unable to work as her registration had been cancelled because of years of severe mental disturbance. She was taking lithium 500mg and moclobemide 600mg per day but she had had many other drugs in the past. She didn't like the drugs as they made her feel "more dead than alive" and caused steady weight gain but she didn't dare stop them herself as she knew she would suffer severe withdrawal effects. At the time she was seen, she was living with her partner of about 15 years but he worked away two weeks in three, so she spent a lot of time alone. They had recently built a new house on their 10ha block (25ac), about ten minutes drive from the town. At home, she was busy with the garden and caring for the animals but she felt unable to mix with people and preferred to stay on their property while her partner was away.

Presenting Complaints

In general, she said, she was feeling "not too bad." She was sleeping solidly, about ten hours each night, and her appetite was good but she was slowly gaining weight. She had enough energy for a fairly busy day but she didn't take any extra exercise. She was interested in her usual activities and liked to get things done as she didn't like sitting around. She had no social life of her own: "I don't want to see people. I have a sense of not fitting in and I'm embarrassed over not working." She had very little sexual interest.

She felt her memory and concentration were poor but she was able to drive to the city and home again after each appointment. She was able to think clearly and make decisions and there were no abnormal perceptions. She described her mood as "waves of anxiety" and was feeling low and miserable about half the time. This was "sad, not suicidal" but she added that she often felt "passively suicidal." Four months previously, she had been feeling it would be better if she simply dropped dead but there was no specific reason: "I have no job, no purpose, no future." She had not experienced elevated moods for years although she had done in the distant past.

She described bouts of intense agitation with many somatic symptoms of anxiety, including shaking, sweating, palpitations, churning stomach and shortness of breath. During them, she stammered and was unable to think or make decisions. She felt irritable and frightened but wasn't sure why. She was having several bouts per week but they lasted for hours on end and she was unable to do anything during them. On questioning, she had always been frightened of public speaking, interviews, threats and criticism, and of arguments or disputes. She feared confrontation, letting people down, causing trouble or giving offence, and always tried to keep the peace. She was fearful of loneliness, humiliation and disapproval and, in particular, of making mistakes or failing at anything. She had always been frightened of mental illness and feared aggressive people.

There were no paranoid symptoms. She had always been fussy about cleanliness, tidiness, order and punctuality but there were no true obsessive-compulsive symptoms. Physically, she was well.

Her history leading to and since her involvement with mental health services was tortuous so it's probably easier to look at her background first, so the psychiatric history can be seen in proper context.

Personal Background:

She was born and raised in the city but later moved to rural areas. Her father, a retired Army sergeant-major, died in 2005, aged about 75yrs. She described him as "a bit up and down, moody and very strict, controlling, domineering, brought the military home." His own father was severely abusive and had been convicted of sexual offences. She thought the grandfather was an alcoholic and she was sure there was sexual abuse in the family. Her father was a militant atheist but his wife, who died about ten years later, aged 89yrs, was a "raving Christian, totally obsessed." She had a long psychiatric history. After the youngest child was born, she suffered a puerperal psychosis and was in and out of hospitals for decades, on large doses of drugs, "completely ruined as a person." Valerie never got on with her mother but somewhat better with her father. Their marriage was poor and she often argued with her father over the way he treated his wife after her breakdowns.

Valerie was the second of three children, the first a brother then aged about 58yrs. He was also ex-Army, working as a technician. He had divorced and was living alone, "OK but domineering and judgemental." The younger brother, aged about 54yrs, was "a tragic psychiatric case." After leaving school, he had joined the Navy but was soon discharged on psychiatric grounds. He then tried to study but again broke down and was detained in hospital where he was given ECT and large doses of drugs. Subsequently, he lived on the streets then went back to live with his parents but he disappeared after his mother gave him a very large sum of money and hadn't been seen for years.

She attended local church schools to the age of 16yrs, passing Year 10 with bare average marks as she wasn't interested in school. She got on reasonably well with the teachers and the other children but didn't play much sport. Out of school, her home life wasn't very good but she was interested in animals and had friends. She began an apprenticeship but quickly became pregnant and had to stop work. At home, she decided that she would keep the baby which caused a ferocious brawl with her mother who saw the pregnancy as a mortal sin: "She never let me forget it, she brought it up every day until she died." To her surprise, her father was much more accepting of the baby and always supported her against her mother.

She tried living with the father of the baby but this lasted only long enough for her to become pregnant again. She then married in order to get out of her parents' home but separated after only a few months and had to go back again with her two infant children. Soon after, she remarried and this lasted 15yrs and gave her two more children. However, this was poor and she suffered recurrent bouts of depression and eating disorder. She was prescribed fluoxetine, which caused a manic reaction so she was taken to a mental hospital. Soon after, the marriage ended, leaving her with four teenage children so she married yet again. This was worse and she finally separated after her husband assaulted her, breaking her leg. Some time later, she met her current partner and they had been together about 15yrs. At the time she was seen, she was leading a very quiet social life, didn't drink, used no drugs, didn't gamble and had no police record.

Self-Assessment:

She saw herself as "nice but useless." Surprisingly, and despite suffering "waves of anxiety," she said she was not a nervous person although she was bothered by guilt, shame and self-consciousness. She was assertive to the point of arguing, mistrustful, impatient, tidy and followed rules. She was not a social person and was not jealous but sometimes held grudges. In the main, she got on fairly well with authority. She saw her temper as "even," her intellect as "reasonably intelligent" and her self-esteem as "fairly good."

Mental State Examination:

The mental state showed a healthy, somewhat overweight middle-aged woman in clean plain casual clothes, with no visible tattoos, studs, scars or jewellery. She was talkative, rambling on in vast detail in a rather flat and monotonous voice. She was somewhat wary and guarded, and not very happy but was neither hostile nor suspicious. There were no psychotic features and she appeared to be at least of bright normal intellect, if not superior.

Psychiatric history:

While with her third partner, she suffered recurrent bouts of depression so she was prescribed fluoxetine by her GP. However, she developed a manic state which led to her first involuntary admission to hospital. Being taken into hospital on an order was the worst experience of her life as she thought it meant she would end up like her mother. She was diagnosed with "bipolar disorder," not a drug reaction, and was given a variety of other drugs but she has never been settled since then. In hospital, she was placed in a mixed ward and, in her agitated state, became promiscuous with the male patients which still troubled her thirty years later.

Because of her breakdown, the marriage ended but soon after, while still in a disturbed state, she married impulsively. This was poor and ended in her leaving after she was assaulted. After the fractured leg was treated, she decided to go on an overseas holiday but her ex-husband got an emergency order to have her detained. She was taken off the aircraft by police and taken to hospital. After she was discharged, she began seeing a private psychiatrist even though she couldn't afford the fees. She studied teaching and eventually graduated but had not worked for years as she felt she couldn't think properly because of the drugs.

Prior to being referred, she had seen a psychiatrist for about four years but wasn't happy with the treatment: "I never liked her, she was a snob. She never once discussed my life or took my history. She'd talk about the weather but if I started to talk about what had happened to me, she'd laugh and say, 'Look at all this psychoanalysis, now what about your tablets?' It cost a lot of money."

I would say the psychiatrist wasn't so much a snob, refusing to deal with the patient's distress, but she didn't know what to do. Because she hadn't taken a history, she had no idea, no understanding of the patient and, above all, no model of mental disorder to tell her what to do. That's not entirely her fault, it's the fault of the system that trained her but she knew, or ought to have known, that she wasn't paid to talk about the weather. But that's a minor gripe compared with the main point of Valerie's history, that her treatment turned her into a mental case.

I've mentioned before that the incidence of mental disorder is rising relentlessly, even as the number of people taking psychiatric drugs rises. In fact, these figures are rising in lock-step. The more people take antidepressants, the more suicides we see. And the more people who take these drugs, the higher the rate of so-called bipolar disorder. Now if a person takes methamphetamine and develops a paranoid psychotic state, we call it a "drug-induced psychosis." We expect that if he stops taking them, he will recover but if he tries them again, he's very likely to go mad again. But if a person takes drugs designed to lift mood, drugs we call antidepressants, and his mood does indeed lift but goes a bit too far, we don't call that a case of drug-induced hypomania. Instead, and with the full authority of the American Psychiatric Association's DSM-5, we call it "bipolar disorder." We say that the drug uncovered a latent tendency to bipolar disorder, even though he had never shown any such behaviour before taking the antidepressant:

Note: A full manic episode that emerges during antidepressant treatment (e.g., medication, electroconvulsive therapy) but persists at a fully syndromal level beyond the physiological effect of that treatment *is sufficient evidence* for a manic episode and therefore, a bipolar I diagnosis (p124, emphasis added).

However, the plot thickens because the previous edition, DSM-IV, specifically excluded drug-induced hypomania as contributing toward a diagnosis of bipolar disorder:

Note: Manic-like episodes that are clearly caused by somatic antidepressant treatment (e.g., medication, electroconvulsive therapy, light therapy) *should not count toward* a diagnosis of Bipolar I Disorder (p332, emphasis added).

Philip Hickey, a retired psychologist who lives in Colorado, neatly shafts the medical approach. In his blog from January 12th, 2015, he said:

Psychiatry defines "bipolar disorder" by the presence of certain behaviours and feelings. If a person meets these criteria, he/she is said to *have* bipolar disorder. What immediately needs to be noted is that bipolar disorder, in common with psychiatry's other "disorders" has no explanatory value. To illustrate this, consider the following hypothetical conversation.

Parent: Why does my son behave in these extreme ways?
Psychiatrist: Because he has bipolar disorder.
Parent: How do you know he has bipolar disorder?
Psychiatrist: Because he behaves in these extreme ways.
The *only* evidence for the illness is the very behaviour that it claims to explain.

This fingers a huge and unacknowledged problem in psychiatry, how it mixes or conflates description and explanation. In philosophical terms, you cannot nominate *and* define an entity in a single illocutionary act. But psychiatry wants its cake and eats it too. It tries both to define a mental disorder and explain it by the single act of applying a name to it. Hickey continues:

As spurious as this is from a logical point of view, the notion of a *latent* bipolar disorder is even worse.
Parent: Why did my son become manic after starting on antidepressant drugs?
Psychiatrist: Because he had a latent bipolar disorder.
Parent: How do you know he had a latent bipolar disorder?
Psychiatrist: Because he became manic.

What psychiatry is doing here is applying their spurious explanation *retrospectively*. *Before* the individual showed any signs of mania, he must have had bipolar disorder because he became manic at a later date. But nobody could ever have verified that hypothesis, because the occurrence of a manic or hypomanic episode is the primary criterion for such a "diagnosis".

There is another long-standing philosophical principle we should invoke, Ockham's Razor, or the principle of parsimony. This dates back at least to early middle ages, possibly much more. It says that the number of explanatory entities must not expand beyond the minimum needed to complete the explanation. So: a person is sick with a chest infection. We give him an antibiotic. He develops a rash. The parsimonious explanation is that he developed a drug reaction. Another man smokes. He develops lung cancer. The parsimonious explanation is that the cigarettes caused the lung cancer, we don't invoke another disease process unless we have to. A third man is taking morphine. He stops it abruptly and develops a range of unpleasant physical and mental symptoms. The parsimonious explanation is that cessation of morphine caused the symptoms (better known as withdrawal).

In Valerie's case, she was depressed. She was given an antidepressant, a drug designed to lift mood. Her mood lifted—and kept going, until she was frankly hypomanic (which she recognises). Psychiatry's explanation is that she had two entirely separate mental diseases, one of which was unsuspected until she took the drug. The parsimonious explanation is that the drug *caused* (in every sense of the word) her hypomanic state. Now why would psychiatry even bother trying to invoke another of what they would call genetically separate mental diseases to explain this? Well, that's better than admitting that your treatment made her worse, isn't it? In this sense, psychiatry is doing just what the tobacco industry, then the asbestos industry, and now the fossil fuel industry, have always done, introducing extra explanatory entities to cloud the line of causation, thereby hiding their culpability (this is now called the Tobacco Playbook).

However, you ask, why didn't she just get better? Because nobody ever took her off the drugs: once a bipolar, always a bipolar. Thus, they kept adding more, stopping this one and adding another two so of course she couldn't get better. Her brain was constantly battered by chemicals that nobody understands. But this doesn't read well in the media, so psychiatry resolutely insists that constantly chopping and changing powerful psychoactive chemicals has no effect whatsoever on mental function (it may be of interest that although 10% of adult Australians take antidepressants for their 'genetic' disease of the brain, very few psychiatrists take them).

In simple terms, Valerie's initial state of depression was a reaction to her very unhappy life. The drugs she was prescribed couldn't improve a poor marriage but she took them anyway, except they drove her mad. She is now coming off the drugs, and her mental state is steadily improving. Coming off lithium, she said, was "like coming out of a dark tunnel." Her so-called bipolar disorder was entirely iatrogenic (adj: doctor-caused, from Gk *iatros*, doctor, and Latin *genere*, to breed or cause). The new epidemic of bipolar disorder is almost entirely caused by psychoactive drugs prescribed by physicians. Either that or we have to invoke a further explanatory entity called "mass mutation of brain enzymes taking place in a single generation." As an explanation, that little monster should have its throat cut by Ockham's Razor. Until proven otherwise, I think we have to accept that it's the drugs what done it. Trouble is, the institution of orthodox psychiatry is so scared of this that it won't go near it until somebody threatens to cut its throat.

15

Treatment and Review of Case Studies

This book isn't about treatment, it's a book about the concept of anxiety, how to see it from a different stance and how to come to grips with it. Before we say anything about treatment, all readers need to be very aware of two important rules:

1. Do NOT attempt to diagnose yourself. It cannot be done.

2. Do NOT attempt to treat yourself. It cannot be done.

In order to stop people trying to diagnose and treat themselves, I will give only half of the program here, the easy half, just to show what this model can achieve. The difficult part, the part that actually does most of the work, requires a separate book.

Treatment should follow rationally from the model. In simplest terms, the model says that anxiety is a self-reinforcing disorder, amplified by feedback loops until the sufferer must do something to stop it. Depending on what he does, it may work or it may make things worse, like drinking, until eventually, the anxiety destroys him. Treatment is therefore directed at breaking the feedback loops. We do that by two means, drugs and psychotherapy. In this chapter, we will only talk about drugs. Let's look at the somatic symptoms of anxiety again:

- Shaking or jelly-like feeling in limbs
- Sweating, especially palms
- Racing heart or heart thudding violently in chest or throat
- Churning or knotted stomach, or butterflies sensation
- Shortness of breath or tightness in chest
- Dry mouth
- Tightness or lump in throat
- Quavering voice
- Stammering or stuttering

- Light-headedness, dizziness or clumsiness.

At the same time, the cognitive symptoms include a sense of the walls closing in, or being trapped; an awareness that the world is in some vital sense different; or that you are different, either from other people or from your normal sense. Your mind may go blank or there may be too many thoughts tumbling through the head.

Clearly, the somatic symptoms are the signs of over-arousal in the sympathetic nervous system, or what is commonly called an "adrenaline rush." These symptoms feed back to the individual, either directly, as in:

> Oh dear, I'm starting to shake/my heart is starting to race/my stomach is churning/etc, which means I'm going to have one of my dreadful turns, *and the thought of a dreadful turn is itself terrifying.*

They can also feed back indirectly, as in:

> Oh dear, I'm starting to shake/sweat/stammer etc, that means everybody will see it and think I'm a drunk or a loser, *and the thought of their disapproval is itself terrifying.*

The expression "a terrifying thought" means "a thought which causes terror just by having it."

How do we block the symptoms of sympathetic over-arousal? That's not difficult, we use the class of drugs called beta adrenaline-blockers. They have a dramatic effect on generalised over-arousal *but* only the old-fashioned ones. Modern beta blockers have been engineered to be cardio-specific and don't have the same range of effects as the originals, propranolol and oxprenolol.

Propranolol is the most effective. It is safe, predictable, rapidly absorbed, non-cumulative, non-addictive, cheap, and has only slight side-effects which tend to wear off in a week or so. Most importantly, it doesn't have much direct effect on the brain itself. However, it has one major disadvantage: in people with active asthma, it can provoke asthma attacks. Normally, asthmatics can't take it but it is surprising the numbers of people who have been prescribed asthma puffers on the basis of shortness of breath, who don't have any wheeze in their chests, who can take propranolol and who are then able to stop using their puffers. That is, the diagnosis was wrong. Almost always, they were prescribed asthma drugs just on the complaint "I get short of breath." But anxiety, in which subjective shortness of breath or dyspnoea is such a prominent feature, is far more common than asthma.

I ask every patient I see if they have asthma. About one in twenty says they do. Of this group, most don't have any signs of the disease and tolerate propranolol very well. For perhaps 50% of the people who genuinely can't take it because it causes chest tightness and wheezing, oxprenolol will be effective. As the bronchoconstrictive effect of beta blockers is doseo-related, quite a few people can take one or two tablets before they start to experience chest tightness, so they can often get the short-term advantage when they need it, e.g. giving a lecture, before a flight etc. A small proportion of people can't take either so they need other remedies.

In my practice, all patients who have the target symptoms listed above will be prescribed beta blockers in the first instance. It doesn't matter how depressed they are, the mere fact of somebody taking a proper history and providing a firm diagnosis gives them a couple of weeks grace. During this short time, the drug is able to prove its merits. Over the past forty years, I estimate I have prescribed it for about 8,000 people, if not more. I prescribe it because it works and it has huge benefits:

1. ECT: Since I graduated as a psychiatrist in 1977, I have never once used electroconvulsive treatment (ECT). My series of perhaps 15,000 consecutive, unselected, public patients is possibly the world's biggest naturalistic study of ECT (*not* using ECT is also a study of ECT). This has *not* unleashed an epidemic of suicide. The repeated claims that ECT is essential, or indispensable, or even useful, are false. Any psychiatrist can learn how to practice without using ECT. The fact that they don't says only that they are attached to it, partly because they firmly believe the dogma that mental disorder is biological, partly because it pays so well but mostly for lack of knowing what to do.

2. Antidepressants: I hardly ever prescribe antidepressants. Perhaps twice a year, I will start an antidepressant but it will be a moderate dose of a mild drug for a limited period only. I never allow patients to take them for life. As a result, my patients do not gain weight. More to the point, by allowing them to discontinue their psychiatric drugs, beta blockers allow people to lose the massive amounts of weight they have gained from conventional drugs.

3. Mood stabilisers: I never prescribe the group of drugs known as "mood-stabilisers." The original drug in this class was lithium, which I stopped prescribing in 1987 when I moved to the monsoonal region in the far north of Western Australia. With day time temperatures normally well over 40C (104F) and punishing levels of humidity, lithium was far too risky as it can cause convulsions, coma and death even in partial dehydration. However, this experience showed me that a drug I had been taught was essential in psychiatry was not, in fact, essential at all. It was very dispensable, so I've never used it since.

Starting in the early 1970s, psychiatrists began prescribing anticonvulsants or antiepileptic drugs as "adjuncts" to drug management of manic-depressive psychosis. As the incidence of epilepsy was steadily dropping in western countries, this gave the manufacturers a new and ever-expanding market for their products. The story of how this came about is simply bizarre. In the 1950s, and apparently as an act of desperation, the family doctor of a decidedly unpleasant American financier named Jack Dreyfus prescribed phenytoin, a powerful anticonvulsant. *Mirabile dictu*, it calmed him down. His previous volcanic rages and ghastly behaviour moderated, so he wrote a book praising the drug and sent a copy to every American doctor. From this small nut grew the mighty tree of anticonvulsant mood stabilisers. Except I don't use them. They aren't mood stabilisers, they are just non-specific tranquillisers that don't wear off. No psychiatrist *needs* to use them, a fact established beyond doubt by my forty years of not using them.

4. Antipsychotics: I never prescribe these drugs unless the patient is actually psychotic. In Australia over the past quarter century, prescription rates for antipsychotic drugs have rocketed. Specifically, between 1992-93 and 2015-16, when the population increased by 33%, Medicare prescriptions of these drugs rose 359%, almost 1100% more than could be predicted (the real increase was even larger because the national Medicare insurance scheme doesn't pay for admissions to state hospitals). The reason is that they are being given to ever-expanding numbers of people for ever-expanding lists of reasons *but...* once started, they can't be stopped. Hospitals now routinely use olanzapine and quetiapine as hypnotics, to help non-psychotic people sleep, but once they go home, the unhappy patients can't do without them. If they try, they may well develop a withdrawal psychosis, and the drugs will be doubled.

Drug companies push their products relentlessly, knowing full well that the so-called "second generation antipsychotics" are often hundreds of times more expensive than the drugs they have replaced but are no better in terms of efficacy or side-effects. A month's injections of the modern antipsychotic drug risperidone 50mg costs AU$847.00. In India, where it is manufactured, a monthly injection of fluphenazine decanoate 50mg, which risperidone has replaced, costs R72. That's... wait for it... AU$1.48. That is, the new drug costs 57,228% *more* than the drug it replaced with practically no demonstrable therapeutic advantage.

Another point which is rarely recognised is that the smallest dose of a drug available is actually much larger than the maximum dose to reduce them. For example, the smallest dose of amisulpride is 100mg but it carries the warning: "Do not stop this drug abruptly." How anybody can get off it without stopping it abruptly is not known. The smallest dose of aripiprazole available on the national health scheme is 10mg. That is far too big to stop abruptly. A five mg tablet is marketed but is not available on the benefits scheme. Why not? Because the manufacturers did not apply to have it registered.

Depot injections of olanzapine are available in two sizes, 300mg and 400mg, at a cost of about AU$300 for 300mg, which is enough for a month. If the injection is to be reduced, it is necessary to buy the expensive preparation and squirt the rest out. Smaller volumes are not available.

I checked whether it would be possible to start a company which imported small doses of drugs but was told that approval of each preparation of each previously-approved drug would cost $150,000. Let's say we wanted to import amisulpride in doses of 50mg, 20mg and 10mg, which would be needed to allow a 10% reduction in each drug. That would cost AU $450,000 just for regulatory approval of drugs which were widely in use, even if they came from the same manufacturer.

You have to hand it to the drug companies, they certainly know which side their bread is buttered. In the alternative, you could say psychiatrists are easily fooled. Anyway, I prescribe these drugs strictly according to their name: for psychosis.

5. Hospitals: I hardly ever admit people to hospital. In any year, I see about 500 individual cases, of whom at least 250 are new cases. Only about five of these people (or 1%) will go to hospital in any year. Practically all of them will be either floridly psychotic and either homeless or unmanageable at home, or they will be people with long psychiatric histories with numerous previous admissions to hospital who take themselves to hospital. It is possible to manage the great bulk of unselected, public patients without ever admitting them to hospital. Granted, managing disturbed people at home is more difficult but it certainly can be done *if the will is there*. Of course, it cannot be offered when patients are dragged into emergency departments by police, to be assessed by nurses using checklists.

An accessible outreach service will prevent about 90% of hospital admissions. This, however, is exactly what the owners of the very lucrative private hospitals don't want to hear. They make their money by keeping their luxurious establishments stuffed full of wealthy people who shouldn't be there, or not-so-wealthy people who foolishly believe that if you want the best for your relatives, you must pay for it. Ultimately, most of the costs are paid from the public purse.

Public hospitals are no better. Some years ago, I stood in the psychiatric assessment unit of the emergency department of a major teaching hospital in a large American city. Their grotesquely medieval approach to mental disorder left me astounded and appalled. All patients coming into the hospital entered via the locked unit where they were stripped of their clothes and dressed in little gowns. They were then left beside a bed for hours until an elderly nurse arrived with a computer on a trolley. She took their history according to the laborious format on the screen, in full sight and sound of the other patients who wandered around like lost souls. Hours later, a psychiatric resident checked the checklist and wrote a prescription. Some people were allowed to go home, some went back to police custody but the majority were admitted to the hospital psychiatric ward or sent to the state hospital about 30 miles away. I had never seen anything quite so depraved but didn't want to say so for fear of offending my hosts.

"This must be costing you quite a bit," I mused. "I'd say it's about $1000 each time a patient comes through that door."

"It's $1032 per admission," replied the chief psychiatrist, a charming, cultured and very experienced chap of Middle Eastern origin who spoke about six languages.

"If you had a proper outreach service, most of these people wouldn't be here," I said as mildly as I could. "I could show you how to do it for about $250 each."

"Not here you couldn't," he replied briskly. "Corruption and institution-alised inefficiency, that's what we deal with. Shall we go?"

Corruption and institutionalised inefficiency. If you had to characterise the institution of modern psychiatry, you'd be hard-pressed to beat that.

According to the Australian Institute of Health and Welfare, this country spends about $8.5 billion a year on mental health treatment for four million patients. If we take into account all the services trying to rectify the damage wrought by alcohol and drugs, family disruption, school failure and so on, I'm sure that figure would be very much higher, but that's the figure we deal with. My figures indicate that at least half of that money is wasted on unnecessary admissions to hospital. Half of the rest is wasted on unnecessary prescriptions of drugs. If people are given the choice of being managed at home by a psychiatrist working in their local area in a readily accessible centre, or going to hospital, almost invariably, they choose to stay at home. Most of them can in fact be managed at home but *not* if the psychiatrist believes that all mental disorder is biological in nature.

6. Suicide: Any psychiatrist seeing 250 new cases a year in a socially-deprived area, many of them poor and socially-isolated or with drug and alcohol problems and prison records, is going to see some seriously disturbed people. Very few of my patients commit suicide. In the past twenty-two years, I can recall five patients who took their lives while still being treated. One was a very isolated and secretive man who lost his job after he was injured in a work accident. He did not reveal that he was having an affair with a married woman. She decided to end the relationship, whereupon he went to a secluded place in the bush and took a carefully planned, lethal overdose.

The second was a middle-aged man whose wife had moved in with their neighbour, taking the children and denying him access even though he could see them and hear them from his house. He was seen on a Thursday and appeared to be doing tolerably well. The next morning, he went to a mandatory mediation conference with his ex-wife. That night, without contacting anybody, he hanged himself.

The third was a 38yo man who had separated from his second wife and had gone back to the first, who had custody of his child. He seemed to be managing but had a series of further upsets including losing his job. He stopped attending and some weeks later gassed himself in his car. The fourth was a 32yo man with a long psychiatric history who had been diagnosed and treated as schizophrenic although his disorder started as a drug-induced psychosis. He was severely disabled by social phobia but agreed to start a training course. On his way to the first day of his course, he suddenly killed himself in front of the passers-by. Not one of these people had given any indication they were in danger.

The last was a 26yo single man with severe social phobia and drug addiction who had made a number of half-hearted attempts on his life over the years. He appeared to be doing reasonably well but failed to attend an appointment to get his supplies for the next two weeks. Several days later, he was found dead of an overdose but no details have been released so it may have been accidental. It seems extremely unlikely that he used his prescribed drugs to end his life.

There will always be suicides. We cannot prevent suicides altogether, and I don't believe we should try. My view is that suicide is the last, inalienable right of any person. There are people for whom life has become intolerable. If we take all conceivable precautions to prevent them ending their torture, we will necessarily remove all reasons for them to live.

7. **Overdoses:** My patients rarely take overdoses, perhaps one or two a year out of five hundred individuals. Almost always, these are people with previous psychiatric histories who have taken overdoses in the past. That is, taking an overdose is their standard response to various forms of distress. If the anxiety is controlled, life is much less awful and the need to escape the intolerable quickly fades. Another factor is the outreach service. If people can get to their appointments with a ten minute bus trip, or can find free parking at the door after ten minutes drive, they are much more likely to seek treatment in the first place, and to continue. As long as they know that "their psychiatrist" is readily available at a location convenient to their homes, or will answer emails and phone calls after hours, most of them manage. My pattern is to see patients frequently for short appointments. This appears to be more effective, and more acceptable, than long appointments every month or two.

Very often, people take overdoses of the drugs they have been prescribed. Partly this is due to the akathisia induced by all psychiatric drugs, but partly it is because they aren't working. It is very unusual for anybody to take an overdose of beta blockers, perhaps one in every 300-400 cases. The reason is that beta blockers quickly and directly relieve the anxiety that drives most impulsive overdoses. I can think of three in the past six years who have overdosed on their beta blockers. All had lengthy psychiatric histories and had taken overdoses before they were referred.

8. **Side effects:** The side effects of psychiatric drugs are terrible and almost invariable. These include the so-called 'metabolic syndrome' of obesity, hypertension, hypercholesterolaemia and diabetes; sexual dysfunc-

tion; drowsiness; lethargy and loss of energy and initiative; poor coordination; acne; hirsuitism (excessive hair in women); addiction; and early death. If patients are given a list of the side effects of psychiatric drugs, almost all will refuse them. By comparison, and apart from the asthma, the side effects of beta blockers are minor and transient. It is rare for a person to stop them due to side effects. Most commonly, this is because the patient is lactose-sensitive as the pills are made using lactose. In contrast, it is fair to say that the side effects of psychiatric medication now cost the nation more than the benefit they give.

As mentioned above, people taking psychiatric drugs in the long term lose an average of 19yrs of life. This doesn't count the huge increases in people who are unable to work just because they have been addicted to psychiatric drugs and are either too fat or too apathetic to get work. In addition, psychiatric drugs do not address the cardinal problem of anxiety, which is the single most powerful factor preventing people working. In any event, the cost of most side effects is incalculable: what dollar value should the society put on eliminating a person's sex life? Be honest: How much money would you want before you would agree to become a eunuch? Bear in mind that the overwhelming majority of people who are put on these drugs weren't given any information, and a substantial proportion of them are involuntary patients who have no choice.

A recent major review of SSRI drugs by the Copenhagen Trial Unit, Centre for Clinical Intervention Research, in Denmark, concluded:

> The evidence on selective serotonin reuptake inhibitors (SSRIs) for major depressive disorder is unclear.... Our results show that the harmful effects of SSRIs versus placebo for major depressive disorder seem to outweigh any potentially small beneficial effects.

If that is the latest opinion, then why have Medicare prescriptions of antidepressants in Australia risen 279% in the past 25yrs? Because drug companies have used their prodigious wealth to influence mainstream psychiatrists who want to believe that all mental disorder is just a case of brain disorder. The last thing they want publicised is that a quick, economical and acceptable form of management is available, because that will destroy their business model. It will also put a lot of luxury private hospitals and rich psychiatrists out of business.

Specific Treatment.

Let's now look at the cases used in this book, starting with Chapter 3.

Case 3.1: Melissa F, aged 19yrs

She lives with her parents and younger brother in a fairly expensive outer suburb and is studying occupational therapy. She drove to the appointment in the car her parents had given her for her eighteenth birthday. She was referred by her general practitioner (GP) after she had been seeing a psychologist for about a year. She was not sure what approach was being followed but the psychologist had told her she needed antidepressants. As she came into the interview, Melissa was decidedly wary. She understood that everybody who saw a psychiatrist would be prescribed drugs but she made it clear she didn't want them.

This intelligent young woman was prescribed beta blockers and made a rapid improvement. No antidepressants, no adverse side effects and certainly no weight gain. After six weeks, she reported she was "lots better." Seen for about five months: total cost of treatment about $820.00.

Case 3.2: Gerry T, an apprentice mechanic aged 30

He was referred because of recurrent depression. Over the years, he had been seen several times by public mental health services and had been given a number of diagnoses: major depression, panic disorder, bipolar disorder and borderline personality. He was first prescribed antidepressants at age thirteen and had taken them on and off over the years but he didn't like them, partly because of side effects (weight gain, sexual effects, severe withdrawal) but mostly because they never seemed to work. His concern was that he had changed careers and had had several "turns" at work so he was worried about losing his job. He lived with his wife and two small children and was taking no drugs at the time.

After three weeks on beta blockers, he reported he was feeling "positive, a lot calmer, handling things better." However, his social problems were endless, e.g. after four months, his partner was diagnosed with a serious malignancy and required extensive treatment; recurring problems with access to his children; constant friction between his partner and his step-mother, who kept close contact with his ex-wife; problems at work, solved by getting a new job, etc. He is doing well but his is a long course. Total cost of treatment after one year: about $1100.00 (a day in hospital costs about $1500).

Case 4.1: Cameron S, aged 48yrs.

This man is a district manager for IT services for a large government department whose IT division is notoriously disorganised. He was referred after he saw his GP to ask whether he should resume antidepressants. For five years after his first marriage ended, ten years before, he had taken escitalopram but he wasn't keen on it. It caused weight gain and loss of libido and he didn't believe he was really depressed. At some stage, he had been told he was suffering PTSD due to his first wife's "malignant narcissism" but he didn't know if he had been given specific treatment. He lived with his partner and their two small children, and also had 40% custody of his two teenage children.

After one week, he reported: "I feel better, more stable. I'm hardly shaking at all, there's been no bad bouts of agitation." Next week, he said: "I'm still crazy anxious at work but the tablets are working, I couldn't be there without them." He started to look for a new job and often made comments about the "magic little red pills." He is seen every 3-4wks at a cost of $73.20.

Case 4.2. Mark C, aged 27yrs.

This man was referred for assessment by the local probation office as he had been convicted of possession of small amounts of marijuana and amphetamines. His probation officer wanted to know if he was suitable for a drug diversion program as he had been diagnosed as schizophrenic at the age of 13yrs and his mental state was very unsettled. He had moved back to stay with his parents and had stopped all drugs, legal and illegal, although he later revealed he hadn't taken psychiatric drugs for years as he didn't like them. Mostly he worked as a labourer on building sites but he had never been able to hold jobs and had been unemployed for over a year. Mark was of average height and weight, with long dark hair, unshaven and with extensive Yakuza-type tattoos over his arms and legs. He always wore heavy metal T-shirts and had several large skull rings on his hands. The striking thing about him was that he was never still. He moved and fidgeted a lot and his talk was jerky and impulsive. His eyes darted around the room constantly but rarely landed on the interviewer.

After five months, he is dramatically better but still not fit for work. He never misses his appointments and is able to get around freely. He is not drinking, is not using any illegal drugs and takes no psychotropic drugs so he is losing weight. He still has a lot of difficulty asserting himself, especially with his brothers, who take advantage of him but he has been able to warn them off. The beta blockers control his agitation and allow him to attend for the psychotherapy component, which is crucial. He will need up to two years of therapy but the total cost of his treatment over that time will be about half the cost of a week in hospital. Total cost of his first year of treatment: $1650.

Case 5.2: Adam B.

Adam was sitting in the waiting room with two people aged about sixty, whom I assumed were his parents. He was muttering as he came through the door. He was solidly-built, dressed in scruffy and ill-fitting clothes and he smelled. He dragged his chair around and sprawled on his arms across the desk, complaining that he was exhausted and nobody understood him. He said he had lost his job but he was living with friends and his father, but they didn't get on. He was taking no medication. Practically every second word was a swear word, which is fairly normal in his area, but mostly it has been deleted because it gets boring.

Adam is not very reliable with his appointments but he is always cheerful. Two months later, he said: "I'm going very well, there's no rows." He was not arguing with either his father or his landlady-cum-partner and was delighted that his sexual performance had improved dramatically. He dropped out after about four months but he lives nearby: if there had been any trouble, he would have come back. Total cost: $510.00

Case 5.3: Samantha, 22yo social work student.

This young woman very reluctantly referred herself after she had self-diagnosed Asperger's syndrome by completing some on-line questionnaires. She attended with her mother. She lived with her parents who both worked, her father as an accountant and her mother as a dental nurse.

This case was not a brilliant success. Yes, the beta blockers were very effective but her social life wasn't much improved. The difference was that she was no longer troubled by having to mix because she knew she could do it if she needed to. Total cost: $433.00

Case 5.4: Karen L, 17yo high school student.

Karen is in her final year at a well-known private school. She lives with her parents in a fairly expensive suburb and has never gone without in her life. Over a period of four months, she has become distressed and agitated, with poor sleep and concentration. At first, her parents thought it was due to the pressure of her school work but then they realised it had started quite abruptly, at the beginning of the mid-year break. Karen described more or less constant, low-grade anxiety with 2-3 "meltdowns" a week, i.e. bouts of intense agitation during which she was "frozen with fear, terrified that something terrible will happen."

The panic symptoms settled quickly with beta blockers but managing her damaged sense of self is a longer-term project. Fortunately, she is intelligent and insightful and has no difficulty with the cognitive therapy. Actually, this is true of younger people: millennials understand self-reinforcing programs as easily as we old people understood running out of fuel. Karen has done very well and has been discharged. Total cost: $784.00

Case 5.5: Aaron H, 22yo single unemployed man.

This young man's mother attended the interview with him. He complained of vomiting and anxiety which led to him giving up his degree course in IT, but no physical cause has been found. He lives with his family and is taking no medication although he was previously prescribed sertraline, which he didn't like. At present, he feels miserable most of the time.

This man lives about a kilometre from my office. After three appointments, he was able to walk to the office alone, something he had not done for a year or more. He has joined a group of gamers and meets them socially, and is planning to resume his course next year. Once again, his management will be a long-term project. It's not uncommon for young people to attend for a few months and show an improvement, then disappear for a year or more. When they return, they explain that they were feeling much better and decided they could manage by themselves, but either something has gone wrong or they have felt the need to deal with other matters, most commonly self-esteem. This man stopped coming for about four months but has recently resumed contact. He has started studying again and has joined a computer group, which is a big improvement. Total cost so far: about $650.00

Case 5.6: Timothy B, 29yo single man.

Tim is a 29yo single man who recently resigned his job in IT in order to treat his "crippling social anxiety." He lives in shared accommodation and is taking no medication apart from asthma puffers, which he uses regularly. At present, he feels "pretty bad." His sleep is poor and he has little appetite, energy, interest or motivation, except he wants to fix these problems so he can get back to work.

This man showed a fairly common pattern, an initial dramatic reduction in the level of anxiety symptoms, followed by a flat patch as he realised the full extent of his mental disabilities. He is happy with the medication and his depressed mood has improved very significantly but he struggles with his severe social anxiety as it is based in his terrible self-esteem. Nonetheless, he is optimistic that he can work to reverse the effects of his dreadful childhood and looks forward to his appointments. He now attends weekly and takes propranolol religiously. After eight months, total cost of treatment has just topped $2000.00, the second most expensive patient of the year.

Case 5.7: Former SUB-LT Walter K.

I met Mr Walter K in 1984, when he was 89. He was a courtly old gentleman, dressed in an old-fashioned linen suit which hung loosely on his bony frame. Carefully placing his panama on his knees, he explained that his wife had recently died and, pressured by his daughter, he had applied for pension benefits relating to his military service—in the Great War.

This old chap didn't get any specific treatment. I felt that the risk of dropping his blood pressure or inducing heart block was too great. In any event, he didn't need it. Simply knowing that his claim had finally been accepted was enough to bring him a degree of peace he hadn't known for seventy years.

Case 5.8: SGT Allan F.

A 33yo career Army sergeant, Allan was referred for assessment of his mental state. He was in an elite unit and, until three years before, had performed extremely well. However, he had developed severe mental symptoms during his first deployment to a combat zone and, despite his efforts to conceal his symptoms, his medical officer wondered whether he was fit for continued service on the basis of possible PTSD.

This man did not do well. He responded to the beta blockers in that his agitation largely settled and he was able to function in daily life, but it was not enough. He was discharged medically unfit, which shattered him. His sense of failure and loss went too deep and although he made an adjustment of sorts, he was, as he said, a latter-day Humpty Dumpty.

Case 6.1: PTE Nathan L, 19yo soldier.

Nathan was referred for psychiatric assessment as part of his discharge procedure following a severe injury to his right shoulder. He enlisted at eighteen and was initially extremely happy in the Army. However, on a combat training exercise one night, running in full kit with his rifle firmly wedged against his right shoulder, he fell face forward into a hole. The whole of his weight smashed on to his rifle butt. The shoulder was dislocated with extensive ligamentous tearing and he had months of conventional treatment without success so, nearly a year after the injury, he was booked for surgery. Following the operation, he could hardly move the shoulder and was unable to put on his uniform.

This man has had a stormy course. He doesn't want to take drugs of any sort as he regards medication as a sign of personal weakness. He freely says the beta blockers work but, after a few months of feeling half-reasonable, he stops them as he feels he should be able to manage by himself. Needless to say, within a month, his world starts to fall apart again as the anxiety bites. Complicating his management, he remains bitterly angry at the way he was treated by the military. Unresolved anger always detracts from the prognosis. In fact, he is coping fairly well but he can't see it. He is preoccupied with the grievous losses he has sustained to the point where black rage takes over and he doesn't want to see anybody, including his very caring and supportive partner. He doesn't attend regularly, dropping out as soon as he starts to feel better, and only returns when his partner reaches breaking point. He doesn't drink or use drugs and keeps himself busy around the house but he can't see a future for himself. That's because the only future he had ever considered was the military, and it was taken away from him. For him, the worst injury of all was the betrayal.

Case 6.2: Gavin T, 29yo interstate truck driver.

This man requested a referral after he had suffered two severe panic attacks at work in a month. The second occurred when he was about to leave the depot at the other end of his route to head home. He was unable to get into his truck for three hours, which caused big problems with his schedule and he had been threatened with dismissal. He lived with his partner and their baby, her two children, and also had his other three children about one third of the time. The family were totally dependent on him working and he was very worried he would lose his job. He also had another weekend job to make ends meet. He was taking no medication but he had taken antidepressants on and off since age thirteen. Over the years, he had seen public psychiatric services who had given him the diagnosis of "borderline personality disorder." He didn't think they'd done much to help him although he added that he was scared of their reputation and didn't trust them.

This man responded quickly to beta blockers. His panic attacks stopped and, for the first time in his life, he was able to go to work and deal with people without dissolving in fear. His depressive state lifted but only to reveal the major, life-long personality problems that nobody had previously asked him about. At one stage, buffeted by problems at work, at home and with his ex-wife, he cut himself and went to hospital. It was his good luck that they had a look at his previous diagnosis, of borderline personality disorder, and sent him home again. Nobody wants to deal with PDs.

Case 7.1: Justin T. 31yo mechanic.

While at work, Justin slipped on some grease and fell into an in-spection pit, fracturing his right ankle. Almost immediately, things started to go wrong. At the hospital, somebody thought he smelled strange and wondered whether he had been drinking. The surgeon decided to treat it conservatively with a plaster cast and rest so he was sent home on crutches.

This man was treated with the combination of beta blockers and a benzodiazepine, diazepam. This will quickly and effectively reduce signs of over-arousal, even when it has reached psychotic intensity. In this state, sleep is critical so it is common to use a sedating antipsychotic drug such as olanzapine as well. However, it should be reduced as soon as the sleep pattern starts to return to normal, and ceased shortly after. There is no reason or justification for leaving people on antipsychotics a moment longer than is absolutely necessary. They act to induce a "chemical imbalance of the brain," otherwise known as addiction. Before anybody realises, the patient has swapped his original short-term problem for a very real and serious long-term problem, from which he may never recover.

It is critically important to recognise when psychotic symptoms are reactive to events, including drug abuse. More and more people are prescribed long-term antipsychotic drugs for drug-induced psychosis, long after the symptoms have abated, just because nobody realises they are addicted. Another point to remember about the combination of beta blockers and benzos: it costs next to nothing. Even seriously agitated people can be managed at home with three propranolol per day (cost 20c) and four diazepam (48c). Compare that with a day's admission to hospital (up to $1500) and antipsychotic drugs (from $20 to $100 per day).

Some years ago, I heard a rather strange thing. A "very senior psychiatrist," a professor and head of a government department and so on, gave a lecture to a group of his senior staff. As it happens, they were in the habit of referring patients to me and liked the rapid response provided by my program. The senior gentleman went out of his way to tell his staff that they were not, under any circumstances, to refer patients to psychiatrists who used beta blockers as they (the drugs, and possibly the psychiatrists) were dangerous. He gave no figures and no citations to support his vehement opposition to this very widely used group of drugs. How did he know they are dangerous? We're not quite sure. He certainly didn't get it from the medical and psychiatric literature, which is generally supportive of them, and he couldn't have got it from personal experience as why would he use a dangerous drug? Very mysterious, but I can state one thing quite bluntly: Any psychiatrist who says beta blockers are dangerous is talking rubbish. Moreover, he knows it.

Case 7.2: Mrs Jenny M, 34yo teacher's aide.

This lady, the mother of two small children, worked only during school hours, although she had been off work for about three months. She was referred by her GP for assessment after two years' unsuccessful treatment of depression. The referring letter said: "She has treatment-resistant depression. I have gently suggested that you may decide she needs to go to hospital for ECT."

Without saying it, her husband's made it quite clear that his wife would get ECT only over his dead body. She has been managed with beta blockers but the neurosis is deep-seated. Two years later, she is coping with home and work but her need to prove to everybody she is as tough and capable as her husband may yet be her undoing. Total cost of treatment: about $1500.00.

Case 7.3. Liam C. A life of anxiety.

Liam was 29yrs old when he was referred for treatment of "agoraphobia and mood swings from low to hyperactivity." He was living with a partner and their 2yo daughter but, because of his mental symptoms, had not worked for about eight years. He was taking no medication at the time but had been referred to a psychologist who suggested he needed to see a psychiatrist for antidepressants. At the appointed time, he crept into the room, a picture of abject and rather smelly misery several sizes too small for his rumpled old clothes.

This man is managed with beta blockers alone and is coping. Sort of. The drugs control the worst of his anxiety and he can do a lot more but his intense self-loathing makes further change very difficult, especially social rehabilitation. He's what we might call "a work in progress." After about eight months, total cost of treatment is $1450.00.

Case 8.1: Rudolph K. Classic avoidance.

Rudolph is a 42yo single doctoral-level student who receives a disability pension for psychiatric problems. He studies part-time a course quite as abstruse as Sanskrit sonnets. During the week, he lives in a small flat near the university while on weekends, he travels by bus to stay with his elderly father in a distant outlying suburb. He has had ten years of private psychiatric treatment, including several admissions to hospital, but could no longer afford the fees.

This chap is managed with beta blockers alone and is doing very well. Since the antidepressants and other drugs were slowly stopped, his depressive symptoms have almost entirely abated. He has been elected chairman of his church vestry, which requires him to chair regular meetings and attend various conferences. These days, he is too busy to worry whether he is in contact with reality. It now seems that the very large sums he and his family spent on seeing private psychiatrists, admissions to expensive private hospitals and buckets of drugs were not necessary. Total cost of treatment so far: about $2150.00. Bear in mind that that is about the cost of 36hrs in one of the expensive private hospitals he has been in.

His case is similar to that of a policeman from a country town whom I saw years ago. He had been injured at work and developed a post-traumatic state. Twice his department sent him interstate for treatment but he didn't respond well. One admission was for three months and the other for two months, which caused huge disruption at home, but he didn't do well either time. Finally, he was advised to have ECT, which he refused. He was sent to me for a second opinion, although it was actually about his twentieth. After being treated with beta blockers for two months, he was able to start a return to work program.

"I don't believe this," he said. "I spent five months in those big hospitals, I've seen dozens of top psychiatrists and professors but nothing helped. But a shrink who wears shorts to work gives me a $10 bottle of pills and I'm ready for work."

Well, yes, but I had the singular advantage of relying on a proper history. Having reviewed his files from those prestigious and prodigiously expensive institutions, I know that their psychiatrists didn't. That is, despite charging well in excess of $250,000 in fees, not one of them had taken a proper history. Unfortunately, that's pretty well normal these days. The more senior the psychiatrist, the more he relies on his unequalled intuition to reach a diagnosis which, mostly, means admission to hospital for some nice expensive treatment.

Case 8.2: Harry L, 60yrs.

Harry is a retired man who had a small business in a distant city but had to close it because of depression (that's his depression, not the economy's). He is now sustained on insurance payments, which also fund his private health insurance. Over the years, he has had about 22 admissions to private hospitals for "treatment-resistant depression." He has been prescribed at least 30 different drugs as well as ECT and a new form of treatment called transcranial magnetic stimulation. He moved to my city to be closer to relatives and immediately asked to be referred to a psychiatrist. At his first appointment, he came through the door plaintively announcing that he suffered severe clinical depression confirmed by Professors X and Y and he felt the need to go to hospital.

Despite his worst fears, this man did reasonably well while his psychiatric drugs were reduced under cover of beta blockers. Amazingly, it emerged that in all his admissions to expensive hospitals, he had never had any psychotherapy. Of course, he had gone to CBT and DBT and ACT and all the other acronyms that bloom in private hospitals, but nobody had ever done anything about, for example, his tribe of parasitic relatives who drove him mad. After six months, he said he was going back to his former city to settle some business matters but he never returned. Months after, I heard that he was not able to manage the negotiations (essentially, telling his relatives there would be no more money for any of them) and fled into a private hospital where all his drugs were resumed. My informant intimated that the relatives didn't get the money they had hoped for because the psychiatrists got it. Cost of his treatment with me: $640.00. Total cost of his many admissions to private hospitals elsewhere: probably about $2million.

Case 8.3: Avoidance at the extreme.

When Kallym D was referred, he was 25yrs of age and had spent the last six years, a quarter of his life, in his bedroom. During that time, he had had no contact with his family. He came out for perhaps an hour or two a day, after his flatmates had gone to work, then spent the rest of the day asleep. Sometimes he went a week without showering or shaving. He had been taking desvenlafaxine 200mg per day for about eight years (this is a very large dose of a powerful and highly addictive antidepressant) and also used diazepam so that he could go to the shops.

Kallym was commenced on beta blockers and the slow and arduous process of reducing the antidepressant began. However, he then revealed he was addicted to oxycodone (narcotic) and alprazolam (benzodiazepine). Initially, there were signs of progress. He showered most days and his clothes were clean. He was able to walk around the shops. He met a lady friend and was seeing her regularly although I was fairly sure her interest in him did not extend beyond the drugs she extracted from him. The relationship ended acrimoniously and about a month later, as this section was being written, I was advised that he had been found dead in his flat, apparently of an overdose.

Case 8.4: Mrs Elizabeth C. 64yo single woman.

Elizabeth has lived alone for eighteen years since her husband abruptly left her for another woman. She has one daughter who constantly worries about her because she has swelling of her ankles and is quite breathless. She has no social life and won't go to see her doctor or dentist. Her diet is poor as she rarely eats fresh fruit or vegetables and the daughter is sure that most of the meat she takes to her mother goes to her pair of very fat cats.

This went nowhere. She refused to accept that she was anxious, or indeed that she had any problems at all, and didn't come back. However, her GP felt the review was valuable as it allowed her to accept very limited goals for her patient. Total cost: $385.00 (a few blood tests and an X-ray can easily add up to this sum).

Case 8.5: Mrs Yvonne K.

This 49yo care worker loudly insisted she wanted "to be tested for autism." She lives with her partner, two sons, a fostered niece and her partner's mother but she is the only person in the house who works. She has had many antidepressants and other psychiatric drugs over the past thirty years but they were no help. She said both sons are "ADHD and ASD," and two nephews are "autistic," as was their father before he committed suicide.

Again, no go. There wasn't the slightest doubt she suffered fairly severe anxiety but it didn't match with her self-diagnosis so she didn't come back. She wouldn't accept that she was anxious because it would mean she was "mental" and probably putting it on. People talk about the "stigma" of mental disorder but all too often, most of the stigma comes from the sufferers. This is difficult when dealing with younger people, as I mostly do, as their families often react angrily to being told their offspring is not suffering the genetic disorder they diagnosed with the aid of Dr Google. If it's not genetic, what is it? Whatever you do, don't say "It's bad parenting."

That's just what they don't want to hear. There are people who would rather condemn their children to a life of drugs than accept they may have made a few mistakes back then. But that's human. Total cost: $223.00.

Case 8.6: Trevor W.

Thank you for referring this 39yo unemployed man whom I saw with his gay partner. He complained of "severe akathisia and tardive dyskinesia" for two years. He has been taking sertraline (antidepressant) since age 15yrs but has been unable to stop it. Whenever he has tried, he becomes agitated and irritable. Two years ago, he was prescribed an antibiotic whereupon his agitation suddenly got much worse. He is now essentially disabled and unable to work.

Same again. Stamped out, never to be seen again. Total cost: $385.00.

Case 8.7: Norman J, 44yo mechanic.

This 44yo man announced at the outset that he is "Asperger's, ASD and autistic and not coping but I wanted to see a female psychologist, not a male psychiatrist." This is never a good start to an interview. He lives with his wife and step-son and is taking no medication. At present, he feels "overwhelmed," which is code for anxious.

He came into the room grumbling and complaining. He resented answering questions ("Do we have to go through all this stuff? I don't see the point") and kept looking at his watch as though he hadn't been told the appointment was for one hour. I don't take it personally.

Case 9.1: Gambling as distraction from anxiety.

Scott B, aged 34yrs,. has a problem. In fact, he has two problems. He has the problem he's had for several years, and he has the problem of what to do when his wife hears of Problem No. 1. He gambles, and soon she's going to find out that the money she thought was going to the mortgage is actually being fed into poker machines when he's supposed to be at work. He thinks he's lost about $150,000 in four years but he isn't sure as he doesn't dare add it up. What he is sure of is that he can't borrow any more, the credit cards (plural) are at the limit, and his plumbing business is about to go down the gurgler.

This man settled quickly with beta blockers but his business and family problems eventually overwhelmed him and he was forced to declare bankruptcy. His marriage ended and he left town. Total cost: $364.00. He had lost a small fortune on gambling; if he had come earlier, he could well have saved all that money, and his family, and his business.

Case 9.2: Eating as distraction.

William McK. is a 44yo single carpenter employed as a building sites inspector by the local council. He lives alone in a small rented flat, drives a battered old car and wears anything he can buy that fits. That isn't easy, as he is 175cm tall, weighs 165kg (BMI 54, dangerously overweight), and has three credit cards sitting on the limit with not a penny to his name. He has been working 28yrs, he doesn't drink, smoke, gamble or use drugs, he never takes holidays, doesn't own a boat, dog, motorbike, racehorse, plane or shares in a goldmine. He doesn't have a girlfriend, his elderly parents live on a farm about an hour away and he has very few relatives in the state but he doesn't go to see them because he can't fit in aircraft seats. He doesn't belong to any clubs or organisations of any sort, and doesn't go to church, football, brothels, casinos or seances, yet he is completely broke. In fact, he doesn't do anything but it takes all his time and money.

Beta blockers controlled the worst of his anxiety but he couldn't commit himself to a proper diet. At the first sign of any pressure, he hurried to the nearest shop, bought a heap of sticky food and shoved it down. He then felt guilty so he had to buy more food to assuage his guilt. Which made him even more guilty. After about eighteen months, he had lost only 15kg so I warned him that he has six months to lose another 15kg or he'd be sent to the surgeon for gastric banding. Five months and two weeks later, he didn't attend his appointment, first time he'd missed in two years. I rang him several times but each time he said he was terribly busy and couldn't talk. Busy at 8.00pm? Two years later, I heard he had had surgery and was losing weight and was active in a support group for anxiety so I put him down as a success. Total cost of psychiatric treatment: about $2500.00. Cost of bariatric surgery: about $22,500. Cost of all that food: hundreds of thousands.

Case 9.3: Drugs as a distraction from anxiety.

A 25yo man was addicted to morphine and was on a controlled reducing program as part of his probation terms. One day, he arrived in a state of intense agitation, saying somebody had stolen his drugs and he was already in a severe withdrawal state.

A lost cause, he could not accept he was mentally-disordered. As far as he was concerned, he had an addiction from too much partying, not because the drugs controlled his anxiety.

Case 9.4: Brian, aged 28yrs: Crime as a distraction from anxiety.

This highly intelligent man used serial crime to distract himself from his performance-related anxiety. As a child, growing up in the shadow of his older siblings, he was quite shy and nervous. He was convinced he could never achieve at their level, could never satisfy his increasingly critical and demanding parents who had used all their tolerance by the time he was born. In his teenage years, his insecurity became much worse. By the time of his final year of school, he was barely able to enter the classrooms for fear of making a mistake or looking stupid. He gave up his sport, stopped music lessons and spent most of his time in his room reading ancient history.

He was commenced on beta blockers and reported an immediate improvement. He engaged in psychotherapy but after six months, was transferred to a low security prison. To my knowledge, he never reoffended, but that could be because he had had enough of prison. Through his stealing and the costs of police, courts and imprisonment, he must have cost the community about $1million. That doesn't include his lost productivity. If he had been referred while he was still at school, then he could have been sorted out for under $1000.

Case 9.5: Jenny M. Cutting as distraction from anxiety.

Jenny was a single woman aged 34yrs who was admitted one night after threatening suicide. She had been abandoned as a child and spent most of her early life in institutions where she was routinely abused sexually, by men and by women. At age seventeen, she was admitted to the psychiatric hospital, the first of many times, where she was given large doses of drugs and eventually had over a hundred ECT.

Cutters are severely anxious, that's why they cut. This case comes from very early in my career, before I had any real idea of anxiety and before I worked out how to assess and manage it. These days, any cutters I see get beta blockers and cognitive therapy, and the results are much better. Most of them will stop cutting although if they experience severe pressure, they are likely to reach for the razor, just as Bill in Case 9.2 reached for food, or drinkers reach for the bottle. But what about the obsessive-compulsives? Two recent cutters, admittedly not as bad as this case, have settled quickly for a total cost each of about $500.

Case 10.1: Jasmine B, 24yo single student.

Jasmine lives with her parents and her younger sister. Her mother attended the interview with her but took notes and said practically nothing. Jasmine is enrolled in a social work course but hasn't passed any units for two years and, it emerges, hasn't been to any classes for over eight months. She presents as attractive, neatly-dressed, bright and cheerful and well-spoken. She was attending, she said with an endearing smile, because her OCD was getting a bit out of control. She wasn't convinced she needed to see a psychiatrist as she had been prescribed antidepressants in the past but they caused weight gain. Instead, she would like some strategies so she could get back to normal life, or perhaps a referral to a psychologist for CBT.

After eighteen months, it was clear that Jasmine firmly believed she had a chemical imbalance of the brain, not that she would ever say so. It seemed likely that she was taking her drugs but she was highly resistant to anything that involves change to her routine. She was definitely less anxious than before but she confirmed a quote from the psychologist, Fritz Perls: "Most people come to therapy, not to get rid of their neuroses, but to feel better about their crazy behavior." She finally stopped attending after a total cost of about $2500, or less than two days in hospital.

Case 10.2: Michael B, 43yo anankastic Army sergeant.

Until he arrived, I didn't know that Michael was in the Army. His referral was from a civilian GP and he had registered using his Medicare number, but everything about him screamed 'military.' He was sitting in the waiting room dressed in spotless sports clothes, receding hair trimmed, a neat moustache, feet and knees together, hands resting on a folder on his lap and staring straight ahead.

As expected, this man took his medication religiously and his panic attacks promptly resolved. However, like his marriage, his career was at an end and he was in a very deep, dark hole. He has been managed over about three years with beta blockers alone and is coping as well as can be expected. He has not had any psychiatric drugs; he remains fit and healthy, maintaining an exercise schedule that would be the envy of many men half his age. He has regained joint care of his children and it seems likely that his ex will lose interest in the children and he will get them (or her latest boyfriend will lose interest in them, same thing). Critically, for him, his sexual interest and performance are as good as ever. He has heard from many other veterans what happens when they take antidepressants and anti-psychotics, and he regularly arranges for me to see his friends so they too can get off the "nutty tablets" and recover their sex lives. Every now and then, we all need a grateful patient. Total cost of treatment so far: about $3500. Cost of one month in hospital: about $45,000, plus plus plus.

Case 12.1: Brendan McC, failed criminal.

Brendan McC is a 31yo single unemployed man, recently released from prison for a botched armed robbery of a chemist shop. Just before closing time, he ran inside with a stocking over his head, reached into his bag and found he had forgotten his knife. In the drama, he grabbed a packet of oral contraceptives and ran out, only to slip on the wet street and twist his ankle badly. The chemist's assistant followed him at some distance as he hobbled up the street, and called the police who found him hiding behind a rubbish bin in the rain, crying (people sometimes accuse me of exaggerating but I don't need to).

Because of the swelling of his ankles, it took some time to get this man on beta blockers. He appeared to be responding reasonably well but then he was arrested for some trivial matter which took place while he was quite calm, and his parole was revoked. No doubt he will turn up one day.

Case 12.2: David L, aged 38yrs.

This 38yo homeless, unemployed pensioner was living in his sister's shed. Some years ago, he was diagnosed with "bipolar disorder and others" and is still taking quetiapine 300mg. In general, he feels very poor.

After two weeks, he reported a dramatic improvement with "them magic pills." It took him six months to come off quetiapine, after which he began to lose weight. Intellectually, he is not suitable for psychotherapy but he is happy to do as he is told, as long as it leads to a calm life. Total cost of treatment so far is a tiny proportion of the total cost of all the psychiatric drugs he has been prescribed.

Weight loss after people stop psychotropic drugs can be remarkable. For example, a businesswoman had been taking antidepressants for about fifteen years and her weight had ballooned from 70kg to 125kg, or nearly 80%. This means a lot to people. She had tried everything to lose weight but nothing worked and was considering surgery. By simply replacing the antidepressants with beta blockers, her weight plummeted.

Psychiatric drugs seem to have two effects. Firstly, they make people selectively want to eat a diet of sweet, rich and fatty food, which can itself induce Type II diabetes. People say they know they have had enough to eat but they can't stop, they have to go back to the fridge or the shop and gorge on food that they know is not good for them. Second, it seems that while taking these drugs, the body's metabolism is changed to conserve fat at all costs. People have to get right off them before they will notice much or even any weight loss, but then the weight seems to come off by itself.

Weight gain of 60%, 80% or even 100% is normal on psychiatric drugs but psychiatrists don't seem to think this is serious. The Queensland Dept of Health maintains a website on psychiatric drugs (at http://www.choiceandmedication.org/queenslandhealth/printable-leaflets) and I'm sure lots of others do the same. For venlafaxine, which the lady above had been taking, it does not mention weight gain. It also specifically says: "Venlafaxine is not addictive," which will be news to all the people who have ever tried to get off it. As for the intense loss of sexual function which it almost invariably causes, the leaflet cheerfully says that "more than one in ten people will experience this... finding it hard to have an orgasm." True, 98% is indeed more than one in ten but the lesser figure doesn't convey quite the same impact. It continues: "(will experience) no desire for sex." Their suggestion? "Discuss with your doctor." What it doesn't say is that s/he will ignore you, because they have no treatment.

This is a seriously neglected aspect of modern medical practice. On the one hand, we know that obesity is a major problem in western countries, and a rapidly developing problem among less-developed countries such as Mexico and South Africa. On the other hand, we are pushing a class of drugs which we have always known cause weight gain, until about 15% of the population are taking them. And nobody seems to have put two and two together and wondered whether there may be a connection.

Case 12.3: Brett L, aged 28yrs.

Thank you for referring this 28yo single unemployed man who was recently released from prison and is scared of being sent back as he has pending trafficking charges. While in prison, he was seen by forensic mental health services but was not prescribed medication, which is most unusual for them. At present, he feels very bad, with poor sleep, loss of appetite, energy, interest and motivation, and no sexual interest.

It later emerged that the reason he wasn't prescribed drugs in prison was because he was terrified of being put on "crazy drugs," antipsychotics, as everybody else seemed to be taking them, so he lied through the interview. He improved dramatically with beta blockers and cognitive therapy and found work, which was probably why he was given extended parole for his additional charges rather than being sent back to prison. Again, a very grateful patient, and a nice chap. Total cost of treatment: about $850.00. Cost of a trial: I have no idea, probably about $25,000. Cost of a day in prison: don't know but it would not be less than $500.

Case 12.4: Kerryn B.

This 30yo single mother of three said her family and friends want her assessed because of her bad temper and "mood swings." At present, she feels reasonable but her sleep is quite erratic. Her appetite is steady and she is physically active but her levels of interest and motivation vary greatly, depending on how she is feeling. Socially, she doesn't mix well. She feels low and miserable about half the time and sometimes feels death would be a relief but is not suicidal. She has brief bouts of feeling good when she is cheerful and talkative but these last minutes, not hours. The main problem is frequent bouts of intense agitation with many somatic symptoms of anxiety, secondary to a long list of social fears. After even trivial upsets, she becomes very angry, yells and throws things. These moods last for hours each day, sometimes extending for days on end.

It's good when a patient comes in smiling and says: "I don't believe this. What's in those tablets you gave me? Look at my hand, steady as a rock. The family can't believe it, I haven't lost my temper for nearly a week. That's a record."

I tell them: "If this drug works for you, that confirms your diagnosis is anxiety. They only work on anxiety, they don't work on anything else. If you feel they have relieved your depression, then that shows the anxiety was causing the depression. That's good news, it proves you're not bipolar or anything like that." Mentally-disturbed people need to get a bit of good news now and then, most of them have had nothing but trouble for most of their lives. She has returned to work, saving the government about $600 a week in benefits. Total cost of treatment so far: under $500.

Case 12.5: Dr Cory V, aged 34yrs.

This man would never have seen a psychiatrist without the most intense pressure. A medical practitioner, he was referred for assessment by his medical defence lawyer after his ex-wife complained to the Medical Board that he was "psychotic and dangerous." They had separated about eighteen months before and were locked in a bitter divorce case. He was working full-time in a solo practice in a small country town and was not taking any medication.

At the time this man was seen, medical boards imposed very strict conditions on any practitioner taking psychiatric drugs, so it was important for his management that he avoided them. He responded immediately to beta blockers, although he was angry at himself for not realising himself that they would work on his symptoms. But that confirms what I said at the beginning of this chapter: You can't diagnose yourself, and you can't treat yourself, so don't try. If a highly intelligent and experienced physician can't recognise the syndrome of anxiety in himself, then there is practically no chance for an ordinary citizen to do so. Total cost: about $3000.

That reminds me of another doctor I saw when I was first starting to use beta blockers. He was about 28yrs of age and was training to be an anaesthetist. Michael was born in Australia of parents from a poor and war-torn eastern European country. As is so common, as the eldest child, the whole of the family hopes rested on him. His parents had sacrificed everything to educate their children but he came into my office looking as though he was about to be led out and shot. After a great deal of silent staring out the window, he finally revealed his terrible secret: he was addicted to diazepam (valium). Addiction is a major risk with anaesthetists as they have ready access to every known drug and it is quite easy for them to steal drugs by fudging the records. By this stage, he was in tears, thinking his career was ruined, so we pressed ahead with the history.

Twice a day, before the operating sessions began, he had to take 5mg of diazepam because without it, he couldn't start work. There's something to know about anaesthetics. When the patient is brought into the operating theatre, everybody stops buzzing around, banging metal pots or talking about the football, to watch the anaesthetist insert the cannula into the patient's veins then give the drugs. The reason is that if there is a sudden noise, the patient may panic and try to get up. Early on, Michael had found the attention quite nerve-wracking and he noticed that as he picked up the cannula, he started to shake. Rather unwisely, from time to time, he took a small dose of diazepam; before long, he was unable to perform the procedure without a full dose. He hid it as long as he could but finally gave in and had to ask for help as he feared a notification to the medical board.

In fact, he wasn't addicted as he didn't take any diazepam on his days off or on holiday. He had classic performance anxiety, dating back to the intense pressure he had experienced at school to perform at the highest level. He was told to substitute propranolol for the diazepam and come back in a week.

Next week, he bounded into the room glowingly happy. It had worked brilliantly, he crowed, he was able to insert them one-handed and had helped some of the junior doctors who were having trouble with them. He was just about in tears: "I can't tell you how grateful I am. When I drove away from here last week, I felt I was flying, it was such a relief. I kept hearing you saying I wasn't addicted, it was just anxiety. That was the best thing you could have said. But why didn't I realise it myself?" Total cost: $230.00.

For him, being anxious was better than being addicted. Not everybody sees it that way. A 21yo public servant was referred to see if he was suitable for service as he had been diagnosed as having "pseudoseizures," or feigning epilepsy. It was obvious to everybody in his office that he only had his "fits" when he was under pressure or being criticised, and the other staff thought he did it to get them to take over his work or to evade trouble. However, he showed the full book of anxiety symptoms, including hyperventilation, which had been present since early teenage years. Hyperventilation, as every epileptic knows, can induce seizures; neurologists use it when testing for epilepsy to see if it can provoke instability in the EEG. A quick examination showed a defect in his field of vision so he was sent for a scan, which showed a temporal tumor. He went straight to the neurosurgeons and, three weeks later, came back, still with the bandages on his head. He was, he said, immensely grateful for the diagnosis as it proved he wasn't lying. Such is the power of the herd instinct in humans that he would rather have a brain tumor than be regarded as a fraud.

Case 13.1: Charles W. 43yo lecturer, writer and actor.

Charles had been admitted to a public mental hospital five months previously. Prior to that, he had been attending a private psychiatrist for several years who had diagnosed "rapid cycling bipolar disorder." Charles had not responded to a range of drugs including valproate, antidepressants and antipsychotics and became suicidally depressed. While in hospital, he was given quetiapine 300mg per day (antipsychotic) and mirtazepine 45mg (antidepressant). He had also been given four ECT. He was advised he should take lithium but he declined and decided he wanted another opinion.

A very complex case, but the first step was to stabilise him on beta blockers then begin the fraught process of slowly withdrawing his other drugs. It was fraught because if he had gone into a withdrawal state, he would almost certainly have been detained in hospital and given more ECT. Everything worked against him but most of all, he was driven to extremes by his perfectionism and his need to satisfy everybody at all times. Clearly, given the people he had to deal with every day, this was impossible. The most you can hope to do in this life is satisfy some of the people some of the time; for the rest, you need to be able to look them in the eye and say "That's your problem, sunshine, so just get on with it." Above all, you have to mean it.

Over the next two years, he had one bout of severe hyperarousal in which he began to hallucinate, partly due to prolonged sleep deprivation (from worrying how he would satisfy everybody) and partly as a direct effect of the arousal itself. This was treated with a small dose of olanzapine for a few weeks. He disliked the drug as it turned him into a "zombie" so he stopped it as soon as he could. He preferred to be agitated than inert, although there are people who are happy in a vegetative state. The beta blockers were helpful but could not overcome his constant and intensely conflicted drives. In this respect, the psychotherapy was crucial but it is a slow and arduous process. Nonetheless, there is progress but one thing is clear: had he been maintained on the large dose of quetiapine with no attempt to resolve his personality conflict, he would either have slipped into a permanent state of self-sustaining hyperarousal (known as psychosis) or he would have acted on his chronic suicidal ideas. Total cost over 29 months: $5550, or the cost of about four days in hospital.

Case 13.2: CPL Jeremy V aged 28.

Jeremy is an Air Force police officer who injured his back in a fall at work. Six months after the injury, he underwent surgery for intractable pain and rapidly-developing nerve damage but the operation was only partially successful. Despite being in constant pain, he managed to get back to work but because he didn't want to lose his career, he did his best to conceal it. Over the next few years, he became increasingly disturbed and was drinking heavily so he was finally sent to a psychiatrist who diagnosed bipolar affective disorder—as one of ten separate diagnoses. He was prescribed olanzapine, paroxetine and lorazepam but was not offered psychotherapy.

Some people seemed destined to have a stormy time and this man was one. Covered by propranolol, the olanzapine and paroxetine were relatively easy to withdraw but, two years after the reduction process started, he is still struggling to get off lorazepam. He was most definitely not told it was addictive and would not have taken it if he had known its effects. Every attempt was made to get him back to work, including retraining, but nothing worked so he was discharged medically unfit. This provoked a series of crises, including in his marriage, which led to more distress and more drinking. One morning after an argument with his wife, he left home and walked close to the railway line. He was picked up by military police and taken to a mental hospital but, fortunately, he knew the law better than the hospital staff did and was able to walk out after six hours. This close encounter with the dark side shocked him and he realised he had to stop drinking or he could lose everything. Since then, he has completed his degree and is now working full-time in his new profession.

He applies himself diligently to the process of understanding how his agitation builds up to screaming pitch but sometimes, it seems nothing ever runs smoothly for him. I have not the slightest doubt that if he had continued with his previous treatment, meaning drugs, drugs and more drugs, he would now be dead. He agrees. He could not have been managed without beta blockers. Total cost over two years: $7200, or less than the cost of five days in hospital.

Case 14.1: Kevin G, 31yo single, unemployed man.

This case was assessed for reports only and wasn't treated.

Case 14.2: Valerie S, 56yo unemployed nurse.

Because of the length and complexity of her history, this lady was commenced on beta blockers and very slowly reduced the psychotropic drugs. She soon began to improve, with the goal of being able to work as a nurse. And for the first time in her life, she is able to talk about the incidents and pressures that led to her breakdowns. It's pretty sad, you know, to be 56yrs of age and saying: "Nobody has ever asked me these questions, nobody has ever let me tell my story."

16 Conclusion

"When truth is replaced by silence, the silence is a lie."
Yevgeny Yevtushenko.

In a recent article in the *Sydney Morning Herald*, a 21yo writer, Louis Hanson, pointed out that Australians are very big users of antidepressants, with the second highest rate in the world after Iceland:

> The defined daily dosage of medication intake in adults more than doubled in Australia between 2000 and 2013.

This, he noted, was a bit strange because there is almost no public discussion about these drugs, or of the phenomenon of mass drugging. He thought it would be a good idea to start the conversation:

> So many Australians are taking these medications; we should be talking about it...[1]

Why does this silence prevail? I don't think it's an accident. According to the Australian Institute of Health and Welfare, in 2016 four million Australians were taking psychiatric drugs. That's just under 17% of the total population. Since most of them are adults, it means more than one adult in five is taking prescribed psychotropic drugs. The rate doubled between 2001-11. Thirty years ago, it was barely one in twenty; forty years ago, barely one in fifty. What's going on? Why are we seeing an exponential increase in drug use? Are the tough-minded, independent Australian people succumbing to an epidemic of mental fragility? Actually, it's not just Down Here, it's worse in the US and in parts of Europe, with other countries rapidly catching up.

Some people will try to tell us that this is justified, that all these people have been assessed according to the latest scientific standards and they require the very effective medication which science has made available to relieve human suffering. In one word, this is bullshit.[2] I submit that there is no convincing medical reason for this to happen. It is a sociological trend similar to other secular trends such as the explosive increase in obesity, the trend away from marriage, rising inequality, the spread of illegal drugs and increasing time spent seated before screens. However, it is driven by two very powerful social imperatives.

The first is the simple fact that psychiatry doesn't have a model of mental disorder. This is a little embarrassing, as governments around the world have granted psychiatrists vast powers to detain and drug people against their will just on the basis that psychiatrists know something about mental disorder that nobody else knows. It isn't true. In the absence of a compelling *scientific* reason, this means people lose their freedom for no better reason than somebody thinks it would be a good idea to lock them up. The notion that compulsory treatment saves lives is devoid of any evidential basis: there has never been anything like a proper controlled study. People were not better for being locked up for life. People were not better for having their brains cut. They were not better for being sterilised, nor for having many hundreds of unmodified ECT. And, most emphatically, people's lives are not better for being forced to take drugs that are known to lead to early death.

If the drugs were effective, perhaps there may be a case for them although I'm still not convinced it would justify enforced treatment. However, we know that many of them aren't much more effective than sugar pills but, unlike placebos, psychiatric drugs come with a vast raft of serious side effects. Increasingly, there is strong reason to believe that, in the long term, modern psychiatric treatment actually makes things worse, not better. Practically all clinical research on psychiatric drugs is of the order of six to eight weeks but people routinely take them for 25-30 years. There has never been a long-term study of the efficacy or side effects of these drugs that could justify that pattern of usage. Nonetheless, all of this is hidden from the general public by a veritable typhoon of propaganda insisting that psychiatrists know all about mental disorder. There has never been a proper debate; the silence behind the barrage of bluster is a lie, which needs to be investigated thoroughly by impartial researchers.

The second imperative is Big Pharma. Drug companies like to say they are an ethical industry but they're an industry first and anything else a very distant second. Their role and their goal is to make money. As it happens, they've hit upon a gold mine, pandering to human frailty, just as alcohol, cosmetics and arms manufacturers do. But their gold mine depends on people believing that mental disorder is the sort of thing that warrants taking drugs. There is no known model of mental disorder that justifies this belief.[3] It doesn't matter what the professors say, or what the DSM com-mittee says, the plain and unadorned fact is that mainstream psychiatry has no published model of mental disorder. Into this intellectual vacuum rode the drug companies but as I said, drug companies are in the business of making money and, like all good capitalists, they aren't too concerned how they do it. If, for want of a better word, they must bribe influential psychiatrists to spread the word that mental disorder is brain disorder, then that's what they will do. Essentially, they paid "key opinion leaders" in psychiatry to tout their wares. And there are just enough academically ambitious psychiatrists who are also lazy, or venal, or mendacious (or all four) for this to happen.

My case is that it is time to draw a line under the mass drugging of the population (20% is mass drugging). We need to stop and reappraise what we are doing. However, the impetus to do so will never come from psychiatry itself. We know that conservative professions actively resist change, and psychiatry is *very* conservative. There will be no change until it is imposed from the outside. For example, today I heard of a psychiatrist in private practice who charges $735 for an initial consultation of one hour, and $480 for each subsequent appointment. The Medicare rebate for an initial consultation (Item 296, one hour) is $221.30, which is what I get in my government-funded private practice. The rebate for each subsequent hour of treatment (Item 306) is $156.15. A patient who pays the full price to that private psychiatrist will only be refunded the approved rebate; the rest must come from his pocket. There are plenty of people in need of psychiatric treatment whose take-home pay for a week's work is $735, and the psychiatrist wants all that for one hour?

I don't believe any psychiatrist is worth that sort of money, especially when the service will consist of a slapdash history followed by "Try these. They didn't work? OK, try these." It is difficult to know what kind of reasoning would lead a psychiatrist to believe that he or she could be worth a week of somebody's wages for an hour of flimflam, so why does it happen? We know the answer: reason has nothing to do with it. It happens because the psychiatrist can get away with it. This will not change spontaneously because it is so immensely profitable to the psychiatrist.[4] At the same time, Principle Two of the Code of Ethics of the Royal Australian and New Zealand College of Psychiatrists says just this: Psychiatrists shall not exploit patients.

If ripping some frightened, insecure citizen of $735 for what is, let's not mince words, shit service doesn't constitute exploitation, then I don't know what would.

We see this in other settings. For example, when I see a patient for assessment and treatment, I am expected to attend to him or her with all diligence. I must apply my full knowledge and experience to the case, working with all care and consideration to get the patient better quickly and with the minimum inconvenience and complications. For this, the Australian government assesses my worth as $223 per hour for the initial assessment (there are reports to read and letters to write) and $156 hourly thereafter for treatment. From this sum, I run my business and make my

living. By this objecttive measure, psychiatrists are worth $156 an hour at
most. However, when people are required to provide a psychiatric report in
a court case, they must choose a name from a list of approved psychiatrists
who, *mirabile dictu,* award themselves from $550-650 an hour *for doing
exactly the same work.* Only the setting has changed, their knowledge and
diligence certainly hasn't.

Because the poor stiffs who end up in court have no choice in the matter,
court-appointed psychiatrists feel comfortable charging three to four times
as much as normal, and the stiffs have to pay. If they baulk at the cost, they
will lose their case. If it's your children you're fighting for, then you have to
shell out. It's common for working or even unemployed people to be
charged $3500-5500, or more, for a psychiatric report to submit to court
(the great part of that cost comes from the psychiatrist reading other
people's reports, not from seeing the patient, which can be knocked over in
as little as half an hour).

If the psychiatric reports analysed and reported on the litigant in terms
of a valid scientific model that is unique to psychiatry, then there may be a
case for that sort of charge but they don't. And, of course, if they did that,
then there would be an even more powerful case for the government taking
over and ordering reports at the standard rate of $156 an hour, just as they
control the fees for blood tests and X-rays. What we are seeing in these
examples is psychiatrists taking advantage of a captive market and milking
it for all they can get. This is not science, it is the ugly face of capitalism
running riot.

How does this little gold mine come about? On the one hand, psychiatrists tell the government that, by virtue of their scientific training, they are
experts and are therefore entitled to all sorts of exorbitant privileges and
benefits. If, however, anybody criticises them *as scientists,* as is a scientist's
duty, thereby threatening their business model, they suddenly change hats
and become capitalists. Eschewing the proper standards of science (i.e.
open, unrestricted debate on any topic), they threaten to use civil laws such
as defamation or trade practice law to block the criticism—as I know too
well. That is, they convert their exorbitant privilege into an extortionate
privilege.

What this says is that, by virtue of their phantom science, psychiatrists
have convinced themselves, governments and insurers that there is no need
for any official body to look at what they are doing. At the same time, by
virtue of all the money they are making, they have compelling reason to
make sure nobody else does, either. This says that change will not come
from within psychiatry. It will only come when the community realises what
is being done, such as massive over-drugging or fee-gouging, and insists on
an impartial enquiry at the level of the recent Royal Commission into
Institutional Sexual Abuse.[5] Above all, psychiatrists must not be permitted

to act as investigators and judges of themselves. They've got away with this for two hundred years, which is more than long enough.

This extended essay has been written to be readable, so the main points emerge by degrees. We can summarise them as follow:

1. Modern mainstream psychiatry does not have an *articulated, published model of mental disorder* to guide its *practice, teaching and research*. It is therefore not a scientific field.

2. The claim that mental disorder is a form of brain disorder, or that the biology of the brain will tell us everything we need to know about mental disorder, is an *ideological claim*, not scientific. It is a *narrative* of mental disorder, in the most disparaging sense of that term. Psychiatrists have control of the narrative and resist all attempts at investigation.

3. The concept of separate categories of mental disorder derives primarily from the need to find biological "causes" for mental disorder, not by empirical observations on the nature of mental disorder. At present, all our concepts of the phenomena of mental disorder are biased by psychiatrists looking at them through a biological lens.

4. The endlessly proliferating diagnostic categories seen in DSM5 are testimony to the power of committees of the self-interested, not to any firm knowledge of mental disorder or any rational scientific process.

5. In one word, modern psychiatry is a pseudoscience.

6. The ever-increasing reliance on drugs to resolve even trivial distress in humans has no scientific justification. Humans like taking drugs while drug companies like selling drugs. Excluding alcohol, in the past 25 years, people have consumed more psychotropic drugs than the rest of human history put together. We have no idea what long-term effects this will have; we also have no idea what happens to these drugs once they enter the natural environment.[6]

7. By any objective measure, psychiatric drugs are dangerous, costly and ineffective in terms of their stated goals.

8. Mainstream psychiatry does not understand the role of anxiety in human life nor its primary role in the precipitation and maintenance of other mental disorders.

9. Treating the complications of anxiety without treating the primary anxiety problem cannot be successful.

10. Psychiatry's failure to incorporate anxiety into a formal model of mental disorder condemns ever-increasing numbers of people to

lives of abject misery complicated by the toxic effects of psychotropic drugs.

11. Effective treatment of anxiety results in massive reductions in the
    amounts of different drugs prescribed, and in the numbers of people
    admitted to and detained in mental hospitals.

12. With effective treatment of anxiety based in a cognitive model of
    mental disorder (specifically, the biocognitive model), it is possible
    to practice psychiatry without resort to ECT or other forms of brain
    stimulation.

13. Using a proper approach, it should be possible to reduce the costs
    of mental disorder, both direct and indirect, by at least 50-75% per
    capita while greatly improving the outcome.

14. There are the most powerful institutional and financial pressures
    holding the current approach to mental disorder in place. In short,
    too many people are making too much money while eagerly advan-
    cing their careers at the expense of the general public. Change will
    not be led, for example, by drug companies or their academic shills.

When I was thirty-four, a senior consultant psychiatrist and head of
psychiatry in a 400 bed general hospital, I went back to university to study
philosophy. I wasn't an average student, I had a publication list and regularly gave lectures to a variety of groups so, on the strength of this, I was
accepted at second year level. However, my first week back at school was
shocking. I was in a class with eighteen year olds, and there was no escaping
the fact that they could think better than I could. I had come through six
years of medical school and four years of psychiatry in one of the richest
and safest countries in the world, yet I hadn't been trained in critical
analysis. The trouble was, the more I learned to think critically, the more I
was alienated from my former psychiatric colleagues. Increasingly, they
didn't like what I had to say about what they were doing and their reasons.

Over the years, my lectures have regularly been interrupted; at least
twice, a distinguished researcher has stormed down the aisle of the lecture
theatre and snatched the microphone from my hand. This is bizarre because,
as solid members of the educated upper middle class, psychiatrists will all
say they support the noble concept of freedom of speech. If asked, they will
all immediately affirm that they have been trained to think critically and
they regard this as an essential part of their education and their status as
professionals. Further, they would all agree that science progresses by
critical reappraisal of the status quo, that theories are put up, criticised, and
knocked down, only to be replaced by something better. Criticism, they
would agree, is the engine of scientific progress.

However, when it comes to criticising them, everything changes. Any
attempt to criticise mainstream psychiatry will be met by hostility. Instead

of reasoned debate, there will be retaliation, mostly covertly effected by a sinister manipulation of artfully-constructed rules designed to exact vengeance and suppress criticism. Making it worse, it is practically impossible in this country to react to this retaliation under threat of the draconian laws on defamation. For example, on a number of occasions, psychiatrists have complained to, say, the Royal Australian and New Zealand College of Psychiatrists, of which I am a member, or the Medical Board, that they didn't like what I had to say about, for example, ECT or involuntary treatment. Each time, the complainant was anonymous. I was not permitted to see the complaint. It was investigated by an unnamed committee meeting in camera allowing me no right of cross-examination of the complainant. When the committee delivered its decision, any attempt on my part to redress the matter was blocked by statute, meaning I had no practical means of appeal. The process isn't trivial: the Medical Board, for example, has the power to suspend or even cancel my registration.

In Queensland, for example, it is the case that a psychiatrist can lodge a complaint with the Medical Board to the effect that I am dangerous. The anonymous and unseen complaint does not require any evidence and the burden of proof is reversed, i.e. I must prove to the Board that I am *not* dangerous. So if you chose to lie to the Board about me, and your complaint were dismissed under S254 of the Act (relating to false, misleading or vexatious complaints), there is nothing I could do because S251 of the Act says that any action that can be seen as "reprisal" attracts a fine of up to $24,000 *and* up to two years imprisonment. Mainstream psychiatrists know this and have no compunction using the various acts to repress all criticism of their business model.

We need to distinguish with adamantine clarity between two models: a scientific model, and a business model. These are absolutely separate, with no points of epistemological contact, yet it suits psychiatrists to conflate them. If, on the one hand, psychiatrists are practising a form of science, they are duty-bound to subject themselves to the most rigorous public criticism. We know they do not. On the other hand, if they are simply following a very successful business model, then they have no right to claim professional status, and must take their chances down in the capitalist arena among the herbalists, colonic irrigators and tarot card readers.

In October 2017, the president of Britain's Royal College of Psychiatrists, Professor Wendy Burn, issued an apology for psychiatry's use of "aversion therapy," the long-standing practice of using electric shocks and nauseating drugs to "cure" people of their homosexuality.[7] This followed nearly half a century of agitation by LGBT activists to stop the policy and acknowledge its brutality. On behalf of the profession, Burns expressed "profound regret":

> There are no words that can repair the damage done to anyone who
> has ever been deemed 'mentally unwell' simply for loving a person of

the same sex. For those who were then 'treated' ... up until as late as the 1970s, the trauma of such experiences can never be erased.

However, a closer reading of her statement raises the suspicion that psychiatry has learned nothing from this shameful episode.

Throughout her statement, Burns repeatedly qualifies her "apology." Firstly, she doesn't use the word "psychiatrists" but blames "mental health professionals," whoever they are. Moreover, it was not so much their fault as the result of "...a wider societal attitude of fear and hatred towards homosexuals." Yes, she says, it was cruel and destructive but that's how society was in those days. These days, we're all enlightened and "...there is no feasible scenario in which a fully trained mental health professional would administer such treatment." Warming to her task, and clearly unaware of Guantanamo, she concludes:

> The injustice of those within the LGB community who were treated as mentally unwell due to their sexual orientation alone is keenly felt by mental health professionals... today, our doors are open and that principles of equality and diversity will be passionately upheld... It is with profound regret that we hear of the lifelong impact that treatments such as 'aversion therapy' had... It is with openness, kindness and humility that we hold our hands up, open our doors, and fight tirelessly to provide the ethical, evidenced-based mental health treatment that all of us deserve.

Let's look at this point by point. Firstly, it is highly unlikely that a psychiatrist trained in the last twenty years would know about aversion therapy, much less be "keenly aware of the injustice." Psychiatrists don't talk about their history and the older generation certainly don't teach it. How many psychiatrists under the age of fifty know of the disgraceful treatment dished out by British psychiatrists to Dr Harold Bourne who, in 1954, showed that insulin treatment of schizophrenia was nothing more than a dangerous and very expensive placebo? None. Nor do they know the scandalous history of "lobotomy," the practice of cutting brains using, in Walter Freeman's case, truly barbaric methods.[8] My experience of mainstream psychiatrists is that they have remarkably little sense of injustice, as they turn their backs on their own history and manage to excuse everything they do today on the basis that their motives are noble.

Second, "our doors are open." Actually, if she looks more closely, she'll see they're locked. Third, "principles of equality" are subject to the proviso that the rich will get the greater proportion of the mental health dollar; the poor can queue in the rain. Four, mainstream psychiatry believes that mental disorder is genetic; even if an experience provokes a life-long disturbance, it's still biological in nature and needs chemicals and shocks, not care and support. "Kindness and humility"? The concept of a kind and humble professor of anything is almost an oxymoron. "Hold our hands up"? I have never once heard a psychiatrist apologise, for anything. Inevitably, if a patient doesn't like what is being done, it's because he or she is thought-disordered, lacking insight and paranoid to boot, and needs more drugs.

Finally, if psychiatry has a leitmotiv, it is "Don't criticise us, we have the science, we can do no wrong." The proof of this lies in Burns' last sentence:

> It is with openness, kindness and humility that we hold our hands up, open our doors, and fight tirelessly to provide the ethical, evidenced-based mental health treatment that all of us deserve.

Here, we see her escape clause, her "Get out of prison free" card. Regardless of what happened in the past (and please, we psychiatrists are delicate, we'd rather not talk about it), regardless of past mistakes and crimes, psychiatrists don't have to worry because now we've got a fool-proof process of sorting fallacies from science. It's called "evidence-based treatment," and with this, we can't possibly go wrong. Whatever we do is sanctified by a rigorous process of winnowing faulty methods from effective, and keeping only the effective. So: using what they like to call the "gold standard" of the double-blind, placebo-controlled drug trial, they compare antidepressants and decide which one works best. Regardless of sentiment, they discard the less effective drug. By this objective means, they claim, they build an armoury of methods that can be applied, knowing that they will be more effective than the rest: "We test different methods of ECT and conclude that one particular procedure is slightly more effective and less risky than the others, so that's the one we adopt" (and nobody can argue).

But hang on. Where is the double-blind, placebo-controlled trial of anti-depressants prescribed over thirty years? Because every working day, I see people who have been taking them that long. Aha, say the clever psychia-trists, the proof is that if the patients try to stop their drugs, their depression comes back. Yes, but if the antidepressants are addictive how would you distinguish between a genuine recurrence of depression and a drug with-drawal state? We solve that problem, say the mainstream psychiatrists, by declaring that psychiatric drugs are safe, effective *and* non-addictive. By general agreement among ourselves, we dismiss the possibility of addiction and never investigate it. That is, nobody need worry about addiction because there is never any *evidence* that these drugs are addictive. "Yes," they say, rubbing their hands in pleasure, "we made sure of that."

GIGO[9]: the evidence-base is only as good as the data fed into it.

But: even when there is evidence, we can always get rid of it by changing the definition of "addictive." Look at this gem from the Queensland Health Department's leaflets on drugs for patients: "Venlafaxine is not addictive." That will come as a pleasant surprise to all the people who have tried to get off it and failed due to severe withdrawal effects. But here's the rub: in order to prove it's *not* addictive, they changed the definition of addiction: "e.g.

you don't get craving or a reward from a dose." This is vaguely true, it's not like cigarettes or grog, which do give a lift of sorts, but that's only because psychiatric drugs are so unpleasant anyway. In addition, abrupt withdrawal from psychiatric drugs takes much longer to come on, maybe as much as four days, but then wow, it gets you! And it's much, much worse than simply withdrawing from the booze or running out of fags. It affects your whole body and mind and it goes on and on, endlessly, until you give in and chuck down some more of the drug. All the leaflets on antidepressants on that site say the same thing: This drug is not addictive. That is simply false, or it would be if the people who posted it had thought about it. Instead, they just got it from the drug companies and did a cut-and-paste job. So much easier than thinking.

Moreover, it's one thing to be able to say that unilateral ECT produces less memory disturbance than bilateral, so that's what we should use, except lots of psychiatrists around the world don't use ECT at all. Before we try to decide which form is preferable, shouldn't we first work out whether there is any evidence that ECT is essential? Be assured, that question elicits only a stony silence from the advocates of ECT. Point-blank, they refuse to investigate that question on the basis it is vexatious and therefore non-scientific, meaning it annoys them and they can't answer it. By selectively seeing what they want to see and ignoring the rest, science becomes what they say it is. This is not new, as Lord Lister (1827-1912) ruefully noted:

> "I remember at an early period of my own life showing to a man of high reputation as a teacher some matters which I happened to have observed. And I was very much struck and grieved to find that, while all the facts lay equally clear before him, only those that squared with his previous theories seemed to affect his organs of vision."

The notion that "evidence-based practice" renders psychiatry immune to criticism is just the latest version of "Don't criticise us, we have the science, we can do no wrong." All too often, their "evidence-based practice" is just eminence-based or market-based.

If we go back to epistemology (which you study in philosophy, not in psychiatry), it is the case that any analysis of evidence is valid only in the context of an agreed, declared, articulated and openly criticised model of the subject matter. This, of course, is something that psychiatry hasn't quite got around to.

But nobody is allowed to say this.

Truth has been replaced by silence, and the silence is a lie.

Footnotes:

1. *Sydney Morning Herald,* Dec 13, 2017. At: https://tinyurl.com/anxiety1000.

2. Bullshit. While the concept of truth has been debated for millennia, its opposites are fairly well-defined. The philosopher, Harry Frankfurt, of Princeton, pinned down the concept of a lie:

> Telling a lie is an act with a sharp focus. It is designed to insert a particular falsehood at a specific point in a set or system of beliefs, in order to avoid the consequences of having that point occupied by the truth. This requires a degree of craftsmanship...

However, that doesn't exhaust the possibilities of non-truth, as we all know intuitively. There is a very large epistemological space he called "bullshit," which he defined as:

> ...a statement which is neither true nor false, but which is designed to influence the audience in favor of the speaker's position. (Compared with a lie, bullshit is) more expansive and independent, with more spacious opportunities for improvisation, color, and imaginative play... less a matter of craft than of art.

For example, practically everything a politician says is bullshit. Statements such as "This great country of ours..." are pure bullshit, being neither true nor false, but designed to sway the audience. Any statement about the future is bullshit: "We will provide jobs and growth" (a particular favorite of the latest Australian prime minister). "Our wonderful fighting men" is bullshit, but it's probably not such a good idea to trumpet that too loudly. Not to be outdone, religion is replete with bullshit, economics, commercial sport, practically all poetry and romance and... psychiatry. The claim "mental disorder is a form of brain disorder" is pure bullshit. How do we know? Simply ask for the proof. You will be told: "Er, we haven't quite got the final proof but don't worry, we're working on it. By the way, could we have some more grant money?"

McLaren N (2016). Psychiatry as Bullshit. *Ethical Human Psychology and Psychiatry* 18: 48-57.

3. McLaren N (2013) Psychiatry as Ideology. *Ethical Human Psychology and Psychiatry* 15: 7-18.

4. Believe it or not, but this particular psychiatrist loudly claims to be devoutly religious. He or she likes to tell people that his or her choice of psychiatry as a specialty was led by God. We don't know which God, perhaps it was Mammon.

5. A Royal Commission is the highest form of investigation in Australia. A Commission is established by an Act of Parliament to investigate a particular question, much as the Chilcott Commission in the UK investigated the British role in invading Iraq, or the current Mueller investigation of the possible Russian interference in the 2016 presidential election. A Royal Commission is chaired by a respected judge and has very broad powers of investigation and subpoena. The recent enquiry into institutional sexual abuse of children lasted five years and cost about $500million. It brought this dreadful secret into the open in a way no other enquiry could have done.

6. We know that when carbamazepine (*Tegretol*, an anticonvulsant) enters streams and lakes, fish are born with severe neurological disturbances which prevent them swimming properly and they don't survive.

7. https://www.buzzfeed.com/patrickstrudwick/uk-psychiatrists-have-issued-an-historic-admission-of-the?utm_term=.htMY6Po1W#.mgd7ya6q1

8. *PBS Frontline. The American Experience: The Lobotomist* (documentary on Dr Walter Freeman, 1895-1972). The following quote comes from Wikipedia's entry on Walter Jackson Freeman II:

> Up to 40% of Freeman's patients were gay individuals subjected to a lobotomy in order to change their homosexual orientation, leaving most of these perfectly healthy individuals severely disabled for the rest of their life.

9. Garbage in, garbage out.

About the Author

Niall McLaren is an Australian psychiatrist, author and critic. He was born and educated in rural Western Australia, graduating in medicine at the University of WA in Perth in 1970. He completed his postgraduate training in psychiatry in 1977 and subsequently worked in prisons and then in the Veterans' Hospital, with a year's break working in the far southern region of Thailand. From 1983-87, he studied philosophy in order to undertake a PhD jointly in psychiatry and philosophy of science. In 1987, he left Perth city to travel to the remote Kimberley Region of Western Australia as the region's first psychiatrist.

As a psychiatrist with no staff, no hospital beds, no clinic and not even an office, nearly 2000km from the nearest psychiatrist, he was the world's most isolated psychiatrist. While there, he continued studying and writing and began publishing work highly critical of mainstream psychiatry. After six years in the bush, he moved to Darwin, the capital of Australia's Northern Territory, first as chief psychiatrist for the Top End, then in private practice, where he concentrated on the large military population. He has since moved to Brisbane, in Queensland, and is emphatic that there will be no more moves.

His work is highly original and he does not admit to any intellectual debt to psychiatrists, living or dead. When he graduated in psychiatry, he was aware that the field was not what it claimed to be. It was clear that psychiatrists routinely made major claims on the nature of mind and of mental disorder that were not justified in the literature and, he intuited, could never be justified. This led him to the philosophy of science which established that psychiatry lacked a formal model of mental disorder. In turn, this problem arose just because it had no model of mind. As a result, modern psychiatry lacks a basis in any known concept of science. It is, in fact, at best a proto-science and, at worst, crude and highly misleading pseudoscience.

Almost invariably, his work provokes bitter antagonism from mainstream psychiatrists. Over the past forty years, orthodox psychiatry has committed itself totally to the reductionist biological approach to mental disorder, with no possible alternatives. Despite massive increases in expenditure on mental health, there is absolutely no evidence to support the oft-repeated claims that psychiatry is making great advances and people are better off than they have ever been. Every figure indicates that as psychiatry extends its reach, the mental health of the population declines. McLaren argues that this is just because psychiatry is not a science.

Because it lacks a formal model of its field of study, mental disorder, psychiatry is perpetually at the mercy of social and political fads and fashions. He maintains that biological psychiatry is nothing more than a passing fad and must eventually go the way of psychoanalysis, behaviourism and possession theory. In the meantime, it is doing an immeasurable amount of damage.

Bibliography

As this is not intended as a textbook, I have included neither references nor citations in the traditional sense. However, over the years, my work has been influenced by a considerable number of authors. While assembling this list, it occurred to me that there are no psychiatrists among them.

Archer, J. (2004). Testosterone and human aggression: an evaluation of the Challenge Hypothesis. *Neuroscience and Biobehaviral Reviews* 30: 319–345.

Boole, G. (1854). *The Laws of Thought*. London: McMillan. Reprinted 1958. New York: Dover.

Chalmers, D.J. (1996). *The Conscious Mind: in search of a fundamental theory*. Oxford: University Press.

Chalmers, D.J. (2010). A computational foundation for the study of cognition. *Journal of Consciousness Studies* 17:7-65.

Chomsky, N. (1959). Review of B. F. Skinner's *Verbal Behavior* in *Language*. 35 (1): 26-58.

Chomsky, N. (2000). *New Horizons in the study of language and mind*. New York: Cambridge University Press.

Crews, F. (1998). *Unauthorised Freud: doubters confront a legend*. Penguin Putnam; New York.

Dean, E.T. (1997). *Shook over hell: Post-traumatic stress, Vietnam and the Civil War*. Harvard: University Press.

Evans, V. (2014). *The Language Myth: Why language is not an instinct*. Cambridge: University Press.

Everett, D.L. (2017). *How Language Began: The story of humanity's greatest invention*. Liveright/Norton: New York.

Floridi, L. (2011). *The Philosophy of Information*. Oxford: University Press.

Frankfurt, H. (1986). On Bullshit. *Raritan Quarterly Review* 6, No. 2 (Fall 1986).

Gotzsche, P. (2015). *Deadly Psychiatry and Organised Denial*. London: Artpeople.

Horwitz, A.V. & Wakefield, J.C. (2007). *The Loss of Sadness: how psychiatry transformed normal sorrow into Depressive Disorder*. New York: Oxford University Press.

Kuhn, T.S. (1970). *The Structure of Scientific Revolutions. (Third Edition).* Chicago, Ill: University Press (International Encyclopedia of Unified Science, Vol. 2, No. 2).

Luria, A.R. (1980) *Higher cortical functions in man.* New York: Basic Books.

Masson, J.M. (1984). *The Assault on Truth: Freud's suppression of the seduction theory.* New York: Simon and Schuster.

Moore, W. (1974) *The Thin Yellow Line.* Ware, Hertsfordshire: Wordsworth Press.

Morone, J.G. & Woodhouse, E.J. (1989). *The Demise of Nuclear Energy: lessons for democratic control of technology.* Yale University Press: New Haven.

Popper, K. R. (1969). *Conjectures and refutations: the growth of scientific knowledge. (Third edition, revised.).* London: Routledge & Kegan Paul.

Shannon, C.E. (1937). *A Symbolic Analysis of Relay and Switching Circuits.* unpublished MS Thesis, Massachusetts Institute of Technology, Aug. 10, 1937. Available at http://dspace.mit.edu/bitstream/handle/1721.1/11173/34541425.pdf?sequence=1

Shannon, C.E. (1948). A Mathematical Theory of Communication. *Bell System Technical Journal* 27: 379–423, 623–656 (July, October).

Shepherd B (2000). *A War of Nerves. Soldiers and Psychiatrists 1914-1994.* London: Pimlico.

Sokal, A. (2008). *Beyond the Hoax: Science, Philosophy and Culture.* Oxford: University Press.

Stoljar, D. (2010). *Physicalism.* Oxford: Routledge.

Turing, A.M. (1937). On computable numbers, with an application to the Entscheidungsproblem. *Proceedings of the London Mathematical Society* (1936 - 37) Series 2; 42:230-65.

Turing, A.M. (1950). Computing machinery and intelligence. *Mind* 59: 433-60.

Whitaker, R. (2002). *Mad in America: Bad Science, Bad Medicine and the Enduring Mistreatment of the Mentally Ill.* New York: Perseus Books.

Whitaker, R. (2009). *Anatomy of an Epidemic: Magic Bullets, Psychiatric Drugs and the Astonishing Rise of Mental Illness in America.* New York: Random House.

Whitaker, R. & Cosgrove, L. (2015). *Psychiatry Under the Influence: Institutional Corruption, Social Injury, and Prescriptions for Reform.* New York: Palgrave MacMillan.

Youngson, R. (1998). *Scientific blunders: a brief history of how wrong scientists can sometimes be.* London: Robinson.

Index

Cracking the Mind-Body Cipher

Dr. Niall (Jock) McLaren is an Australian psychiatrist who uses philosophical analysis to show that modern psychiatry has no scientific basis. This startling conclusion dovetails neatly with the growing evidence that psychiatric drug treatment is crude and damaging. Needless to say, this message is not popular with mainstream psychiatrists. However, in this book, he shows how the principles of information processing give a formal theory of mind that generates a model of mental disorder as a psychological phenomenon. This book shows...

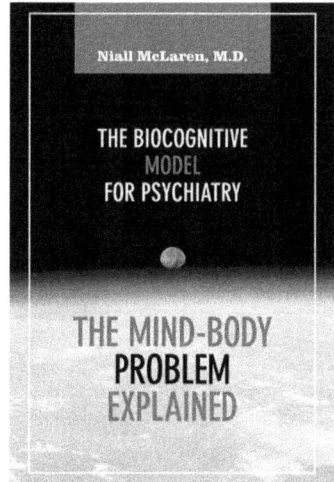

Niall McLaren, M.D.

THE BIOCOGNITIVE MODEL FOR PSYCHIATRY

THE MIND-BODY PROBLEM EXPLAINED

- How, for ideological reasons, modern philosophy misses the point of the duality of mind and body;
- How to resolve the mind-body problem using well-defined principles;
- Why the entire DSM project is doomed to fail;
- Why the ideas of Thomas Szasz have failed to influence psychiatry;
- Where we go from here.

~ ~ ~

"*The Mind Body Problem Explained* is a thoughtful, insightful and provocative exploration of the nature of the human mind, and sets forth a powerful argument for rethinking the medical model of mental disorders. The current paradigm of psychiatric care has failed us, and Niall McLaren's book will stir readers to think of new possibilities."
--Robert B. Whitaker, author *Mad in America*

"It is impossible to do justice to this ambitious, erudite, and intrepid attempt to dictate to psychiatry a new, 'scientifically-correct' model theory. The author offers a devastating critique of the shortcomings and pretensions of psychiatry, not least its all-pervasive, jargon-camouflaged nescience."
--Sam Vaknin, PhD, author
Malignant Self Love: Narcissism Revisited

ISBN 978-1-61599-170-9
From Future Psychiatry Press
www.FuturePsychiatry.com

How do we know what we know?

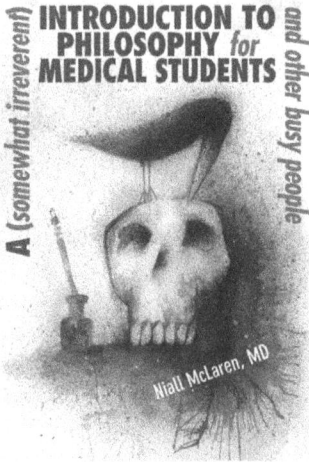

INTRODUCTION TO PHILOSOPHY for MEDICAL STUDENTS

A (somewhat irreverent)

and other busy people

Niall McLaren, MD

During their careers, many students become aware that, lurking in the background, there are complex and conceptually difficult questions that, all too often, their teachers either can't answer, or can't even understand. These are traditionally the questions addressed by philosophy, and this little primer is the result of another student's journey over many years. Niall McLaren MD has spent over three decades banging his head against the Really Difficult questions behind psychiatry, and offers his a personal view of how these questions should be approached. Very deliberately, he simplifies the convoluted language and reasoning that set philosophers apart, making it accessible to students of scientific fields in particular.

In this book, you will gain a background in the following fields:

- Religion and the origins of philosophy
- Mentalism, antimentalism and behaviorism
- Epistemology, as the study of knowledge itself
- Philosophy and the nature of science
- Philosophy and the nature of ethics

Included is a glossary explaining some of the many -isms that can be so daunting to non-philosophers because philosophers too have their jargon but it is not meant to intimidate. True, it can be complex, but the issues involved are complex. The goal of this book is to show that, with clear thinking, the complexities need not be overwhelming.

"This is one of the very few books I have every intention of reading several times in rapid succession. It is such a bounty of iconoclastic observations emanating from an in-depth acquaintance with psychiatry and a love of philosophy that no single reading can do it justice: it just keeps giving."

---Sam Vaknin, PhD, author,
Malignant Self-love: Narcissism Revisited

ISBN 978-1-61599-156-3
From Future Psychiatry Press
www.FuturePsychiatry.com